NOTES FROM HIGHER GROUNDS

AN ALTITUDE TRAINING GUIDE FOR ENDURANCE ATHLETES

Elizabeth Egan, PhD, BSc

Kukimbia Huru Publishing

Published by Kukimbia Huru Publishing
Barmoney, Enniscorthy, Co. Wexford, Ireland

Copyright © 2013 Elizabeth Egan

All rights reserved. No part of this book may be reproduced, stored in a retrieval system, or transmitted in any form or by any means, electronic, mechanical, photocopying, recording or otherwise without permission in writing from the publisher, except by a reviewer, who may quote short passages within a book review.

ISBN 978-0-9927552-0-1

Printed and bound in Ireland by Naas Printing

Every effort has been made to ensure that information in this book is accurate and up to date at time of publishing, but some details are subject to change and should be checked before travel. The publisher cannot accept responsibility for any consequences arising from the use of this book, nor for any material on third-party websites.

Dedicated to the memory of Professor Tom Reilly.

I hope that some of his passion for sport, excellence, language and the pursuit of knowledge has rubbed off on me, and that the pages which follow would have made him proud.

Our deepest fear is not that we are inadequate

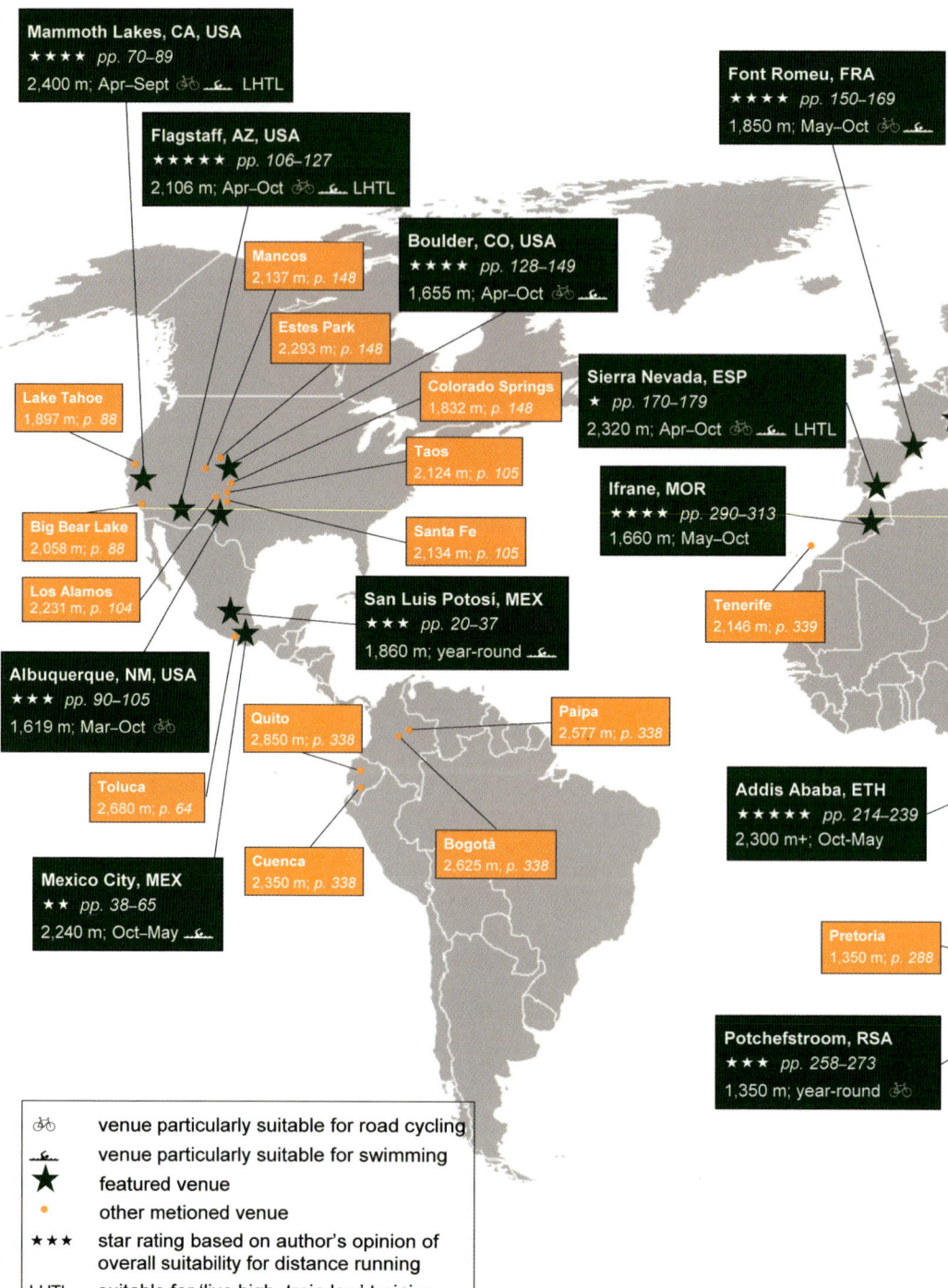

ALTITUDE TRAINING VENUES AROUND THE WORLD

Contents

Preface xv

1. Introduction 1
2. San Luis Potosí 20
3. Mexico City 38
4. Mammoth Lakes 70
5. Albuquerque 90
6. Flagstaff 106
7. Boulder 128
8. Font Romeu 150
9. Sierra Nevada 170
10. Iten 180
11. Addis Ababa 215
12. Falls Creek 240
13. Potchefstroom 258
14. Dullstroom 274
15. Ifrane 290
16. St. Moritz 314

Acknowledgements 341

Appendix 1 French, Spanish and German phrases 342

Appendix 2 Conversion charts 345

Detailed Contents

Preface	xv
1. Introduction	1
Other features of this book	1
Disclaimer	1
Clearing up a few things	2
Scientific basis for altitude training	3
Background	3
How it works	3
Current trends	4
Responders and non-responders	4
The how of altitude training	5
Altitude training in other sports	5
Health and nutrition at altitude	6
Iron and altitude training	6
Anaemia	7
Racing at altitude	8
Tips for racing at altitude	8
Pre-acclimatisation	9
References and further reading	9
Travel and the life of the elite athlete	10
Preparation checklist	10
Packing checklist	10
Essential packing list for altitude	11
Medical preparation	11
Some tropical illnesses that you may need to protect against	11
Travel nutrition	13
Food for the journey	13
Buffet dining	13
Food safety	13
Long haul flights: jet lag and travel fatigue	14
Travel fatigue	14
Jet lag	14
DVT	14
Choosing your altitude training venue	16
Booking your accommodation	17
Training full-time: striking the right balance	18
Dealing with injury at altitude	19
2. San Luis Potosí	20
Author's verdict	22
Mexico: an introduction	23
Getting in	24
Getting around	26
Weather and when to visit	26
Accommodation	26
Food	26
Shopping	26
Language	28
Communication	28
Health and safety	28
Money	29
Power	29
Time	29
Laundry	30
Culture and respect	30
Sports facilities and services	31
Training camps and tour operators	31
Trails and running routes	31
Track facilities	31
Gym facilities	31
Cross-training options	31
Sports medicine and sports science support	31
Local races	32
Running community	32
Suitability for other sports	32
Things to see and do between training	36
Rest day excursions	37
A note on living here long-term	37
Further information	37
3. Mexico City	38
Author's verdict	40
Getting in	42
Getting around	44
Weather and when to visit	46
Accommodation	47
Food	48
Shopping	48
Language	50
Communication	50
Health and safety	51
Money	52
Power	52
Time	52
Laundry	52
Culture and respect	52
Sports facilities and services	56
Trails and running routes	56
Track facilities	58
Local races	58
Gym facilities and facilities for other sports	60
Things to see and do between training	62
Rest day excursions	63
A note on living here long-term	64
Further information	64
Other altitude training sites in Mexico	64
Toluca de Lerdo	64
United States general practicalities	66
Getting in	66
Getting around	66
Shopping and clothes sizes	68
Langage	68
Communication	68
Health and safety	68
Money	68
Power	69
Laundry	69
Culture and respect	69
4. Mammoth Lakes	70
Author's verdict	72
California	73
Getting in	74
Getting around	74
Weather and when to visit	75
Accommodation	75
Food	76
Shopping	76
Communication	76
Health and safety	76
Money	78
Time	78
Laundry	78
Other practicalities	78

Sports facilities and services	79
Training camps and tour operators	79
Trails and running routes	79
Track facilities	80
Gym facilities	80
Cross-training options	81
Sports medicine and sports science support	82
Local races	82
Running community	82
Suitability for other sports	82
Things to see and do between training	86
Rest day excursions	86
Further information	87
A note on living here long-term	87
Other altitude training sites in California	88
Lake Tahoe	88
Big Bear Lake	88
5. Albuquerque	90
Author's verdict	92
New Mexico	93
Getting in	94
Getting around	94
Weather and when to visit	96
Accommodation	96
Food	97
Shopping	97
Communication	97
Health and safety	98
Time	98
Other practicalities	98
Sports facilities and services	99
Trails and running routes	99
Track facilities	100
Gym facilities	100
Cross-training options	100
Local races	100
Running community	101
Suitability for other sports	101
Things to see and do between training	102
Rest day excursions	103
A note on living here long-term	104
Further information	104
Other altitude training sites in New Mexico	104
Los Alamos	104
Santa Fe	105
Taos	105
6. Flagstaff	106
Author's verdict	108
Arizona	109
Getting in	110
Getting around	110
Weather and when to visit	110
Accommodation	111
Food	112
Shopping	112
Communication	112
Health and safety	112
Time	112
Other practicalities	112
Sports facilities and services	116
Training camps and tour operators	116
Trails and running routes	116
Track facilities	120
Gym facilities	120
Cross-training options	120
Sports medicine and sports science support	120
Local races	120
Running community	122
Suitability for other sports	122
Things to see and do between training	126
Rest day excursions	126
A note on living here long-term	127
Further information	127
7. Boulder	128
Author's verdict	130
Colorado	131
Getting in	131
Getting around	132
Weather and when to visit	133
Accommodation	134
Food	134
Shopping	134
Communication	135
Health and safety	135
Time	135
Other practicalities	135
Sports facilities and services	138
Training camps and tour operators	138
Trails and running routes	138
Track facilities	139
Gym facilities	142
Cross-training options	142
Sports medicine and sports science support	142
Local races	143
Running community	143
Suitability for other sports	143
Things to see and do between training	146
Rest day excursions	147
A note on living here long-term	147
Further information	147
Other altitude training sites in Colorado	147
Colorado Springs	148
Estes Park	148
Mancos	148
Other options	149
8. Font Romeu	150
Author's verdict	152
Getting in	154
Getting around	156
Weather and when to visit	157
Accommodation	157
Food	157
Shopping	158
Language	158
Communication	158
Health and safety	158
Money	159
Power	159
Time	159
Laundry	159
Culture and respect	159
Sports facilities and services	162
Training camps and tour operators	162
Trails and running routes	162
Track facilities	166
Gym facilities	166
Cross-training options	166
Sports medicine and sports science support	166

Running community	166
Suitability for other sports	166
Things to see and do between training	168
Rest day excursions	168
A note on living here long-term	169
Further information	169

9. Sierra Nevada — 170

Author's verdict	172
Getting in	173
Getting around	174
Weather	174
Accommodation	174
Language	174
Health and safety	174
Time	174
Sports facilities and services	178
Things to see and do between training	178
A note on living here long-term	178
Further information	178

10. Iten — 180

Author's verdict	182
A bit about Kenya	183
Getting in	186
Getting around	187
Weather and when to visit	188
Accommodation	189
Food	189
Shopping	190
Language	190
Communication	190
Health and safety	192
Money	193
Power	193
Time	193
Laundry	194
Culture and respect	194
Sports facilities and services	198
Training camps and tour operators	198
Trails and running routes	198
Track facilities	202
Gym facilities	204
Cross-training options	204
Sports medicine and sports science support	204
Local races	204
Running community	204
Suitability for other sports	204
Things to see and do between training	207
Rest day excursions	207
A note on living here long-term	208
Further information	208
Other altitude training sites in Kenya	208

11. Addis Ababa — 215

Author's verdict	216
Getting in	220
Getting around	221
Weather and when to visit	222
Accommodation	222
Food	223
Shopping	224
Language	224
Communication	224
Health and safety	224
Money	226
Power	226
Time	226
Laundry	227
Culture and respect	227
Sports facilities and services	228
Training camps and tour operators	228
Trails and running routes	228
Track facilities	229
Gym facilities	229
Cross-training options	229
Sports medicine and sports science support	229
Local races	229
Running community	229
Suitability for other sports	229
Things to see and do between training	236
Rest day excursions	237
A note on living here long-term	237
Further information	237
Other altitude training sites in Ethiopia	238
Bekoji	238

12. Falls Creek — 240

Author's verdict	242
Getting in	244
Getting around	246
Weather and when to visit	247
Accommodation	247
Food	248
Shopping	248
Language	248
Communication	248
Health and safety	249
Money	249
Power	249
Time	250
Laundry	250
Culture and respect	250
Sports facilities and services	254
Trails and running routes	254
Track facilities	254
Gym facilities	254
Cross-training options	254
Sports medicine and sports science support	256
Local races	256
Running community	256
Suitability for other sports	256
Things to see and do between training	257
A note on living here long-term	257
Further information	257
Other altitude training sites in Australia	257
Mount Hotham	257

13. Potchefstroom — 258

Author's verdict	260
South Africa: a brief history	261
Getting in	262
Getting around	263
Weather and when to visit	264
Accommodation	264
Food	265
Shopping	266
Language	266
Communication	266
Health and safety	266
Money	267
Power	267

Time	267
Laundry	267
Culture and respect	267
Sports facilities and services	268
Training camps and tour operators	268
Trails and running routes	268
Track facilities	268
Gym facilities	268
Cross-training options	268
Sports medicine and sports science support	270
Local races	270
Running community	270
Suitability for other sports	270
Things to see and do between training	271
A note on living here long-term	271
Further information	271
14. Dullstroom	**274**
Author's verdict	276
Getting in	277
Getting around	278
Weather and when to visit	278
Accommodation	279
Food	279
Shopping	280
Language	280
Communication	280
Health and safety	280
Money	281
Power	281
Time	281
Laundry	281
Culture and respect	281
Sports facilities and services	284
Trails and running routes	284
Track facilities	286
Gym facilities	286
Cross-training options	286
Sports medicine and sports science support	286
Local races	286
Suitability for other sports	287
Things to see and do between training	287
A note on living here long-term	288
Further information	288
Other altitude training sites in Southern Africa	288
Pretoria	288
Lesotho	288
15. Ifrane	**290**
Author's verdict	292
Moroccan history in a nutshell	293
Getting in	294
Getting around	295
Weather and when to visit	296
Accommodation	296
Food	296
Shopping	297
Language	300
Communication	300
Health and safety	300
Money	301
Power	302
Time	302
Laundry	302
Culture and respect	302
Sports facilities and services	304
Training camps and tour operators	304
Trails and running routes	304
Track facilities	304
Gym facilities	304
Cross-training options	306
Local races	306
Running community	306
Suitability for other sports	306
Things to see and do between training	312
A note on living here long-term	312
Further information	312
16. St. Moritz	**314**
Author's verdict	316
A bit about Switzerland	317
Getting in	317
Getting around	319
Weather and when to visit	322
Accommodation	322
Food	323
Shopping	323
Language	323
Communication	323
Health and safety	324
Money	324
Power	324
Time	324
Laundry	324
Culture and respect	324
Sports facilities and services	328
Trails and running routes	328
Track facilities	330
Gym facilities	330
Cross-training options	330
Sports medicine and sport science support	330
Local races	330
Running community	330
Suitability for other sports	330
Things to see and do between training	333
Rest day excursions	333
A note on living here long-term	334
Further information	334
Other altitude training sites in Switzerland	335
Pontresina	335
Davos	335
Altitude training sites in South America	338
Bogota, Colombia	338
Paipa, Colombia	338
Cuenca, Ecuador	338
Quito, Ecuador	338
Other altitude training sites in Europe	339
Turracher Höhe, Austria	339
Kühtai, Austria	339
Tenerife, Canary Islands	339
Rila Mountains, Bulgaria	339
Acknowledgement	**341**
Appendices	**342**
Appendix 1 French, Spanish and German phrases	342
Appendix 2 Conversion tables	344
Legend for maps	**345**
Photo credits	**345**

Maps

Outline map of San Luis Potosí	25
Outline map of Mexico City	45
Map of Bosque de Chapultepec with some running trails	59
Map of Mammoth Lakes	75
Map of area east of Mammoth Lakes showing training facilties and trails	81
Map of main routes and major areas of Albuquerque	95
Map of main routes and major areas of Flagstaff	117
Outline map of Boulder	133
Map of airports, cities and main roads linking to Font Romeu	155
Map of Font Romeu with training facilities and some trails	163
Map of Granada, Pradollano and surrounding area	175
Map of Iten and suggested trails	187
Overview map of Eldoret and Iten	203
Map of Addis Ababa with main access routes	221
Overview map of Eastern Victoria	246
Map of Falls Creek Trails	255
Overview map of Potchefstroom	263
Overview map of Dullstroom and surrounding area	278
Map of Dullstroom trails	285
Map of Ifrane	296
Map of airports close to St. Moritz	321
Overview map of St. Moritz	321
Map of St. Moritz Trails	329

Information boxes

Normal values	7
Iron content of various foods	7
Comparison of men's athletics winning performances at 1964 and 1968 Olympic Games	8
Tips for travel	10
Packing list	11
Good foods to pack	13
Mexico quick facts	23
US quick facts	66
Driving in the US	67
American-English translations	69
France quick facts	153
Spain quick facts	1
Kenya quick facts	183
Some useful Swahili phrases	191
Ethiopia quick facts	216
Australia quick facts	242
Driving in Australia	245
South Africa quick facts	261
Driving in South Africa	264
Staying safe in the city	267
Morocco quick facts	293
Some useful Moroccan Arabic phrases	301
Switzerland quick facts	317

From the blog

Why Mexico?	xiii
How not to travel around the world,	15
Lost in translation	29
Beetle Mania	43
Driving me crazy	47
Living the life of an elite athlete	89
Hot-air balloons	103
Fabulous Flagstaff	123
Bolder Boulder	149
This is Kenya	184
This is Ethiopia	217
Addis Ababa by picture	218
The carb queen is dead and gone,	223
Eliz's Great Ethiopian Run experience	234
Australia in a nutshell	243
I'm in heaven	250
A thousand camel?	310
One last trip	320
Fifteen venues later	337

Special Features

El Camino Real de Tierra Adentro	23
The Tarahumara: Mexico's Running Tribe	32
Mexico City Olympic Games, 1968	41
California's giant trees	73
Pueblos	93
Running among the Navajo and Hopi people	109
Solar furnaces	168
What's in a name	191
Some of the key players in Kenyan distance-running history	196
Kenya: the ultimate experience	206
Rift valley rivals: Kenya v Ethiopia	210
Some of the key players in Ethiopian distance-running history	232
Ethiopia: the ultimate experience	236
Moroccan glossary	301
Morocco's distance running success	308
The Albula/Bernia World Heritage Railway	319
Swiss German	325
St. Moritz and winter sports	332

Training camps

La Loma Altitude Training Camps	34
Centre National d'Entrainement en altitude (CNEA)	167
Centro de Alto rendimiento (CAR) Sierra Navada	170
High Altitude Training Centre (HATC)	200
Yaya Village	230
Kenenisa Athletic Resort	231

Preface

This book was written as a travel guide for athletes who wish to train at altitude. But it is more than just a travel guide. It's a log of a personal journey and adventure. While the main part of the book details the facts about each of the venues, it is accompanied by sections from a blog that I kept while carrying out the research. To add to the sense of journey, the venue chapters fall in the order in which research for the book was carried out between March 2010 and June 2012.

Much has been written about the proposed benefits of altitude, but the scientific evidence is far from conclusive. Personally, I have no doubt but that altitude training works, but I care less about the effect of hypoxic conditions on my red blood cells, than I do about the effects that running on soft trails in the fresh mountain air have on my mind and my soul.

Why I quit my stable job with a steady income, packed everything into a suitcase, and took a massive leap into the unknown, is probably best answered with the first of my chosen blog excerpts.

WHY MEXICO?
Adapted from the blog, 1 April & 3 April, 2010

When out for a run one cold Saturday morning in December 2009, I realised that the cause of my recent frustration was that I wasn't doing anything special with my life. Now, I don't have a burning desire for fame or fortune, but I do think there is a desire within all of us to achieve something significant in life. I quickly revisited some old ideas I'd had, and there it was; the idea that was going to make me happy. In less time than it takes the average human to decide what they're going to have for dinner, I'd decided that it was time to move along. Brief chats with some of my closest friends banished any tiny doubts that I might have had and by lunchtime that Monday (21 December) I had given notice that I was quitting my job for a life on the road.

Ever since I knew what a book was, I wanted to be a writer. I've always wanted to create something that others can read and enjoy. As a child I thought that my publication was going to be of the fictional type, but it soon became clear that I'm much more of a factual writer. Any project that I did at school was at least twice as long as required; each topic an opportunity for me to form the basis of a possible future book. I can't have been much more than eight or nine when the two-page project on insects that we were assigned, became a six-page masterpiece—well that's if you can forgive the hundreds of spelling mistakes. A few years later I was assigning myself projects, and set about putting together 'books' about clothing through the ages, the counties of Ireland, and a world encyclopaedia, among others. By the time I reached Leaving Cert, my Home Economics bathroom design assignment became a mini DIY -manual that earned me an A+++.

My obsession with the written word doesn't stop there. I can't go shopping without spending hours in a bookshop. I own how-to books on skills that I will never master, travel guides for countries that I will never visit, and biographies that I will never have time to read. And reading a book is never just enough—I've got to own it. I visit charity shops to buy books, not to donate them. Books take up far more space than clothes in my bedroom.

Like writing, athletics has long been a major part of my life. I love to run in all weathers, but sometimes, just sometimes, I need to escape the cold and the rain and do some training somewhere else in the world. I like to travel, and running gives me a great opportunity to do that. In 2004 I began to plan my first trip to Kenya. It was almost impossible to find the information that I needed. Subsequent warm-weather training trips around Europe have proved to be just as difficult to organise. Where do you find information on the best places to train? What venues have access to weight training equipment? How do you arrange access to the local track? Where is the best place to stay? Do you need a car to get around? Is it safe? Is it suitable for solo travellers? And most importantly, as someone who generally dislikes running on the roads, what are the trails like?

I had an idea a few years back about putting together a book to answer these questions about the best altitude training venues around the world, but for a long time this has only been a crazy idea at the back of my head. On Tuesday March 30, 2010, I set off on the first leg of my exploration journey; a quest to gather information for what I hope is the first of many books. Time to achieve something significant!

Introduction

This book is a resource designed for any athlete or sportsperson looking to train at altitude. It provides information on each of 15 venues around the world as if it was a travel guide, but with reference to sport-related considerations. Every athlete and sportsperson from every country in the world, however, would be a very broad target audience, and a book relevant to all would make for a very long and tedious book.

To enhance reader experience, distance running is used as the main target sport. Brief reference is, however, made to other sports, where relevant. Flight details, visa requirements, and other travel-related information is targeted at a British and Irish audience, but reference is also made, where possible, to other European countries, and other major English-speaking nations (i.e. US, Canada, South Africa, Australia and New Zealand). Readers from countries other than the targeted ones should, however, still benefit from the information provided.

You don't have to be an elite athlete to train at altitude. Athletes of all levels can benefit from a few weeks exposure to moderate altitude. Even if you're not concerned with achieving Olympic qualification standards, or indeed even improving your performance, you may still wish to travel to some of the venues included here. Iten and Addis Ababa are great places to visit if you have any interest in distance running, and the trails of Flagstaff, St. Moritz and some of the other venues, make for a very enjoyable running experience. And you don't need some sort of special invitation to train in these places. The information in this book should provide all the information you require to arrange your own trip.

OTHER FEATURES OF THE BOOK

As well as providing details on where to go, how to get there, where to stay and other practicalities on each of the world's most popular altitude training venues, special features on items of historical, cultural, practical and social interest are included in each chapter. For those who don't like to spend all their time eating, sleeping and breathing athletics or for those who have a significant other to keep occupied while they eat, sleep and breath athletics, pointers are given to local tourist attractions and other ways to pass the time. Additional points of interest for athletes are noted, including races in those venues, famous athletes that train there, and how to find the best routes in each location.

Every effort has been made to ensure that the information is objective and I acknowledge that what might be an attraction for one athlete might be a turn-off for another. In all sections except the 'Author's verdict' paragraph, I have stated the facts to the best of my ability and encourage the reader to decide for themselves whether or not a venue suits their needs and tastes.

One of the questions that I often hear about altitude training venues is whether or not they are a suitable place to move to for training. I have tried to answer this for each of the venues, and mention work and educational opportunities, training variety, access to races, and cost of living. This is, however, a very difficult question to answer, as each individual will look for different things in a training base.

DISCLAIMER

Every effort has been made to ensure that the information in this book is up to date at the time of publishing. However, things are constantly changing. A new track has been built in Mammoth Lakes since I visited there, a new camp has been set up in Addis Ababa, the Gautrain system in Johannesburg has been extended to link the airport with the city of Johannesburg, and a new restaurant has opened at the HATC in Iten. It's likely that even more facilities will pop up over the coming years, and that transport links will be established where there previously were none. Likewise, flights between cities may be discontinued, and bus service numbers may change. The information in this book should be used as a starting point, and all details should be checked before travel.

Weblinks have been included where possible and relevant, and every effort has been made to ensure that these links are correct. Any change to independent websites after publication is beyond the control of the author.

I do not condone doping in sport. Athletes who have doping convictions (at time of publishing) are not referenced in this book, with the exception of the section on Moroccan athletes where specific reference is made to Morocco's considerable list of doping offenders. However, I have no control over which athletes may receive a doping conviction in the future. Reference to any athlete who receives a drug suspension in the future, should not be taken as my approval of their behaviour.

CLEARING UP A FEW THINGS

There are two separate aspects to the physiology of altitude training and the rationale behind exercising at altitude. Mountaineers spend time acclimatising to altitude, and preparing themselves for the physiological demands of high altitude and low oxygen pressure before embarking on a trip up the mountains. They are most concerned with how their body will cope at altitudes of 3,000 m or more above sea level (high altitude), and want to reduce acute mountain sickness, and the most debilitating physiological consequences of extreme hypoxia. On the other hand, athletes utilise the physiological adaptations which occur at moderate altitude (1,500–3,000 m above sea level), to enhance their performance at sea level. This book is targeted at the second group (though there is some reference to preparing for races that are held at moderate altitude), and refers to places that people go to get the physiological benefits of moderate altitude, rather than base camps for climbing expeditions.

Often when athletes refer to high altitude training, they mean training at moderate altitudes of 1,500–3,000 m. For the purposes of this book, we will simply refer to it as altitude or altitude training.

Most people have some perception of what altitude training is like before they go. Many of these perceptions tend to be inaccurate.

Hill training and altitude training are not the same thing
Many people associate altitude training with running up the side of a mountain. True, some of the best venues are located on or between the slopes (e.g. Font Romeu, Mammoth Lakes, St. Moritz), but others (e.g. Iten, Addis Ababa, Mexico City and Dullstroom), are located on high plateau, far from any significant mountain range. Conversely, being at the top of a mountain doesn't mean that you are at any significant altitude. The highest mountain peak in Ireland is 1,038 m and the peak of Ben Nevis, the highest peak in the British Isles, is a mere 1,344 m above sea level. Much of the floor of the Rift Valley, as it runs through Kenya and Ethiopia, is approximately 1,200 m above sea level!

Just because it's near the equator doesn't mean that it doesn't get cold there too.
The equator cuts right through Kenya, yet, the evenings in Iten, just north of the equator, can get quite cold. The further you go above sea level, the colder it gets, and the lower humidity associated with high altitude means that when the sun sets, the temperature drops dramatically. Don't go to Kenya (or any altitude training venue for that matter) without packing some warm clothes for the evenings!

Just because it's a ski resort in the winter, doesn't mean that it's not warm enough to run there in the summer.
The mountains of Switzerland and France experience similar seasonal temperature changes as elsewhere in Europe, and while places like Font Romeu and St, Moritz are well known as winter ski resorts, the snow doesn't last forever. The snow across central and southern Europe has usually melted by April, leaving beautiful mountainsides and high valleys ready for hiking, mountain biking, and, of course, running. Many ski resorts provide good training venues with lots of scenic runs, good transport networks and cheap accommodation during the summer.

Dullstroom, at 2,100 m, isn't exactly what you would call mountainous

SCIENTIFIC BASIS FOR ALTITUDE TRAINING

The following pages provide a brief outline of the physiological effects and benefits of training at altitude and suggestions of how to adjust training while at altitude. Some reference will be made to the supporting literature, and current best practices, but this is not intended to be a comprehensive review of the literature, or a detailed scientific analysis. A list of further readings is included on *p. 9* for those interested in finding out more about the science behind altitude training.

Normally altitudes of between 1,500 m and 3,000 m are used to initiate a physiological training response which may, in turn, enhance performance at sea level. While the scientific evidence to support the benefits of altitude training when competing at sea level are far from conclusive, the anecdotal evidence is undeniable, and these days most world-class distance runners spend long periods training at altitude. How they train at altitude, and for how long they stay, varies considerably from individual to individual. Modern training methods such as 'live high, train low', stimulated altitude and oxygen supplementation are also discussed briefly.

BACKGROUND

Much of the original anecdotal evidence in support of altitude training originates from the successes of the East African athletes at the Mexico City Olympics in 1968. Hailing from altitude, these athletes were better able to cope with the difficult conditions for endurance performance at 2,240 m above sea level. While training at altitude improves beyond doubt competitive performance at altitude, it is less clear whether or not living and training at altitude provides an advantage for competitions held at sea level. Living and training at altitude is one of the factors attributed to East African distance running success, but while anecdotal evidence supporting altitude training abounds, well-controlled studies have found mixed results.

Prior to the Mexico City Olympic Games, a number of countries anticipated the difficulties that racing at 2,240 m would pose. A track was purpose-built in the forest above Lake Tahoe for the US team's preparations; the French established the CNEA in Font Romeu, and St. Moritz was utilised by the Swiss team for their preparation. In the end, almost every medallist in distances of 1500 m or longer, were either from altitude, or had trained extensively at altitude prior to the Games. There is no doubt but that acclimatisation is important prior to racing at altitude.

Around the same time, athletes from Ethiopia and Kenya, all of whom hailed from altitude, began to compete more extensively on the world circuit than they had previously, and were performing way above what would have been expected of countries with such little previous success at world level. Could training at altitude, as they did on a daily basis, help performance at sea level?

HOW IT WORKS

Put simply, the higher the altitude, the less oxygen there is available. Barometric pressure decreases as altitude increases, and the quantity of oxygen per volume of air decreases. The percentage of oxygen in the air remains unchanged.

In response to decreased oxygen in the air, acute or initial altitude exposure results in a number of physiological and physical responses which can be observed and measured. Most notably, resting and submaximal exercise heart rates increase in an attempt to increase oxygen transport to the tissues. Maximum oxygen consumption begins to decrease at altitudes above 1,500 m and decreases exponentially with increased altitude/decreased barometric pressure. Resting and submaximal ventilation increase, blood pressure increases, and catecholamine secretion increases, resulting in increased lactate production. Perceived exertion also increases.

You will notice that you find it harder to breathe, or that your breathing is faster, that you are more tired, that your sleep is disrupted and that your appetite may be suppressed. Though unusual at altitudes below 3,000 m, acute mountain sickness results in a number of additional symptoms including headache, insomnia, vomiting, irregular heart rate, diarrhoea, irritability and disturbance of breathing. Anyone who is suffering from altitude sickness should rest, or return to a lower altitude if possible, until the symptoms disappear.

On a positive note, due to the reduced air resistance and affect of gravity, you will find it easier to sprint over short distances. To maintain leg speed, consider adding a series of short sprints or strides to the end of each run.

After exposure to altitude for several weeks, exercise capacity increases significantly, but maximum oxygen consumption doesn't change. The adaptation to altitude, and the resultant improvement in exercise performance, are largely biochemical in nature.

Plasma volume decreases, haemoglobin, red blood cell count and haematocrit increase in an attempt to improve the oxygen carrying capacity of the blood. Skeletal muscle vascularity and tissue myoglobin increase, resulting in improved oxygen transport to muscles and cells, and increased mitochondrial size and number increases muscle metabolism.

Over time, catecholamine secretion begins to reduce, but never return to levels seen at sea-level. Similarly, resting and submaximal heart rate reduce, but don't return to normal, irrespective of how long is spent at altitude.

Decreased blood oxygen levels at altitude are detected by the kidneys, which increase the production and secretion of erythropoietin (EPO). Erythropoietin is a naturally occurring hormone which is responsible for the regulation of haemoglobin and red blood cell (erythrocyte) production. Red blood cell maturation generally takes 5-7 days from the initial increase in serum EPO following altitude exposure. The threshold for increased EPO production appears to be 1,600 m of altitude, though there are large individual variations in erythropoietic responses to altitude.

Most scientific studies show no improvement in maximal work capacity or maximal oxygen consumption on return to sea level. Many of the physiological adaptations that occur are of little benefit to exercise at sea level, with the notable exception of increased haemoglobin.

Indeed, there are some disadvantages to training at altitude. Because of the reduced oxygen content of the air, training at the same intensity as at sea level is not possible. Reduced intensity and volume have the potential to reduce the fitness of the athlete, though with clever planning, a balance between the intensity of training and the exposure to altitude can be achieved. Risk of infection and over-training are higher at altitude, and close monitoring is advised. Additionally, the humidity at altitude is lower than at sea-level, and any athlete training to compete in endurance events in high-humidity environments should not carry out the last stages of their preparation at altitude. At least 10 days will be required to reacclimatise to humidity. Additionally, altitude training is expensive, and not all athletes can afford the time required to carry out a full block of training at altitude.

Despite the disadvantages of training at altitude, and the lack of definitive scientific evidence to support the use of training at altitude to improve sea level performance, many elite distance runners live and train at altitude. In an attempt to overcome some of the disadvantages of training at altitude, other approaches to altitude training are gaining popularity.

CURRENT TRENDS

It appears that many of the benefits of altitude can be attained just by living or sleeping at altitude, and thus a method known as 'live high, train low', (often referred to as 'LHTL' in the research), whereby athletes live at altitude and travel to lower altitudes to carry out all or some of their training, is often used. This procedure can also be stimulated by use of altitude tents, altitude houses or nitrogen apartments. Some such products (e.g. altitude tents) maintain sea-level air pressure, but reduce the concentration of oxygen, while others (hypobaric chamber) are both hypobaric (low pressure) and hypoxic (low oxygen).

Supplemental oxygen training, a stimulated form of 'live high, train low' training, may help overcome some of the disadvantages of traditional altitude training. Hyperoxic medical grade gas is used to enable training in stimulated altitude conditions.

Intermittent hypoxic exposure (IHE) and intermittent hypoxic training (IHT) are essentially 'live low, train high' (LLTH) approaches to altitude training. Altitude training masks, which reduce inspired oxygen concentration, and a form of intermittent hypoxic training, are becoming increasingly popular but while they may have some advantages for mountaineers, or those looking to compete at very high altitudes, they have minimal benefit for sea level performance.

Traditional 'live high, train high', is far from extinct, but may be more beneficial for responders than non-responders.

RESPONDERS AND NON-RESPONDERS

Some research has indicated that not everyone responds to altitude exposure in the same way and that there are those that respond to hypoxic conditions (responders) and those that don't (non-responders). However, more recent research has indicated that the state of responder or non-responder is not necessarily permanent. Underlying factors such as iron deficiency, illness, training or training too hard, too soon, may turn a potential responder into a non-responder. Mental stress, sleep deprivation and emotional distress can also blunt an athlete's response to altitude.

THE HOW OF ALTITUDE TRAINING

The essential elements of altitude training are mentioned briefly here. For further depth, refer to Randall Wilber's excellent *Altitude training and athletic performance*, which examines a range of altitude training programmes in detail.

Optimal altitude

The optimal altitude at which to live is somewhere between 2,100 m and 2,500 m. Training and recovery may be reduced at higher altitudes, and though altitudes of 1,600 m initiate some response, it may not be optimal. Where possible, quality sessions should be carried out at a lower altitude. The phase of the season, and an individual's previous altitude exposure may also influence the choice of height to live and train at.

Duration required

The minimal time required at altitude is between 3 and 4 weeks, though up to 6 weeks is ideal. Not all athletes can afford the time or money to spend this long at altitude. Some pre-acclimatisation can be used *(p. 9)* in such cases.

Training

Basic acclimatisation to altitude takes approximately 7 days during the first visit (acclimatisation may be slightly quicker on subsequent visits), though this varies depending on the individual. After this time, resting heart rate will have returned close to baseline. Submaximal heart rate will remain elevated even after weeks of acclimatisation.

Overall training volume should be reduced by 10–20 percent during the first week and increased gradually over the following 3–4 weeks. Submaximal efforts and tempo run pace should be measured by heart rate and effort rather than time or speed.

The intensity of interval work should be reduced by approximately 5–7 percent initially and increased gradually. Interval work in the first week will be difficult and should be confined to 100–200 m efforts. These distances can be doubled in the second week (i.e. 200–400 m) and doubled again the following week.

Rest between efforts should be longer than during the same session at sea level. Use heart rate to determine recovery (e.g. return to 120 BPM). In the absence of heart rate a safe starting point may be to double the normal rest used, and reduce by 2–3 percent per week.

You'll also need longer recovery between sessions. Take resting HR and reduce the intensity or duration of any planned exercise if this is more elevated than normal. Some of the benefits of altitude will be gained just from living there, so athletes shouldn't be concerned if they have to miss a session or two.

Remember that there are huge individual variations in response to altitude. Athletes are encouraged to listen to their own body and not to measure themselves against others.

The biggest mistake that athletes make when training at altitude, is that they train too hard. This is especially true for runners who are not used to training full-time, and who want to make the most of not having to fit their training around work or study. Remember, with altitude training, less is more, particularly during the first two weeks.

Returning to sea level

As with all aspects of altitude training, there are huge individual variations in the optimal timing of return to sea level. Not only is there differences between individuals, but some individuals respond differently from one trip to the next. Many athletes race within 3 days of returning from altitude (jet lag and travel fatigue should be considered) and again 14-16 days later. Others like to race approximately 10 days after returning to sea level.

Many believe that the beneficial effects of training at altitude last just 2 weeks, though others observe benefits for up to 2 months after returning from altitude. Carrying out base-level preseason training at altitude may have prolonged benefits, as a wide base is laid for the season ahead. In such cases the inability to train at high intensities is of less concern to the athlete.

ALTITUDE TRAINING IN OTHER SPORTS

Altitude training is popular in endurance sports such as cycling, triathlon and rowing. Swimmers also tend to train at altitude. More recently, team sports players have been using altitude training as part of their preseason training. Altitude training in team sports players was the subject of an Aspetar conference in March 2013. Conference proceedings were published in a special supplement of the British Journal of Sport and Exercise Medicine in December 2013.

HEALTH AND NUTRITION AT ALTITUDE

A high altitude environment can pose a number of minor risks to the health and wellbeing of an athlete. These are some of the areas that require attention.

The sun
The sun's UV rays are much stronger at altitude than at sea level, even though the temperatures may be cooler. Always use sunscreen, even if it doesn't feel particularly warm, wear sunglasses and avoid prolonged exposure to the sun.

Muscle wastage
The reduced effect of gravity at altitude may cause muscle wastage, though this is minimal at altitudes below 3,000 m. Maintain resistance training to minimise muscle loss and ensure that you consume adequate calories.

Diet
Diet is very important when training at altitude. Basal metabolic rate increases for the first 4 days of altitude exposure, particularly in females. After 4 days metabolic rate begins to return to normal, but remains above sea level values.

Since more oxygen is required to break down fat than carbohydrates, 80 percent of calories should be derived from low glycaemic carbohydrates. Meals should be taken at least every 4 hr. Increased carbohydrate utilisation may result in the depletion of glycogen stores, and a conscious effort should be made to replace carbohydrates during and after training.

Reduced nutrient absorption in the gut at altitude results in greater faecal losses. Maintaining a high proportion of carbohydrate, and ensuring that overall calorie intake is adequate, may reduce or offset this faecal loss.

Some individuals may experience reduced appetite. Small but regular meals, and eating a variety of fresh products, may help. Apples and grapes in particular have natural chemicals which increase appetite.

Iron levels are also very important *(see opposite)*.

There is a risk of immunosuppression, and a subsequent increased risk of upper respiratory tract infections and gastrointestinal infections. Ensure that you have adequate vitamins (A, folic acid, B_6, B_{12}, C and E) and minerals (copper, selenium and zinc) in your diet, and replace carbohydrates quickly after exercise.

Hydration
Because of increased ventilation, increased urinary water loss, and low humidity at altitude, the potential for dehydration is increased. Intake of caffeine-free fluids should be increased by as much as 4 litres per day. Monitor morning urine colour to ensure that fluid needs are being met, and reduce caffeine consumption.

Other side effects
Some individuals may experience other side effects to living and training at altitude. Stomach cramps and digestive system discomfort, difficulty getting to sleep, disrupted sleep and intense dreams are among the side effects of living at altitude, though they usually reduce with acclimatisation. Afternoon naps may help replace lost sleep at night.

Acute mountain sickness
Exposure to more extreme altitude (>3,000 m) can induce acute mountain sickness. Extreme headaches, blunted appetite, nausea and vomiting, tiredness and dizziness are among the symptoms. Symptomatic athletes should omit or reduce training until recovered.

IRON AND ALTITUDE TRAINING

Adequate iron stores are essential when training at altitude, and iron deficiency is one of the reasons why some people don't respond to altitude *(p. 4)*. Iron is a mineral that is essential in the production of haemoglobin. Haemoglobin is the part of the red blood cell which attaches to oxygen and transports it around the body.

As the body turns iron stores into additional red blood cells in response to the hypoxic conditions and subsequent increased erythropoietin syntheses, the demand for iron rises, and with it the risk of developing anaemia, even in healthy runners.

However, it is not just iron that's important. Folic acid and vitamin B_{12} are also essential in the formation of red blood cells, and vitamin C plays a role in the absorption of iron.

Iron needs an acidic environment to be absorbed. Meat produces acid in the stomach when it is being digested, but vegetable/fruit sources of iron must be eaten with acidic foods (e.g. ones which contain Vitamin C) for them to be absorbed properly. Antacid tablets and certain foods (milk, eggs rhubarb, caffeine beverages) may decrease iron absorption. Calcium can inhibit the absorption of iron from non-meat sources.

Megaloblastic anaemia, where red blood cells do form, but are defective or abnormally large, and are ineffective in carrying oxygen, results from vitamin B_{12} deficiency. Since vitamin B_{12} is only found in animal products vegans are at particular risk of deficiency.

Both iron stores (ferritin) and haemoglobin levels should be measured well in advance of any planned trip to altitude. As it takes at least two months for inadequate haemoglobin levels to be rectified through supplements, planning is important. It is also a good idea to have ferritin and haemoglobin levels checked on returning to sea level.

ANAEMIA

Anaemia is measured by the amount of haemoglobin per measure of blood (i.e. < 12 g/dl). It is usually caused by insufficient dietary intake of iron (deficiency anaemia) though in can also be caused by factors which inhibit iron absorption (caffeine, digestive disorder), increase iron consumption (pregnancy), increase iron loss (bleeding) or alter iron turnover (prolonged infection). Repetitive pounding associated with running may cause trauma to the feet, bladder and digestive track which results in loss of blood or haemoglobin in the urine or faeces.

Females and vegetarians are particularly susceptible to anaemia, but it can occur in males too. Low ferritin (iron stores), yet normal haemoglobin levels, are common in athletes. The cause of this (latent iron deficiency) is unknown.

Symptoms of anaemia include tiredness, breathlessness during exercise, headaches, light-

NORMAL VALUES

	Male	Female
Haemoglobin values	13.5–17 g/do	12–15 g/do
Ferritin levels	15–445 µg/L	10–235 µg/L
Haematocrit	40–50 %	36–46 %
RDA of iron	6.7 mg/day	14.8 mg/day

headedness, a pale complexion, rapid heart rate, an unexplained dip in performance, moodiness, cold and numbness in the fingers and toes due to poor circulation, brittle or soft nails, and mild depression. Those suffering from iron deficiency anaemia may also be more susceptible to infections. None of the symptoms are exclusive to anaemia, and anaemia can often go undetected for some time. Regular blood tests are the best way of preventing and diagnosing the illness early.

More iron is not always better and unless you have an iron shortage, iron supplements will not increase performance. However, a lack of iron can greatly reduce performance, and the normal benefits of altitude are not evident in those who have low iron availability.

Generally, iron supplements should not be administered for longer than six months and are not advised if you have a stomach ulcer or any stomach or bowel disorder. Iron preparations are best taken before a meal on an empty stomach. Do not take within an hour of bedtime. Side effects include nausea, stomach upset, heartburn, vomiting, and diarrhoea. Continuous use may cause constipation and darkening of the stools.

IRON CONTENT OF VARIOUS FOODS

Food	Iron (mg) per 100 g	Food	Iron (mg) per 100 g	Food	Iron (mg) per 100 g
Liver (calf)	12.2	Chicken liver pâté	9.2	Spinach (cooked)	3.6
Liver (lamb)	10.2	Chicken (lean, cooked)	0.9-1.2	Broccoli (cooked)	1.9
Liver (chicken)	3.3	Egg yolks (raw)	2.7	Kale (cooked)	0.9
Clams (boiled)	14.0	Bran flakes*	20.0	Cabbage (cooked)	0.4
Oysters	12.0	Cornflakes*	7.0	Prunes	2.6
Venison steak (cooked)	4.2	Teff (uncooked)	7.0	Dry roasted peanuts	2.0
Beef (cooked)	2.5-4.0	Brown rice (raw)	1.5	Cashew nuts	6.7
Minced beef (cooked)	3.1	White rice (raw)	0.8	Almonds	3.7
Lamb (lean, cooked)	2.5	Pasta (uncooked)	1.3	Dried apricots	3.5
Veal (lean, cooked)	2.1	Wholemeal bread	3.1	Raisins	3.8
Pork (lean, cooked)	1.1	Wholemeal roll	3.6	Red lentils (boiled)	3.0
Mackerel (smoked)	1.2	baked beans	1.4	Red kidney beans	2.0

* Fortified with iron

Racing at Altitude

The Mexico City Olympics in 1968, was the greatest example to date of the difficulties of racing at altitude. The winning times in all distance races were slower than at the previous Games, and many athletes, particularly those who did not live at altitude, struggled to run times that they would have had no difficulty with at sea-level.

Though the Summer Olympic Games are unlikely to be held at altitude again in the near future, it is not unusual for important competitions to be held at or above 1,500 m of altitude. The US indoor athletics championships have regularly been held at altitude in Albuquerque, and colleges competing in the Mountain West Conference and the Big Sky Conference of NCAA competition, are regularly subjected to regional qualifiers at altitude. Thanks to altitude adjustment that the NCAA accepts, athletes competing in these conferences can run qualifiers for national championships without having to travel to sea level. The 2011 Pan American Games were also held at altitude in Guadalajara (1,570 m).

Winter sports athletes regularly compete at altitude, and the Nordic events of the 2002 Salt Lake City Winter Olympic Games were held at altitudes between 1,650 m and 1,800 m.

Perhaps one of the most infamous competition venues at altitude is Estadio Hernando Siles, the national football stadium in La Paz, Bolivia. It is located at 3,637 m of altitude, and the stresses of the altitude are so great that players resort to using bottled oxygen during half-time. Unsurprisingly, the locals are somewhat acclimatised and a 2-0 defeat of Brazil in 1993 and a 6-1 trashing of Argentina in 2009 are among their successes in the stadium. In 2007, FIFA banned stadiums above 2,500 m from holding World Cup qualifying games, but, after protests, the level was raised to 3,000 m in 2008, and Estadio Hernando Siles was given a special exemption and can continue to host international games. It's not a venue that visiting teams enjoy.

As mentioned previously, each individual responds differently to altitude. Some athletes perform much worse at altitude than their peers, even peers who have had the same previous exposure to altitude. Kenyan steeplechaser Paul Kipsiele Koech is an example of an athlete who struggles to race at altitude. He has the third fastest time in history (7:54.31) and was the world number 1 in 2008 and 2012. However, he did not represent his native Kenya at the Olympic Games in either of those years, because he failed to perform at the Kenyan trials which were held at altitude in Nairobi. Koech was born at altitude in Cheplanget.

Air resistance and the effect of gravity decrease with increased altitude, and as a result, performance is generally improved in sprint and jumping events. While performance was greatly hindered in endurance events at the Mexico City Olympics, new world or Olympic records were set in almost every sprint and jump event. Performance is also improved in the heavy throws (shot put and hammer), but in the discus and javelin, where air density provides lift to the throwing implement, performance tends to be hindered at altitude.

Tips for Racing at Altitude

Acclimatise

If possible, spend 14 days acclimatising to the altitude that you will be competing at. Some people suggest that if you are racing at altitude but don't have adequate time to acclimatise, then you should arrive less than 24 hr before your race, before the body realises you are at altitude. This is debatable, and others suggest that you should

Comparison of Men's Athletics Winning Performances at 1964 and 1968 Olympic Games

	1964 Tokyo (sea level)	1968 Mexico City (2,290 m)
5,000 m	Bob Schul (USA) 13:48.8	Mohammed Gammoudi (TUN) 14:05.01
10,000 m	Billy Mills (USA) 28:24.4 **OR**	Naflati Temu (KEN) 29:27.40
marathon	Abebe Bikila (ETH) 2:12:11.2	Mamo Wolde (ETH) 2:20:27
20 km walk	Ken Matthews (GBR) 1:29:34.0	Volodymyr Holubnychy (URS) 1:33:58
50 km walk	Abdon Pamich (ITL) 4:11:12.4	Chritoph Hohne (GDR) 4:20:14
3,000 m steeplechase	Not held	Amos Biwott (KEN) 8:51.02

OR—Olympic record

spend as much time as possible at altitude before you race (i.e. that 4 days is better than 3).

Lower your expectations
You're going to run slower at altitude than you would at sea level. And it's going to feel more difficult, even if you've had some time to acclimatise. The higher the race, the more difficult it will be to replicate your personal best times. If you've never raced at altitude before, you won't know how you are going to respond.

Run according to feel rather than pace
Don't expect to be able to hit the same split times as at sea level. It may be a good idea not to even set yourself target split times. The NCAA have set time adjustments for qualification races run at altitude, and Jack Daniels has calculated altitude adjustments for different race durations at different elevations, but remember that each individual responds differently to altitude and these adjustments are only estimates. Heart rate may be a better indicator of effort. Respect the altitude.

Be prepared
Racing at altitude is difficult, even for locals. Make sure that you are well hydrated, have suitable clothing and sun protection, and know the route well. Hydration is very important at altitude, and while you might not take fluid onboard during 10 km at sea level, you should make use of all available water and feed stations at altitude.

Work on your kick
Distance races held at altitude are even more likely to be tactical, sit-and-kick affairs than normal. Athletes competing in championship events at altitude should be prepared for very tactical races.

Enjoy the atmosphere
Races like the Great Ethiopian Run and Bolder Boulder are great ways to experience racing at altitude. With an aim of completing the course rather than racing against the clock, you will have the opportunity to relax and enjoy the atmosphere.

PRE-ACCLIMITISATION

Pre-acclimatisation, i.e. exposure to stimulated altitude, through the use of altitude tents, altitude chambers or altitude training masks prior to travel, may help speed up acclimatisation after travelling to altitude. However, studies looking at pre-acclimatisation have largely been conducted on sedentary populations or hikers preparing for high-altitude treks.

REFERENCES AND FURTHER READING

You may find the following publications useful if you would like to learn more about the physiological adaptations to altitude, and recent advances and evidence in support of altitude training for sea level performance.

Books
Wilber, R.L., *Altitude Training and Athletic Performance,* Human Kinetics, Champaign, 2004.

Daniels, J., *Daniels' Running Formula*, Human Kinetics, Champaign, 2005.

Brooks, G.A., Fahey, T.D. & White, T.P., Exercise Physiology: *Human Bioenergetics and Its Applications*, 2nd Ed., Mayfield, Mountain View, 1996.

Journals
Lundy, C. et al., Does 'altitude training' increase exercise performance in elite athletes? British Journal of Sports Medicine, 2012; 46: 792-795.

Wilber, R.L., Application of altitude/hypoxic training by elite athletes. *Medicine and Science in Sport and Exercise*, 2007; 39: 1610-1624.

Chapman, R.F. et al., Defining the 'dose' of altitude training: how high to live for optimal sea level performance enhancement. *Journal of Applied Physiology*, 2013; published online, Oct 2013.

IAAF, Training at altitude. IAAF @-Letter for CECS Level II Coaches, 2003; 6: 1-19.

Pedlar, C. et al., The BASES expert statement on human performance in hypoxia inducing environments: natural and stimulated altitude. *The Sport and Exercise Scientist*, 2011; 30: 6-7.

Altitude Training and Team Sports, *British Journal of Sport and Exercise Medicine*, 2013; 47 (Supplement 1), Entire supplement.

Levine, D.L & Stray-Gundersen, J. Dose-Response of Altitude training: How Much Altitude is Enough? *Advances in Experimental Medicine & Biology*, 2007; 588 (Hypoxia and Exercise supplement): 233-247.

Stray-Gundersen, J. et al., 'Living high – training low' altitude training improves sea level performance in male and female elite runners. *Journal of Applied Physiology*, 2001; 91: 1113-1120.

Travel and the Life of the Elite Athlete

The average high performance athlete spends a considerable amount of their time on the road, and getting to and from some of the venues in this book, can involve a day or more of travel. For many athletes travel can be a stressful experience, but when properly planned, it can be productive, motivational and even enjoyable!

Good planning and organisation are essential. Always have a back-up plan, and emergency contact details close to hand for when things go wrong. Most importantly, don't stress. Stress rarely solves travel problems. So long as you have a back-up plan, the worst that can happen is that your travel plans are delayed by a few hours.

Preparation Checklist

Paperwork
- Passport—does it have at least six months validity?
- Visa requirements—do you need to apply in advance?
- Travel insurance—do you have valid travel insurance for the destination to which you're travelling

Medical *(see p. 11)*
- Dental check-up
- Iron level check
- Prescription renewal
- Vaccine requirements

Logistics
- Arrange transport to/from airport
- Book accommodation
- Check expected weather

Money
- Money/currency - Arrange money/currency and alternative access to money should anything go wrong
- Inform bank of travels

Packing Checklist

Before you embark on a trip, it's a good idea to put together a list of everything that you need to pack. Not only will this help you remember important items; it will also make you more efficient and ensure that you have the correct items in your hand luggage. It's particularly useful to have items that can only be packed at the last minute on a checklist. And the next time you travel, you only have to adjust the list rather than start from scratch.

Tips for Travel

Email a copy of important travel documents (passport, visa, driving licence, travel vaccine records, itinerary, travel insurance, and important telephone numbers) to yourself so that you can still access this information, even if all your belongings are stolen.

Be aware of hand luggage allowances. Liquids greater than 100 ml are not permitted in hand luggage and many budget airlines have a strict hand luggage allowance.

Inform your bank of dates that you will be abroad to avoid your credit/debit card being blocked.

Pack important training kit in your hand luggage so that you can still train if your checked baggage doesn't arrive.

If you travel frequently, duplicating toiletry items such as hairbrush, razor, toothbrush, and shampoo can make packing and unpacking easier.

Roll rather than fold clothes to prevent wrinkles and create more space.

Label luggage clearly on both inside and outside to avoid confusion if outer label gets ripped off.

Keep any medicines in their original packaging; it will help airport security to identify what you have, and avoid delays.

When buying bus or train tickets in a country where you can't speak the language, use a phrase book to write down the destination, ticket type and travel date in the local language before approaching the ticket counter.

Give yourself some peace of mind. Travel insurance is inexpensive. Consider annual multi-trip insurance if you are a frequent traveller. It works out cheaper, and saves you having to worry about insurance every time you travel.

Always pack toiletries in a plastic bag to prevent spillages in your luggage.

If you find travel a useless waste of time, try to be productive. Drive with a language CD on; do some study on the plane; take up a needlecraft, write your Christmas cards on the train, use the time to catch up on sleep.

Essential packing list for altitude

Sunscreen and sunglasses The sun's UV rays are much stronger at altitude than at sea level even though the temperatures may be cooler.

High carbohydrate snacks Carbohydrate replacement is very important at altitude, so it is probably a good idea to bring a supply of your favourite cereal bars (at least enough for the first few days until you source supplies locally).

Warm clothes Low humidity means that temperatures can drop drastically and quickly once the sun sets.

Vitamin supplements Altitude training places additional iron and antioxidant needs on the body. Where possible athletes should eat a varied diet high in fresh fruit and vegetables, but supplements are advised if this is not possible.

Hand sanitiser Hygiene levels in most African countries are not what would be expected in the Western world. Eating on-the-go also often involves using the hands.

Entertainment Training camps can be boring, with lots of free time to kill between sessions. Many of the popular training destinations offer little in way of entertainment.

Heart rate monitor Training to heart rate zones prevents overtraining at altitude, when the same pace will represent a higher percentage of your maximal oxygen consumption.

Useful resources

UK travellers can find further information on the Foreign and Commonwealth Office website (www.fco.gov.uk), which has up-to-date travel advice for each country in the world. The Department of Foreign Affairs and Trade website (www.dfa.ie) provides similar information for Irish travellers.

Suggested items to pack

Passport	Study material
Visa	Sleep mask/ear plugs
Other travel documents	Travel pillow
Driving licence	Massage balls
Travel itinerary	Travel socks
Passport-size photos	Travel adaptors
Vaccination certificates	First aid kit
Travel insurance	Hand sanitiser
Currency	Suitable clothing
Travellers cheques	Training kit
Travel guide and maps	Training equipment
Phrase book	Umbrella
Sunglasses	Suncream
Phone plus charger	Toiletries
Laptop plus charger	Tissues/toilet roll
Camera plus charger	Snacks
Entertainment	Dietary supplements
Reading material	Medication

Medical preparation

From a medical perspective, at least three things (blood screening, dental check, travel vaccinations) should be done before any trip to altitude. A general medical check-up is also advised. Medical preparation should start two months in advance, or longer if you are trying to fit it in around important races. Purchasing travel insurance with medical cover is also important

Blood screening It is important that you have a blood screen to assess haemoglobin and ferritin levels *(see p. 6)*, and to check for any underlying infections or deficiencies.

Dental check Teeth are one of the most neglected parts of the body. A tooth infection can, however, have a severe detrimental effect on training, at any time, but toothache can be even more severe at altitude, and while flying. It is important to ensure that your teeth are in good health if planning on travelling to a country where emergency dental care may be inadequate (e.g. Kenya or Ethiopia). An infection of any kind, but particularly a tooth infection, can also use up valuable iron stores.

Travel vaccines and medication If you are travelling to Africa or South America, it is likely that you will require vaccination against various diseases and prophylactics against malaria. Seek the advice of a medical practitioner at least two months in advance, and try to avoid receiving vaccines during a heavy period of training, or just before a race (as some vaccines may make you feel slightly ill for a few days).

Renew all prescriptions Ensure that you have adequate supplies of any prescribed medication that you take. Your medications may not be available abroad, or may contain different ingredients when purchased abroad (and put you at risk of inadvertently committing a doping offence).

Some tropical illnesses that you may need to protect against

Cholera is an acute diarrhoeal disease contracted by consuming contaminated food and water. Cholera can be fatal without medical treatment. The risk to travellers is low, and sticking to safe water and food reduces that risk further. Diarrhoea is typically sudden, profuse and watery in those infected with the disease. Prompt replacement of lost fluids is vital. There is currently no widely-available effective vaccine.

Hepatitis A is common in most countries outside of North America, Northern Europe and Australia, and is particularly common in countries with a warm climate, poor hygiene standards and overcrowding. The highly-incapacitating viral disease is normally spread by the faecal–oral route, most often by consuming faecal-contaminated water or food. Vaccination, which lasts for approximately 12 months in the first instance (a booster injection 6–12 months later provides immunity for up to 10 years), is required at least two weeks in advance of travel. Strict personal hygiene, and avoiding inadequately cooked shellfish, unpasteurised milk, raw vegetables and untreated water in infected countries is also strongly advised.

Hepatitis B is a viral infection often followed by chronic liver disease, and occurs throughout the world. Currently available vaccines are expensive, but should be considered by those intending to spend six months or longer in an endemic area and those who are involved in heath care. Transmission is most likely through unscreened blood transfusions, inadequately sterilised medical equipment, shared needles or razors, and unprotected sex, though it may be spread in other ways.

Malaria, a tropical disease carried and spread by mosquitoes, is a major cause of death in Africa, Asia and Latin America, and is the disease most likely to cause illness in the modern traveller. Using appropriate malarial prophylactics and minimising exposure to mosquito bites may virtually eliminate the risk to tourists. Lower temperatures at high altitude increase the length of time it takes for the malaria-causing parasite to develop within infected mosquitoes. There is a significantly reduced chance that the mosquito is still alive by the time the parasite has developed at altitudes above 1,600 m. Epidemics are possible above this height in some regions in warm, wet years, and though malaria has recently been recorded at altitudes above 2,400 m, this is the exception rather than the rule. There is minimal risk of contracting malaria in the venues featured in this book, but travellers should seek the most up-to-date medical advice in advance of travelling. Malaria is present in low-lying areas of Ethiopia, Kenya, South Africa and Mexico, and the risk should be considered if excursions to affected areas are planned. Prophylactics are required to be taken for up to two weeks before exposure, and for up to four weeks after potential exposure to malaria-carrying mosquitoes. No drug is 100 percent effective in the prevention of malaria and you should make every effort to avoid being bitten by mosquitoes – sleep under a mosquito net, use insect repellent, and wear long sleeved tops and trousers after dark.

Rabies is a serious, potentially fatal disease and is most often contracted through the bite of an infected dog (or similar animal). Vaccines are expensive, and do not negate the need for treatment after exposure. If you are travelling to a high-risk area, seek medical advice in advance, and check that there is sufficient medical care within easy travel should you be bitten.

Typhoid, like cholera, is potentially fatal if untreated. It is typified by diarrhoea, abdominal pain, vomiting and fever and is caused by the bacterium *Salmonella typhi*. Vaccination is recommended for travellers to Africa and rural areas of developing countries in other parts of the world. Vaccination doesn't result in complete protection, and care should be taken to avoid unsafe water and food in infected areas. Standard vaccines are effective for three years.

Yellow fever is a potentially fatal virus spread by mosquitoes. It occurs in jungle and urban areas of South America and West and Central Africa. A sudden high fever, muscle ache, headache, nausea and vomiting may indicate the onset of the disease. Most cases of yellow fever are mild, but the worst cases can result in liver failure. This liver failure causes the jaundice which gives the disease its name. Vaccination is essential for visitors to all endemic areas, even if there have been no recently reported cases of the disease. A single vaccine provides immunity for at least 10 years. Obtaining an International Certificate of Vaccination when inoculated is essential, as travel to certain countries is restricted without it (e.g. if you are flying to South Africa via Ethiopia, you will need a certificate, even if you are only changing aircraft in Addis Ababa). Certificates are only valid from 10 days after vaccination. Mosquito bites should be avoided.

Booster immunisation against tetanus, diphtheria and polio is recommended for all travellers

Further information
This information should not replace the advice of a trained medical practitioner. Those who want to know more may find the following sources useful:
Darwood, R. *Travellers' Health: How to stay healthy abroad*, 5th Edition, Oxford University Press, 2012 (www.travellers-health.info).
National Travel Health Network and Centre (UK) – www.nathnac.org
Centers for Disease Control and Prevention (US) – www.cdc.gov/travel

TRAVEL NUTRITION

Managing your diet can be one of the most difficult things to do while travelling and training abroad. Micro-nutrients are important to prevent illnesses (colds, virus, infections) which the stress of travel and air-conditioned aircraft cabins may expose you to. In a new environment, with different foods, calorie requirements still need to be met. Care should be taken to avoid traveller's diarrhoea and other food-borne illnesses.

FOOD FOR THE JOURNEY

Pack as much fresh food as reasonably possible for your outward journey. If you are travelling late at night, you may not be able to get food at your final destination. Snacks may also be required to supplement or replace the food provided on long-haul flights and if your flight is delayed you may not have time at the airport to eat before catching a connecting flight.

When packing food, consider airport restrictions on hand luggage allowance (only one item of hand luggage allowed onboard some budget airlines), fluids (no liquids in hand luggage), and taking animal products from one country to another.

Food at airports tends to be expensive and finding nutritious options can be difficult. Always choose nutritional content over price. Fresh-made sandwiches; fresh meat with salad and hot meals are better than pre-packaged sandwiches and microwave pasties.

After clearing security, purchase adequate fluid supplies for your flight and, if there's a chance that you won't be able to buy fluids at your arrival airport, for the next leg of your journey. Aircraft humidity is around 10–15 percent, and moisture is drained from your body during flights. Don't drink alcohol on the flight and avoid drinking tea, coffee and cola; all of which may increase dehydration.

Bring a range of healthy snacks onboard long-haul flights and avoid large bags of sweets or crisps which you may eat purely out of boredom. Travelling can upset the digestive system. Drink lots of fluid and eat fibre-rich foods such as fresh and dried fruit and wholemeal bread.

BUFFET DINING

Athletes often struggle with buffet meals and the dining-hall experience. The food in most altitude training camps is well balanced and nutritious, but individuals may try every food available, eat too much, or miss out on some key nutrients. Your meal should be mostly carbohydrate (noodles, potatoes, cereal, bread), with some protein (eggs, meat, fish, cheese), and ample fresh vegetables. A treat is reasonable, but sampling every desert on the menu is unlikely to fuel your training.

If you feel that your nutritional requirements are not being met, or that you don't like the food provided, ask for alternatives. A large establishment is unlikely to completely change its menu just to accommodate one resident, but is likely to make small adjustments where required. If you have specific dietary requirements (e.g. lactose or gluten intolerance) check well in advance that your accommodation can cater for your needs. Unless you're willing to eat rice for breakfast, those with celiac disease are likely to struggle in Kenya, for example.

FOOD SAFETY

Particular care should be taken when sourcing and preparing food in African, Asian and South American countries where food hygiene doesn't meet Western standards. The general rule is 'peel it, cook it, shell it, or forget it'. Eat only in well-known or recommended establishments and avoid stalls. Food should always be well cooked, and served piping hot. If the local water is unsafe to drink, use only sealed, bottled water and drinks, avoid ice in drinks, clean teeth with bottled water and avoid salad vegetables which may have been washed in contaminated water.

If vomiting or diarrhoea does occur, replace lost fluids and electrolytes using oral rehydration solutions and safe water. Eat bland foods (e.g. dry toast, crackers, biscuits and rice). Avoid alcohol, fatty foods and dairy products until you feel better. If you are using oral contraceptives, beware that absorption may not have occurred.

GOOD FOODS TO PACK

Dried fruit	Jam*, honey*
Nuts and seeds	Peanut butter*
Tinned fruit*	Instant noodles
Cereal bars	Baked beans*
Breakfast cereal	Powdered sports drinks
Crackers and oatcakes	Jellies and sweets
Fig rolls, Jaffa cakes	Tinned spaghetti*
Dutch breakfast cake	Powdered milk
Rice cakes	Fruit squash*
Liga, Rusks and other fortified baby food	Malt loaf Halva

* Not suitable for hand luggage on international flights

Long-haul flights: jet lag and travel fatigue

Travel can negatively affect health and performance in a number of ways. Doing a hard session straight after getting off a long-haul flight will increase injury-risk; breathing recirculated cabin air when flying can increase the risk of infection; and getting stressed can wear you down. Travel fatigue can affect how well you feel for a day or two after you reach your chosen destination and jet lag can affect how you feel, and how well you perform, for a week or longer.

Travel fatigue

Long-distance travel, irrespective of the number of time zones crossed, can result in travel fatigue. A feeling of extreme tiredness, due to a combination of disruption to normal routine, sleep and eating patterns; boredom; cramped conditions; travel stress and dehydration, tends to follow travel.

Jet lag

Travelling across multiple time zones results in a specific form of fatigue associated with disruptions to the body's daily (circadian) rhythm. These disruptions arise from discrepancies between the body's internal 'clock', which is adjusted to the time where you have travelled from, and the actual time in your destination. The human circadian rhythm is tuned to enhance activity and performance during daylight hours and to promote sleep and recovery during hours of darkness, but adjustment to a new environment, and a new set of day/night cues takes time.

It normally takes 1 day per time zone travelled, to adjust to the new environment, though individual variations do exist. Travel westward results in less severe symptoms than travelling eastwards. Lark-type personalities (early risers), are better suited to eastward travel, and owl-types (those who are most active late in the evening), are better suited to westward travel, though neither are immune.

Symptoms of jet lag include an inability to sleep at night, difficulty waking, and feeling sleepy during the day. Mood, appetite and bowel movement are suppressed. Mental confusion, disorientation and decrements in concentration can have negative effects on performance, and headaches, nausea and general malice make training difficult.

Avoid sleep deprivation in the days before travel. Being tired before you start will exacerbate the effects of jet lag.

Book flights for a time that will best help you adapt to a new routine. Arriving in the evening when you will naturally want to go to bed may be better than arriving in the morning, when the temptation to go to bed may be too great to overcome. On the other hand, if you arrive very late at night and get to bed later than usual, you will already have missed valuable sleep time.

Consider pre-adapting your sleep–wake cycle before you travel. If travelling eastwards, get up a few minutes earlier each day, and go to bed earlier each night, and vice versa. Adjust your watch to the time at the final destination when you board the plane, and start adjusting immediately.

Fit into sleep/wake patterns and meal patterns straight away, no matter how tired (or awake) you feel. When travelling westwards, make use of evening light by exercising or taking a walk to stay awake later. Sleep in a room with windows, so as to adjust to the light/dark cues quicker.

During the first few days, where possible, training should take place during the overlap period in time zones. Doing so will help maintain the quality of training and reduce the risk of injury.

Don't forget that you need to adapt to travel on both the outward, and the home journeys.

DVT

DVT is the clotting of deep veins, usually in the calves, resulting in swollen legs, and more severe consequences if the clots become loose, travel to the lungs, and cause a pulmonary embolism. DVT is most common during long-haul flights, but can occur as a result of any situation involving prolonged sitting and cramped conditions, including car and bus journeys.

Regular walks to the toilet, to get fluids, or to look out of the window, will help prevent stiffness and DVT. Heel raises, knee extensions, ankle rotations and light calf and hamstring stretches should be performed during the flight.

Always wear compression socks during the flight. Keep well hydrated, avoid sleeping pills, and book an isle seat, so that you can walk around when you wish. These precautions will not only help prevent DVT, but will also prevent stiffness.

Avoid intense sessions immediately before or immediately after a long flight, as this will increase your injury and infection risks. Instead use mild exercise to loosen out your legs.

HOW NOT TO TRAVEL AROUND THE WORLD
Adapted from the blog, 3 April 2010

This trip probably hasn't got off to the best of starts. Two days ago I thought I had been April-fooled when I went online to check that I had been paid this week. To my dismay, my current account didn't appear on my online banking. Yes, that's right, it didn't appear at all. A credit card account for which I don't yet have the card, and a savings account which I have no account to transfer money from, are a fat lot of good when I'm stuck in Mexico with no money! A trip to the ATM confirmed my worst fears - my card didn't work. It looked like the fraud squad have spotted some international action on my account and blocked it. One long-distance phone call from the hotel (I'm scared how much that will cost) later it's all been sorted, but the woman in the bank clearly didn't pay any attention when I told her that I was going to Mexico in a few days, and that I wasn't coming back any time soon.

And that's not the only thing to go wrong so far. I'm just four days into a two month trip and the list of mishaps is already getting very long.

1. A few days before the trip started I realised that my credit card was about to expire, and that the new one had probably been sent to my old address. I ordered a replacement card, but there wasn't enough time for it to arrive before I left.

2. When I went to confirm the dates with the camp that I was hoping to stay at (3 days before I was due to leave), I learned that they were booked out. I'm not sure where I get this reputation for being organised from!

3. I didn't have enough time to locate and book alternative accommodation. Taking the term 'no fixed abode' to a whole new level, I left without knowing where I was going to be spending my first night in Mexico.

4. I arrived at Birmingham International Airport at 06:30 on Tuesday morning having finished work just 13 hours before that. Starting a 19 hour journey on 20 minutes sleep isn't a good idea.

5. I forgot how annoying the questioning can be before boarding a flight to the US. Travelling on an Irish passport, from the UK, with no current UK address, and no current employment, doesn't go down too well. Going on vacation alone is not viewed as normal, and one large suitcase, a rucksack, and a large carrier-bag is seen as inadequate for a 10-week trip (little do they know, that I'm travelling unusually heavily for me). And a Jordanian visa in your passport seems to get you noticed for all the wrong reasons.

6. I completely forgot to request an aisle seat at check-in, and was put next to the window. The confinement of my seating was compounded by the fact that it was just a small plane, and I couldn't stand and stretch during the flight.

7. I attempted to book accommodation at Newark airport, but realised that the only way I could get internet access was by paying for it with credit card, but as we know, I don't have a valid one of those! Luckily, when I got to Huston, I was able to get a complimentary 45 minutes internet access, and managed to book accommodation for two nights. Things were finally starting to look up.

8. When I arrived at the airport in San Luis Potosí, I couldn't find my luggage. The one with the plastic film wrapped all around looked closest, but wasn't it... or was it? Yes, the helpful baggage man confirmed that it was indeed mine. The handle for pulling it had been broken off, and the whole thing was about to burst open.

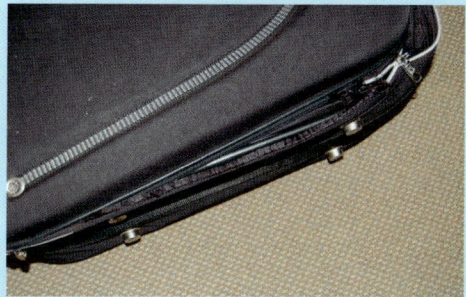

Note to self: before travelling, make sure that suitcase is in full working order

9. When I arrived at the hotel they had no confirmation of my booking, and had not received payment. Luckily they had a room, but at 22:00 local time, and potentially nowhere to stay, I really was living life on the edge.

10. My mobile phone hadn't worked since leaving Birmingham, so I couldn't let the people that I had promised to text know that I had arrived safely.

12. Stupidly unprepared for the weather I got sunburnt on my first day here. Hopefully this was the last in a long line of things to go wrong.

So, now that I've learned what not to do, I'm hoping that the rest of my trip will go ok.

CHOOSING YOUR ALTITUDE TRAINING VENUE

There is a huge variety of venues suitable for altitude training. There are regions of high altitude on each continent and on both sides of the equator. Selection of a suitable venue comes down to an individual's budget, training requirements and personal preferences. These are just some of the things to consider when considering where to train.

The time of year
A lot of the high altitude venues in Europe and America are covered in snow during the winter and spring months, while the opposite is true for Australia. Most venues in Africa (with the notable exception of Ifrane in Morocco), and Central and South America are available all year-round.

The phase of your training year
The height and location at which you choose to train, may be determined by the stage of your training cycle. Higher altitudes may be more appropriate for early season base work, while having access to a track and gym may be essential closer to the season.

The amount of time you have available
While a minimum of 3 weeks at altitude is recommended for maximum adaptation, individuals don't always have that much time available to them. Spending a day travelling to some exotic location (and a day travelling back) may eat into valuable time.

Time to get there
The time it takes to get there may not be as it seems. You can reach Addis Ababa after a 7 hr direct flight from London Heathrow. Getting to St. Moritz from London may involve a 2 hr flight to Zurich, an overnight stay in Zurich, followed by a 3 hr 30 min train journey to St. Moritz, meaning that you reach your destination some 15 hr after boarding an aircraft in London.

The type of training protocol you are planning on implementing
'Live high, train low' training procedures are only possible in some of the altitude training venues featured in this book.

Race plans
Jet lag and travel fatigue may hinder performance upon return to sea level. Additional thought may need to go into whether or not facilities are adequate for race-specific sessions, and whether the altitude is too high to carry out the required quality sessions.

Training preference and requirements
Do you need a track or gym? Are there any alternative training options if you get injured? Can you continue to cross-train? Is there a suitable variety of off-road trails? Are there traffic-free roads to carry out race-specific marathon sessions? These are just some of the questions you might want to ask yourself when choosing a venue.

Who you're travelling with
If you are travelling with non-running partners or friends, make sure that there is something for them to do while you're training. Mexico City is one example of a city with lots to do. Smaller towns like Falls Creek may not be so appealing to people who like to keep busy. Kenya and Ethiopia are good for the full cultural experience, and great for solo travellers looking to meet and befriend like-minded individuals.

Your budget
Travelling in groups may help save money in some venues, but travelling alone in others (e.g. Kenya), may not be a financial disadvantage. Car hire is a hidden cost, but some venues don't require access to your own transport. While the flight to most African countries may be expensive, the cost of living is much lower than in Europe; a balance which swings in Africa's favour if you plan on being away for a long period. Self-catering accommodation usually works out cheaper than hotels, especially if travelling in groups, but not all venues in this book have suitable self-catering rental properties. While all-inclusive camps are less hassle, they are usually more expensive than booking everything yourself.

US While the cost of travelling in the US will generally depend on the strength of the dollar against the British pound or euro, it's fair to say that accommodation, eating out, car hire and clothing will usually be cheaper than in Europe, and groceries, physiotherapy and massage, and gym membership will be more expensive. A car is almost essential in most US venues, and the cost of car hire should not be forgotten when budgeting for a trip. The ski resort of Mammoth Lakes and trendy Boulder are more expensive than Albuquerque and Flagstaff. Health care is expensive, and travel insurance is essential.

Africa Flights to East and Southern Africa will be expensive, but the costs once you get there, will be much cheaper than anywhere else in the book. Flight prices do vary depending on the time of year, and booking well in advance is strongly advised. As driving is not recommended, car hire doesn't have to be factored in, and public transport is usually very cheap. The cost of all-inclusive camps such as Yaya Village (Addis Ababa) and HATC (Iten), includes food, accommodation and facility hire, and very little spending money is required. Budget flights to Ifrane make it a particularly attractive option.

Europe Europe is expensive, particularly as the best venues are upmarket ski resorts. Budget flights reduce the cost, and accommodation may be cheaper outside the main tourist seasons. Groceries tend to be expensive, but of a high standard, and fresh fruit, vegetables and bread can easily be sourced.

Australia Flights from Europe will set you back a considerable amount, a car is essential to get around Australia, and groceries are expensive. Accommodation in Falls Creek can be cheap outside of the ski season, but the relative value for money depends largely on the strength of the Australian dollar against other currencies. The value of the dollar against the euro and British pound has fluctuated dramatically in recent years.

BOOKING YOUR ACCOMMODATION

There are a number of things to consider when choosing and booking accommodation. Price is important, but given that you are likely to be spending a few weeks in the same accommodation, and want to be in the best shape to carry out a reasonable block of training, there are other things which should be considered.

Cost This is one of the most important factors when booking accommodation, especially if your stay is going to be over a prolonged period. Apartments and other rental properties will generally be cheaper than other accommodations, particularly if travelling in medium or large groups. However, in some cases, for example Kenya or Ethiopia, the convenience of all-inclusive training camps will far outweigh the cheaper prices of rental properties which often don't have running water or hot showers. Bear in mind that holiday apartments are charged per week from Saturday to Saturday in some popular tourist destinations (e.g. St. Moritz). Some property owners may be willing to negotiate on price if you are staying for a prolonged period. American hotel tax doesn't apply for stays of more than one month in some cities.

Location Some venues (e.g. Flagstaff, Font Romeu, Falls Creek) are so small or compact, that it doesn't matter where you choose your accommodation. Others, most notably Mexico City and Albuquerque, are large sprawling cities, and care must be taken when choosing accommodation. It's useful to stay close to at least one trail suitable for recovery runs, and to stay at a higher altitude than you will be training at. If you are not planning on hiring a car, you will need to stay close to the main trail system, track and gym. It's useful to have a supermarket close by, and a choice of restaurants if you plan on eating out regularly.

Before you book your accommodation, double-check where it is located. Hotels are not always correctly located on Google Maps or generic hotel search engines. You may think that you're staying right next to the best park for running in a city, but actually end up at the other side of the city, kilometres from a public transport link.

Type of accommodation As discussed previously, self-catering accommodation tends to work out cheaper, and allows athletes to cook food to meet their own nutritional needs. This is more difficult in venues without large supermarkets (e.g. Falls Creek or Sierra Nevada). All-inclusive camps tend to be more convenient, especially in Kenya and Ethiopia, but are more expensive than other options. If moving around a lot, and travelling on your own, long-stay hotels, or hotels with suites, can be a more suitable option, especially in the US. They are likely to work out cheaper than renting an apartment on your own, but still allow you to prepare your own food.

Space and facilities You are likely to be spending a considerable amount of time in your accommodation recovering or relaxing between training sessions; much more so than with a sightseeing or beach holiday. It is important therefore that your accommodation is comfortable and that you don't feel overcrowded.

Availability Book your accommodation well in advance, particularly if you are travelling in a large group and want to be accommodated together, or are travelling during the busy Christmas and Easter holidays. In some venues (e.g. Ifrane) there is limited apartment accommodation, and booking late may leave you with the more expensive options, located away from the main training venues, or unable to find accommodation which caters for your group size. Some of the training centres (e.g. CAR Sierra Nevada, HATC in Iten and La Loma in San Luis Potosí) are used by large national teams, and tend to get booked up well in advance. This is especially true in the run up to major international competitions.

TRAINING FULL-TIME: STRIKING THE RIGHT BALANCE

Boredom can be an issue when training at altitude. Striking a balance between killing time, relaxing, and embracing the culture of your training home, can be difficult. The balance between training, recovery, and sightseeing will largely be determined by your goals. A serious athlete, looking to carry out a good block of training, shouldn't be spending all the time between training walking from site to site, or risking injury by trying skiing. A recreational athlete looking to do some running while touring a new country will be less concerned about recovery, and will look to experience as many new activities and sites as possible. Most people will fall somewhere in between. They will want to spend their time wisely, and have new experiences, but recover adequately for their next training session, and not increase their injury risk. Students or anyone who has work to complete while away, will have additional balances to strike, but will benefit from the distractions from training. Full-time athletes may be well adjusted to filling the long gaps between training, but those new to full-time training may struggle.

Some of the risks are:
- You become lethargic from boredom, and your training suffers as a consequence.
- You try to fit too much in, and don't get adequate recovery.
- You fail to embrace the culture and miss out on some enjoyable and inspiring experiences
- In an attempt to avoid boredom, you fill the time between training with more training, and get burned out.
- You get addicted to computer games, and delay or skip training.
- You spend all day on your feet visiting sites, and end up getting tight muscles and sore feet, and risk increasing injury.
- You fill all your spare time with sleep, and become generally lethargic, or struggle to sleep at night. You will of course need more sleep at altitude, and afternoon naps are acceptable, but ensure that you don't oversleep.
- You get dragged into other people's routines. Having people to do things with is very positive, but remember that each person responds differently to altitude, and you may need more recovery than your friends.

Here are some ideas on how to strike the balance:

Choose a venue based on your entertainment needs If you don't like to sit around chatting all day then Kenya might not be for you. If you like to shop and visit lots of new sites, then choose Mexico City. Choose a big city like Albuquerque if you like to have lots of things to do, and choose somewhere like Falls Creek if you would prefer to be close to nature.

Decide on one or two things you'd like to do while you're away, and then decide where those activities best fit into your training programme. A rest day might be a good time to fit in an excursion, but ensure that it won't tire you out too much for the following day's training. Having things to do during the first week, when you're trying to curtail your training, may also be a good idea. If you plan on trying cross country skiing (weather permitting), or would like to explore the area on mountain bike, use them as cross training during the first week, or on a recovery day later in your stay.

Bring some entertainment with you A pack of cards is a great way to make friends and fill time. Board games are also a good way to pass the time. DVDs are also a good idea, and many athletes like to play computer games, but consider if spending hours on a Playstation actually has the desired effect of relaxing you. It goes without saying that reading is a good way to pass the time. If English-language reading won't easily be available bring plenty of books, or an e-reader.

Study or do some work It sounds a bit mad, but having some study or work to do, may help distract from training in a very positive way. Doing an online course, completing college work, or carrying out mini projects may be a very rewarding way to fill the time. Internet access may be slow and expensive in some countries, and this should be considered. You may find that there are more interesting things to do when you get there, so keep your targets realistic.

Take up a new hobby or practice a skill Taking photos, learning to knit, painting and drawing the landscape, learning a language or writing a novel are just some ways to productively pass the time. Use the time to do things that you don't get the chance to do when you're at home.

Enjoy your mealtimes Fitting training in around full-time work or study can mean that eating becomes a chore, and is often a rushed process. While away, use the extra time to try cooking new dishes (if self catering) or bake some healthy flapjacks. The dining hall can become a great place to meet new people and make new friends. Your digestive system will also thank you for not rushing your meals all the time.

DEALING WITH INJURY AT ALTITUDE

If you are training at altitude, and get an injury that prevents you from carrying out your normal training, it is best not to panic. Depending on the severity of your injury, your goals, how far you are into the season, and the duration of your planned trip, you have a number of options.

The most important thing is that you get treatment for your injury. If you do not have support personnel with you, cannot find access to a suitable physiotherapist, and do not know what your injury is and how to treat it, you may be best taking complete rest. In this case, if you have a long trip planned, consider shortening your trip.

Even if your ability to train is severely hindered by your injury, you will still benefit from sleeping at altitude. If it's an injury that you would have to rest, even if you were at home, you may still be able to get some benefit from your trip, and the solitude of altitude may help with adherence to rehab exercises.

There may actually be a number of advantages of cross-training at altitude. Sometimes athletes find it difficult to run slow enough to keep their heart rate within the required zones. Cycling, aquajogging, or even just walking, may be sufficient to raise the heart rate to normal easy exercise levels. Cross-training may, therefore, be a good choice of exercise particularly during the first ten days, and during base-building training stints, and may help clear up niggling injuries at the start of a stint at altitude.

Venues which are hilly, or have rough trails may hinder training with certain injuries, but individuals may still be able to carry out a large volume of cross-training. In places like Iten, it is very difficult to find routes that are not hilly or rough, but if you can handle the monotony, the track at Kamariny Stadium has a dirt surface, and is ideal for short runs. Be willing to adapt your training, and to think outside of the box.

If you are susceptible to injury, or have a recurring injury, ensure that you have access to physiotherapy, and/or medical backup, have access to cross-training facilities if required, and have investigated if the trails are suitable for you.

If all else fails, and if it's not practical for you to go home early, consider that your injury may be your body telling you to take a break. Consider whether you actually need a holiday. Make a conscious effort to make the most of the trip, and add in some extra sightseeing, make some new friends, and relax. Make the most of the hypoxic air!

BELOW If the hills of Iten are too much for your Achilles, head to the track at Kamariny for a light off-road recovery run (or walk)

San Luis Potosí

The old colonial mining town of San Luis Potosí, located in Mexico's central plateau, has a pleasant climate year-round. Excellent facilities at La Loma Altitude Training Centre more than meet the needs of high performance athletes. Parque Tangamanga I provides some running trails, with additional options in the mountains surrounding the city. Cost of living is relatively low, once you get there, and the medium-sized city offers both convenience and relaxation. Mexican culture and food are waiting to be sampled in the city's Centro Histórico.

San Luis Potosí, Mexico (1,860 m)

The colonial city of San Luis Potosí is relatively small by Mexican standards, and has a population of just under 750,000. It is located on the central plateau that connects the Sierra Madre Oriental and Sierra Madre Occidental, the two mountain ranges that run down through Mexico. San Luis Potosí is just over 400 km north of Mexico City. It is the capital of a state of the same name, and is named after Louis IX of France (San Louis), and the rich mines of Potosí in Bolivia. The city was founded in 1592 following the discovery of gold and silver mines in nearby Cerro de San Pedro.

San Luis Potosí is located in the centre of the triangle formed by Mexico's three largest cities—Mexico City, Guadalajara and Monterrey—and halfway between Mexico City and the US border. Today the city has a prolific manufacturing industry, and the economy, previously based around gold, silver, copper and zinc mines, is now based around the city's many flour mills, tanneries, textile mills, furniture factories, breweries and smelters, and the distribution of domestic and foreign goods.

The city's historic centre (Centro Histórico), which contains buildings constructed in an eclectic mix of artistic and architectural styles, has been named a UNESCO World Heritage site as part of the El Camino Real de Tierra Adentro *(p. 23)*. It is affectionately known as La Ciudad de los Jardínes (*City of Gardens*).

Prior to the arrival of Spanish conquistadores, the area in which San Luis Potosí is located was inhabited by groups of nomadic tribes known generally as Chichimeca. As the Chichimeca didn't build permanent settlements, it was the Spaniards who founded the first villages and towns in the area in the late 1500s. The mines of Cerro de San Pedro were discovered in 1952, and when a lack of water prevented the building of a new settlement next to the mines, San Luis Potosí was legally founded.

The city has twice served as the national capital—in 1863 and 1867—and the Mexican national anthem was written in the city in 1854. While Francisco Ignacio Madero Gonzalez was imprisoned in the city by the dictator Porfirio Díaz, he drafted the Plan of San Luis Potosí. This document called for democracy to be reintroduced and for the people of Mexico to revolt. It led the way for the Revolution of 1910 *(see p. 23)*.

PREVIOUS *Plaza del Carmen in Centro Histórico*

Author's verdict

Year-round sunshine, excellent facilities, and a low cost of living make the city an attractive option, though without driving into the countryside, the trail options are limited. The medium-sized city provides all the services, conveniences and entertainment an athlete would need. Long-haul flights may make it a less attractive destination for European athletes, but North Americans can easily escape to spring sunshine. San Luis Potosí is better for middle distance athletes doing a block of quality training, than it is for long distance runners. The city is nice enough, but I'm not sure I would want to spend any more than a couple of weeks there at any one time, and I would have enjoyed the trip more if I could speak Spanish.

Running ★★★★★ - Adequate runs for middle distance athletes; endurance runners may need to drive out of the city for variety; synthetic track for sessions; limited cross-training options.

Convenience ★★★★★ - Conveniently located airport; well connected with major US airports; long flight from Europe; medium-sized city is easy to get around; English not widely spoken; weather good year-round; all-inclusive camp at La Loma

Safety ★★★★★ - Not particularly affected by violent or drug-related crime; some pickpocketing and petty theft; good medical service; hepatitis A and typhoid vaccination recommended.

Cost ★★★★★ - Low cost of living in the city itself; La Loma rates comparable with similar all-inclusive facilities; flights from Europe are expensive; car useful, though not essential.

Cultural experience ★★★★★ - Exciting cultural experience for first-time visitors to Mexico; some interesting sites and museums; regular festivals and cultural activities; good day-trips.

Things to do between training ★★★★★ - Exploring the beautiful historic centre, shopping for cheap souvenirs and picnicking in the park are some of the popular activities; some good museums and other forms of entertainment.

Suitability for solo travellers ★★★★★ - English is not widely spoken, and a good command of Spanish is useful for solo travellers; most athletes training at La Loma will be in groups or teams, though there is some opportunity to meet other athletes if staying there.

Must do Explore the beautiful plazas in the city's historic centre; run around Parque Tangamanga I where all the locals come to play; do a track session at La Loma while overlooking the city.

Ideal for Athletes in North America looking for some winter sun, and a change of scenery.

MEXICO: AN INTRODUCTION

The country that makes up present-day Mexico has been inhabited for more than 13,000 years, first by indigenous civilisations (the Aztec, Maya, Olmec, Teotihuacan and Toltec), and later by the descendants of Spanish conquistadors. Mexico was part of the Spanish Empire for three centuries, and declared independence in 1810, following a prolonged struggle with Spain. The Mexican-American War broke out in 1846, and when it ended two years later, Mexico ceded almost half of its territory (including the current states of Texas, California, Nevada, Utah, Arizona, New Mexico, and parts of Colorado, Wyoming and Kansas) to the US. France invaded Mexico in 1861, and Maximilian I, backed by Napoleon III, was placed on the throne in an attempt to revive the Mexican monarchy. The US government, among others, refused to recognise his administration, which helped the plight of the Benito Juarez-led republican forces. Maximilian was captured and executed in 1867. Mexico's economy was modernised in the years that followed, and political stability resulted in dramatic improvements in the country's infrastructure. The Mexican Revolution (1910-1929) saw the country's poor revolt against the government, who they believed did little to improve their plight. A tenth of the population were killed, but the system of large haciendas, which originated with the Spanish conquest, was ended. After centuries of conquest and revolution, Mexico is now politically stable. Today, stabilising violent drug wars between rival drug cartels dominates the attentions of the Mexican military.

The language, architecture, religion, art and cuisine of modern Mexico are a product of the fusion that has occurred between the customs and traditions of the ancient native civilisations and the European invaders. Mexico is the most populous Spanish-speaking country in the world, yet has the largest number of Native American language speakers in North America with 62 nationally recognised indigenous languages.

MEXICO QUICK FACTS

Capital/largest city Mexico City
Official language Spanish
Public holidays New Year's Day (Jan 1); Constitution Day (Feb 5); Benito Juarez's birthday (Mar 21); Maundy Thursday*; Good Friday*; Labor Day (May 1); Independence Day (Sept 16); Revolution Day (Nov 20); Change of Federal Government (Dec 1); Christmas Day (Dec 25)
Currency Mexican peso ($/MEX$; MXN), divided into 100 centavo
Time zone Various; Mexico City and San Luis Potosí operate on Central Time Zone (CST; GMT-6) with daylight saving (Apr–Oct)
International dialling code +52
Outgoing access code 98
Emergency contacts 066 (police), 065 (medical), 068 (fire)
Power 127 V; 60 Hz supply; Type A (NEMA 1-15) and Type B (NEMA 5-15) American-style plugs and sockets with two flat vertical pins
Driving Right side
Measurement Metric

* varies according to Christian calendar

Special feature
EL CAMINO REAL DE TIERRA ADENTRO

El Camino Real de Tierra Adentro ('the Royal Road of the Interior Land') was a trade route which stretched over 2,500 km between Mexico City and Santa Fe in New Mexico. Unofficially used by native tribes for trade since early times, the route was officially operational between 1598 and 1882, when railroads replaced the need for travel by horse and wagon. In 2010, a southern section of the trail, which includes the historic centre of San Luis Potosí, was declared a UNESCO World Heritage site.

The route, also known as the Silver Route, was used to transport silver from the mines of Guanajuato, Zacatecas and San Luis Potosí, and mercury imports from Europe. In addition to trade, the route fostered cultural, social and religious links between the peoples along its course. The route runs through Mexico City, San Louis Potosí, Albuquerque and Santa Fe, all featured or mentioned in this book.

LEFT *Detail of the facade of the Templo del Carmen, an 18th century church in Plaza del Carmen*

Getting in

Flying into San Louis Potosí's small international airport is the most convenient way to get in from outside of Mexico, though flights are generally more expensive than flying to Mexico City. The excellent intercity bus network provides a great way of seeing the country while travelling in comfort.

By air

San Louis Potosí's Ponciano Arriaga International Airport (SLP) is situated off MEX-57, 18 km north of Centro Histórico, and approximately 25 km from La Loma Altitude Training Centre. It has just two gates and operates direct international flights to Dallas (American Airlines) and Houston (Continental Airlines), as well as several daily flights to Mexico City.

Flights from the UK, including connections, take 14–21 hr. British Airways, with American Airways, operates a service from London which requires a single change in Dallas. Most other flights involve two changes. Flights are usually more expensive than flying to Mexico City and taking the bus from there, though getting through Mexico City airport takes a lot longer than at SLP, and the time required to travel across Mexico City to the bus terminal should also be factored in.

Taxis from the airport to the city are inexpensive, and take approximately 20–25 min at non-peak times. Taxis operate a 24-hour service from outside the terminal building. Purchase a ticket from the taxi kiosk within the terminal building. Cars can be hired at the airport from Budget, Hertz, Sixt, Thrifty and Avis, and the Mexican company Green Motion (www.greenmotion.mx).

By bus

The large bus terminal (Central Camionera), located 2.5 km east of Centro Histórico, operates services to and from destinations across Mexico, and overnight services to Austin, San Antonio and Laredo across the border in Texas. Roads between San Luis Potosí and Mexico City are in excellent condition, and the more luxurious buses are extremely comfortable. Bus travel is an excellent and inexpensive substitute for the non-existent passenger train service.

There are frequent services from Mexico City (approximately 5 hr to the south), Monterrey (approximately 5 hr to the north), and Guadalajara (approximately 5 hr south-west), among others. The luxury bus companies Primera Plus (www.primeraplus.com.mx) and ETN–Turistar (www.etn.com.mx) both operate direct, almost hourly services to and from Mexico City. Buses from Mexico City to San Luis Potosí leave from Terminal Autobuses del Norte *(p. 42)*.

These companies, together with Omnibus de Mexico (www.omnibusdemexico.com.mx), operate services across Mexico. Tickets can be booked on their websites. Other smaller companies also operate services to and from San Luis Potosí, and tickets, which may be cheaper, can be booked at the station. Turimex International, part of the Grupo Senda company (www.gruposenda.com), operates services from Texas. Buses from the border take approximately 11 hr.

From the bus station, you can take a taxi to your accommodation. Taxi tickets should be purchased from the booth inside the station. Local bus services operate from outside the station. Any bus marked *'Centro'* will take you to the centre of San Luis Potosí.

By car

Mexico is a very big country, and distance between cities should be carefully considered before attempting to drive between cities. Mexico City, Monterrey and Guadalajara are all approximately 5 hr from San Luis Potosí, and the US border is 7 hr away. While driving in the large cities is advised against, hiring a car may be a good way of travelling between cities. There has been considerable investment in the Mexican interstate network since the 1990s and the roads between the main cities are in good condition. The downside is that many of Mexico's best roads now have an expensive toll (*cuota*). Visitors from the US who are taking their own car across the border should ensure that they complete the required paperwork.

Visa requirements

Citizens of most European countries, including the UK and Ireland; Australia; New Zealand; the US; Canada; and many South American countries, do not require visas to enter Mexico for business or tourist purposes for stays of up to 180 days. Citizens of Russia, Ukraine and Brazil require electronic visa authorisation prior to travel. Citizens of all African countries, including South Africa, and most Middle Eastern and Asian countries require a visa, unless they hold a valid US visa, or are a permanent resident of Canada, US, Japan, the UK, or any of the Schengen area countries. Visas take between two days and three weeks to issue, depending on nationality.

OPPOSITE *Plaza del Carmen in Centro Histórico*

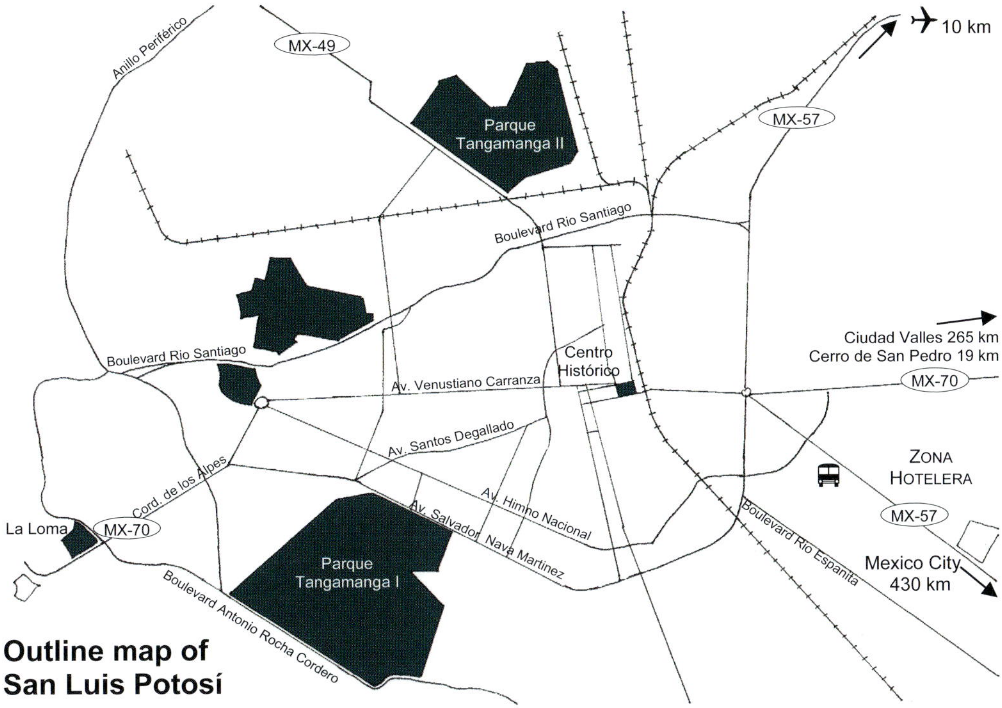

Outline map of San Luis Potosí

Airlines will only allow you to board a flight to Mexico if you have a valid return (or onward) ticket. If, during your stay, you lose the migratory form which you completed on entering the country, you will be required to complete a new one and pay a considerable fine, when leaving.

Getting around

Centro Histórico consists mainly of pedestrianised streets, and getting around on foot is often the best option. The city has a good bus and trolley network. All buses marked '*Centro*' lead to the centre. Bus routes can be mapped at Busca Tu Ruta (www.buscaturuta.com). Taxis are cheap and plentiful, and are a good option if you don't have access to a car and need to pick up groceries.

A car is useful to get to the trails in the hills surrounding the town but is largely useless in the city itself. In addition to the pedestrianised streets of Centro Histórico, there are a number of one-way streets. Often the best way to get across the city is to go around it.

The building number normally follows the street name in physical addresses. The tourism board of the state of San Luis Potosí produces a free map of the city which is available from hotels and information centres.

Weather and when to visit

San Luis Potosí's climate makes it a great destination all year-round. January and December are the coldest months, but even then, average daily highs are approximately 20 °C. April and May, the warmest months, have average daily highs of approximately 28 °C. Temperatures, even at night when it's noticeably cooler, rarely drop below zero.

Rainfall is low. June to September, inclusive, are the wettest months, with an average of 60–70 mm of rain and 7–8 rain days per month. This is much less than the 20 rain days per month that Mexico City experiences during the summer.

Easter is a good time to visit. Temperatures are ideal at this time of year, and there are festivals and lots of things to do in the city. However, this is also the busiest time at La Loma. Book early if you intend to stay at the camp during the holiday period.

Opposite Facade of Templo del Carmen, built between 1749 and 1764

Accommodation

In addition to accommodation at La Loma High Altitude Training Camp *(p. 34)*, there is a variety of accommodation within the city. Most of the chain hotels and motels are located in the '*zona hotelera*' along MEX-57, the main route past the bus station and towards the eastern edge of the city. Most of the independent hotels are centred around the city centre. The area between the cathedral and the railway station has cheaper options for budget travellers. A very limited selection of self-catering homes, holiday apartments, and private rooms in shared houses available for short-term rent, can be found on Airbnb (www.airbnb.com).

Food

Many of the best restaurants, serving traditional and modern Mexican and Spanish dishes, are located along Avenida Venustiano Carranza and surrounding streets in the downtown area. There are also small restaurants selling typical local dishes along Camino a La Presa de San Jose (behind Parque Juan H Sánchez). It is recommended to go to the ones with the most customers, though with tough competition quality is generally good across the board. Food includes the standard Mexican foods. The locals are particularly proud of the bright orange *enchiladas potosinas*, which are usually fried and served with guacamole and refried beans.

Mobile food stands sell roasted corn-on-the-cob (served with butter, cheese, mayonnaise, chilli, lime or a combination of the above), *tamales* (corn bread covered and steamed in corn leaves), *tacos sudados*, *gorditas de horno* (thick tortillas stuffed with various savoury fillings and coated in hot salsa), and tumblers of peeled and cut tropical fruit (including mango, pineapple and coconut).

Anyone catering for themselves should have no problem finding cheap foodstuffs in the many large supermarkets around the city.

Shopping

Various supermarket chains operate in the city with the main commercial centres located at Plaza Tangamanga, Plaza Sendero, Plaza El Dorado and Plaza Sanborns San Luis. There are smaller grocery stores, and a number of bakeries in and around the city centre.

There are shops and markets selling a variety of goods, throughout Centro Histórico. Mexican

handicrafts and tacky souvenirs are sold alongside just about every household and personal item imaginable. Mercado Hidalgo, north from Plaza de Armas, sells a variety of products including pottery, baskets, and fine shawl-like garments called Santa Maria rebozos. Handcrafted items can also be purchased from the Fonart crafts store around the corner from the Church of San Agustín, and from La Casa del Artesano (www.lacasadelartesano.gob.mx) at Jardín Colón. Calle Hidalgo, the pedestrian mall linking Plaza de Armas and the mercado hosts some of the city's finest stores and shops. There are several outlets of the popular candy producer Costanzo.

There is a fruit shop, DVD store and other shops in the Plaza La Loma just outside La Loma and a large Walmart supermarket about 10 min drive away close to the entrance of Parque Tangamanga I.

The general sports shops in the main shopping area in the centre of the city, and in the large shopping malls on the edges of the city should be sufficient for basic fitness clothing and running footwear.

Above Cartons of freshly cut fruit, sold from food stands, make healthy snacks

LANGUAGE

Since few locals speak fluent English, basic conversational Spanish will greatly improve the enjoyability of your trip. Some restaurants have menus in English, though you may have to ask for these. The staff at La Loma usually have good multi-lingual skills. Apart from the main tourist services, however, very few people speak English. The lack of English-speaking tourists make San Luis Potosí a great place to learn and improve your Spanish.

COMMUNICATION

Mexico phone networks operate on the same 850/1900 MHz GMS frequency as most networks in the US and Canada. Some European phones (which normally operate on 900/1800 MHz) will not pick up network signal. A SIM card (called a 'chip') on the Telcel or Movistar networks can be purchased for unlocked mobile handsets that operate on the required frequencies. Prepaid Mexican phone kits, which are a good option if staying in San Luis Potosí for a prolonged period, usually include at least half the value of the phone in airtime. Phones are registered in the region they are issued, and roaming fees, which can be high, apply if used outside of that region. A prefix is added to Mexican mobile number when calling from a landline—044 for numbers registered in the local area, and 045 for all non-local mobile numbers. The digit '1' is added between the international dialling code, and the mobile number when calling a Mexican mobile from outside the country. Most payphones require a prepaid Ladatel calling card which can be purchased from news-stands, pharmacies and grocery shops.

Internet cafes are reasonably cheap. Many larger hotels offer Wi-Fi internet access, though speed of service can vary greatly between establishments. Wi-Fi hotspots in public places, usually operated by Mexican phone company Telmex, are becoming more popular. Prepaid cards for this service are available in telephone-related stores,

The Mexican postal service (Sepomex) is slow and unreliable. Courier services are recommended for packages and important letters. Stamps can be purchased in some hotels. The city's main post office is located on Avenida Universidad in Centro Histórico.

HEALTH AND SAFETY

Vaccination against yellow fever is required for those arriving from or through affected areas.

LOST IN TRANSLATION
Adapted from blog, 6 April 2010

San Luis Potosí is a relatively small city and a lovely place to begin my travels. However, I think I will try to learn Spanish before I visit again. There are a few competitors from the World Senior Tennis Championships (which is currently being held in the city), staying at my hotel, but apart from that, I haven't encountered anyone that can speak English. But then why should they? I should be a little less lazy with my languages.

Two days ago, I inadvertently ordered a whole pitcher of papaya juice in a restaurant. I can see now that the waitress was questioning my choice, but at the time I thought she was making sure that it was papaya juice I wanted (in truth I had chosen that purely because it was the only fruit I recognised), and convinced her that was what I actually wanted. I was a little embarrassed when she put a massive pitcher of red-orange coloured juice on the table. There must have been three litres of the stuff in there. Too proud to admit my mistake, I drank glasses and glasses of it until it was all gone, as if it was exactly what I wanted. Thankfully, I haven't suffered from vitamin poisoning, but it must have been close.

Tonight when I visited the same restaurant, I was handed a menu in English. Now that's much easier!

For the record, jarro de jugo de papaya *is a pitcher of papaya juice. Other useful Spanish phrases can be found in appendix 1.*

Hepatitis A and typhoid vaccines are highly recommended. There is a risk of malaria at lower altitudes, but not in San Luis Potosí and the central highlands.

Street food, part of the Mexican culture, is widely available. Eating it, however, may pose a health risk, and illness from poorly prepared food is not unheard of. Eat in reputable restaurants where possible, avoid spicy foods to begin with, drink lots of fluid, and stick to dry foods if diarrhoea does strike. Tap water is drinkable but not recommended. Bottled water is widely available in shops and supermarkets.

Medical care is good, but travel insurance with medical cover which includes repatriation in the event of serious illness or injury, is definitely recommended. Nuestra Señora de los Angeles Hospital, located on Avenida Adolfo López Mateos just north of Parque Tangamanga II, is a private medical institution with an emergency (*emergencia*) department and Hospital Centro Médico, on Calle Antonio Aguilar is one of the best hospitals in the country.

Mexico has a reputation for violent gang and drug-related crime, though San Luis Potosí is not one of the affected areas, and tourists are not normally affected by the notorious criminals who give the country such a bad name. Less serious crime, such as pickpocketing, does affect tourists, but is rarer here than in the larger cities. Be careful around busy areas such as Centro Histórico and the bus station.

Mexican police officers have a reputation for corruption. If you are approached by a police officer, remain calm, explain that you are a tourist, and phone your embassy immediately if asked for a bribe.

Seismic activity is frequent in Mexico. While tremors from earthquakes further south are often felt in San Luis Potosí, the city is north of the main risk area.

MONEY

The Mexican peso (sign: $ or MEX$; code: MXN), divided into 100 centavo, is the currency of Mexico. Conversion rates are not uniform, so shop around for the best deals. Currency exchange offices (*casas de cambio*), which offer better rates than the banks, can be found near the main post office. Credit and debit cards are widely accepted, and ATMs are relatively plentiful.

POWER

Mexico operates on 127 V; 60 Hz electrical supply with Type A (NEMA 1-15) and, recently more common, Type B earthed (NEMA 5-15) American plugs and sockets with two vertical flat pins. American plugs with a third round pin won't physically fit into the older Type A sockets which lack the third 'ground' contact. Standard travel adaptors usually don't have the ground pin, and should work in both socket types.

TIME

San Louis Potosí, like most of the rest of Mexico, operates on Central Standard Time (GMT-6). Daylight saving operates between the first Sunday in April and the last Sunday in October.

Mexicans tend to use the 24-hour clock when writing time.

Because of its relative proximity to the equator, there isn't a large variation in daylight hours from month to month, though due to daylight saving, sunset occurs around 18:00 during November and December. Streets are well lit in and around the city centre but running after dark away from the main streets is not advised.

	Mar	Jun	Sept	Dec
Sunrise	06:53	07:00	07:31	07:16
Sunset	18:53	20:29	19:47	18:03

LAUNDRY

There are various laundries (*lavanderías*) around the city. Each apartment at La Loma has a washer and dryer. There is also a launderette in Plaza La Loma, just outside the centre.

CULTURE AND RESPECT

To avoid looking like a tourist don't wear shorts or revealing tops when sightseeing. The locals in this predominantly Catholic country always tend to dress on the conservative side. You should avoid wearing shorts or low cut tops, and take off sunglasses, hats and caps when entering churches.

Mexicans are quite relaxed about time, and arriving 15 minutes late is not unusual. That said, those who work in the tourist sector are usually punctual, and public transport generally runs on time.

Mexican men are courteous towards women, particularly older women, and will often hold a door open or offer up a seat. Resisting such gestures is considered rude. If gestures go beyond politeness, and you feel harassed, a simple 'no' usually suffices. Females should dress conservatively to avoid unwanted male attention.

Tips of approximately 10 percent are adequate in restaurants, though some restaurants will already have added a service charge to the bill. Taxi drivers can be tipped if they provide a special service. Porters would expect a tip of approximately 10 pesos for helping with your luggage.

TOP RIGHT *The churches feature detailed craftsmanship*
RIGHT *Templo del Carmen in Plaza del Carmen*

SPORTS FACILITIES AND SERVICES

The facilities at La Loma Altitude Training Centre make St Louis Potosí a popular destination for athletes in a variety of sports. The 400 m track, well-equipped gym, and mile-long running trail on the camp grounds are ideal for middle distance runners. The nearby Parque Tangamanga I has off-road routes for longer runs, and there are trails in the hills a short drive from the city. As San Luis Potosí is located within Mexico's elevated central plateau and surrounded by mountains, 'live high, train low' is not possible, and in many cases the trails outside the city are actually at a higher altitude than the city itself.

TRAINING CAMPS AND TOUR OPERATORS

The excellent facilities at La Loma (p. 34) make it one of the most popular training camps of its kind in the world. It is particularly well equipped to cater for competitive swimmers, but is also popular among middle-distance runners.

TRAILS AND RUNNING ROUTES

The main area for trails is Parque Tangamanga I which is located in the south of the city, approximately 3.5 km from Centro Histórico, and 4.5 km from La Loma.

There is a 1 km jogging trail, with a dirt surface, within Parque Tangamanga I. It is located amid the trees to the right as you enter the park via the main (Calle Tatanacho) entrance. You are likely to have to share the trail with other users, many of them recreational joggers and walkers. There are road, dirt and grass surfaces, suitable for various runs and sessions, elsewhere in the park.

Within La Loma there is a one-mile trail which can be used for warm-up and cool-down for track sessions, or for interval training. It is ideally located for combining track intervals with longer off-track mile repetitions.

There are additional options outside the city if you have access to a car. The hills to the south-east of the city (the La Loma end) are particularly good, with some of the minor roads having a dirt surface. Many athletes drive to the village of Bledos, about 45 minutes away, for longer runs.

The park is relatively flat, and the road surfaces within the park would be suitable for race-walking. Mexico has a long tradition of race-walking success, and those practicing the event would not be out of place. Marathon runners will find the options within the park very limiting and will need to drive out of the city for more variety.

TRACK FACILITIES

In addition to the eight-lane 400 m Mondo track at La Loma, there is a track located within the eastern section of Parque Tangamanga II, and there are other clay and synthetic tracks across the city. Those staying outside of La Loma can use the track at the camp for a fee.

GYM FACILITIES

Most of the main hotels have their own sports facilities, including a swimming pool, weight training equipment and squash and racquetball courts. La Loma has excellent gym facilities which those staying outside of the centre can access for a fee, and the centre itself serves as a major fitness facility for locals. Xtreme Sport Centre (www.xtremeslp.com) is a large company with three well-equipped gyms in the city.

For those who don't wish to pay for gym use, but who still want to carry out some level of strength training, there is some outdoor gym equipment, including ladders, monkey bars and parallel bars, near the jogging trail in Parque Tangamanga I. There is some similar equipment at La Loma next to a section of the jogging trail.

CROSS-TRAINING OPTIONS

Swimming is one of the easiest forms of cross-training to partake in. There are swimming pools at La Loma, but lanes are often booked up by swim teams training there. Many of the hotels have small swimming pools suitable for recovery swims or aqua jogging. It is possible to rent small mountain bikes and tandems in Parque Tangamanga I which is an ideal place for relaxed recovery rides.

There are good cardio fitness facilities and a designated spin bike studio at La Loma. Racquetball courts, tennis courts, and a basketball court at the centre, make it possible for athletes to use other sports for cross-training purposes. The broad range of classes offered at La Loma can be used as cross-training. The city's parks have basketball courts, football fields and grass areas for informal games.

SPORTS MEDICINE AND SPORTS SCIENCE SUPPORT

Physiotherapy and sports massage support is available for guests at La Loma. Paramedics are available at the centre all day, and doctors are available in emergencies. Laboratory tests are available, and there is access to a nutritionist and psychologist. The Physiotherapy and Sports Medicine Centre, located at Plaza Del Valle on Avenida Nereo Rodriguez Barragán, also offers a range of services.

Local races

The city's annual marathon, Maratón Internacional Tangamanga (www.maratontangamanga.com), takes place in June each year. The event also features races over half marathon and 10 km distances, and a 2.5 km fun run.

Running community

American athletes Shalane Flanagan, Shannon Rowbury and Leo Manzano are among the athletes who have regularly trained in San Luis Potosí. Germán Silva, two-time Olympian and former New York marathon winner, lives in the city. He is head of the athletics academy at La Loma, owns the successful German Silva Coaching (www.germansilva.com), and coaches some of Mexico's top distance runners. Runners and joggers of all levels use Parque Tangamanga I for their daily runs.

Suitability for other sports

San Luis Potosí is particularly popular among swimmers thanks to the excellent facilities at La Loma Altitude Training Centre. The centre's facilities are also suitable for tennis, basketball, racquetball and martial arts.

Swimming La Loma has an indoor 50 m pool and an outdoor 25 m pool. The centre is particularly popular among national swim teams. Pool time is at a premium at key points during the year, and 2 hr training slots are reserved on a 'first-come, first-served' basis. There are other pools in the city, but La Loma offers the best training environment for high performance swimmers.

Cycling Cycling in or close to the city centre is not advisable, and the best options are out into the countryside. Cerro de San Pedro, the mining ghost town east of the city is particularly good for mountain biking. Absolutamente Ciclismo is a specialised cycling shop located on Avenida Himno Nacional, just north of the park.

Triathlon The swimming and athletics facilities at La Loma, and the running trails at Parque Tangamanga I combine to make San Luis Potosí a suitable, though not outstanding, venue for triathlon training. As cycling routes are limited, some triathletes may find training here suboptimal, and somewhat monotonous.

Team sports There are basketball and volleyball courts, softball fields, a football field and an outdoor beach volleyball court at La Loma. The all-inclusive nature of La Loma may be particularly appealing to athletes in team sports.

Other sports Athletes in martial arts, racquetball, squash, golf, gymnastics and tennis are well catered for at La Loma. A dedicated rowing machine area at the centre, together with spin bikes, other cardiovascular equipment and excellent weight training facilities, may be suitable for rowers carrying out dry-land training. The International Challenger Tennis Tournament, which forms part of the ATP Tour, has been held in the city each Easter since 1984 and, together with the increasingly popular San Luis Open, is increasing the city's reputation for tennis.

Special feature
THE TARAHUMARA: MEXICO'S RUNNING TRIBE

The Tarahumara are an indigenous barefoot running tribe based in the Copper Canyon area of the state of Chihuahua. They were brought to public attention as the subject of Christopher McDougall's book, *Born to Run (2010)*. Most of the tribe practice the traditional Tarahumara lifestyle and inhabit cliff overhangs and caves or small cabins constructed of stone or wood. They grow beans and corn and raise cattle, goats and sheep. Almost all Tarahumara perform some form of migration during the year. The term *Rarámuri,* the word which they use for themselves, is proposed to mean 'those who run fast', or 'runners on foot'.

The Tarahumara developed a tradition of long-distance running for transportation, inter-village communication and hunting. It would not be unusual for a Tarahumara to run up to 200 km in a single two-day trip through rough canyon countryside. The Tarahumara are noted for their toe-strike running technique typical of barefooted runners. The long-distance running also has competitive and ceremonial aspects. Foot throwing races, which involve groups of male runners kicking wooden balls in a relay fashion as they run, can last from a couple of hours, to a couple of days, without a break. Before a long-distance run, large quantities of *tesgüino*, a high-carbohydrate, low-alcohol corn beer, are consumed.

Trails and facilities in Parque Tangamanga I

Training camp
LA LOMA ALTITUDE TRAINING CAMP
(CENTRO DEPORTIVO LA LOMA)

La Loma is one of the most popular and best-equipped altitude training camps in the world. It is located in the south-west of San Luis Potosí, 8 km from Centro Histórico. The altitude of the centre is approximately 1,900 m.

The centre, which was opened in 2003, has hosted teams in the sports of athletics, swimming, gymnastics, racquetball, tennis and football, from United Kingdom, Canada, US, Sweden, Germany, France, Spain and most countries in South America.

La Loma is particularly popular among swimmers and specifically targets teams of swimmers from around the world. The centre has an indoor 50 m swimming pool and an outdoor 25 m pool. Both are equipped for high performance training, with starting blocks, and timing facilities.

There are 12 tennis courts, a fully equipped gymnastics hall suitable for artistic and rhythmic gymnastics, a boxing ring and boxing training facilities, a large matted area for judo and other martial arts, and a large indoor sports hall which can be used for volleyball, basketball, handball and other sports. There are a number of glass-backed racquetball and squash courts, and outdoor facilities for football, softball and beach volleyball. There is also a Jack Nicklaus Signature golf course and academy at the centre (www.lalomagolf.com.mx).

Athletics facilities include an 8-lane 400 m Mondo track, a mile-long gravel jogging track, and a grass infield which can be used for drills and strides.

Gym facilities are excellent and include a gym with free and machine weights, a room with cardiovascular equipment, a large high performance strength and conditioning area, a studio suitable for yoga, boxercise and other fitness classes and areas dedicated to spin bike training and rowing ergometer training.

A range of exercise classes are run at the centre including spinning, fitness ball training, yoga, Zumba, CrossFit and Pilates.

Sports medicine, physiotherapy, massage, nutrition and psychology support is available at the centre, and a variety of laboratory tests can be arranged.

The centre also serves as a sport and leisure facility. It employs some 150 people and supports

over 2,000 people through it's various programmes. It operates academies in a number of sports, including athletics, triathlon, gymnastics, golf and swimming.

Apartment-style accommodation, complete with kitchen facilities, satellite TV, and a washing machine, is located just 200 m from the entrance to the sports facilities. Security staff patrol the entire campus, including the accommodation, 24 hours per day.

The Real Inn San Luis Potosi by Camino Real (www.caminoreal.com) overlooks the athletics track, and can provide accommodation for coaches who don't wish to share apartment accommodation with athletes. Guests at the hotel have access to the pool, gym, track and some other facilities at the camp, but food and some other benefits are not included in the hotel price.

Rates include access to facilities, accommodation, and three all-you-can-eat buffet-style meals per day. Internet access is available in both the accommodation and the training centre. Transport to and from the airport can also be arranged.

When to visit
The accommodation and facilities at La Loma often get booked up, especially during the Easter and Christmas holidays. Book early, or avoid the busy holiday times. La Loma also hosts regular competitions and tournaments meaning that facilities are often booked out. No matter what time of the year you're visiting, you are advised to book early to avoid disappointment.

Contact
Website: www.altitudeswimming.com (in English and specifically targeted at foreign groups) and www.lalomacd.com.mx (in Spanish and targeted at local users, but with additional information on the facilities and services within the centre)
Postal address: Avenida de la Victoria, #100. Fracc. La Loma CP 78216, San Luis Potosí, S.L.P., Mexico

OPPOSITE The Real Inn by Camino Real overlooks the Mondo track at La Loma
ABOVE The 1-mile gravel track which circles the track and other facilities at La Loma

THINGS TO SEE AND DO BETWEEN TRAINING

San Luis Potosí's historic central zone is a UNESCO World Heritage site and one of the most beautiful urban centres in Mexico. Big and bold architecture in baroque and neoclassical styles combine with beautiful plazas, garden-like parks and cobblestone streets within the well preserved Centro Histórico.

The 16th century cathedral in Plaza de Armas seamlessly blends baroque and neoclassical architecture. The Governor's Palace, also in the Plaza de Armas; Templo de Nuestra Señora del Carmen with its beautiful altars and colourful tiled domes; Basilica Menor de Guadalupe; the beautiful Jardín de San Francisco, and adjacent Templo de San Francisco; and the Palacio de Gobierno, twice the base of the Mexican leader are among the other highlights. You can get a feel for the city by walking through the series of plazas and the narrow streets that connect them. Walking tours, and guided tours on double-decker sightseeing trolleys (Tranvía Turístico SLP) are also available.

Museo de las Tradiciones, a fascinating folklore and traditions museum located in a beautiful early 20th century mansion in the heart of the city, is a great place to discover local traditions. Museo Federico Silva features the work of famous Mexican sculptor Federico Silva and is the site of regular dance and painting workshops, sculpture classes, concerts and temporary exhibitions. The Museo Nacional de la Mascara, displays a collection of some 1200 Mexican masks of cultural importance, and explains their mystic, religious and philosophical connections. The Labyrinth Museum of Science and Arts (Museo Laberinto de las Ciencias y las Artes) is a large modern museum in Parque Tangamanga I. The museum occupies 6.5 hectares, and features an interactive tour through art, science and technology galleries. Casa de la Cultura, located a taxi ride away on the west side of the city, is the best museum for Mexican art, crafts and archaeological artefacts.

The city's small plazas are brought to life over Christmas and Easter with street sellers and funfairs. The Procession of Silence, one of the world's largest commemorations of the Stations of the Cross, takes place in the city on Good Friday each year. Dia de Muertos (Day of the Dead), on 2 November is also an important religious and cultural day. During holiday times, the night is lit up with spectacular lightshows on the walls of the cathedral, the university building in Plaza Fundadores, and Templo del Carmen.

Bullfights take place at the Plaza España bullring on Avenida Universidad. San Luis FC (www.clubsanluis.com.mx), a Mexican first division team, plays its home games at Estadio Alfonso Lastras, located close to the centre of town. Car racing events regularly take place on the racetrack which incorporates the runway of the city's old airport at Parque Tangamanga II. Tickets for football games, ballet, music concerts and other events can be purchased through Super Boletos (www.superboletos.com).

Both Parque Tangamanga I and Parque Tangamanga II have recreational facilities including grills for barbecues; grass areas for rounders, football and picnics; and BMX, quad bike and motocross tracks. The road surface is suitable for rollerblading. There is a 19-target archery range and a mini aerodrome with model aircraft.

Cinemas are generally located in or near the large shopping malls. There is a Cinépolis cinema by Plaza Sanborns, near La Loma. Hollywood releases are often shown in English with Spanish subtitles, rather than with Spanish dubbing.

ABOVE Another church in Centro Histórico
RIGHT A statue in one of the many pretty plazas

REST DAY EXCURSIONS

The ancient streets of Cerro de San Pedro, where the silver mines were discovered in 1592, host a beautiful church dedicated to San Pedro among other buildings. Old mining tunnels can be visited, and the area is used for extreme sports. Cerro de San Pedro is located just 8 km from the east of San Luis Potosí.

There are some 20 haciendas (colonial estates and villas) of architectural, historical and cultural interest and open to the public, in the surroundings of San Luis Potosí. Many of the haciendas feature chapels, museums, elegant buildings, and expansive gardens. Hacienda de Gogorrón, located in Villa de Reyes (55 km south of the city) was used as a backdrop to many of the main scenes in the Legend of Zorro. Other Haciendas worth visiting include Peñasco, located close to the airport; La Pila, with its imposing central house; Jesús María, which has an interesting religious museum; Corcovada, with local food and handicrafts for sale; and the elegant Pozo del Carmen, located near Santa Maria del Rio.

The town of Santa Maria del Rio, 60 km southeast of San Luis Potosí, hosts several religious and cultural festivals and celebrations, and has spas, an ancient aqueduct, a beautiful waterfall, and a number of other haciendas. The historic centre of San Miguel de Allende, located south of Santa Maria del Rio, and approximately 180 km from San Luis Potosí, and the nearby Sanctuary of Atotonilco, a church complex with exquisite baroque murals, are together a UNESCO World Heritage site. The area also has a number of thermal and hot springs. Real de Catorce, in the heart of the old silver mines approximately 200 km north of San Luis Potosí, is interesting and scenic, and a great place for exploring by bike or on horseback.

The region known as la Huasteca Potosina, in the eastern portion of the state of San Luis Potosí, is home to some of Mexico's most important ecotourism sites. Ciudad Valles, the second largest city in the state, is located approximately 3 hr by car from San Luis Potosí and forms the heart of the region. Tancanhuitz de Santos is home to two groups of Native Americans living in traditional ways. The town of Xilitla, with its jungle castle and gardens (Las Pozas), and the 376-m deep El Sótano de las Golondrinas (cave of the swallows) are located within easy reach of Ciudad Valles. The area is full of amazing waterfalls and beautiful scenery. White-water rafting, hiking, kayaking, mountain biking, river rafting and abseiling are popular.

A NOTE ON LIVING HERE LONG-TERM

San Luis Potosí is cheap, the climate is ideal for training throughout the year, and the city provides all the amenities and entertainment needed for prolonged stays. Living at La Loma or in any of the hotels in the city would be too expensive for prolonged visits, but anyone who speaks Spanish should be able to arrange rental accommodation. While the city has the potential to provide employment opportunities, work visas for non-Mexican citizens are notoriously difficult to obtain. There are some opportunities for races within the city, but getting to races at sea level would incur significant time and expense. Most significantly, the trail options are not particularly appealing for distance runners, and while adequate for a short stay, may quickly become monotonous.

FURTHER INFORMATION

Information on San Luis Potosí is relatively difficult to find. While it is mentioned in most travel books alongside the other colonial cities of the north, websites providing practical information on travel to and within the city are difficult to find, or are in Spanish only. The city does have a tourism sector, but is far more popular among Mexicans, than among international visitors to the country.

The official website of the San Luis Potosí state tourism office (www.visitasanluispotosi.com), available in English and Spanish, has suggestions on sites and activities across the state. Heraldo (www.heraldo.com.mx) highlights shops and businesses in each area of the city on a map. San Luis Potosí Municipal website (www.sanluis.gob.mx), in Spanish only, may also be useful. The San Luis Potosí Municipal tourist office is located in Palacio Municipal, Jardin Hidalgo No 5, and the state tourist office is located at Alvaro Obregon No 520.

Mexico City

As the only city at altitude to host a Summer Olympic Games, Mexico City holds a special place in distance running history. Many of the original Olympic facilities survive, and modern sports centres, athletics tracks and swimming pools are plentiful. Bosque de Chapultepec provides relatively peaceful running routes near the centre of one of the world's largest cities. The forest parks south-west of the city provide the best running trails, but they are a little difficult to reach. The hills surrounding Toluca, about 40 min from the city, offers the extra challenge of training at more than 3,000 m above sea level. There is always plenty to do on rest days, and lots to entertain non-running travel partners. Noise, pollution and traffic jams can, however, be a problem.

Mexico City, Mexico (2,240 m)

It could be said that Mexico City is where it all began; where the effects of altitude, both positive and negative, were first observed; and where the notion of moving to altitude to train stemmed from. For the Kenyans, it was where distance-running domination began. But there's more to Mexico City than its Olympic Legacy. As a former major Aztec and Spanish Empire centre, and now the Mexican capital, it is one of the world's most important cultural centres. It has more museums than any other city, and only London and New York have more theatres.

Mexico City, known locally as Cuidad de México and officially as México, DF, is not part of any one of the 31 states of Mexico. The Federal District is a separate area, similar to Washington DC in the US.

AUTHOR'S VERDICT

Mexico City is the perfect destination to combine a training and cultural holiday, and offers plenty for non-running travel partners. The cost of living is low, and I found an affordable 4-star hotel right by Bosque de Chapultepec where I did all of my training and spent most of my downtime. As one of the largest cities in the world, Mexico City has its drawbacks, and I was a little put-off by the large crowds on my first visit to the city centre. Pollution and traffic are also a problem. There is a large running community, but there are probably cities which are more suitable for high-performance training. Information about training here was difficult to find, and basic fluency in Spanish would have been useful. That said, Mexico City holds a special place in the history of altitude training and acclimatisation, and I wasn't going to let a language barrier stop me visiting.

Running ★★☆☆☆ - Moderate variety of routes in Bosque de Chapultepec, Bosque de Tlalpan and other parks around the city; good options in the hills surrounding the city, but difficult to get to; most streets are busy and unsuitable for running; tracks throughout the city.

Convenience ★★★☆☆ - Large international airport with direct connections around the world; long, but reasonably direct flights from Europe; good public transport network; very big city; getting accommodation close to the main training venues is essential.

Safety ★★★☆☆ - Risk of pickpocketing in the city centre and on the Metro; good medical service; hepatitis A and typhoid vaccination recommended; some risk of food-related illness.

Cost ★★★☆☆ - Low cost of living; flights from Europe expensive, but justifiable when combining a cultural trip with a training one; a car is not required (and driving is not recommended).

Cultural experience ★★★★★ - Cultural experiences are plentiful and a true insight into Mexican life possible; lots to see and do; difficult not to learn about Mexicans and their ancestors during your stay.

Things to do between training ★★★★★ - Lots to see and do; excursions are easy to organise; many shopping and entertainment opportunities; non-running travel partners are well catered for.

Suitability for solo travellers ★★★☆☆ - English reasonably widely spoken though Spanish is useful; with lots to do between training, it hardly matters if you don't interact with other runners.

Must do Visit the Olympic Stadium where all the 'hype' about altitude training began; spend a lazy afternoon exploring the sites of Bosque de Chapultepec; take a trip to Toluca where the real hardy train at 2,700 m of altitude and higher.

Ideal for Anyone looking to combine a cultural experience with a training holiday

ABOVE and OPPOSITE *The Olympic stadium in Mexico City*
PREVIOUS *A fountain in Bosque de Chapultepec*

Did you know?
John Stephen Akhwari fell during the marathon race at the 1968 Games and badly cut and dislocated his knee. He continued running, and finished last among the 57 finishers. Akhwari was more than an hour behind the winner, Mamo Wolde of Ethiopia, and completed the race after the sun had set. When asked why he continued running, Akhwari simply replied, 'My country did not send me 5,000 miles to Mexico City to start the race. They sent me 5,000 miles to finish the race'. Akhwari recovered from his injuries, and went on to compete for a further 10 years. He finished 5th in the marathon at the 1970 Commonwealth Games.

Special feature
MEXICO CITY OLYMPIC GAMES, 1968

Each Olympics has its own controversies, breakthroughs, and memorable performance, but the Games of the XIX Olympiad, held in Mexico City in 1968, is of particular significance from an athletics perspective. The Fosbury Flop, fully automatic timing, drug testing and Tartan tracks made their Olympic debuts, and Black Power salutes and 'Beamonesque' long jumping were among the memorable moments. However, it is altitude, and its effects, that have truly given Mexico City its place in athletics history. Distance running, as we then knew it, would never be the same again.

A total of 5,530 sportspeople from 112 nations competed for 172 sets of medals in 20 sports. The US, the Soviet Union and Japan filled the top three places on the medal table, but it was the eight athletics medals won by Kenya that was the most newsworthy achievement. Prior to 1968, Kenya had not won a single gold medal at the Olympics (and only one medal in total), but in 1968 they won three, all in distance events (Kipchoge Keino, 1500 m; Naftali Temu, 10,000 m; Amos Biwott, 3,000 m Steeplechase). Ethiopia won their third consecutive men's marathon gold. It seemed that athletes born and living at altitude may have an endurance performance advantage when competing at altitude.

The altitude didn't just affect the outcome of the distance events. The reduced air resistance resulted in a number of world records being broken. Bob Beamon improved the long jump record by 55 cm; his 8.90 m leap wasn't bettered until 1991. There were also world records in the men's 100 m, 200 m, 400 m, 400 m hurdles, triple jump (improved 5 times during the competition), pole vault, 4 x 100 m relay and 4 x 400 m relay; and in the women's 100 m, 200 m, long jump and 4 x 100 m relay.

During the 200 m medal ceremony, African-Americans Tommie Smith, the gold medallist, and John Carlos, who won bronze, raised their black-gloved fists as a symbol of 'Black Power'. They were later banned from the Games for life as punishment. Dick Fosbury won gold in the high jump utilising a technique which became known as the Fosbury flop, and quickly became the dominant technique utilised in the event. Daniel Rudisha, who won silver with Kenya in the men's 4 x 400 m relay, is father to world 800 m record holder David Rudisha.

Drug testing made its first Olympic appearance, though tests were primarily for narcotics and stimulants. Having drunk several beers to calm his nerves just prior to the shooting phase of the modern pentathlon competition, Swede Hans-Gunnar Liljenwall became the first Olympian to be disqualified because of a doping offence. The Swedish team, who originally finished third in the competition, had to return their bronze medals.

The Olympic Stadium (Estadio Olímpico Universitario) was built to represent the crater of a volcano. Today it is home to the football and American football teams of the National Autonomous University of Mexico (UNAM). The Stadium is located within the Ciudad Universitaria (University City), the campus of UNAM. The university is the largest in Latin America and has a student population of over 300,000, and almost 35,000 staff members. The campus is a UNESCO World Heritage site.

Getting in

Mexico City is well served both domestically and internationally by air. A cheap and efficient bus network provides links with cities across Mexico.

By air

Benito Juárez International Airport (MEX), the second largest airport in Latin America, is located approximately 10 km east of Centro Histórico. There are direct flights from more than 100 destinations worldwide, including Amsterdam, Frankfurt, London, Madrid and Paris, most of the main South American and North America cities, and the vast majority of airports within Mexico. The airport has two terminals which are linked by a free light rail system and a bus line which charges a small fee.

Passing through immigration and customs at Mexico Airport usually takes approximately an hour. The arrivals area is usually quite busy. Bag carriers will usually take your trolley from you and assist you with transporting it; a service for which they will expect a small tip.

The easiest way to get to the city centre from the airport is by taxi. Tickets should be purchased at marked counters within the airport terminal. Larger cars cost more, so ensure that you are sold a ticket for the size of car suitable for your group and quantity of luggage.

There is a Metro station (Line 5; yellow line) next to the domestic flight arrivals hall in Terminal 1. While the Metro provides a cheaper option for getting into the city, the Metro station is not suitable for carrying luggage, with lots of stairs and narrow gates. Large bags on the Metro are usually frowned upon. Avoid the Metro during rush hour, and keep an eye on your belongings, as pickpocketing is common.

Toluca's Licenciado Adolfo Lopez Mateos International Airport (TLC) approximately 60 km south-west of Mexico City, provides an alternative if travelling from within Mexico or the US. Low-cost and regional carriers such as Volaris, Aeroméxico Connect and Interjet operate flights from many of the major Mexican airports, and from Dallas, San Antonio, Las Vegas and Fort Lauderdale in the US. Getting from the airport to Mexico City will require taking a direct taxi or shuttle service, or taking a taxi to the large bus terminal in Toluca and transferring to one of the frequent bus services from there to Mexico City. Because of the longer transfers, flying to Toluca may work out more expensive.

By bus

Travel by bus in Mexico is relatively comfortable and is by far the cheapest way to get around the country. There are usually more than one service operating on a given route, and even the more expensive luxury services are cheap by European standards. There are direct services from most cities within Mexico, and links to international networks. Mexico is a large country, and distances which may not look far on a map, may be half a day of travelling away.

Greyhound services in the US link with Mexico's bus system, with transfers onto a partner Grupo Estrella Blanca (www.estrellablanca.com.mx) services at the US border. Buses from Guatemala and other Central American countries travel as far as Tapachula, where they connect with Grupo ADO (www.ado.com.mx) services to Mexico City.

There are four major bus stations in Mexico City, one in each of the north, south, east and west of the city, and each serving buses from a different area of the country. All four stations are connected to the main Metro system. The Metro system is not suitable for transporting large amounts of luggage, and a taxi may be a better way of getting from the station to your accommodation. Like in the airport, the licensed taxi will have a ticket counter in the station where you purchase a ticket before going to the taxi rank, and baggage carriers will be on hand to help you with your luggage for a small tip.

Terminal de Autobuses del Norte is located on Eje Central Lázaro Cárdenas in Colonia Magdalena de las Salinas. The station is situated on Line 5 (yellow) of the Metro system (stop: Autobuses del Norte) and serves buses from the US and most cities in the north of Mexico including San Luis Potosí, Guadalajara, Monterrey, Guanajuato and León.

Terminal de Autobuses del Sur, also known as Tasqueña, is located on Avenue Tasqueña in Colonia Campestre Churubusco. It is on Line 2 (blue) of the Metro (stop: Tasqueña), and is used for services to and from destinations south of the city including Taxco and Acapulco.

Terminal de Autobuses de Pasajeros de Oriente, or TAPO for short, is located on Calzada Ignacio Zaragoza, east of the city, and just west of the airport. It serves destinations in the east and south-east of Mexico including Veracruz, Oaxaca, and the Yucatán Peninsula. Terminal Oriente is situated next to San Lázaro Metro station on Line 1 (pink).

BEETLE MANIA
Adapted from the blog, 8 April 2010

It was on my taxi ride to the bus station this morning that I realised just how many Beetles there are in Mexico. In the space of just two minutes, I had counted 10 of them, and when I arrived in Mexico City, there were even more. I have seen hundreds today! No I don't mean the hard skinned creepy-crawly type, nor do I mean the shaggy-haired 1960s pop stars (because then I'd have spelt it wrong!). No, I mean the car. And I don't mean the ugly remake. I mean the proper clapped-out original. I've never seen so many of them in my life. What a great place to play the Beetle-Box game! It begs the question: is Mexico where Beetles go to die, or is it where they go to live forever?

Apart from my car spotting, I've had a fun day. I resisted the temptation to fly from San Luis Potosí to the capital, and went for the cheaper bus option. I've read good things about the bus service in Mexico, but I was blown away by just how amazing bus transport is here. After paying for my taxi, which incidentally cost next to nothing, I entered what looked more like an airport terminal than a bus station. I couldn't get over how clean, tidy and safe it looked. Before boarding the bus, we were given a complimentary drink and ham sandwich. There were only 24 seats on a bus the size of a normal 52-seat coach, plenty of space, a nice footrest, two toilets, neither of which smelled like a bus toilet, and a TV. Oh, and the six-hour journey only cost about £25. Bargain!

The journey flew by too. The scenery was amazing and the roads were excellent. We even arrived at the final destination half an hour early. The place is huge, but much nicer than I expected. I'm staying in a very nice hotel, English is more widely spoken than it was in San Luis, and I've just had pasta for the first time in nine days. Spaghetti bolognese never tasted so good!

Terminal de Autobuses del Poniente is located on the west of the city at the junction between Sur 122 and Avenida Rio Tacubaya, and served by Line 1 (pink) of the Metro (stop: Observatorio). Terminal Poniente is usually used for services to and from cities in the western states of Jalisco, Michoacán and Toluca.

Traffic around all the stations, but particularly TAPO, can get very congested during rush hours. Allow adequate time to get to and from the station.

Visa requirements
See p. 42

GETTING AROUND

Mexico City is the most populous city in the Americas and one of the largest in the world. Getting around it can take some time. While officially divided into 16 boroughs consisting of approximately 250 neighbourhoods, districts are a more common and useful way of subdividing the city. Centro Histórico is linked to Bosque de Chapultepec in the west via the beautiful Paseo de la Reforma. The MEX-85 runs west of the centre in a roughly north-east–south-west direction. The 57D brings traffic into the east of the city from the north, and the Circuito Interior circumnavigates the central districts.

Driving is not recommended. There are large traffic jams and numerous complicated junctions, which foreign drivers struggle to negotiate. Mexican drivers are generally reckless, street parking is scarce and relatively expensive, and the labyrinth-like street network makes it incredibly easy to get lost. Those who do wish to drive should be aware of the *Hoy No Circula* (today it does not circulate) anti-traffic and anti-pollution initiative which limits the times that you can travel depending on the final digits of your number plate.

Despite the distances between the main sites, getting around by public transport is relatively convenient. In addition to the efficient Metro system, the RTP bus system, an electric trolleybus, several franchised private buses and thousands of taxis make the city a well connected one. Route maps for the Metro, Metrobús, light rail line, trolleybuses, and RTP buses can be found on the respective service websites and on www.mexicometro.org, a website in English.

Busca Tu Ruta (www.buscaturuta.com) which covers the whole country, and Via DF (www.viadf.com) which only covers Mexico City and requires complete addresses, are useful websites for planning routes by public transport, car or bicycle. The latter is available in English, Spanish, German and French, and the former allows you to search by clicking on points on a map of the city.

Mexico's address system is relatively simple. The street name is followed by the house or building number, colonia (neighbourhood), city, state and postal code. Even numbered buildings are on one side of the street, and odd numbers on the other.

Main districts

Centro Histórico, situated in roughly the centre of the city, consists of the original city, and features Aztec archaeological sites and many important colonial landmarks. The district is centred around the Zócalo (Plaza de la Constitución), the third largest square in the world, and features mostly narrow cobbled streets, and large crowds, especially at the weekend. Many of the main tourist attractions and older department stores and shops are in this district. Metro is the easiest way to get to the centre, with Lines 1 (pink), Line 2 (blue) and Line 3 (green) running through Centro Histórico, and walking is the best way to get around.

Chapultepec-Lomas is an important district on the west of the city. Bosque de Chapultepec is one of the largest urban parks in the world, the centre of outdoor activities in the city, and one of the best places in the city to run. Metro stops Chapultepec (Line 1/pink) and Auditorio (Line 7/orange) are located on the east and north sides of the park respectively. Nearby Lomas de Chapultepec is the city's wealthiest neighbourhood.

Polanco, the area just north of Chapultepec Park is a wealthy area with expensive designer boutiques, embassies, hotels and upscale restaurants. Santa Fe, west of the park, consists of a high-rise business area surrounding a large shopping mall.

Zona Rosa is the district linking Chapultepec-Lomas with Centro Histórico and consists of Paseo de la Reforma and the surrounding streets. It is an important business and entertainment area, and has a high density of hotels, restaurants and clubs. Condesa and Roma, immediately south of Zona Rosa also have many places to eat, with trendy bistros and restaurants.

South of Condesa and Roma are Del Valle, a business and shopping district; Coyoacán, an area of art and learning encompassing Ciudad Universitaria and Villa Olímpica; and Xochimilco,

44

an important tourist area featuring a series of Aztec irrigation canals.

By public transport

The Metro (www.metro.df.gob.mx) is the easiest and cheapest way to get around the city. Lines 1–8, Line A, Line B and a light railway line between Tasqueña and Xochimilco, link most of the important areas within the city, the main tourist attractions, and the four main bus terminals. Approximately four million people use the Metro each day, it can become very busy during peak times, and pickpocketing is common. Trains are quick, and run frequently between 05:00 and midnight on weekdays, with a later start on Saturdays (06:00) and Sundays (07:00). Lines are indicated by a number (or letter) and a colour, and stations by name and by symbol. Carry a Metro map with you, as there are usually no maps on board the Metro, and only a few on the platforms. Tickets are for a single journey (regardless of length), and multiple tickets can be purchased at a time. When you approach a ticket booth just state in Spanish how many tickets you want, and drop the money in the tray. A ticket will allow you to enter the turnstile to the platforms. Unlike many other transport systems, your ticket won't be returned from the turnstile.

Outline map of Mexico City

The Mexico City Government operates the full-sized orange and white RTP buses (www.rtp.gob.mx) with standard, exact change, fare across the city. The privately operated green and white microbuses or shared taxis called *peseros* are slightly more expensive (though still very cheap) and considerably less safe than the RTP buses. Both types of bus operate similar routes. Stops tend to be unmarked, and are usually just before intersections. While routes are generally complex and somewhat flexible, particularly on peseros, major stops are usually indicated in the windscreen. To get to a Metro station, look for a bus displaying an 'M', followed by the station name. Taking the bus can be confusing to begin with, but is a useful way of getting around some of the main avenues.

The Metrobús (www.metrobus.df.gob.mx) operates on four lines across the city and has stops at approximately 500 m intervals. An electronic ticket card, onto which credit is loaded, must be purchased at vending machines before using the Metrobús for the first time. There is a standard fare, which covers transfer between lines if the journey is completed within 2 hr.

There are 15 trolleybus lines (*líneas de Trolebús*; www.ste.df.gob.mx) operating over a network of more than 400 km. They are less crowded and more comfortable and reliable than regular buses, though they do travel a little slower. There is a flat fare across the service, and no change is given. Line A links the north and south bus terminals.

A light rail line (*Línea de Tren Ligero*; www.ste.df.gob.mx) operates in the south of the city linking Tasqueña Metro station with Xochimilco and the Azteca Stadium (Estadio Azteca). The ticketing system is similar to the Metro system, though they are different tickets, and must be purchased in addition to any Metro ticket that you may have used on your journey.

A regular sightseeing bus (Turibus; www.turibus.com.mx) operates 'hop-on, hop-off' trips around the city. While this would be an expensive way to get around, it is a good way of getting to know the city's layout, and a hassle-free way of getting between all the main sites. *Circuito centro* has stops in Centro Histórico, along Paseo de la Reforma, and in Bosque de Chapultepec while *circuito sur* takes in the Olympic Stadium and sites in the south of the city.

By taxi
Taxis are particularly useful when getting to and from the airport and bus stations, as detailed in the 'Getting in' section. A taxi may also be useful when travelling to some of the sites on the edge of the city, and if shopping in the more remotely located shopping malls and discount outlets.

The city has approximately 250,000 taxis and prices are generally cheap. Catching a taxi in the street is not advised, especially at night. Radio taxis, which are called by phone, are more expensive than regular taxis, but are more reliable, very safe and operate right through the night. Regular taxis are divided into free-roaming taxis (with licence plates beginning with 'A'), and *sitio* taxis (with licence plates beginning with a 'B'), which operate from a certain base. Sitios are safer than free-roaming taxis, though slightly more expensive. Ensure that the licence is displayed inside the taxi and that the photo of the driver on the licence is the actual driver. Also, check for a meter. All taxis have meters, and though some taxis do not operate meters at night, you should be able to negotiate a fair fare in advance with the driver. Hotel taxis are more expensive than either radio or sitio taxis.

The city is large and duplicate street names are very common, so drivers won't know where you are going without the colonia (neighbourhood), district or postcode. Even then, you will be expected to give some direction. If possible, mark your destination on a map and use the well-practised tradition of pointing and smiling if your Spanish is insufficient or your sense of direction poor. Knowing some local landmarks is also useful.

By bicycle
Mexico City is not a particularly cycling friendly city, though that is improving. Paseo de la Reforma and some of the streets in Centro Histórico are closed to motor vehicles every Sunday morning, allowing thousands of cyclists, skateboarders, rollerbladers and joggers to take to the streets. Once a month, other routes are added, making a traffic-free circuit of more than 30 km, called the Cicloton (www.deporte.df.gob.mx). Proof of residency is required to register for Ecobici (www.ecobici.df.gob.mx), Mexico City's bike rental programme.

WEATHER AND WHEN TO VISIT

Mexico City has a subtropical highland climate with two seasons. The season between November and April, is mostly dry, and has a colder part (Nov–Feb) and a warmer part (Mar–May). The rainy season, which sees most of the

DRIVING ME CRAZY
Adapted from the blog, 13 April 2010

If there is one thing that annoys me about the Mexicans, it's their lack of indicator use when driving. That annoys me about drivers in any part of the world, but the Mexicans are particularly big offenders. In a country like this, where a green pedestrian light does not mean that you have the right of way (as cars that are turning right can still proceed), it's not only annoying, but also dangerous.

And that's not the only crazy thing about the driving here. A huge round monument in the centre of two intersecting roads suggests roundabout to me. Not so to the Mexicans. Right in the middle of one of the main roads through the city, is the craziest junction I have ever seen.

It's a bit difficult to explain, but I'll try. Road A is a two-way dual carriageway running roughly east–west. Road B is a one-way dual carriageway, but with six lanes, running from south to north. There is a big circular monument in the centre of where they meet. Traffic going south to north splits and goes either side of the monument (3 lanes either side). Traffic from the east goes north of the monument if turning right, and splits and goes either side of the monument if going west. Similarly, the traffic from the west can go either side of the monument if going east. This is all fine when the traffic lights are working, and everybody is obeying them, but when the traffic is heavy, and cars are sneaking through amber lights, it's total mayhem. Dozens of cars end up facing each other on the same piece of road, on every rotation of the lights.

Some of Mexico City's crazy traffic

It's estimated that 4 million cars use Mexico City streets every day. Imagine the entire population of Ireland getting into a car (not the same car of course; each into a different car) and converging on one city, not using indicators, going around roundabouts whatever way they please, and not obeying traffic lights. I think the Road Safety Authority might have a very large headache all of a sudden!

city's 820 mm of annual rainfall, runs from June to October and there is an average of 22 rain days per month in July and August. Dense hail showers are common, but the city has not experienced snow since the 1960s. Average daily highs range from just over 21 °C in November, December and January, to over 26 °C in April and May. Temperatures and rainfall vary across the city due to variations in elevation and proximity to mountains. The period between March to May, when temperatures are high and rainfall low, is the best time to visit. However, pollution is at its highest during these months. June to September should be avoided if you want to catch some sun and don't like running in the rain. Apart from very cool evenings, the winter months are pleasant enough for training.

ACCOMMODATION

There are hotels catering for all budgets across the city though where you choose to stay will depend on the aim of the trip, and the sports facilities that will be used during the stay. Having accommodation with self-catering facilities is useful as Mexican food may become monotonous, can cause stomach upset, and is not particularly nutritious.

There are some holiday rentals and serviced apartments with kitchen facilities around the city. Rental accommodation can be found on Room Lenders (www.roomlenders.com), Mexico City Apartments (www.bestmexicoapartments.com), HomeAway (www.homeaway.co.uk) and

TripAdvisor (www.tripadvisor.com) and Some hotels have suites, and Lombardo Suites (www.lombardosuites.com), which comes with a fitness centre, is located right next to Bosque de Chapultepec. Hotel booking website Bookings.com (www.bookings.com) lists apartments, apartment hotels and suites, but doesn't necessarily enable you to avail of discounts for extended stays.

Those who wish to do some running while on holiday in Mexico City should stay close to Bosque de Chapultepec where there are good transport links, many sites, and a reasonable choice of running trails. The area around Paseo de la Reforma immediately east of the park, and the Polanco district north of the park, have many hotels. Paseo de la Reforma is traditionally a business district, and good value deals may be available in some hotels here during the Easter and Christmas holidays. Rates are sometimes negotiable, particularly if you are staying for a long period or are willing to pay in cash. Many of the higher end hotels either have their own fitness centres, or have access to fitness centres that guests can use.

For those less interested in spending time in the city and touring the sites, there are a number of running options on the outskirts of the city, particularly in the south-west in the direction of Toluca. You are unlikely to find accommodation by the national parks, but the Santa Fe district is a short drive from the best running trails, and some good hotels and suites. It is situated above 2,500 m of altitude.

Serious runners, particularly those who will be using a track, may wish to stay in the south of the city, near Bosque de Tlalpan and the excellent facilities of Deportivo Villa Olímpica, or near the tracks in Ciudad Deportivo close to the airport in the east of the city. Participants in team sports, and other disciplines which are dependent on facilities, may wish to stay close to the facilities that they will be using. The best advice is to investigate facility options before booking accommodation.

Food

There is no shortage of places to eat, and you can find a broad range of national and international restaurants. Centro Histórico, Zona Rosa, Polanco and Condesa districts contain the main restaurant areas. La Merced (by Metro stop 'Merced' on the pink Line 1) and Mercado San Juan Arcos de Belem (Metro stop Salto del Agua (on Line 1 and Line 8) are excellent places to try cheap authentic Mexican food. Popular and reputable Mexican chain restaurants include Vips, Sanborns and Toks. Zona Rosa is a good place to find European and Asian cuisine.

Comida corrida (set menu) restaurants and *fondas* are popular at lunchtime, and serve a series of small courses, with authentic home-cooked flavours, for very reasonable prices. This is a great way to try local dishes, and to get a substantial meal without spending a fortune. Lunch is traditionally the main meal of the day, so tends to be substantial and not rushed.

Other popular eatery types include street food stalls, found outside most Metro stations and on busy street corners; *taquerías* which are small restaurants selling similar food to street-food stalls but with better hygiene standards; and *cantinas* which serve food and alcohol in the evening.

Dinner has traditionally been a small meal, though many restaurants now offer a full dinner menu. There are vegetarian options available at the larger restaurants, but vegetarians are not well catered for at the street vendors.

Pastelería Madrid, on 5 de Febrero, just south of Zócalo in Centro Histórico is a traditional bakery which sells a variety of fresh bread, pastries and cakes, and tacos, tamales and other hot food. Bread is baked at least twice per day and prices are very low. There are many other bakeries around the city.

Eating in is less convenient, but is the best way to ensure that you are eating healthy, nutritious food. There are many supermarkets and smaller food stores around the city. Markets (*mercados*) are a good place to buy fresh products, including meat and vegetables and bakeries sell cheap fresh bread.

Shopping

There are many places to shop, with department stores, shopping malls and specialty shops plentiful in most of the main districts. While shopping malls in the less crowded suburban districts have become popular over the last 40 to 50 years, Centro Histórico, which includes all the older department stores, still has lots to offer.

Shopping malls and department stores are generally open between 10:00 and 19:00 Monday to Saturday with some boutiques and smaller shops closed for lunchtime (usually between

Torre Mayor, Mexico City's tallest building. The 225 m, 55-story block is built to withstand earthquakes measuring up to 8.5 on the Richter Scale.

13:00 and 15:00). Smaller shops may also close on Sundays, particularly away from the main tourist areas. Bargaining is not entertained in most boutiques and department stores, but is part of the shopping experience in the markets (*mercados*). Mercados are the most interesting place to shop and there is usually at least one in each neighbourhood.

The main department store chains are Liverpool, which sells a wide range of affordable clothing and other products, and El Palacio de Hierro, which specialises in designer clothes. Centro Santa Fe (www.centrosantafe.com.mx), the largest shopping centre in Mexico, is located on Avenida Vasco de Quiroga in Lamos de Santa Fe. Perisur (www.galerias.com/perisur) is a large shopping centre located between Ciudad Universitaria and Villa Olímpica in Coyoacán.

Altavista is an upscale shopping street in San Ángel, Condesa has a number of alternative stores and boutiques, and Polanco has an upmarket shopping area centred around Avenida Presidente Masaryk and Campos Eliseos, just north of Bosque de Chapultepec. There is a large indoor market with food, clothing and shoe vendors located near Pino Suárez Metro stop (lines 1 and 2).

Arts, crafts and souvenirs can be purchased across the city. Mercado de Curiosidades is a large building with many small art and craft shops in Centro Histórico. The Mercado Insurgentes on Calle Londres in Zona Rosa sells silver and ceramics at reasonable prices. Mercado Artesanías de la Ciudadela, located on Calle de Balderas, is an excellent place to bulk-buy gifts and souvenirs. Museum shops sell an interesting range of merchandise. The gift shop at Villa de Guadalupe is the best place to purchase religious art. There are a number of large bookshops, many selling books in English.

Supermarkets are plentiful. Walmart has a number of large stores, the most accessible of which is next to Nativitas Metro station on Line 2 (blue). Superama and City Market are high-end supermarkets, and Chedraui, Comercial Mexicana and Soriana are other popular supermarket chains. There are supermarkets within most mini-malls, and small corner stores in all neighbourhoods.

Central de Abasto is a massive wholesale fresh produce market located in the Iztapalapa neighbourhood in the south-east of the city. Produce is fresher here than anywhere else in the city, as it is here that the mercados, supermarkets and restaurants source their goods. Mercado de San Juan, near Salto del Agua Metro station, is a good place for exotic meats, and for any vegetables and spices which are difficult to find elsewhere in the city.

Finding shops which sell running footwear and sports clothing shouldn't be difficult. There are a number of Nike Factory stores, including one on 16 de Septiembre in Centro Histórico. Mexican sports retailer Marti (www.marti.mx) has several stores around the city selling running footwear, clothing and accessories, leisurewear, and a limited range of triathlon and cycling clothing. One of the best places to purchase running kit is from the retailers who set up stalls at the main running trails. Stalls are usually set up at the weekend near the entrance of El Sope in Bosque de Chapultepec and in Bosque de Tlalpan.

LANGUAGE

Spanish is the main language spoken in the city. Some tour guides, hotel staff, hotel taxi drivers, and many young people speak some English, but being able to communicate in basic Spanish will greatly enhance your experience. Knowing some polite phrases and greetings, being able to count to ten, and having the confidence to use hand signals and point at a map, will help those that are not proficient in the language. The Metro system was designed with the city's then high illiteracy rates in mind, and is easy to use even by those that don't speak Spanish. Menus often come in English, or have photos, and some tourist sites have guides who speak English.

Written Mexican Spanish has few differences from Standard European Spanish. The colloquial Mexican Spanish has regional variations, and can differ from standard Spanish in both vocabulary and pronunciation. Some words have been borrowed or Hispanicised from indigenous languages, especially from the Aztec language Nahuatl. Pronunciation is more similar to the dialects of southern Spain than of other regions. Those who speak standard Spanish shouldn't have any difficulty being understood; the differences are somewhat similar to the difference between British and American English.

COMMUNICATION

Mexico phone networks operate on the same GMS 850/1900 MHz frequency as most networks in the US and Canada. Some European phones (which normally operate on 900/1800 MHz) will not pick up network signal. A SIM card (called a 'chip') on the Telcel or Movistar networks can be purchased for unlocked mobile handsets that operate on the required frequencies. Prepaid Mexican phone kits, which are a good option if staying in Mexico City for a prolonged period, usually include at least half the value of the phone in airtime. Phones are registered locally, and roaming fees apply if used outside of Mexico City. A prefix is added to Mexican mobile number when calling from a landline - The digits 044 are added before 10-digit Mexico City registered mobile numbers (i.e. numbers starting '55'), and 045 is added to mobile numbers registered in other areas. The digit '1' is added between the international dialling code and the mobile number when calling a mobile from outside the country.

Most payphones require a prepaid 'Ladatel Card' which can be purchased from news-stands and grocery shops. Payphones can be found along main streets, in petrol stations and in Metro stations.

Reasonably priced internet cafes are plentiful, particularly in Zona Rosa, and there are Wi-Fi hotspots, operated by Telmex, in several malls, restaurants and cafes around the city. Prepaid cards for the hotspot service, called 'Tarjeta Multifon', are available from Telmex and other telephone-related stores. Many of the larger hotels offer Wi-Fi internet access, though speed of service can vary greatly between establishments.

The Mexican postal service is slow and unreliable and courier services are recommended for packages and important letters. Stamps can be purchased in many hotels, and hotels will often post letters and postcards. The city's main post office is located on Calle de Tacuba just opposite the Palacio de Bellas Artes in Centro Histórico.

The News is the only English language newspaper available at news-stands, though you can find a greater choice of English and foreign language newspapers at Sanborns stores.

HEALTH AND SAFETY

Medical care is relatively good, but travel insurance with medical cover is recommended. American British Cowdray Hospital (Centro Medico ABC; www.abchospital.com), one of the best hospitals in Mexico, has facilities in Observatorio and Santa Fe, and has English-speaking staff and an outpatient department. Hospitals Angeles (www.hospitalesangeles.com) has facilities right across the city.

There is some risk of diarrhoea from poorly prepared food. While sampling street food is part of the cultural experience, care should be taken to avoid illness. Eat in reputable restaurants where possible, avoid too much spicy foods to begin with, and, if diarrhoea does strike, drink lots of water and stick to dry food. Tap water is drinkable but isn't recommended. Hotels often provide limited bottled water free of charge. Additional supplies are widely available in shops and supermarkets.

Vaccination against yellow fever is required for those arriving from affected areas. Hepatitis A and typhoid vaccines are recommended. There is a risk of malaria at lower altitudes, but not in Mexico City.

Mexico has a reputation for violent gang and drug-related crime, though Mexico City is not within the affected areas, and tourists are not normally victims of violent crime. Pickpocketing, especially on the Metro system and in the often crowded Centro Histórico, and taxi robberies ('express kidnappings'), do affect tourists. To reduce your risk of taxi robberies, which involve victims being taken to various ATMs to max out credit cards, use only official licensed cabs, and inform a friend of the licence plate number of the cab in which you are travelling. Taxiaviso (www.taxiaviso.com) is a free mobile app which can be used to verify if a cab is official, and to report any emergencies. Keep your valuable personal items out of sight when on the Metro or in crowded streets, and avoid gathering around street performers and magicians outside Metro stations. Try not to look like a lost and vulnerable tourist. Streets are generally well patrolled and well lit, and you will rarely find yourself alone. Crime rates are falling, and the city is not particularly unsafe.

Mexican police officers often rely on bribes to top up their moderate wages, and may look for money if you are found to be breaking a law. If you are approached by a police officer, remain calm, explain that you are a tourist, and phone your embassy immediately if asked for a bribe. Specially trained tourist police, who are often more helpful than regular police officers, can usually be found near the major attractions. If you are affected by crime or robberies contact the Ministerio Público, a specialised prosecution office for foreigners with multilingual staff and located at Victoria Street 76 in Centro Histórico.

Driving poses a serious risk to both your health and your sanity. There are almost endless traffic jams as some four million cars make their way through the city's streets each day. Drivers are generally reckless, some junctions are rather complex, and it's easy to get lost. Fissures, potholes and large speed bumps, all with the potential to damage a car, are common along the city's suburban roads. Avoid driving if possible.

Mexico City is located along the Trans-Mexican Volcanic Belt and seismic activity is frequent. A very large earthquake, measuring 8.1 on the Richter scale, struck the city in 1985 and killed thousands of people. The epicentre of this earthquake was in fact 600 km away in the Pacific, and it affected other urban areas in Mexico, but had particular destructive consequences in the capital. Following this catastrophic earthquake, a number of the city's major buildings have been reinforced and new buildings have been designed to meet legally required structural criteria.

The city's location, geography, and weather systems combine with car fumes and industrial waste to make one of the most polluted areas in the world. The weak winds associated with the anti-cyclone weather systems in the Valley of Mexico are inadequate to disperse the air pollution created by four million vehicles and more than 50,000 industries. Initiatives have been introduced to improve the city's air quality, and levels of lead, ozone, carbon monoxide and sulfur dioxide have all fallen considerably in the last 25 years.

Money

See p. 29

Power

See p. 29

Time

Mexico City operates on Central Standard Time (CST; GMT-6). Daylight saving operates between the first Sunday in April and the last Sunday in October. Mexicans use the 24-hour clock.

Because of its relative proximity to the equator, there is little variation in daylight hours from month to month, with just under 11 hr of daylight in December and almost 13 hr 20 min of daylight in midsummer. Daylight saving means that sunset occurs around 18:00 during the months of November and December. Streets are usually well lit, but running after dark anywhere other than the main streets, is not advised.

	Mar	Jun	Sept	Dec
Sunrise	06:45	06:58	07:24	07:03
Sunset	18:46	20:16	19:39	18:01

Laundry

Laundries (*lavanderías*) can be found practically everywhere in the city but coin-operated self-service laundries are rare. The standard service usually involves having your clothes washed, dried and folded, and is charged based on the weight of the clothes. Many self-catering accommodations have a washing machine, and a very small number of hotels have coin-operated machines.

Culture and respect

Though locals are used to seeing tourists dressed provocatively, avoiding revealing clothing will help you blend in and will show respect. Collared shirts and trousers or skirts are normal attire when visiting nicer areas of the city including museums and official buildings. Some churches won't allow people who are wearing shorts or inappropriate clothing to enter. You should remove sunglasses, hats and caps when entering religious buildings.

Mexicans are quite relaxed about time, and arriving 15 minutes late is not unusual. That said, those who work in the tourist sector are usually punctual, and public transport runs on time. Mexicans are used to coming in contact with tourists who do not speak Spanish, and being able to speak any level of Spanish will both surprise, and impress them.

Mexican men are generally courteous towards women, particularly older women, and will often hold a door open or offer up a seat. Resisting such gestures is considered rude. If gestures go beyond politeness, and you feel harassed, a simple 'no' usually suffices. Females should dress conservatively to avoid the wrong type of male attention.

Tips of approximately 10 percent are adequate in restaurants, though some restaurants will already have added a service charge to the bill. Taxi drivers can be tipped if they provide a special service. Porters expect a tip of approximately 10 pesos for helping with your luggage. Tour guides should also be tipped.

Opposite Monumento a la Independencia on Paseo de la Reforma
Following Gravel trail in the centre of Paseo de la Reforma as it passes through Bosque de Chapultepec

Sports facilities and services

Mexico City is probably more suitable for recreational runners looking for a running holiday than for elite athletes wishing to carry out a hard block of training. That said, those who want to spend a week or two here, combined with training elsewhere in Mexico, will find their stay enjoyable.

The official altitude of Mexico City is 2,220 m, and though the central districts are relatively flat, some of the western and south-western suburbs reach 2,500 m and above. The national parks between Mexico City and Toluca are 3,000 m and higher. There is no opportunity to 'live high, train low', though you can live high, train higher'. The Olympic Stadium is situated 2,290 m above sea level.

Trails and running routes

Bosque de Chapultepec is the main place to run within the city itself. There are a number of other parks around the city, many of them with running trails, and there are a number of great options in the forests and mountains south-west of the city limits. The websites En Donde Correr (www.endondecorrer.com) and Asdeporte (www.asdeporte.com) have descriptions, maps, and photos, of running trails in the city. Some secured trails close at 17:00. Run early in the morning to avoid the worst of the pollution.

Bosque de Chapultepec

Bosque de Chapultepec, one of the largest urban parks in the world, is a good place for those who are holidaying in the city to run. The park is unsuitable for long fast runs, and long-distance runners may become frustrated with the lack of variety and constantly having to cross the large roads that intersect the park.

As you enter the park from the east along Paseo de la Reforma, follow Calzada Mahatma Gandhi around to the right. Amid the first section of trees beyond the swimming pools, there is a 1 km loop trail which has every 100 m marked. The area, known as Circuito Gandhi, is well shaded from the midday sun, though probably not suitable for fast interval work as the course is narrow, has lots of bends, and other park users tend to wander onto the course from time to time. There is a single straight 100 m trail down the centre of this track, and various tree stumps and outdoor gym stations which can be used for stretching and core work.

If you continue roughly following the perimeter of the park, you will come to a busy junction between Calle Rubén Darío, Calzada Chivatito and Avenida Paseo de la Reforma. Continue west, past the military camp, and join the second section of the park by taking one of the pedestrian bridges across Periférico Bulevar Manuel Ávila Camacho and head for the amusement park, Lago Mayor and Bosque de Chapultepec II. Just west of Lago Mayor is another measured trail. Known as El Sope, this 2 km trail, which was renovated in 2011, has a fenced perimeter. It is slightly undulating, and the surface is composed of fine volcanic rock gravel. There is a 100 m straight for sprints or strides. El Sope is a good place to buy running kit and footwear, especially at the weekend, and to find out about upcoming races and running events. It is open daily from 05:30 until 17:00 and gets very busy at the weekend. Toilets on site can be used for a small fee. There are weight training facilities and outdoor gym equipment in this area.

The flat concrete route around Lago Mayo is popular among joggers and rollerbladers but isn't the most suitable surface for running. A better road option is the tarmac cycle lane beside the almost traffic-free road around the lake area. These routes are quietest during the week and in the early mornings. Weekends in the park are always very busy.

Avenida College Military and Gran Avenida provide a circular asphalt route around the Castle to the south of the park. The hill up to the castle is a good place for doing hill efforts, but can become crowded in the afternoon and at weekends. The dirt path which runs down the centre of Paseo de la Reforma, as it passes through the park, can be used for warm-up and cool-down, or to add variety to runs. There are some junctions to cross, however.

Viveros de Coyoacán

Viveros de Coyoacán is a smaller park in the Coyoacán district south of the city that has a compacted 2 km dirt trail around it. No roads run through the park, so running here can be more enjoyable than at Bosque de Chapultepec, and it is easily accessible from Coyoacán Metro station.

Bosque de Tlalpan

Bosque de Tlalpan is one of the busiest running spots in the city. There is a variety of trails of varying lengths around the park. Snacks and

OPPOSITE Jogging tracks and running trails in Bosque de Chapultepec (CLOCKWISE FROM TOP LEFT) Cycle track around Logo Mayor; El Sope, Circuito Ghandi, centre of Paseo de la Reforma and path around Lago Mayor

fresh fruit juices can be purchased from nearby vendors, and running footwear and clothing is often available near the park entrance. There are also restaurants, picnic areas, playgrounds, football fields and a zoo. To get to the park take a bus to Centro de Tlalpan from Estadio Azteca Metro station.

Autódromo Hermanos Rodríguez
There are three main running routes by the Autódromo Hermanos Rodríguez in Ciudad Deportiva Magdalena Mixhuca. Entrances to the area are within walking distance of the Velodrome, Ciudad Deportivo and Puebla Metro stations (Line 9; brown). A gravel track, similar to the other ones around the city, runs on the inside of the main, eastern portion of the racetrack; a second dirt track runs along the outside of the eastern portion of the racetrack, and the racetrack itself is a popular asphalt route for joggers, rollerbladers and cyclists.

Virgilio Uribe
A completely flat paved, traffic-free route of 5 km circles the Virgilio Uribe (Cuemanco) regatta course. Each 1 km of the course, which may be particularly appealing to race walkers, is marked. There is public parking (small charge), toilets, and running kit and fruit juice stands.

Circuit Mario de la Cueva
Circuit Mario de la Cueva at Ciudad Universitaria is also a popular place to run and walk, and makes use of the quite asphalt roads in the south of the campus. It is advised to run here early to avoid the walkers. The 4 km circuit, which is closed to traffic at weekends has many twists and turns, is popular among cyclists.

Xochimilco Ecological Park
Xochimilco Ecological Park in the south of the city has approximately 4 km of flat asphalt road suitable for running and other activities. There is a small entry fee to the park. Bicycle rental is available.

Bosque de Aragón
Bosque de Aragón, located just north of the airport and of Deportivo Oceania (Metro: Bosque de Aragón, Line B), combines well-marked asphalt and dirt routes to make a flat course of approximately 5 km in length surrounded by trees and grass. There is also a fitness area.

OPPOSITE Weight training equipment near El Sope jogging track in Bosque de Chapultepec

The following options are outside the city limits, and though accessible by public transport, are probably best reached by car. They are popular choices for local elite athletes, and are especially good for marathon runners not wishing to run endless laps of the city's jogging tracks. These options are at a higher altitude than the city, and are all in the forested area off the Mexico–Toluca toll road, 30–40 km from the city centre.

El Ocotal
El Ocotal is one of the main sites at which to spot elite athletes in Mexico City. The moderately hilly forest loop, approximately 5 km long, is located at an altitude of approximately 2,900 m on the city side of Acopilco, north of the Mexico–Toluca motorway. To get there by public transport take a bus to Acopilco from Metro station Observatorio (Line 1; pink) and ask the driver to let you out at 'el Ocotal enfrente (opposite) *de las fresas*'. There are stalls selling sportswear and fresh fruit juices.

La Pila
La Pila is a 12 km out-and-back dirt trail (24 km in total) located south of the Mexico-Toluca motorway approximately 5 km further from El Ocotal. It is located at an altitude of 3,300 m, is relatively flat and like El Ocotal is popular among serious runners. It begins just after the Our Lady of the Pillar Church (La Virgen del Pila). To get there by public transport, take the bus 'Ruta 110C Metro Tacubaya—La Pila' from Tacubaya Metro Station to the yellow footbridge by the church. Climb to the trail from here (opposite side from the church).

Parque Nacional Desierto de los Leones
The forested area before la Pila, and more or less opposite el Ocotal is known as the Desierto de los Leones and it provides additional running routes in the area.

TRACK FACILITIES

There are a number of synthetic athletics tracks across the city, including 400 m tracks at Deportivo Villa Olímpica, Ciudad Universitaria, Deportivo Xochimilco, and Ciudad Deportivo.

LOCAL RACES

There are road races in the city, almost every weekend. The Mexico City International Marathon is held each September and takes in sites in Centro Histórico, Basque de Chapultepec and Polanco, and the main thoroughfares Avenida Revolución, Insurgents Sur and Paseo de la

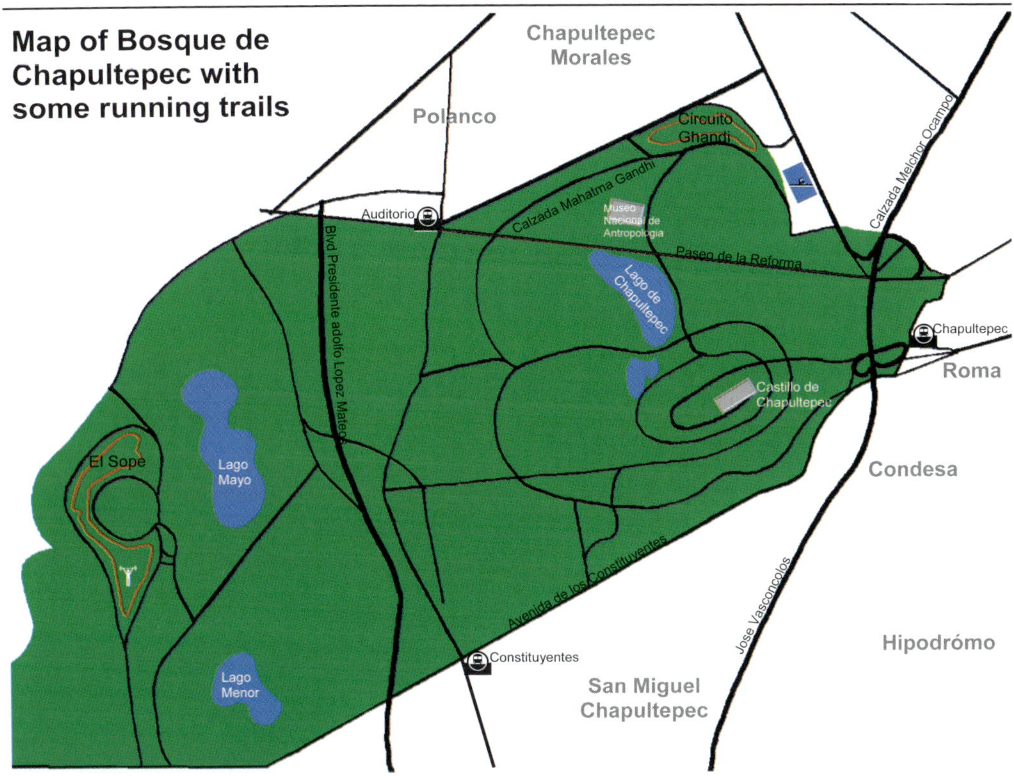
Map of Bosque de Chapultepec with some running trails
Chapultepec Morales
Polanco
Circuito Ghandi
Calzada Mahatma Gandhi
Museo Nacional de Antropologia
Auditorio
Calzada Melchor Ocampo
Paseo de la Reforma
Lago de Chapultepec
Chapultepec
Roma
Castillo de Chapultepec
Blvd Presidente adolfo Lopez Mateos
Condesa
El Sope
Lago Mayo
Avenida de los Constituyentes
Jose Vasconcolos
Hipodrómo
Constituyentes
San Miguel Chapultepec
Lago Menor

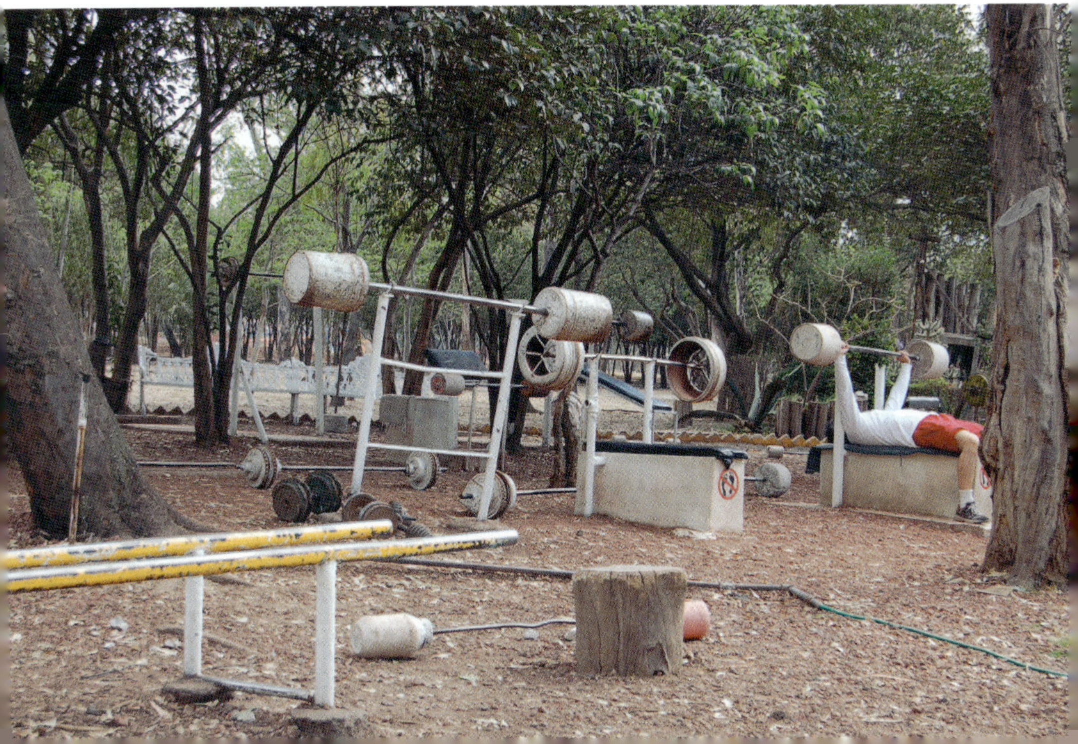

Reforma. Good websites for information on upcoming events include those of event organisers Club Asdeporte (www.asdeporte.com) and Emoción Deportiva (www.emociondeportiva.com), and the RunMX website (www.runmx.com). The En Donde Correr website (www.endondecorrer.com) has event listings for across Mexico. All these sites are in Spanish. You may also find fliers in sports stores, at the kiosk in Bosque de Tlalpan, and in fitness centres around the city.

GYM FACILITIES AND FACILITIES FOR OTHER SPORTS

As a city that has hosted an Olympic Summer Games in the modern era, it is unsurprising that Mexico City has sports facilities for just about every sport imaginable. Most of the original Olympic facilities remain, though the use of some has been adapted. Finding information on public access to facilities is difficult. The following outlines the main facilities and how to find them. The city sports institute website (www.deporte.df.gob.mx) has some useful information, including maps of public sports facilities in various districts.

The majority of the city's sports facilities are concentrated in two main areas – Ciudad Deportivo near the airport in the east of the city, and the Ciudad Universitaria and Villa Olímpica areas in the south of the city. There are also a number of fitness centres in the tourist areas of the city.

Magdalena Mixhuca Sports City (Ciudad Deportivo), not to be confused with Ciudad de los Deportes, an area containing Azul Stadium and La Monumental bullring in the south of the city, is located near the airport, and has a number of sports arenas, facilities and complexes. The area, accessed via the Velódromo, Ciudad Deportiva and Puebla Metro stations (Line 9; brown) hosted the basketball, cycling, fencing and hockey events during the 1968 Olympics. Palacio de los Deportes, an indoor arena, hosts volleyball and basketball matches, exhibitions and pop concerts and can facilitate boxing, wrestling, fencing, weightlifting, ice hockey, cycling, equestrian and athletics competitions. Autódromo Hermanos Rodríguez, Foro Sol, and the Velodrome are other major sports facilities within the area. There are also a number of playing fields, a skatepark and athletics tracks. CNAR Mexico (www.cnar.gob.mx) is a national high performance centre based at the Ciudad Deportivo. It has access to extensive physical conditioning facilities and facilities for swimming, gymnastics, combat sports, ball sports, athletics, archery and cycling.

Ciudad Universitaria, UNAM's main campus, was built on an ancient solidified lava bed in the Coyoacán borough in the south of the city. It encloses the Olympic Stadium, other sports facilities, around 40 faculties and institutes, the Central Library, some museums and an ecological reserve. The track within the stadium is used only for international competitions. Football and American football fields, martial arts gyms, boxing gyms and other sports facilities near the stadium are intended mostly for students.

El Centro Deportivo Villa Olímpica, as the name suggests, is built on the site of the main 1968 Olympic Village, just south of Ciudad Universitaria. It has become one of the most important leisure centres in the south of the city and has facilities for swimming and other aquatic sports, judo, tennis, athletics, football, boxing, taekwondo, beach volleyball, and wrestling, and a rehab department. The area is just north of Bosque de Tlalpan, and is approximately 1 km walk from the Villa Olímpica Metrobús station (Metrobús Line 1).

There are excellent swimming, diving, syncronised and water polo facilities at the CEFORMA Aquatics Centre (Centro Acuático CEFORMA; www.centroacuaticoceforma.jimdo.com) also in the Tlalpan area. In addition to an Olympic standard 50 m pool, there are two 25 m pools, diving boards, and a separate water polo area. CEFORMA also has areas suitable for martial arts and combat sports including judo, taekwondo, boxing and wrestling.

Sport Care (www.sportcare.com.mx) offers rehabilitation and sports medicine services, and is located in Perisur, just west of Ciudad Universitaria and Villa Olímpica.

Club Casablanca San Angel (www.clubcasablanca.com.mx), also located in the south-west of the city has 25 m and 50 m swimming pools, 24 tennis courts, football fields, gymnastics facilities, CV fitness equipment, a dojo and a spinning room. It is located beside Deportivo Torres de Ixtapantongo which also has outdoor pools and an athletics track, and opposite an equestrian centre (Club Hípico El Oliver).

There are also a number of other sports facilities around the Xochimilco area in the south-east of the city. Virgilio Uribe, the regatta course and training/warm-up lane used for rowing and canoeing events at the 1968 Games, is located just west of Lake Xochimilco. The area, also known as 'Cuemanco', has other facilities, and there is an athletics track at Deportivo Xochimilco.

There are numerous gym facilities around the city, many with swimming pools, and some with additional sports facilities. Qi (www.centro-qi.com), on Avenida Amsterdam in Colonia Condesa, has a climbing wall, cardio and free weight gym, spa, and a sports medicine department, headed up by a certified sports doctor. Flexible and short-term memberships are available. Nelson Vargas (www.anv.com.mx) sports centres, located across the city, specialise in swimming, but also have cardiovascular and free-weights gyms, and offer spinning, yoga and other exercise classes. Junior club (www.juniorclub.com.mx) is located on Calle Sindicalismo in Colonia Condesa and has 14 tennis courts, a squash court, a 25 m swimming pool, a gym and an aerobics studio. Sport City clubs (www.sportcity.com.mx) have centres, most with swimming facilities, CV equipment, free and machine weights, tennis courts and squash courts, across the city.

For those who don't want to pay for gym membership, but who still want to do some weight training, there is another novel, and somewhat Spartan, option. There are outdoor gym facilities, including improvised barbells and gymnastics-type facilities, near the start/finish areas of El Sope trail and at other running trails around the city.

Due to heavy traffic, Mexico City is not a particularly cycling friendly city, and cyclists would find it difficult to train from here. The velodrome at Ciudad Deportivo offers limited public access. Options for serious mountain biking are also limited within the city itself. Nearby Toluca, and other surrounding towns would be more suitable for serious cyclists and mountain bikers. For the less-serious cyclist, or those looking to use cycling as a form of cross-training, the quieter areas of Bosque de Chapultepec, and the racing circuit at Autódromo Hermanos Rodriguez are good options. The cyclotron events on Sundays, when some of the city roads are closed to traffic, are a good opportunity to cycle. These options, together with the concrete path around Lago Mayor in Bosque de Chapultepec are also good for rollerblading.

BELOW *El Sope jogging track in Bosque de Chapultepec*

THINGS TO SEE AND DO BETWEEN TRAINING

Of all the venues featured in this book, Mexico City stands out in terms of cultural sites and activities. It's an ideal place to take a non-running partner, and to combine a training and cultural holiday. Take the Turibus (www.turibus.com.mx) to get a feel for the city. There are running trails near most of the major tourist and entertainment spots (e.g. Bosque de Tlalpan is next to Six-Flags Mexico; Xochimilco Ecological Park is adjacent to the floating gardens of Xochimilco and there are numerous sites and attractions in Bosque de Chapultepec) facilitating an enjoyable day out for all the family.

Bosque de Chapultepec, the large park at the western extent of the Paseo de la Reforma, is home to many of the city's cultural and leisure activities. The large zoo (Zoológico de Chapultepec) has free entry and features big cats, elephants, white rhino, giraffe, giant panda and selections of birds and monkeys. Among the park's museums are the National Anthropological Museum, the Museum of Modern Art, and the National History Museum. The anthropology museum is the largest museum in Latin America and features a number of important archaeological finds and the world's most significant collection of pre-Hispanic Mexican art. Los Pinos, located on the edge of the park, is the official presidential residence. The park's three lakes (Lago de Chapultepec, Lago Mayor and Lago Menor) are a hive of activity at the weekends and many of the city's residents come here to relax. Numerous vendors, selling a variety of wares and food, fill the walkways, pedal boats fill the lakes, and a festive atmosphere fills the air.

Centro Histórico features a number of historic sites and free attractions. The Zócalo (also known as Plaza de la Constitución), where locals congregate, and events are held, can become very crowded at the weekend. Sites include Catedral Metropolitana, the largest cathedral in the Americas; the Palacio Nacional which lines the entire eastern side of the Zócalo; Templo Mayor, the ruins of a double pyramid complex from Aztec times; the Museo Nacional de Arte housing Mexican masterpieces from a period of five centuries; and the magnificent Palacio de Bellas Artes.

The Xochimilco Floating Gardens, with colourfully decorated barges floating along the Aztec canals; and Villa de Guadalupe, which honours Mexico's patron saint, the Virgin de Guadalupe; are just two of the main attractions in the city's suburbs.

There is plenty of opportunity to watch sport and visit sports venues. Estadio Azteca, with a capacity of 105,000, is one of the largest football stadiums in the world. It was built for the 1968 Olympic Games, and hosted games during the 1970 and 1986 FIFA World Cups. Azteca is home to Club America FC, one of the most famous football clubs in Mexico, and also hosts concerts and American football games. It can be reached by the light rail which connects with the Line 2 Metro service at Tasqueña. Sporting events can also be watched at Estadio Olímpico de Ciudad Universitaria (the Olympic Stadium; UNAM 'Pumas' football team), Foro Sol (baseball), Palacio de los Deportes (indoor events including once-a-year NBA basketball games) and Estadio Azul (Cruz Azul football club home games). Arena Mexico hosts Mexican free wrestling, a popular 'entertainment' sport, and there are almost daily horse races at the Hipódromo de las Américas (www.hipodromo.com.mx). The Autódromo Hermanos Rodríguez, hosted Formula 1 races until the cancellation of the Mexico Grand Prix in 1992. Today it hosts NASCAR races.

La Feria Chapultepec Mágico, the oldest amusement park in Mexico City, is located in Bosque de Chapultepec, and Six Flags México, the largest amusement park in Latin America is located in Tlalpan. Cinemas are plentiful. Cinemex (www.cinemex.com), the most popular, has more than 30 cinemas across the city. Hollywood movies are often shown in English, with Spanish subtitles. Classical music is popular, and a number of orchestras, offer seasonal programmes. The Auditorio Nacional (Bosque de Chapultepec) has regular Spanish and English-language pop and rock performances, operas and other performing arts shows from around the world. Foro Sol (www.ocesa.com.mx) and Palacio de los Deportes are among the many other popular concert venues. Theatres, which are plentiful, stage Spanish versions of popular Broadway shows as well as Spanish-language originals. Rodeo Santa Fe (www.rodeosantafe.com.mx) in Colonia Tlalnepantla is also a popular entertainment spot.

REST DAY EXCURSIONS

There is so much to see and do in Mexico City that it's unlikely that you will want to leave. That said, Teotihuacan, located just 40 km from the city is one of Mexico's main attractions, and there are other options offering solace from the busy city.

Teotihuacan, one of the largest archaeological sites in Central America, is located just 40 km north-east of the city. It features pyramids, museums and palace complexes over an area of 20 km^2. There is a lot of walking involved in exploring the site, so consider that when fitting in between training, and since the site is free for Mexican residents on Sundays, it is wise to choose another day of the week to visit. Buses to the site operate from Terminal Autobuses del Norte, while a number of tour agencies also offer half and full day tours to the site. Try to get to the site early to avoid the worst of the crowds, and the blazing midday sun.

RIGHT (TOP TO BOTTOM) *Palacio de Bellas Artes; Catedral Metropolitiana; Castillo de Chapultepec; Monumento a los Niños Héroes*
OPPOSITE (LEFT TO RIGHT) *Market stalls; Lago de Chapultepec; and tree-lined walkways, all in Bosque de Chapultepec*

Oaxtepec, just 100 km south of the city, has a tourist campus which boasts a large waterpark, a 50 m swimming pool and a diving pool . A bus leaves for Oaxtepec from Tasqueña bus station approximately every 10 min. During the Mexico Olympics, Oaxtepec hosted a world youth championship as part of the Cultural Olympiad.

Other cities and towns worth visiting and within easy reach of Mexico include Taxco, famous for its narrow cobbled streets and colonial architecture; Puebla, a UNESCO World Heritage site renowned throughout Mexico for its cuisine; and Cuernavaca (45 min away) which is known as 'the City of Eternal Spring' thanks to its temperate climate. Valle de Bravo, a lake-side town in the middle of a forest, offers excellent mountain biking, water skiing and paragliding opportunities.

A NOTE ON LIVING HERE LONG-TERM

Not many serious athletes would move to Mexico City to train full-time, but runners who find themselves moving here for work or study-related reasons could benefit from the altitude and training options within the city. The size of the city has both positive and negative aspects, with a low cost of living, a good choice of entertainment and things to do between training, and a large international airport which is well connected to both national and international destinations, just some of the benefits. The weather is relatively conducive to training throughout the year. Sea level races are always at least a flight away, there is little opportunity for training at a lower altitude, and living in a city so large is not for everyone, least of all for runners who like variety in their training. Mexico's strict immigration laws make casual employment almost impossible, and work permits, which are required to work in the country, are notoriously difficult to obtain.

FURTHER INFORMATION

Any good bookshop will provide a choice of excellent guidebooks detailing Mexico City's sites, museums and attractions, and providing practical information. Good English-language websites are a little more difficult to find. Inside Mexico (www.insidemexico.com), 'the English Speaker's Guide to living in Mexico' provides information for those moving to the city and includes news, advice on living in the country, travel information and real estate listings. MexicoCity.com (www.mexicocity.com) has listings of activities, shops, cinemas and other attractions. The official Mexico City Tourism website (www.mexicocity.gob.mx) lists a host of attractions and activities, and details sports facilities in the city in Spanish.

OTHER ALTITUDE TRAINING SITES IN MEXICO

Toluca de Lerdo (2,680 m)
www.toluca.gob.mx

Toluca, at 2,680 m, is the highest city in North America. Toluca is just 66 km from Mexico City, but is much safer (in terms of crime, traffic and sanitation) and considerably less polluted. Temperatures are cooler than in the capital, due to the higher altitude, and heavy hail showers are possible at any time of the year.

Both Mexico City and Toluca international airports are within easy reach. Caminante busses (www.tmt-caminante.com.mx), run hourly services from Mexico City airport to a terminal in the east of Toluca. Other bus services, including services from Mexico City's Observatorio, Terminal Norte and Cuatro Caminos stations, arrive at Toluca's main terminal in the south-east of the city. Taxi travel is both cheap and plentiful, with approximately 5,000 vehicles serving a city of less than a million people. The city is fairly compact and easy to get around. Visitors will find the streets more driveable, and a car more useful, than in Mexico City.

Historically, one of the most popular sites for training was El Nevado de Toluca (also known as Xinantacel), an extinct volcano located approximately 30 km south of the city. An unpaved road, approximately 20 km long, winds up the volcano from pine forests, to the barren crater. With a final altitude of 4,200 m, this run, known to bring even athletes who are well accustomed to altitude to their knees, is probably too difficult to be beneficial. None-the-less, the route maintains much of its former prestige. The unpaved roads which run most of the way between the city and the foot of the volcano provide a more suitable training environment, while training sites within the city include Alamenda 2000 and Parque Nacional Sierra Morelos. The El Ocotal, La Pila and Parque Nacional Desierto de los Leones trails *(p ??)* are also accessible from Toluca.

As a pre-Columbian cultural centre, there is much to see and do in Toluca. The central plaza in the historic centre is surrounded by modern and historic state and municipal buildings, and the city has many parks, museums and churches.

OPPOSITE A polar bear at Chapultepec Zoo

United States General Practacilities

In an attempt to avoid duplication, the following section contains practical information that applies to all US venues.

Getting in

Visa requirements
Residents of Canada and Bermuda do not require visitor visas. Citizens of 37 countries (including UK, Ireland, most other EU and EFTA countries, Australia, New Zealand, Japan and South Korea), are part of the visa waiver programme and must apply for ESTA (Electronic System for Travel Authorization) before boarding a plane. Approval is valid for business and tourism stays of up to 90 days. Passports should have at least six months validity after the planned departure date. Citizens of countries not in the visa waiver programme must apply for a visa which may take 30 days or longer to obtain. Further details on visa requirements and procedures can be found on www.travel.state.gov.

Getting around

The US is a driving and flying nation. The long distances between towns and cities, and the lack of an efficient public transport system away from the main urban areas necessitate access to your own car. Even within medium-sized towns, many of the amenities and larger shopping malls are located outside the main downtown. Locals are normally poor at giving directions for public transport, where it does exist, because they are so used to driving everywhere.

Roads in America
Interstate highways are the straight, wide and fast motorways which transverse the country. They are prefixed with letter 'I' (e.g. I-40), and indicated by a number on a red, blue and white shield on maps. Odd numbered interstates normally run north–south and even numbered ones east–west. US highways and state highways are more or less equivalent to British dual carriageways. US highways are indicated on maps and signs by a number in an empty shield, and state highways symbols vary from state to state, but often feature a number in a circle.

Hiring a car
Hiring a car in the US is relatively cheap, especially for long periods, and currently fuel prices are much lower than in Europe. The best deals are obtained by booking in advance. There are extra charges for picking up and dropping off at different points (drop fee/one way fee). Most cars are automatic. While the minimum age for driving in the US is 16, most companies only hire to experienced drivers over 25. Foreign driving licences are valid for tourists for up to a year. Beware of the distances between cities. Cities that look close together on the map, may be a day's drive apart.

Addresses
A similar street address system is applied in most, but not all (see Albuquerque), towns and cities in the US. In most built-up areas, roads are laid out in a grid of blocks. These blocks are numbered sequentially from a central point (downtown in most cases). Thus, 720 S Broadway will be seven blocks south of downtown along Broadway. In many smaller towns 'streets', which are sometimes named alphabetically, tend to run north–south, and 'avenues' which are generally numbered, run east–west. Once you find your address, remember that what in Britain would be called the ground floor is the first floor in America; the first floor is the second floor, and so on.

US quick facts

Capital Washington DC
Largest city New York
Official language English
Currency US dollar ($; USD), divided into 100 cents
Time zone Four time zones on continental US, with daylight saving operating between the second Sunday in March and the first Sunday in November§; see individual state details
Public holidays New Year's Day (Jan 1)‡, Martin Luther King Jnr's Birthday (Jan 15), Presidents' Day (third Mon Feb), Easter Monday*, Memorial Day (last Mon May)‡, Independence Day (Jul 4)‡, Labor Day (first Mon Sept)‡, Columbus Day (second Mon Oct), Veterans' Day (Nov 11)‡, Thanksgiving Day (last Thurs Nov)‡, Christmas Day (Dec 25)‡, plus state-specific public holidays
International dialling code +1
Outgoing access code 011
Emergency contact 911
Power 120 V; 60 Hz power supply; Type B, American-style (NEMA 1–15 unpolarised) plugs and sockets with two flat parallel pins and a round earthing pin
Driving Right side
Measurement Imperial

§ Most of the state of Arizona does not operate daylight saving
* Varies according to Christian calendar
‡ Celebrated in all states

DRIVING IN THE US

Traffic laws are not uniform across all states, and speed limits and other regulations are set locally. Check state-specific rules on the AAA website (www.drivinglaws.aaa.com). The following are general guidelines for driving in the US.

- Americans drive on the right side of the road.

- Distances are in miles (or sometimes hours) and speeds are in miles per hour. Fuel is priced and sold in US gallons (1 US gallon = 3.8 litres).

- Roundabouts are very rare. Traffic light order is red, green, flashing amber and red. In the absence of traffic light turn signals at junctions, you can turn right if there is no traffic coming from the left. You should not turn right (or left) on a red arrow.

- You must always stop at 'stop' signs. At four-way intersections, where all cars must stop, cars proceed in order that they reached the intersection after they have come to a complete stop. In the event that two cars arrive at the same time, the driver on the right, or a driver who is travelling straight (if a car is turning), has the right of way.

- It is illegal to pass a school bus, in either direction, if it has flashing lights or a 'stop' sign sticking out the side. This law is taken very seriously.

- Exiting and entering motorways can be a daunting experience. Be decisive. You don't have much time to merge with the other traffic on entrances, and though exits are well marked, they sometimes seem to pop up out of nowhere. Some motorways have six or more lanes. American drivers are notoriously poor at using indicators on motorways, and do not give way to traffic changing lanes. Undertaking is not illegal, and occurs regularly, and Americans drive very close to other vehicles.

- There are many toll roads (turnpikes) across the US, especially in the East and Midwest. Some take credit and debit cards, but some are cashless tolls which are billed via a transponder fitted in the car. Car hire companies charge a fee for transponders, which is sometimes extortionate, though cashless toll roads can usually be avoided. Check cashless toll payment procedure with your car hire company.

- The maximum speed limits in most states is 65 miles per hour (105 kph), though there are some differences from state to state. Speed limits by schools are 15 or 20 miles per hour (24 or 32 kph) when lights are flashing. Speeding around roadworks is frowned upon.

- Parking is not permitted facing oncoming traffic on the wrong side of the road or on pavements painted yellow for emergency vehicles. Signs will indicate other limitations such as scheduled street sweeping, zoning restrictions, reservations for business and snow emergency routes.

- Petrol (gas) stations are usually self-pump, but require payment by credit card in advance at the pump. Service stations can take you a long way off the motorway, and onto regular roads, so be prepared to switch from and to motorway mode.

- Black lettering on white signs proclaims federal law that must be obeyed. Yellow signs with black writing indicate advice that should be followed, though this is not a legal requirement.

- Take 'four-wheel drive only' signs seriously. Jeeps are recommended for rugged terrain.

- Sat Nav/GPS is useful, especially around the larger cities, but should be used as a guide, and not at a substitute for reading street signs and motorway exit signs. US ZIP codes don't pinpoint an area as accurately as, say, UK postcodes do, so street addresses are also useful.

- Car pool or HOV (high occupancy vehicle) lanes are marked by signs and tarmac markings of a hollow diamond. This lane is always the left-most lane.

- In some areas, it is a legal requirement to have your headlights on at all times. Signs will indicate these areas.

- Never have open alcohol in the car, and carry any alcohol in the boot.

- If you are pulled over by the police, stay in the car, and keep your hands visible at all times. Under no circumstances reach to get anything from your glove compartment as the police will presume that you are reaching for a gun. Be polite, and do not attempt to make a joke.

SHOPPING AND CLOTHES SIZES

Shopping for cheap clothes and shoes is an important part of any trip to the US. However, to avoid frustration, remember that women's clothing sizes are two figures less than British sizes (e.g. UK size 12 is a US size 10). Women's shoe sizes are generally a half size higher than the British equivalent, and there is one shoe size difference for men.

LANGUAGE

English is the national language, and is spoken by most Americans. Spanish is the primary secondary language in the Southwest and California, and is spoken by Americans from Porto Rico (where Spanish is the primary language) and by Latin American immigrants. Americans will expect visitors to speak and understand English, and while many study a major European language at school (Spanish, German or French), very few reach or retain any level of fluency.

Americans have a number of words which are different from the UK version of English. Because of the popularity of American TV shows and films in Europe, you might understand what an American means when they say elevator, ATM or restroom. However, they are likely to look at you strangely if you ask for the lift, cash machine or loo.

COMMUNICATION

Mobile phones in the US operate on an 850/1900 MHz GMS network, or an 850/1900/1700 or 2100 UMTS (3G) network. These are not the same frequencies as European networks. Due to incompatibility between some European phones and the American networks, signal may not be picked up, or text messaging may not work. Roaming charges are high. For prolonged trips, purchasing a cheap handset with prepaid credit or a US SIM (check that your handset works on the required frequency), may be a cheaper option. Calls to mobile phones in the US are charged at national call rates, but users are charged for incoming calls and incoming text messages. The main network operators are AT&T, T-Mobile, Sprint and Verizon. Check local network signal on the Open Signal website (www.opensignal.com).

Most hotels, and many restaurants and cafes offer free Wi-Fi access. A small number of cafes and hotels provide computers for public use. Wi-Fi access doesn't come as standard in rental accommodation.

The US has an excellent postal system (USPS) and has branches in most towns and villages. Locations and opening times are available on the USPS website (www.usps.com).

HEALTH AND SAFETY

Travellers from Europe do not require vaccines to enter the US, and there are few contagious diseases in the country. HIV is more prevalent than in Canada and Europe.

Natural disasters are a greater threat to your health than disease. Hurricanes, tornados, earthquakes, blizzards, floods and wildfires are prevalent. Though the venues included in this book generally have low risk, just prior to publication (in September 2013), a serious fire caused major damage and disruption in Yosemite National Park, just north of Mammoth Lakes, and major flooding in Colorado, caused major destruction, including significant damage to trails, in Boulder and surrounding towns.
California has a particular earthquake risk, and tornados are common east of the Rocky Mountains. Be aware of risk warnings, and follow official advice.

Violent crime is generally concentrated in inner city neighbourhoods, and tourists should be relatively safe. Be vigilant, especially in areas that you are not familiar with, and take normal precautions.

Travel insurance, though not compulsory, is essential for all travellers to the US. There is no national health system, and without travel insurance, even the smallest injury can cost a fortune. If travelling on multi-trip insurance, ensure that your policy covers North America (not all multi-trip worldwide policies do). A reasonable amount for medical expenses (£1,000,000 GBP or local currency equivalent), and air ambulance transport home in the event of serious injury or illness, should be covered by the policy.

MONEY

The US dollar (sign: $; code: USD), divided into 100 cents, is the currency of the US. The dollar is colloquially referred to as the 'buck', and cent coins are referred to as the 'penny' (1¢), 'nickel' (5¢), 'dime' (10¢) and 'quart' (25¢).

Most ATMs accept foreign bank and debit cards. Many charge a fee for cards from different banks (though not necessarily for ones issued outside the country). ATMs in shops and restaurants charge a higher fee. Some large supermarkets don't charge for cashback with purchases, though your bank may. Major credit and debit cards are widely accepted. The US has been slow in turning to chip-and-PIN technology, so don't be surprised if you are asked to sign for your purchases (and to show identification).

Most states and many cities add a sales tax to the marked price of goods (excluding groceries). The tax varies from state to state, but is usually in the region of 7–10 percent. A hotel tax (of up to 14%) is added in many cities for stays of up to 30 days. Rental accommodation booked for longer than 30 days may not be subject to this tax.

POWER

The US operates on 120 V; 60 Hz power supply, and uses Type B, American-style (NEMA 1–15 unpolarised) plugs and sockets with two flat parallel pins and a round earthing pin.

LAUNDRY

Most hotels in the US have coin-operated washing machines and dryers. Laundrettes (laundromats) are common, and a self-service, coin-operated facility will usually be found in any medium or large shopping centre.

CULTURE AND RESPECT

Tipping in America is very important. Unless the service has been shockingly bad, not leaving a tip of at least 15 percent in restaurants is seriously frowned upon. Waiting staff depend on tips to bolster their very low wages. Similar tips should be added to taxi fares. Hotel porters would expect approximately $1 for each bag they carry for you.

Some useful translations

American English	British English
diaper	nappy
elevator	lift
pants	trousers
restroom	toilet
to-go	takeaway
counter-clockwise	anticlockwise
bill	banknote
cot	camp bed
crib	cot
drugstore	pharmacy/chemist
fall	autumn
line	queue
period	full stop
physician	doctor
push cart	trolley

Sport related terms

athletics	sport
track	athletics
hockey	ice hockey
field hockey	hockey
football	American football
soccer	football
field	pitch
locker rooms	changing rooms
sneakers	trainers/running shoes

Food related terms

eggplant	aubergine
zucchini	courgette
chips	crisps
fries	chips
cookies	biscuits
biscuit	scone
Popsicle	ice lolly
jell-o	jelly
jelly	jam
broiled	grilled
check	bill

Driving related terms

gasoline	petrol or diesel
turnpike	toll road
traffic circle	roundabout
interchange	exit or junction
kerb	pavement
parking lot	car park
deductible	excess (insurance)
transmission	gearbox
trunk	boot
hood	bonnet
fender	bumper
blinkers	indicators
ramp	slip road

Mammoth Lakes

Mammoth Lakes, located in the High Sierra in north-east California, is ideal for anyone wanting to 'live high, train low' in advance of early season track races in California. The town has been the home of Olympic medallists Deena Kastor and Meb Keflezighi, and numerous other American distance runners in recent years. Even when the town is snow-covered, there are lots of snow-free trails and quiet roads within a 30-minute drive of the town. There are good gym facilities at Snow Creek Athletic Club, and a track was opened just outside the town in 2012. Cost of living can be high, especially during the ski season, but accommodation is plentiful, and of a high standard.

Mammoth Lakes, US (2,400 m)

Mammoth Lakes, incorporated in 1984, is a small town of just 7,000 year-round residents. Many of the residents have left an urban lifestyle behind, and have chosen to come to the Eastern Sierra for a quiet life, close to nature. The town, located in Mono County, is surrounded by forest and wilderness areas. Running north–south to the west of the town lies the dramatic mountain, lake and forest landscape of the Sierra Nevada crest. To the east is a rolling escarpment which tapers off towards the valley floor. The dramatic juxtaposition of mountains and plateau give the area a dramatic appearance, and you are often running on undulating desert roads with dramatic snow-capped mountains in the background.

The economy of the town is based around the tourism industry, with almost 3 million visitors to the area each year. There are almost 5,000 rentable units (including hotels, apartments and campgrounds), more than 65 restaurants and a range of shops and stores. Mammoth Mountain Ski Resort, California's premier ski resort, is located just 8 km from the town. The mountain, together with the lake area, provides an outdoor playground in both the winter and the summer. Mammoth Lakes has its own National Monument (Devils Postpile), and is just 45 min drive from Yosemite National Park.

Author's verdict

The town was snow-covered when I visited, but with endless snow-free trails just a short drive down the valley, this hardly mattered. There is a good choice of shops and eateries, and a large supermarket, in the town, but prices are high. Accommodation is also plentiful, but expensive during the ski season. Mammoth is located in a beautiful part of California, and there is a reasonable choice of activities between training. A track has been opened just outside the town since I visited and the high performance athlete is well catered for. I enjoyed my stay, but would love to revisit later in the year after the snow has melted.

Running ★★★★☆ - Good variety of off-road trails in town and within a short drive; trails easy to find; quiet roads suitable for marathon training; synthetic track close to the town; excellent 'live high, train low' and 'live high, train higher' opportunities; good cross-training opportunities.

Convenience ★★★☆☆ - Limited flights into Mammoth airport; easy to get around town; good choice of accommodation; restaurants, entertainment and shops conveniently located; car useful, especially during winter.

Safety ★★★★★ - Low crime rate; no major disease risk.

Cost ★★☆☆☆ - High cost of living, particularly during ski season; car required to get to trails.

Cultural experience ★★☆☆☆ - Locals are friendly and easy-going, but there's nothing that you wouldn't expect to see in any American town.

Things to do between training ★★★☆☆ - Reasonable choice of entertainment and sites; some relaxing day trips within easy reach.

Suitability for solo travellers ★★☆☆☆ - Most athletes are permanent Mammoth Lakes residents; little opportunity to meet other runners, though recent addition of track will develop centre for athletes; area could become dull without travelling companions.

Must do Take the gondola to the top of Mammoth Mountain on a clear day; visit Mono Lake with your camera; drive towards Bishop and pick a completely random trail on which to run.

Ideal for Those who want to combine altitude training with racing on the US circuit.

CALIFORNIA
www.visitcalifornia.com

People
California is the most populous state in America, and one of the most ethnically diverse. There are large populations of African Americans and Asian Americans, more Native Americans than any other state. Approximately 40 percent of the population describe themselves as Hispanic or Latino. Less than 60 percent of Californians speak English as their first language.

Places
California is the third largest state in the US. Greater Los Angeles and the San Francisco Bay Area are among the country's largest urban areas. The state contains both the highest (Mount Whitney) and lowest (Death Valley) points in the contiguous US. Other geographical features include the sandy Pacific coastline in the west, the Sierra Nevada mountain range (east), the Mojave Desert (south-east), redwood forests (north-west), and a large central valley dominated by agriculture. Hollywood in Los Angeles and Silicon Valley in the San Francisco Bay Area are world-famous entertainment and computer technology centres respectively. The state capital is Sacramento.

Practicalities
California operates on Pacific Standard Time (GMT-8), with daylight saving. Distances between cities can be quite large and a lot more than they look on a map, especially given road closures in the highlands during the winter and spring months. Rural freeway maximum speed limit is 70 miles per hour (112 kph) and residential area limits are 25 or 30 miles per hour (32 or 48 kph). California operates a number of additional public holidays to the federal holidays including Christmas Eve, 26 December, and New Year's Eve. Cost of living is higher that in other states.

Possibilities
In addition to altitude training destinations at Mammoth Lakes and Lake Tahoe, and warm weather training centres in Chula Vista, California can provide excellent race opportunities for track runners. For a particularly memorable trip, drop down to sea level for a run on one of California's famous beaches, spend some time shopping and sightseeing in San Francisco, visit the Kings Canyon, Sequoia or Yosemite National Parks, challenge yourself to a short run in the soaring heat of the Death Valley National Monument, pop across the Nevada border to Las Vegas or drive into Arizona and visit the Grand Canyon.

Did you know? California is the only state in the US to have hosted both the Winter and the Summer Olympics. Los Angeles was host to the summer games in both 1932 and 1984, and the Winter Olympics were held in Squaw Valley Ski Resort near Lake Tahoe in 1960. The Los Angeles Memorial Coliseum is the only stadium to host the Summer Olympics twice.

OPPOSITE *Mono Lake located just north of Mammoth Lakes*
PREVIOUS *Gondola, and view from top of Mammoth Mountain*
ABOVE *Trails through the wilderness area south of Mammoth Lakes*

Special feature
CALIFORNIA'S GIANT TREES

California's most famous forests are made up of two indigenous species of ancient giant trees. Both the coastal redwood (*Sequoia sempervirens*) and the giant sequoia (*Sequoiadendron giganteum*) are members of the species of coniferous trees known as redwoods which have fibrous reddish-brown bark and live for over two thousand years. The timber from redwoods is known for its beauty and its resistance to decay, and is much sought after for furniture production.

Coastal redwoods are the world's tallest trees and are found near the northern portion of the Californian coastline. Redwood forests can be visited at Muir Woods National Monument and Redwood National and State Parks in northern California. The tallest specimens can grow to 115 m.

Giant sequoias are the largest organisms on earth, and have the greatest base circumference and total volume of any tree. They are found mainly on western slopes of the Sierra Nevada including in Sequoia, Kings Canyon and Yosemite National Parks. Bark thickness can be up to 90 cm, and the oldest known sequoia is 3,500 years old.

Getting in

Mammoth Lakes is located in the High Sierra, in the east of California. Seasonal flights make getting in and out possible when snow blocks off the most direct routes from the San Francisco Bay Area.

By air

Mammoth Yosemite Airport (MMH) is a small airport located on US 395, approximately 12 km (10 min by car) south-east of the town. Alaska Airlines operates daily, year-round flights from Los Angeles (LAX), while there are seasonal (Dec-Apr) United Airlines flights from San Francisco (SFO), San Diego and Orange County.

Mammoth Taxi (www.mammoth-taxi.com) and My Mammoth Shuttle (www.mymammothshuttle.com) provide airport taxi services which can be reserved online in advance. Many hotels and lodges also offer pick-up from the airport.

There is a larger airport in Reno (Reno–Tahoe International Airport; RNO), a 3-hr drive north of Mammoth Lakes. There are flights to Reno from many major US airports including Dallas, Chicago, Phoenix, Los Angeles, San Francisco and Denver. The Eastern Sierra Transit Authority (www.estransit.com) Reno–Lone Pine service connects Reno-Tahoe International with Mammoth Lakes.

By car

Mammoth Lakes is a scenic 450 km (5 hr) drive from San Francisco, and is 500 km, (5 hr) from Los Angeles. During the winter months, the route from San Francisco will be at least an hour longer, as a diversion around Yosemite National Park is required. Winter showers and blizzards may also delay travel. The California Department of Transportation (Caltrans) website (www.dot.ca.gov) has up-to-date information on highway conditions and winter road closures across the state.

By bus and train

During the summer months, Amtrak operates a Thruway (bus) service from Mammoth Lakes (through Yosemite National Park) to Merced to connect with the San-Joaquin train service that links Bakersfield with Sacramento.

Greyhound operates services from across its network to Reno, 275 km north of Mammoth Lakes, and to Lancaster, 390 km south of Mammoth. Both are connected to Mammoth Lakes by Eastern Sierra Transit services.

Eastern Sierra Transit Authority (www.estransit.com) operates bus services along US-395 between Reno and Lancaster. The Lone Pine–Reno service runs on Monday, Tuesday, Thursday and Friday and links Reno Greyhound Station and Reno Airport with Mammoth Lakes. A Mammoth Lakes–Lancaster service runs on Monday, Wednesday and Friday. The Mammoth Lakes Express service links Mammoth Lakes to Bishop, with three services per day, Monday–Friday. Reservations are recommended on all services. Buses stop at the McDonald's on the corner between Main Street and Sierra Park Road.

Getting around

If staying centrally you will be able to walk to the shops and restaurants. Cycling and using the town's shuttle service are also convenient ways to get around the small but dispersed town. A car is required to get to the best trails, especially during the winter months, and to get to the track.

By car

A car is required to get to snow-free trailheads during the winter months, to exploit the town's 'live high, train low' potential, and to get to the track. The most convenient way to explore the national parks and other sites is also by car. Cars can be hired from Mammoth Yosemite Airport (Enterprise Rent-A-Car) or from Mammoth Car Rental at Mammoth Chevron on Main Street (www.mammothcarrentals.com). Hertz have pick-up points at the airport and in the town.

By bicycle

There is a good network of paved cycle paths through the town, and cycling is a highly recommended way of getting around. Road and mountain bikes can be hired from Footloose Sports on Main Street (www.footloosesports.com) and from Mammoth Sporting Goods (452 Old Mammoth Road). For bicycle sales and repairs, check out Brian's Bicycles and Cross-Country Skis on Chateau Road (summer only).

By bus

Eastern Sierra Transit Authority (www.estransit.com) operates a free winter service (late November –late May) around the town. Services link the Village and Vons to most of the main ski lodges, and the red line runs from Snowcreek in the south of the town, along Old Mammoth Road to the village and on to Main Lodge. Most of the services operate from 07:00 to 17:45, with two less frequent services operating in the evenings. A free weekend shuttle service operates between Mammoth and June Lake and a slightly reduced service, with extensions to Reds Meadows and the lake basin area, operates during the summer months. Eastern Sierra Transit also operates a year-round door-to-door dial-a-ride service between 08:00 and 18:00.

By taxi

Taxi services include Mammoth Cab (+1 760 924 2227), My Mammoth Shuttle (+1 760 709 6459), Mammoth Taxi (+1 760 924 8294) and Mammoth All Weather Shuttle (+1 760 709 2927).

WEATHER AND WHEN TO VISIT

Mammoth Lakes receives the vast majority of its annual snowfall (5.5 m in total) between the months of November and April, with December, January and February all averaging more than a metre of snowfall. Average daily lows for these months can drop below -8 °C. The months between June and September are the warmest and driest months, with average daily highs of 21–26 °C and minimal rainfall. Mammoth Lakes experiences more than 300 days of sunshine during the year. Even during the coldest winter months there are periods of warm sunshine.

While the town is snow-covered for much of the year, there are snow-free routes within a short drive of the town most of the year. Bishop, located just 68 km from Mammoth Lakes, is suitable for training year-round as December to February average daily temperatures are above 12 °C. Bishop experiences on average 21 cm of snow per year, minimal rainfall, and summer daily average temperatures in the region of 30–37 °C.

There is a greater choice of flights into Mammoth during the winter months, though driving distances are shorter during the summer. Ski season is the peak season, and accommodation cost is at its highest between the months of December and April. The 'live high, train low' options in the area mean that quality training can be carried out throughout the year. Road closures and possible delays to flights due to snow showers should be considered when planning getting to Mammoth Lakes or getting out for races.

ACCOMMODATION

There is a large variety of accommodation, with self-catering rental accommodation (studios, apartments, condominiums and town homes) the

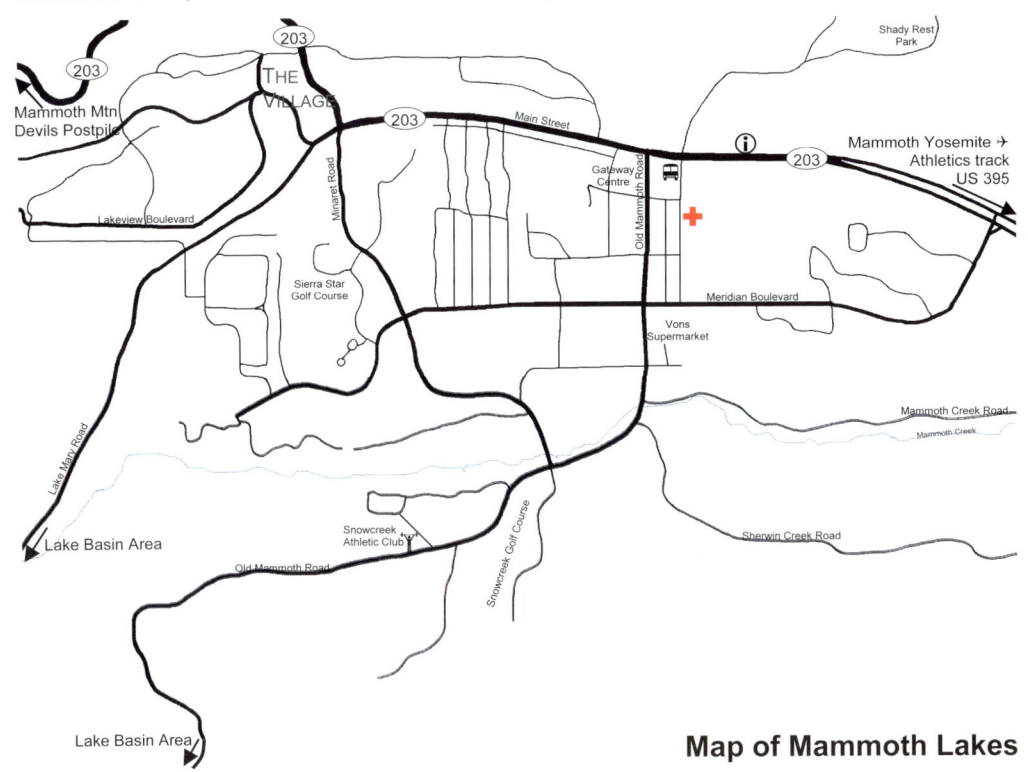

Map of Mammoth Lakes

most popular option. The official Mammoth Lakes website (www.visitmammoth.com) has a lodging booking facility, and links to the websites of all the main resorts, hotels and reservation sites. Apartments are also listed on HomeAway (www.homeaway.co.uk) and on the vacation rentals section of Rentals.com (www.rentals.com) which also includes other self-catering options such as hotel suites and studios.

Prices are higher during the main ski season (mid Dec–early Apr), and at the weekend, and are generally higher than other US altitude training destinations. Some resorts offer special rates for return visitors and for those who fly to Mammoth Yosemite Airport with Amazon Air (check out the 'coupon' tab for each property on the Mammoth Lakes website).

Food

There is a good choice of restaurants with menus to suit all tastes and budgets. Restaurants are located mainly along Old Mammoth Road, Main Street and in the Village. Sierra Menus (www.sierra-menus.com) provides information on each of the restaurants, a map indicating their location, and menus. Von's supermarket, located in Minaret Village by the junction between Old Mammoth Road and Meridian Boulevard, is more than adequate to meet the grocery needs of self-catering visitors.

Shopping

Mammoth has a surprisingly large number of shops for the size of the town, with everything from large supermarkets to fine art galleries and ice cream shops. Prices are generally high. Mammoth Lakes is not somewhere that you would come to shop, but you should be able to find almost anything that you need.

The main shopping areas lie along Old Mammoth Road (supermarkets and other essentials), along Main Street, and in the Village area off Minaret Road north of Main Street (luxury boutiques, and gift stores). There is a Rite-Aid drugstore, and a Do It Centre selling tools and home supplies, at the Gateway Centre. For those looking for a designer bargain, there is a cluster of luxury outlets just off Main Street.

There are a number of sports shops, most of which specialise in ski sales and rentals, and bicycle rentals. Mammoth Outdoor Sports (www.mammothoutdoorsports.com) sell running shoes, and other outdoor and sports shops carry a limited stock of running gear and footwear. Snowcreek Athletics Shop carriers a small range of specialist equipment and clothing. Sage to Summit (www.sagetosummit.com) is a specialist mountain running and fastpacking shop in Bishop.

Communication

The four main mobile network providers have reasonable coverage in Mammoth Lakes. Check coverage before purchasing a handset or SIM card.

Most rental properties have free high-speed or Wi-Fi internet access. Looney Bean cafe in the Gateway Centre is a trendy hangout with Wi-Fi access for customers. The cafe has a computer available for those that don't have their own laptop. Mono County Library (Sierra Park Road) also offers free internet access.

The town's post office is located on Main Street between Forest Trail and Sierra Boulevard.

Health and safety

There is no tropical disease risk, or other serious contagious illness alert. There is a hospital located on Sierra Park Road. The town has a low crime rate. California lies in an earthquake belt, and though several earthquakes occur under Mammoth Mountain every day, these cannot be felt and cause no damage.

In September 2013, just prior to publication of this book, a fire damaged large portions of Stanislaus National Forest and Yosemite National Park, north of Mammoth Lakes. The fire, which was named the Rim Fire, was caused by an illegal hunter's fire. Forest and bush fires can spread quickly in dry wilderness. Warnings should be obeyed, and campfires should never be lit outside of designated areas.

One of the biggest dangers to personal safety comes from the local population of black bears. While bears rarely attack, they should always be treated with respect. Bears are attracted to the town because of readily available food, and to ensure that bears remain wild, all human sources of food should be kept out of reach. Dispose of all litter in bear-resistant bins (be careful you don't catch your hand in the bear-resistant lock). Never feed any of the wildlife. If you are confronted by a bear, don't run. Try to scare the bear away by making noise, making yourself look as big as possible, and standing with other people to intimidate the bear. Never approach a bear.

GB International steeplechaser Luke Gunn on one of the many trails within driving distance of Mammoth Lakes

MONEY

Bank of America, Union Bank and Eastern Sierra Community Bank have branches in Mammoth Lakes and there are ATMs throughout the town.

TIME

California operates on Pacific Standard Time (GMT-8) with daylight saving between the second Sunday in March until the first Sunday in November. Daylight hours vary greatly from month to month, with 9 hr 30 min daylight in December and almost 15 hr of daylight in midsummer. Note the early sunsets if planning on training in Mammoth Lakes during the winter months.

	Mar	Jun	Sept	Dec
Sunrise	07:07	05:34	06:38	07:04
Sunset	19:03	20:19	19:05	16:38

LAUNDRY

Many self-catering houses come with a washing machine and dryer, or have laundry facilities within the complex, as do many of the hotels and resorts. There is a self-service, coin-operated laundry facility in the Gateway Centre on the corner between Main Street and Old Mammoth Road.

OTHER PRACTICALITIES

Details on health and safety, language, communication, money, power, laundry, culture and respect can be found in the US general section *(p. 68-69)*.

ABOVE Snowboarders Mammoth Mountain
BELOW Salt formations on Mono Lake
OPPOSITE Hannah England, one of the world's top 1500 m runners, training on roads of Mammoth Lakes

SPORTS FACILITIES AND SERVICES

Located 2,402 m above sea level, Mammoth Lakes is at an ideal altitude for living at altitude. Trails at altitudes as low as 1,200 m are located within easy reach of the town, making it an ideal venue for a 'live high, train low' approach. The area by Mammoth Airport, 10 min drive from the town, is approximately 2,100 m above sea level; the Pleasant Valley Reservoir area (30 min) is less than 1,400 m above sea level, and the town of Bishop (45 min) is 1,264 m above sea level. During the summer months, there is also the option to 'live high, train higher', as the lake basin area provides beautiful routes above 2,700 m of altitude. The variety of trail surface and terrain, and the recent addition of a synthetic track, make Mammoth Lakes an ideal training venue for everyone from 800 m athletes to marathon runners.

TRAINING CAMPS AND TOUR OPERATORS

A number of companies and organisations (e.g. www.mammothtrackproject.org; www.ccsd.com; www.altitudeproject.com) run week-long running, cycling and triathlon camps in Mammoth Lakes. Coaching, training support, facility access and workshops tend to be included, but not all packages include accommodation. Camps work out more expensive than organising a trip yourself, but are a good option for solo travellers.

TRAILS AND RUNNING ROUTES

The running options can be grouped into three main areas: (i) within the town and its immediate surroundings (ii) off the US 395 between Mammoth Lakes and Bishop and (iii) above the town in the backcountry around the lakes and Reds Meadows. Together these three areas provide trails, tracks and surfaced roads of almost every imaginable surface and terrain. Not all routes are accessible year-round, but with the varying altitude in the region, there is a good variety of snow-free trails even during the winter months.

Trail maps and descriptions can be found on the Mammoth Lakes Trail System (www.mammothtrails.org) and Sage to Summit (www.sagetosummit.com) websites. The Mammoth Lakes visitor centre also has trail maps for the area.

Options for race walkers are largely limited to the slightly undulating Green Church Road, conveniently located next to the athletics track, and other short stretches of flat road off US 395 close to Bishop. Trail runners have options in and around the town once the snow has melted, and marathon runners are spoilt for choice with lots of quiet, paved roads off US 395, and long off-road circuits north and south of the town.

Within the town

There are some trails, and suitable roads in the town itself, though, these are limited to cleared asphalt roads during the winter months.

The various cross country skiing routes around town become ideal running surfaces after the snow has melted. Mammoth Creek Road and Sherwin Creek Road, both just off Old Mammoth Road, are unsurfaced, and provide good training during the summer months. Sherwin Creek Road runs south of the town and eventually joins the US 395. Old Mammoth Road, beyond Snowcreek Athletic Club, and Lake Mary Road, provides hilly road runs with relatively little traffic. Mammoth Mountain Bike Park provides technical routes in the hills to the west of the town.

The Inyo Craters (trailheads off Minaret Road in the north-west of the town), provide more than 20 km of rolling dirt tracks through the forest. The Mountain View Trail, which runs approximately 8 km from Minaret vista down to Earthquake Fault, is a popular option.

Shady Rest Park has a paved road with interval markings for fast road intervals, and is surrounded by dirt trails through the surrounding forests. The entrance is on the right as you enter the town, just beyond the visitor centre.

Mammoth Rock Trail starts just off Sherwin Creek Road. The first half is a steep uphill trail; the second half a relaxing downhill run along Old Mammoth Road. The full loop is approximately 10 km, with a total elevation gain of almost 200 m.

Routes off US 395

No matter how wintery the weather is in the town, a drive south of the town along the US 395 will eventually lead to snow-free areas, trails and roads suitable for training. The altitude drops 1,000 m within 50 km of the town. A drive of 30–45 min towards Bishop will take you to an area which rarely sees snow, even in the winter.

Off the highway, there is every sort of surface and terrain imaginable. The easiest routes to find are the pylon access routes; you will find double track access roads, constructed of a mixture of sand and gravel, almost anywhere that you see electric power lines. The area is desert-like in places, and makes for some interesting scenery away from the forests and the mountain lakes of the town.

Lookout Mountain, located approximately 15 km north of Mammoth Lakes along US 395 just after the junction with Dry Creek Road, provides dirt road routes of between 10 km and 50 km. The trails circumnavigate the mountain. Owens River Road, a quite paved road just north of Lookout Mountain, is great for longer runs

Green Church Road (also called Benton Crossing Road) is popular among race walkers and its slightly undulating, but smooth surface provides an ideal surface for road training. The paved road has a dirt shoulder suitable for running, and leads to a number of off-road single and double track trails. There are half-mile markings for 10 miles (approximately 16 km) along the road. Green Church Road is indicated by a Green Church, just after Mammoth Yosemite Airport and is located to the left of US 395 as you head towards Bishop. Parking and changing facilities are available at the athletics track.

There are additional options at the aptly-named Pleasant Valley Reservoir, at 1400 m above sea level, 50 km south of Mammoth Lakes,

Lake Basin and Reds Meadows

Old Mammoth Road and Lake Mary Road lead from the town to the backcountry Lake Basin area which is located at 2,700 m above sea level. There is a mixture of road and dirt trails, and most of the paved roads have dirt shoulders for off-road running. Intervals of one and two miles, suitable for repeats, are marked along the mostly flat asphalt road. The additional altitude can be a challenge, but the beautiful scenery can help distract from the extra effort.

There are some good trails in the Reds Meadow/Devils Postpile area, north of Mammoth Lakes. Take Minaret Road past Mammoth Mountain Main Lodge and on to the National Monument where many of the trails begin. You will only be able to access the National Monument by car early in the morning during the summer. There is also a shuttle bus connection.

The backcountry routes and trails are accessible between May and September.

TRACK FACILITIES

A nine-lane, synthetic 400 m track was opened just outside the town in 2012. The track is located on Benton Crossing Road/Green Church Road, just beyond Mammoth Yosemite Airport. The track is open from April to November, and visitors to the town are welcome to use it free of charge. For a small fee, the track can be booked for events through www.mammothrecreation.com.

GYM FACILITIES

Located on the edge of the town, Snowcreek Athletic Club (www.snowcreekathleticclub.com) is Mammoth's main fitness facility and is used by the town's elite athletes for strength and conditioning work. Daily, weekly and monthly passes are available for visitors to the town. The club has a well-equipped weight training area, cardiovascular equipment, racquetball courts, a basketball court, and indoor and outdoor swimming pools. There is also a spa, a bistro restaurant, a sports bar and free Wi-Fi. Snowcreek is open 06:00 to 21:00 Monday to Friday and from 08:00 to 21:00 at the weekend.

Many of the other rental properties in the town have access to a fitness room, and all the main hotels have fitness suites.

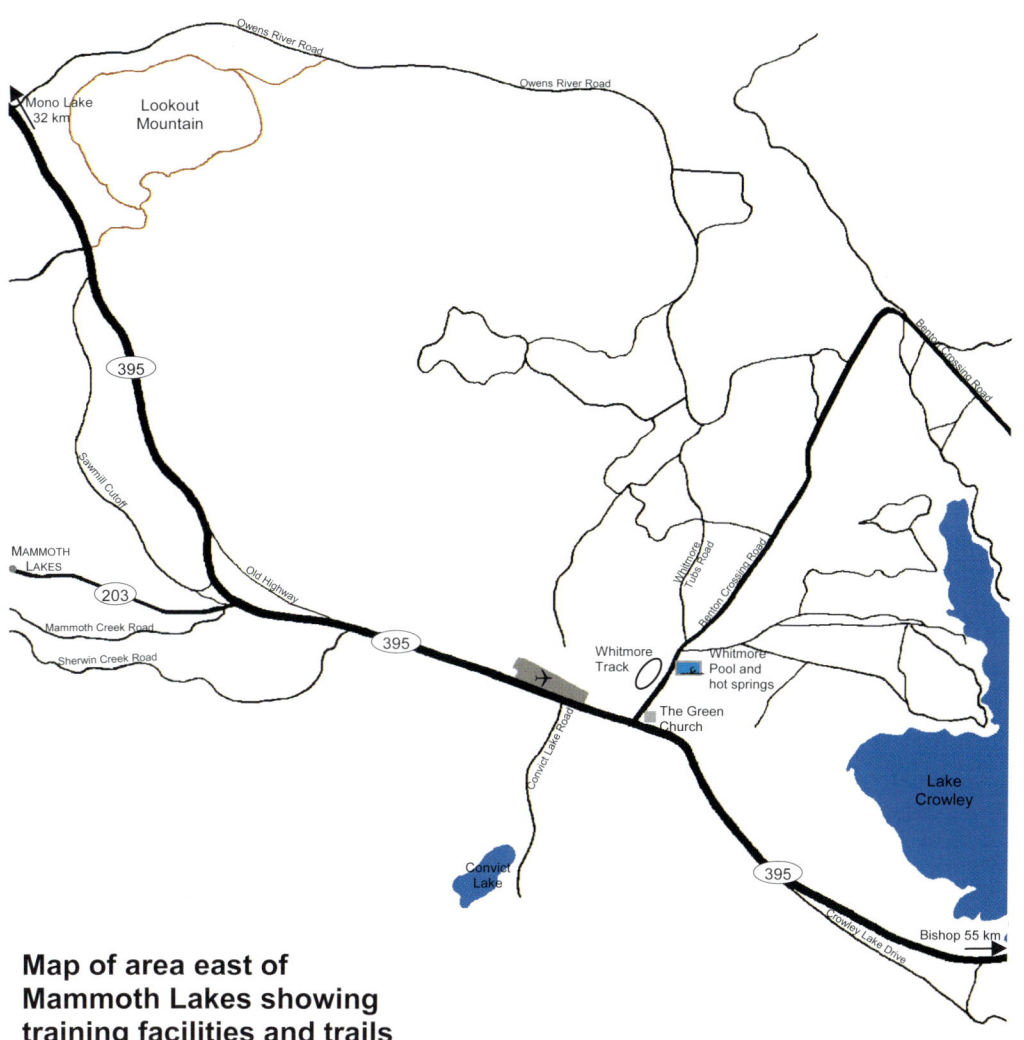

Map of area east of Mammoth Lakes showing training facilities and trails

CROSS-TRAINING OPTIONS

Road cycling and mountain biking (in summer) and cross country skiing (in winter) are the obvious cross-training options, though a number of other activities are also available. Swimming, ice skating, climbing, mountain biking, and canoeing are among the available options. Alpine skiing is available almost year-round.

Mammoth Mountain Bike Park is open during the summer months, and provides trails for beginner and experienced thrill seekers. Many of the dirt tracks and forest trails are also suitable for mountain biking. The roads in the area are suitable for road cycling, and combine hilly mountain routes with gently undulating desert roads. Road and mountain bikes can be hired in the town.

Tamarack Ski Centre (www.tamaracklodge.com), located in the Lake Basin area, has trails for cross country skiing and snowshoeing. Equipment can be rented, and lessons are offered for beginners.

Snowcreek Athletic Club runs fitness classes, and there is indoor, outdoor and open-water swimming available in and around the town. Ice skating (winter) and inline skating (summer) are available at the municipal Mammoth Ice Rink. There are six community tennis courts at the Community Centre and Park, and beach volleyball courts, softball fields and football fields at Shady Rest Park. Climbing is available at Mammoth Mountain.

Sports medicine and sports science support

There is a physical therapist based at Snowcreek Athletics Club. Prices for massage and treatments in Mammoth are high. The one-stop sports medicine centre at Mammoth Hospital on Sierra Park Road has diagnostic, treatment and rehabilitation facilities.

Local races

The Quake and Shake 10 km/Half Marathon (www.sierra-nevada-races.com) is held in the town each August. Ned's Mammoth Rock Run is a trail race organised by High Sierra Striders (www.highsierrastriders.org), the Freedom mile forms part of the Fourth of July celebrations and the Chart House 5 km and 10 km are held in early August.

For those looking to try something a bit different, there are a number of triathlons in the town (www.highsierratri.org), and the Sierra Cycling Foundation organises a 100 mile cycle in the High Sierra/Mono Basin area in early September (www.fallcentury.org).

Excellent sea level track races are just a short flight away. The Stanford Invitational (late Mar) and the Payton Jordan Invitational (late Apr) at Stanford (Palo Alto, San Francisco Bay Area), are among the most popular graded distance running events in the US. These events attract athletes from across the world who are seeking qualifying times, particularly in the 10,000 m, for the Olympic Games and other major championships.

Running community

Most of the town's successful athletes are members of Mammoth Track Club (www.mammothtrackclub.com). 2004 Olympic marathon medallist, Deena Kastor, is president of the club and has been training in Mammoth Lakes since 2001. Other professional athletes include Josh Cox, John Gilbertson and Josphat Boit. A host of other US champions and record holders, and Olympians have been based in Mammoth Lakes over the past decade.

Suitability for other sports

Mammoth Lakes offers excellent facilities for a range of sports. The Recreation Department of Mammoth Lakes Town Government (www.mammothrecreation.com) offers access to most municipal facilities on a pay-as-you-go basis.

Cycling The roads in the area are suitable for road cyclists (see www.eastsidevelo.org for rides in the Eastern Sierra), and the trails and mountain resorts provide perfect terrain for Mountain Biking during the summer months.

Triathlon In addition to the excellent running and cycling options, triathletes can make use of indoor and outdoor swimming pools at Snowcreek Athletic Club, the hot spring-heated Whitmore Pool near the track on Green Church Road/ Benton Crossing Road (late May–early Sept), and open water swimming at Horseshoe Lake (summer only).

Team sports There is a regulation baseball diamond and two softball fields at the Whitmore Recreational Area beside the athletics track, and beach volleyball courts, softball fields and football fields at Shady Rest Park. The indoor facilities at Snowcreek Athletics Club are suitable for a variety of other sports and activities.

Other sports Facilities within the town are excellent for competitive winter sports athletes, and Mammoth Mountain provides suitable terrain for competitive skiers and snowboarders in all disciplines. Rowing, flatwater canoeing and kayaking are possible on most of the lakes in and around the town. There is up to 1,600 m of rowing available on Lake Mary, and up to 7 km available on Crowley Lake (2,066 m above sea level) not far from the town. The facilities at Snowcreek Athletics Club are suitable for judo and other martial arts.

Right Athletics track at Whitmore Recreational Area with snow-capped High Sierra peaks in the background

THINGS TO SEE AND DO BETWEEN TRAINING

Mammoth Mountain provides a range of activities during both the winter and summer months. Once the snow melts, Tamarack cross country ski area and the lake basin area are great for hiking, fishing, camping and horse riding. Companies which provide activities in the area include Sierra Mountain Guides (www.sierramtnguides.com), DJ's Snowmobile Adventures (www.snowmobilemammoth.com) and Sierra Rock Climbing School (www.sierrarockclimbingschool.com).

For spectacular views of the area in both winter and summer, take the gondola ride from Mammoth Mountain Ski Lodge to the top of Mammoth Mountain. The Top of the Sierra Interpretive Centre provides interesting information on the area's geology and volcanic history. The mountain is a dormant volcano, and there are daily earthquakes in the area, though none of these can be felt or cause damage.

There are many hot springs, suitable for bathing, within easy reach of the town. Most notable of these is Benton Hot Springs, located about an hour from the town along Benton Crossing Road.

There are DVD rental shops, a cinema at Minaret Shopping centre (by Vons Supermarket), and performing arts venues (Mammoth Lakes Arts Centre, Mammoth Lakes Repertory Theatre) showing live performances throughout the year. Devils Postpile National Monument is a national monument which protects the Devils Postpile (one of the finest examples of symmetrical basalt formations), the Rainbow Falls, and pristine surrounding mountain scenery. The monument, located 16 km from Mammoth Lakes, is only accessible by car from mid June until late October (exact dates dependent on snowfall), but can be visited at other times on foot or by ski. From the town, take Minaret Road to the Mammoth Mountain Ski Area and transfer to the shuttle service that operates from mid-June to September (tickets can be purchased from Mammoth Mountain Gondola Building). There is no fee to enter the monument.

REST DAY EXCURSIONS

California has a rich and varied landscape, and many of its best and most famous natural parks and sites are within reach of Mammoth Lakes. While destinations such as Yosemite National Park are easier to get to during the summer months when all access routes are open, a little bit extra effort can lead you to spectacular frozen waterfalls and snowscapes during the coldest months.

Mono Lake is a beautiful lake located near Lee Vining, a small tourist town 45 km north of Mammoth Lakes. Formed by tectonic activity, Mono Lake is almost three times as salty as the ocean and too alkaline for fish to survive in it. Despite this, with over 1,000 plant species, and roughly 400 vertebrate species within its watershed, Mono Lake and its surrounding basin encompass one of California's richest natural areas. The mineral structures within the lake, formed from the interaction between freshwater springs and the lake's alkaline waters, make for a dramatic landscape.

Yosemite National Park, a UNESCO World Heritage site, is renowned for its waterfalls, clear streams, granite cliffs and domes, and biological diversity. The park, which covers some 30,000 hectares, contains thousands of lakes, has 1,300 km of hiking trails and 2,600 km of streams, and is the third most visited of the United States' National Parks. Despite its size, the majority of the park's four million annual visitors explore an area around Yosemite Valley which makes up just one percent of the park's total area. At 739 m, Yosemite Falls is the highest waterfall in North America. The park features three groves of Giant Sequoia (Sierra Redwood). The Mariposa Grove, located south of Wawona and accessible March to November, is the largest of these. Glacier Point and Badger Pass, Tuolumne Meadows, Crane

Flat, and Hetch Hetchy Valley are areas of particular beauty and interest within the park.

The park has four main entrances, with the Tioga Pass Road (CA 120) east from Lee Vining the most accessible from Mammoth Lakes. This road, however, is only accessible between June and October. The Yosemite Area Regional Transportation System (YARTS) provides shuttle transportation into Yosemite Valley from Mammoth Lakes, and other nearby towns. A free shuttle service also operates within the valley itself. Bicycles, which can be hired at Curry Village, are a great way of getting around the park. There is a small entry fee.

Sequoia National Park contains the greatest concentration of Giant Sequoia trees anywhere, and some of the largest individual specimens of the tree. The park features dramatic views of Sierra Peaks, canyons, caves and a collection of beautiful meadows. Kings Canyon National Park, which shares a common border with Sequoia, is dominated by the great canyon of the Kings River and is at its most powerful during the snow-melt. Despite their proximity to Mammoth Lakes (as the crow flies), the drive to the parks' entrances on the east takes approximately five hours.

Death Valley, the hottest place on earth, is located approximately 4-hr by car south of the town.

A note on living here long-term

Many US international athletes have moved to Mammoth to train over the years, and it's fair to say that the town is an attractive place to spend more than a few weeks. As with all American venues, obtaining work visas would be an issue, but for US citizens, the nearby Mammoth Mountain ski resort and other tourist-related businesses provide casual employment opportunities. Cost of living is relatively high, even compared with other US venues, and living without a source of income or funding, would be difficult for a sustained period of time.

Despite being snow-covered from December to May, training is possible just south of the town throughout the year. 'Live high, train low' options, make quality training possible at any time of the year. Quality races are just a short flight away.

Further information

Mammoth Lakes Visitors Centre, which stocks maps, books and free brochures and showcases historical and geological exhibits, is located at 2520 Main Street (on the right as you enter the town). The Mammoth Lakes official website (www.visitmammoth.com) contains a wealth of information and resources, including an accommodation booking facility, shopping and restaurant listings, an events calendar, a transport and lodgings map, suggestions of things to do, and a downloadable visitor guide. The website of Mammoth Mountain Resort (www.mammothmountain.com) contains information about summer and winter activities on the mountain and other useful tourist information.

Opposite The top of Mammoth Mountain
Below Salt formations on Mono Lake
Previous Mono Lake just north of Mammoth Lakes

OTHER ALTITUDE TRAINING SITES IN CALIFORNIA

Away from its famous cities and sandy beaches, California has extensive areas of mountains and highlands that provide opportunities for altitude training. Lake Tahoe (1,897 m) and Big Bear Lake (2,058 m) are popular training spots.

Lake Tahoe (1,897 m)
www.visitinglaketahoe.com

Lake Tahoe is a fault-formed, glacial-eroded lake which straddles the border between California and Nevada. South Lake Tahoe is the larger of the two main towns on the lake, and is located on the south shore close to the state border. Tahoe City is situated on the north-west shore of the lake. Squaw Valley, which hosted the 1960 Winter Olympic Games, is located just west of the lake.

During the winter months, the area is a popular ski destination with both alpine and Nordic resorts, while 4-wheel driving, hiking, horse riding and an abundance of other outdoor activities draw tourists during the summer months. Casinos, located in the Nevada half of the area, attract crowds throughout the year and, together with a busy nightlife, mean that Lake Tahoe has a more vibrant feel than most of the other small-town venues featured in this book.

Both South Tahoe and North Lake Tahoe have extensive networks of backcountry trails and paved paths. North Lake Tahoe has one of the most extensive selections of cross country ski trails in North America, and during the summer, these trails provide a paradise for runners, cyclists and other endurance athletes. The 240 km Tahoe Rim Trail makes a circuit of the lake, and offers particularly beautiful views. Tahoe Mountain Milers are a local running club, and their website (www.tahoemtnmilers.org) includes descriptions of many of the best trails and other useful information. They welcome visitors to the area on their runs. Sierra Front (www.sierrafront.org) describes the trails in the Lake Tahoe, Reno and Carson Valley areas, and provides information on other activities. Lake Tahoe Ironman is a popular event. Swimming camps are hosted by Boost Swimming (www.boostswimming.com) at their facility in Incline Village Recreation Center on the north shore.

There are Amtrak stations in both Reno and Truckee, the latter from which there is a Thruway connection to South Lake Tahoe. North Lake Tahoe express (www.northlaketahoeexpress.com) operates a year-round service between Reno airport (just across the border in Nevada) and the northern shores of Lake Tahoe. Tahoe Area Regional Transit (TART), operates a year-round local bus service. South Lake Tahoe is 73 km from Truckee; 47 km from Carson City; and 101 km from Reno. There is a good choice of accommodation in all the towns around the lake. Tahoe's Best (www.tahoesbest.com) has links to lots of vacation rentals, cabins and condominiums.

Big Bear Lake (2,058 m)
www.bigbear.com

Big Bear Lake, situated in the San Bernardino Mountains in Southern California, promotes itself as a 'four-seasons resort', with an emphasis on alpine and cross country skiing in the winter, and adventure sports (water sports, mountain biking, off-roading, zip-lining and helicopter flights), during the spring, summer and autumn. The town is located on the south shores of a reservoir of the same name and has a population of just over 5,000. It is the home town of US Olympic marathon runner Ryan Hall. It has traditionally been a training base for boxers and martial arts fighters, but cyclists and athletes are increasingly making use of the trails around the town.

There are many single and double track forest trails and fire access roads suitable for running, mountain biking and hiking in the hills and mountains surrounding the town. There is an asphalt route around the reservoir. At more than 11 km long and approximately 4 km wide, Big Bear Lake is Southern California's largest recreation lake. Maps and descriptions of some of the trails can be found on the Big Bear Valley Trails Foundation website (www.trailsfoundation.org), or the Big Bear Mountain Bike and Hiking website (www.mountainbikebigbear.com). Numerous trail running races are held in the town.

Mountain biking is very popular and the alpine ski slopes of Snow Summit Ski Resort become a mountain biker's paradise during the summer. A map and description of the Snow Summit trails is available for download on the Big Bear Trails website (www.bigbeartrails.com). Big Bear Cycling Association (www.bigbearcycling.com) organises weekly rides from the town, and their website has lots of useful information on both mountain biking and road cycling in the area. The lake provides opportunities for water sports including rowing and canoeing. The Big Bear Valley Recreation and Park District website (www.bigbearparks.com) has information on other sports activities, and sports facilities which can be hired. Open Air Big Bear (www.openairbigbear.com) has an event calendar and links to trail maps and other useful resources.

Sky High Training (www.skyhightraining.org) is a not-for-profit high altitude training facility equipped specifically for boxing and mixed martial arts (MMA). It can also cater for other strength-based sports. There is an exercise physiologist and a physical therapist on site, and blood profiling, oxygen consumption testing, and body composition assessments are available. Sky High Training provides accommodation in fully furnished 6–10 person houses, and athletes and teams can utilise the centre's 'personal' chef.

LIVING THE LIFE OF AN ELITE ATHLETE
Adapted from the blog, 16 & 24 April, 2010

Following an exhilarating run along Venice Beach in LA, I headed for the hills again. After a delayed flight (due to an electrical fault, and which I shouldn't really complain about since planes right across Europe are grounded due to a rather inconsiderate volcano ash-cloud), I made it to Mammoth Lakes. And when I landed, there were two friendly faces waiting for me. Great Britain internationals and all-round superstars Hannah England and Luke Gunn, who have already spent three weeks training in the town, had come to pick me up. After two weeks in Mexico, it was really good to have a conversation in English!

After dropping my bags at the accommodation, Hannah and Luke took me for a quick tour of the town. We were driving up a road by the forest, looking at some nice (and rather expensive) houses, when I thought I spotted one. After considerable debate with myself, and at the risk of sounding stupid, I decided to mention what I thought I'd seen. Luke and Hannah didn't know whether to believe me or not, and to be honest I didn't know if I trusted my own eyes. Either way, Luke decided to reverse back and at worst put the notion out of my head. And there it was: a black bear, not too long after waking up from hibernation, prowling around on a bank of snow searching for food. Seeing a bear in the wild was special. Some of the athletes who have been living in Mammoth for over a year have not seen a bear yet, and here I was, not in the town a full hour, and I'd spotted one.

Mammoth Lakes is a beautiful place. Weather conditions have fluctuated between cloudless blue skies with temperatures close to 15 degrees, and cold, snowy blizzards with

The nearest passenger service airport is Palm Springs International Airport (PSP), located 140 km south-east of the town. Big Bear Lake is 160 km (2 hr by car) north-east of Los Angeles. San Bernardino, 65 km from Big Bear, is the closest large city, and has a greyhound station, and an Amtrak station served by the daily Southwest Chief service which also stops in Flagstaff and Albuquerque. Local bus services (www.marta.cc) connect San Bernardino Metrolink, Amtrak and Greyhound stations with Big Bear Lake (3 services/day). Links to resort cabins and lodges, condominiums, private homes, hotels, B&Bs and hostels can be found on the official Big Bear website (www.bigbear.com).

temperatures as low as minus six. Luckily, if you get in a car and drive towards the valley, you can find some fine, snow-free weather to train in about half an hour. Even with snow on the ground in the town, it is warm enough in the valley to run in shorts and tee shirts most days.

Two training-related injuries have not stopped me from making progress with training! Injury is a slight exaggeration, but they demonstrate just how clumsy I am. The first—a grazed shin—was incurred during my first training session here. We were running on a rocky trail, when I, just for one second, took my mind off the task, hit a stone, and came crashing to the ground. The fall itself wasn't witnessed by anyone but me (I was at the back of the group), but the subsequent belly-slide across the gravel got everyone's attention. What a way to introduce myself to people that I'd never met before!

The second injury was even more stupid, and a lot more painful. On Wednesday, while doing a weights session, my mind was full of pound to kilogram conversions, when I let a 15.8 kg plate slip while taking it from the rack. My finger was pinned between it and another plate in a real 'jump-around-and-scream-in-pain' moment. The resultant blackened fingernail is slowly healing, and, with any luck, I won't lose it this time.

Between training, there's been some time for sightseeing, and Luke and Hannah have been trying their best to get me hooked on cryptic crosswords. And I think they're succeeding. I'm not brilliant, yet, but as a team, we're unstoppable. In two days, between the three of us, and with the help of the solution and a dictionary, we've almost completed one crossword. By the end of play tomorrow, we should have it done and dusted! What better way is there for elite athletes to pass the time?

Albuquerque

Albuquerque, the largest city in New Mexico, has been a popular training destination for elite athletes for decades. Reportedly one of the fittest cities in the US, Albuquerque offers trails and training facilities for high performance athletes and recreational runners alike. The short winter and warm summer make it a popular place for those seeking sun, and the moderate altitude makes quality training possible at any time of the year. The cost of living is lower than in other US venues, and a large airport, just south of the city, makes getting in and out relatively easy. Albuquerque is ideal for those who prefer city life and having lots to do between training sessions.

Albuquerque, US (1,619 m)

Albuquerque, with a population of just over half a million people, is the largest city in the state of New Mexico. Located in Bernalillo County in the central region of the state, the city straddles the Rio Grande, a river which brings life-sustaining water through the desert. The Sandia Mountains mark the eastern extent of Albuquerque, which is one of the highest major cities within the US. The elevation varies between 1,500 m in the valley by the Rio Grande, to just under 2,000 m in the foothills of Glenwood Hills and Sandia Heights.

Albuquerque was founded as a Spanish colonial outpost in 1706, and the name of the city is believed to have come from the Spanish village of Alburquerque. The name Alburquerque, which may have derived from Arabic or Latin (because of the Spanish town's Moorish and Roman routes), may mean either 'Father of the Cork Oak', or 'White Oak', though Western folklore trace the name of the American city to the Galician word 'albaricoque', meaning 'apricot', a fruit which was introduced to the area by Spanish settlers.

Old Town Albuquerque, the original settlement, was built in traditional Spanish village style with a central plaza surrounded by houses, government buildings, and a church. From 1880, New Albuquerque (the new town) built up around rail yards and a passenger depot 3 km away. This area, now Albuquerque's downtown, became a major mercantile commercial centre and was incorporated as a city in 1891. It wasn't until the 1920s, that Old Town was absorbed into the city. Route 66, which originally ran north–south through the city, began taking travellers to Albuquerque in 1926, and restaurants, motels and gift shops subsequently sprung up along the roadside. In 1937, the route was adjusted to take a more direct east–west path along Central Avenue. The city continues to grow, and today it is one of America's fastest growing metropolitan areas.

Author's verdict

I like to just step out the door and run and, having to travel to run, shop and eat made Albuquerque very frustrating for me. Accommodation close to the foothills would have been preferable to the isolated area around the airport where I was staying, and things would, no doubt, have been easier if I had my own transport. There is a good variety of trails if you are willing to travel, with flat routes by the Rio Grande and a variety of off-road trails in the foothills. The weather was good when I visited in late April, and training is possible year-round. The option of living and training at higher altitude in Santa Fe or Los Alamos, and travelling 'down' to Albuquerque for more quality sessions looks attractive, and there are options for those looking to work or study while training at altitude. Albuquerque is a popular destination, but for me, it didn't tick enough of the boxes.

Running ★★★★★ - Variety of trails and routes around the city, but few are within running distance of accommodation; number of tracks, good options for cross-training.

Convenience ★★★★★ - Many one-connection flights from Europe; amenities, trails and facilities spread out; car required.

Safety ★★★★★ - Moderately-low crime rate associated with big city; no major disease risk

Cost ★★★★★ - Lower cost of living than other US venues; good choice of reasonably priced accommodation, restaurants and supermarkets; car required.

Cultural experience ★★★★★ - Located in the heart of a historic area featuring traditional Native American settlements, numerous museums, and quaint old town centres; good opportunity to sample local culture and food.

Things to do between training ★★★★★ - Plentiful entertainment opportunities; some historic sites within easy reach of the city; relaxing cafes to hang out in with other runners.

Suitability for solo travellers ★★★★★ - Popular spot for athletes from around the world; finding training partners should not be difficult in theory; the size of the city can make solo travellers feel isolated.

Must do Make at least one trip to the foothills; hang out with other runners in the cafes by the Academy; shop for souvenirs in the Old Town.

Ideal for Those who value city life and having lots to do between training sessions.

NEW MEXICO
www.newmexico.org

People
New Mexico, known as the Land of Enchantment, is a former Spanish and Mexican colony. Today it has a large native Spanish speaking population, and Spanish is the state's official second language. There are also large Native American communities, including Pueblo people across the state, and Navajo in the state's portion of Navajo Nation *(p. 109)*. The majority of the state's population of just over two million are concentrated along the Rio Grande in the cities of central and north central New Mexico.

Places
Santa Fe is the state capital, though the majority of the state's population is concentrated in and around Albuquerque. The state is divided into six distinctively different regions. The Rocky Mountains meet the Great Plains in the north-east. The low-lying south-east is mostly desert. North central New Mexico, which includes Santa Fe and Taos, is the main tourist area. North-west New Mexico, which is part of Four Corners and of the Navajo Nation, contains red rocks and other unusual geological formations. Scenic low-lying mountains and farmland dominate the Rio Grande banks in south-west New Mexico. Albuquerque is located in Central New Mexico.

Practicalities
New Mexico operates on Mountain Time (MST; GMT-7) with daylight saving. While the main cities have a public transport network, New Mexico is mainly a driving state. Most roads are in good condition, though drink-driving is a major issue in the northern half of the state. The maximum rural freeway speed limit is 75 miles per hour (120 kph). Speed limits can be as low as 15 miles per hour (24 kph), in urban and residential areas.

Possibilities
New Mexico offers a multitude of outdoor recreation opportunities, distinctive regional cuisine, a thriving fine arts scene, and insights into both Native American and Hispanic cultures. The relatively short distances between the three main training bases (Los Alamos, Santa Fe and Albuquerque) makes it possible to train at different altitudes and in different environments without much effort. Many British athletes have gained scholarships to University of New Mexico, and use the opportunity to carry out prolonged stints of training at altitude. Many students who study in Albuquerque remain after graduation.

Special feature
PUEBLOS

Pueblos are communities of Native Americans in America's Southwest. The term pueblo, meaning town or village, was used by the first Spanish explorers to describe the local communities and their multi-story apartment-like mud and stone adobe homes. Of the 21 federally recognised pueblos which are home to Pueblo people, 19 are located in New Mexico. Modern-day pueblos might have a population of thousands, and though they may not have always been this big, it's estimated that populations would have been in the hundreds in the early Middle Ages. This contrasts sharply with the living arrangements of the semi-nomadic Navajo who live in camps of two to four families.

While some Pueblo people still inhabit century-old pueblo adobe buildings, many maintain an additional home outside of the Pueblo. Adobe construction methods dominate the architecture of much of New Mexico, not just in the pueblos, but also in the towns and cities.

ABOVE Part of an outdoor display at the Albuquerque Museum of Art and History
OPPOSITE The city of Albuquerque at sunset, taken from the hills above the town (© Ryan McLeod, published with permission)
PREVIOUS View from above (© Ryan McLeod, published with permission)

Did you know? Albuquerque has featured in many Bugs Bunny cartoons. As Bugs burrows underground to travel around the world he often gets lost, and remarks, when consulting a map, 'I knew I should have taken that left turn at Albuquerque.' The popular TV series *Breaking Bad* is also based in Albuquerque.

Getting in

With a large airport just south of the city, major north–south and east–west interstates intersecting in the city, and a major trans-American passenger train service making a daily stop in downtown, Albuquerque is easy to get to.

By air

Albuquerque International Sunport (ABQ), approximately 5 km south-east of downtown, serves over six million passengers per year. It is New Mexico's only international airport. American, Delta, Frontier, Continental, United and US Airlines connect Sunport with their respective major hubs (including Atlanta, Denver, Houston, Los Angeles, New York, Phoenix, San Francisco, and Washington) while Southwest Airlines offer direct services to Baltimore, Dallas, Kansas City, Las Vegas, Oakland, San Diego, Seattle, St. Louis, and Tucson.

Afternoon arrivals at ABQ can be extremely bumpy (due to thermals created by a combination of elevation, wind and heat), and while this does not pose a risk to safety, travellers who are prone to air sickness, may wish to arrange a flight that lands in the morning, or after sunset.

The local number 50 bus operates every 30 min during weekdays (and a more limited service on Sat) between the airport and downtown via Yale Boulevard, University of New Mexico (UNM) and Dr Martin Luther King Jnr Avenue. The pick-up stop is located on the lower level towards the left (west) of the shuttle island.

By car

The Pan-American Freeway (I-25), the main north–south highway through Albuquerque, connects the city to Santa Fe and Las Cruces, before continuing north to Denver. Coronado Freeway (I-40) is the main east–west route through the city and an important trans-American route, linking Albuquerque to Oklahoma City in the east and Flagstaff in the west.

Albuquerque is 520 km (5 hr) from Flagstaff, 440 km (4 hr) from El Paso, 720 km (8 hr) from Denver, and approximately 860 km (9 hr) from both Oklahoma City and Phoenix.

By train

Amtrak's daily Southwest Chief service between Chicago and Los Angeles stops at Alvarado Transportation Centre (beside the Greyhound depot) in downtown. The journey from Flagstaff takes approximately 5 hr, while LA is some 16 hr 30 min down the line and Chicago 26 hr away. Pre-booking is essential. Up to 25 percent can be saved off the fare by booking at least a week in advance, and by travelling mid-week.

The New Mexico Rail Runner Express is a commuter railway which connects the city to Santa Fe and other small towns along the Rio Grande. The line has three stops in Albuquerque (the Alvarado Transportation Centre in downtown, Rio Bravo Boulevard in South Valley, and one just off Paseo del Norte in North Valley/Los Ranchos). Services are limited outside of weekday rush hours.

By bus

Greyhound buses serve Albuquerque, with arrivals and departures at the Alvarado Transportation Centre in downtown. There are direct connections with Phoenix (9 hr); via Flagstaff (6 hr); Oklahoma City (11 hr); El Paso (4 hr 30 min); and Denver (17 hr) via Colorado Springs and Santa Fe. Most services operate three times a day. Fares are slightly cheaper when booked online.

Getting around

The city is divided into north and south by the Central Avenue (Route 66), and east and west by the railway tracks, giving rise to four quadrants (NE, NW, SE and SW) which form part of the mailing address. Thus an address ending NW would indicate that it is north of Central Avenue and west of the railway line.

The Northeast Quadrant, the largest quadrant by both area and population, stretches to Sandia Peak Aerial Tram and contains UNM, Balloon Fiesta Park, the Uptown area and much of the affluent foothill neighbourhoods, known simply as the Heights. Northwest Quadrant contains Old Town Albuquerque, most of downtown, Petroglyph National Monument, a number of low and middle-income neighbourhoods, and the affluent North Valley area along the Rio Grande. The Southeast Quadrant contains the airport, a large proportion of the city's hotels, the Kirtland Air Force Base and the trendy Nob Hill neighbourhood. Southwest Quadrant, often referred to as South Valley, is traditionally the rural and agricultural area of Albuquerque, and contains some of the city's older communities, the south end of downtown, the Bosque woodlands, and Albuquerque Biological Park.

While Albuquerque is a large, sprawling city, it is possible to maintain your bearings simply by remembering that the Sandia Mountains are in the east, that the Rio Grande marks the western extent of the city, that I-40 runs east–west, and that I-25 runs north–south through the city.

By car
Because both the amenities and the trailheads are dispersed around the city, a car is recommended. All the major car rental companies have offices at the airport, and many have offices in the city.

Roadworks are commonplace around the city. Local radio station traffic updates and the City of Albuquerque website (www.cabq.gov) may help avoid hotspots. Congestion, particularly during rush hour and on Saturdays, is common along the two interstates (I-25 and I-40), at 'The Big I' interchange between the two interstates, and at the river crossings.

By bus
Local bus transit is operated by ABQ RIDE (www.cabq.gov/transit). While public transport is largely underdeveloped, there are good services along Central Avenue. Rapid Ride's Red Line (Route 766) runs from uptown to west of

Map of main routes and major areas of Albuquerque

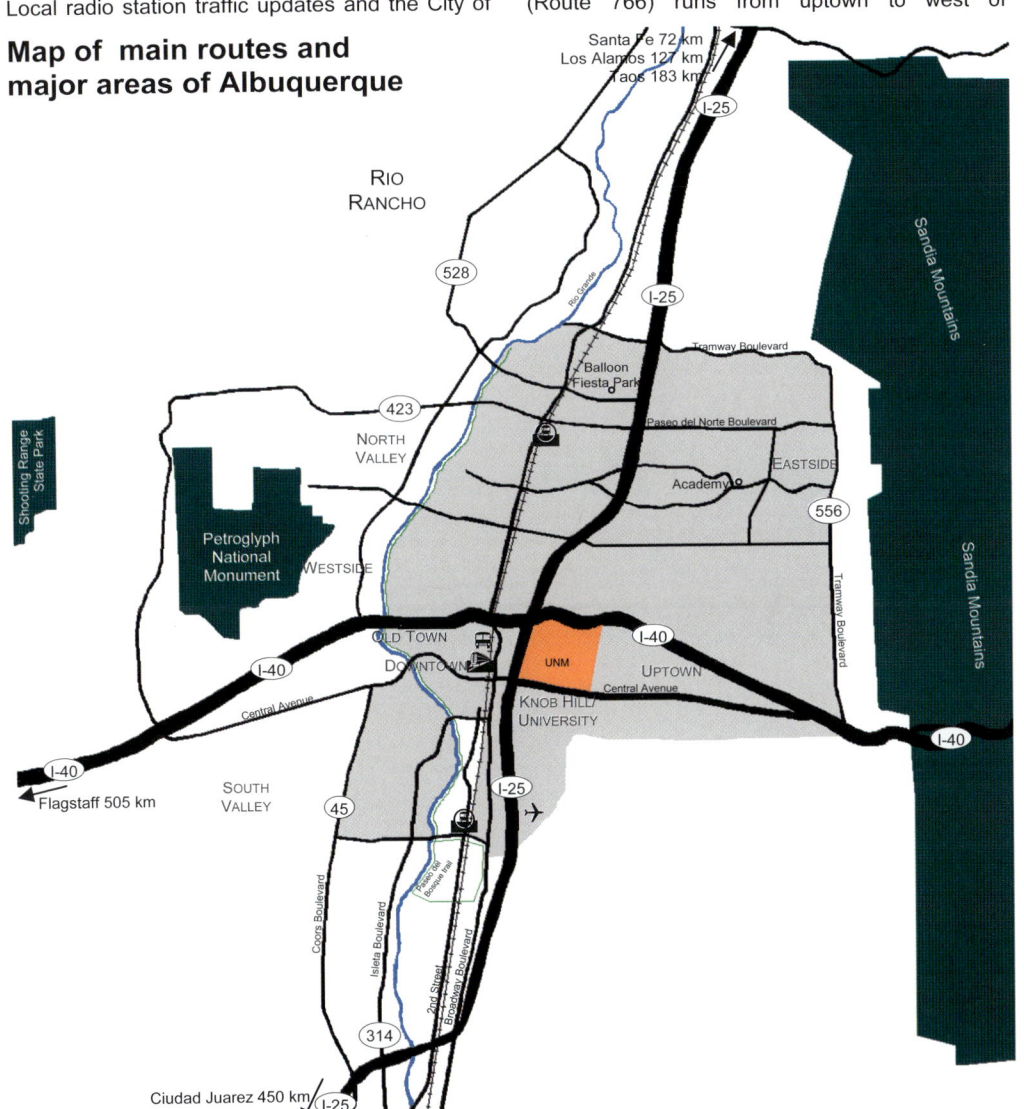

downtown, the Green Line (Route 777), links downtown with Tramway/Central, and the less frequent Blue Line (Route 790) runs between UNM and the Cottonwood Mall in West Side. Many of the services start at the Alvarado Transportation Centre in downtown.

Day passes, which can be purchased when boarding the bus, are valid for unlimited trips, on any route and are the cheapest way to get around. A Rail Runner Express day pass also includes an ABQ RIDE day pass.

By bicycle

Albuquerque is quite spread out, and is hillier than it looks, but getting around by bicycle is just about achievable. Cycling the streets can be risky at times, and using the paved trail network is considerably more enjoyable. All buses have bicycle racks, making a combination of cycling and riding the bus a good option. Details of how to load and unload your bike are available on the Albuquerque government website (www.cabq.gov). The city has an active cycling community and further investment into bike transit is planned.

Paseo del Bosque is a scenic route along the east of the Rio Grande, and is considered the crown jewel in Albuquerque's cycle network. Other good routes include a paved trail on Tramway Boulevard offering access to the Sandia Mountain foothills, and the North Diversion Channel Trail which links UNM North with Balloon Fiesta Park. Maps of trails and cycle lanes can be found on the city's bicycle website.

Road, mountain and hybrid bikes can be rented from the BikeSmith (www.thebikesmithllc.com) on Grande Boulevard. Routes Rental and Tours (1102 Mountain Road, NW) also hire bikes (city cruisers and mountain bikes) and operate cycle tours along Paseo del Bosque.

WEATHER AND WHEN TO VISIT

Albuquerque, lying on the upper reaches of the Chihuahuan Desert ecoregion, has a climate classified as semi-arid. No month has an average temperature below zero, and the average annual rainfall is less than half the average evaporation. Extended cloudiness is rare, and Albuquerque experiences, on average, 278 days of sunshine per year. Winters are short but sharp, and occasional snowfall and below freezing temperatures can be experienced in December and January. It can get windy in March and April, before temperatures rise to average daily highs of 26 °C in May, and above 30 °C for June, July and August. Most of the annual rainfall occurs between early July and mid-September, with an average of 8–10 rain days in July and August.

Albuquerque's temperate climate is one of its major attractions. The city is warmer, and experiences less snow than Mammoth, Flagstaff or Boulder, is cooler than cities like Phoenix, and is less humid than Houston. The hot summers are broken by rain, making temperatures bearable.

Training is possible here almost year-round, with the cold of December and January and the rains of July and August a minor inconvenience. Expect inflated accommodation prices if you visit during the Balloon Fiesta in early October or the Christmas holiday period.

ACCOMMODATION

Meeting the demand for accommodation during the Balloon Fiesta has resulted in a surplus of accommodation at other times, and athletes should have no problem finding accommodation to meet their needs. Prices are inflated in early October (before or during the Balloon Fiesta), and during the Christmas holiday period, and booking early at these times is strongly advised.

Serviced and furnished apartments and rental homes are plentiful, and there are many good options in the foothills area. Many rental properties are spacious, well equipped and some come with large gardens. Prices vary considerably depending on location, property, and duration of stay. Apartments are listed on the Albququerque Convention and Visitors Bureau website (www.itsatrip.org), and sites such as Oakwood Apartments (www.oakwood.com), TripAdvisor (www.tripadvisor.co.uk) and HomeAway (www.homeaway.co.uk).

Extended stay and suite options, offered by the major hotel chains, may be a better option for those travelling alone or as a couple. Most of the hotels with cooking facilities and special rates for stays of five or more days are located in the south of the city, close to the airport.

Hotels, hostels, and guesthouses may also provide suitable accommodation for athletes. The city's Convention and Visitors Bureau website (www.itsatrip.org) is a good starting point for searching accommodation. Guesthouse and B&B listings are available on the Albuquerque Bed & Breakfast Association website (www.abqbandb.com).

Location of accommodation is crucial if you don't have access to a car. Choose accommodation either in the foothills, or very close to Paseo del Bosque (though there is less choice here). Albuquerque is a sprawling city, and distances are further than they look on a map.

Food

Eating out is generally casual and inexpensive. New Mexican food is the most popular, but there are also Italian restaurants, burger joints, and thanks to the city's lively Asian community, Thai, Chinese and Vietnamese restaurants. Restaurant listings and reviews can be found on the Urban Spoon website (www.urbanspoon.com).

New Mexican food combines the cuisine of Mexico, Spain, and the broader Mediterranean, with Pueblo Native American tastes and cowboy chuckwagon flavours. New Mexican food is typically hotter than Mexican food, and sauces are generally made of chillies rather than tomatoes. Popular foods include typical Mexican and Southwestern dishes such as Burritos (typically without rice, and in smaller tortillas than the Californian version), enchiladas (specifically the lasagne-style, and the flat Santa Fe-style varieties), quesadilla and tacos; Spanish foods; and Latin-American favourites.

The green chilli is particularly dominant in everything from burritos to cheeseburgers. The chilli crop is the largest of all agricultural crops within the state of New Mexico. Indeed, the chilli is so important to the state that US senator Pete Domenici, a New Mexico native, had the state's spelling of the vegetable (*chile*), officially entered into Congressional Record.

Pozole is a thick stew made with corn, pork and chilli; *atole* is a thick, corn gruel; and *caldillo* is a thin green chilli stew. *Carne adovada* are cubes of spicy marinated pork; *carne asada* is grilled or roasted meat and *chorizo* is a spiced pork sausage often used in dishes as an alternative to chicken or minced beef. *Huevos rancheros* are fried eggs covered with chilli salsa or cheese. Breakfast burritos include scrambled eggs, cheese, potatoes and sometimes meat. *Albóndigas* are meatballs, *frijoles refritos* are refried beans and *piñones* are pine nuts. *Biscochito* is an anise-flavoured cookie, *capirotada* a traditional dessert usually made during Lent and *natillas* is a soft custard dessert.

New Mexican food isn't the healthiest of cuisines, and fried tacos and cheese intake should be moderated. Cooking for yourself is a viable alternative. There are several outlets of the chain grocery stores Smith's and Albertsons around the city. Organic food stores such as La Montanita Natural Foods Co-Op, Whole Foods Market, and Sunflower Market, and the international food stores Talin Market World Food Fare and Pro's Ranch Market (Hispanic food) add further choice.

Shopping

Shops are dispersed around the city, and there are few major shopping areas. Old Town (www.albuquerqueoldtown.com) has a good collection of gift shops selling authentic Native American and Southwestern crafts and art, other speciality shops and some tacky souvenir outlets. Downtown is particularly lacking in shops, though there are some boutiques and art and craft shops along Gold and Central Avenues. Nob Hill, a trendy district along Central Avenue between Girard and Carlisle, has small craft and art shops and some grocery stores.

Uptown has more of the typical suburban malls and major chain outlets. Coronado Mall (www.coronadocenter.com) hosts some of America's popular department stores including Macy's, JCPenney and Sears, while ABQ Uptown (www.simon.com) contains more high-end retail outlets. You're likely to find everything you need, but you have to do a bit of searching, and a fair bit of travel to get it.

There are a number of specialty running stores, most of which are located in the north-east quadrant of the city. They include ABQ Running Shop (Montgomery Boulevard NE), Fleet Feet Sports (Menaul Boulevard NE), Heart and Sole (San Mateo Boulevard NE), Athlete's Edge (Wyoming Boulevard NE), Sport Systems (Montgomery NE) and New Balance (outlets on Juan Tabo Boulevard NE and Ellison Road NW).

Communication

All the major mobile operators offer good mobile reception across Albuquerque.

All branches of the Albuquerque/Bernalillo Country Library network provide free Wi-Fi access, and offer computer-use for a small fee. The main library is located in downtown on Copper Avenue, NW. Other free Wi-Fi spots include the airport, downtown's Civic Plaza, the Old Town Plaza, and the UNM campus. The Nob Hill area, close to the university, contains most of the city's internet cafes.

HEALTH AND SAFETY

There is a small risk of coming in contact with scorpions, black widow spiders and rattlesnakes. Not all are lethal, but any venomous bite or sting can hurt. Avoid long grass, and give snakes a wide berth. If you do get bitten or stung, take note of what the animal that attacked you looked like (including size, colour and any patterning), and seek immediate medical attention.

Albuquerque has had an outbreak of the 'Sin Nombre' hantaviral lung disease, a potentially fatal disease for which there is no known cure. Tourists aren't particularly at risk from the disease, but should apply common sense and not handle dead animals or enter wild animal's dens.

Albuquerque's crime rate is on par with America's average, and tourists are not specifically targeted. Parts of Central Avenue, particularly between the train station and University Boulevard and east of Carlisle, and some smaller streets in the area, should be avoided after dark. Beggars and homeless people are plentiful, but shouldn't pose a significant threat to your safety.

Hospitals with 24-hour accident and emergency services include Presbyterian Hospital (1100 Central Avenue, SE); Presbyterian Kaseman Hospital (8300 Constitution, NE); Presbyterian Rest Hospital (2400 Unser Boulevard, SE, Rio Ranch), and Lovelace Westside (10501 Golf Course Road, NW).

TIME

New Mexico operates on Mountain Standard Time (MST; GMT-7). Daylight saving operates from the second Sunday in March until the first Sunday in November.

Daylight hours vary between the seasons, with just less than 10 hr of daylight in December and 14 hr 30 min of daylight in midsummer.

	Mar	Jun	Sept	Dec
Sunrise	07:18	05:52	06:49	07:07
Sunset	19:14	20:22	19:14	16:56

OTHER PRACTICALITIES

Details on health and safety, language, communication, money, power, laundry, culture and respect can be found in the US general section *(pp. 68-69)*.

BELOW Bandstand in the centre of Old Town

SPORTS FACILITIES AND SERVICES

Albuquerque has long been a favourite training haunt of world marathon record holder Paula Radcliffe and a host of other athletes. Excellent training facilities, the amenities of a large city, an international airport, a running tradition, and an active population combine to make an excellent environment for training. Trails along the Rio Grande and in the Sandia foothills, tracks in high schools across the city, and a variety of excellent gym facilities, mean that athletes training here have everything they need in one city. A car will be required to get around, and a guide to show you some of the best routes is useful.

'Live high, train low' is not possible from Albuquerque, though athletes who live and train in Santa Fe use the city as their 'train low' venue, and would typically travel down once a week for quality workouts.

The flat trails along the Rio Grande are suitable for race walkers, and enable marathon runners to carry out quality asphalt workouts away from traffic. Mountain runners, trail runners and orienteers are well catered for in the Sandia foothills and mountains.

TRAILS AND RUNNING ROUTES

The main collections of trails are in the foothills of the Sandia Mountains, which run along the eastern boundaries of the city (altitudes of 1,800–2,000 m), and in the Rio Grande Valley State Park along the banks of the Rio Grande on the west of the city (altitude approximately 1,520 m). There are a few options within the city itself. A car is required to get to the majority of the trailheads.

Trail maps can be found on the Parks and Recreation section of the City of Albuquerque website (www.cabq.gov). Printed maps can be obtained from any cycling shop or by phoning Municipal Development (+1 505 768 2680). There is parking at most of the trailheads, though spaces are often limited, and a fee sometimes applies.

If you fancy getting out of the city, and doing some running at an even higher altitude, Santa Fe and Los Alamos are both great options within easy reach of Albuquerque *(pp. 104-105)*.

Foothills
There are a number of hilly and challenging trails, of various distances, within the wilderness and open space areas in the Sandia Mountain foothills. Foothills trail (Route 365), running roughly north–south along the base of the hills, is the flattest of the trails. Copper Avenue, Simms Park Road and most of the other roads east of Tramway Boulevard lead to trailheads, with the Indian School Road trailhead a particularly popular starting point. The bicycle lane along Tramway Boulevard is a popular running route in itself.

Sandia Mountain
While it might sound like a bit of a challenge, not least because of the additional altitude (up to 3,000 m), the Sandia Mountains, and Sandia Peak ski area in particular, offer additional choice for forest trails. Service roads which run around the mountain, rather than up it, are popular among hikers, and are suitable for running.

Rio Grande Valley State Park
The Rio Grande Valley State Park runs most of the length of the Albuquerque section of the Rio Grande. In addition to the main asphalt Paseo del Bosque, a flat multi-use asphalt path which stretches for approximately 25 km along the east bank of the river, there are gravel and packed-dirt trails intermittently along both banks of the river, and a network of unmarked trails through the various wooded sections of the park. There are trailhead car parks on both banks at Montano Road, Central Avenue, Bridge Boulevard and Rio Bravo Boulevard, and on the east bank at Alameda Boulevard, Paseo del Norte and Candelaria Road, located by Rio Grande Nature Centre and charging a parking fee.

Albuquerque Academy
The route of approximately 5 km around Albuquerque Academy is very popular among visiting athletes who relax afterwards in the nearby Starbucks and Whole Foods Market cafes. Parking is on Wyoming Boulevard between Harper Street and Academy Street. The loop is mostly flat and offers views of both the Sandia Mountains and the city. This is the best place in Albuquerque to find other athletes.

University of New Mexico North Golf Course
The 3 km packed-dirt route around UNM Golf Course is popular among the student-athletes on their recovery days as they take advantage of not having to drive to trailheads. The route is very slightly undulating.

West of the Rio Grande
There are spectacularly scenic traffic-free paths and trails off Paseo del Norte in the north-west of the city. These are flatter, and at a lower altitude, than the trails in the foothills.

TRACK FACILITIES

There are tracks at Highland High School (just across Jackson Street from Highland Pool parking area), Sandia High School, Manzano High School and Eldorado High School. As all tracks are high school facilities, it is advisable to avoid using during school hours. Highlands is easy to access, but is often busy with walkers and joggers.

During the winter, a 200 m Mondo indoor track is constructed inside the Albuquerque Convention Centre (2nd Street, NW). In addition to hosting competitions (including USATF Championships, and NCAA competitions), and UNM training sessions, there are opportunities for public use. Details of open track times can be found on the Parks and Recreation section of the City of Albuquerque website (www.cabq.gov).

GYM FACILITIES

Despite there being many well equipped commercial fitness centres and personal training gyms around Albuquerque, finding one that does short-term or pay-as-you-go memberships is very difficult. Some do offer week-long trials or free trial guest passes, though non-residents are not always eligible for these. Many of the city's community centres have gym facilities and weight training rooms and offer fitness classes. Details and locations of centres can be found on the parks and recreation section of the City of Albuquerque website (www.cabq.gov).

CROSS-TRAINING OPTIONS

Road cycling, mountain biking and swimming are all accessible forms of cross training. Cross country skiing is possible in the Sandia Mountains during the winter months. There are community tennis facilities at Jerry Cline Tennis Complex (7205 Constitution NE) and Sierra Vista West Tennis Complex (5001 Montano Road NW) and beach volleyball sandpits at the Sandia Peak base facility.

LOCAL RACES

The most popular and most challenging race in Albuquerque is the annual La Luz Trail Race, a 9 mile run to the Sandia Crest. The route, which features a 1,400 m elevation gain, is almost continuously uphill along narrow paved road and single-track dirt trail. There is a participant cap of 400, and entry is via ballot. The Duke City Marathon (www.dukecitymarathon.com) is a somewhat flatter race in and around downtown and the Bosque bike path. It is held in late October each year. Sandia Peak Challenge, held in late July, features 4 mile and 7 mile trail runs. The Albuquerque Road Runners website (www.abqroadrunners.com) has a comprehensive list of races.

Running community

Many of the world's best athletes have spent time training in Albuquerque. The mild climate, moderate altitude and good transport links make it possible among European and American athletes between races on the American road and track circuits. Paula Radcliffe, Lornah Kiplagat, Liz McColgan and Noureddine Morceli are just some of the big names to have trained here over the years. The UNM distance squad is particularly strong, and UNM student-athletes often stay in the city after graduation.

The main club in the area is Albuquerque Road Runners (www.abqroadrunners.com). Fee-based training groups and programmes available include Albuquerque Road Runners' Women in Training; New Mexico Track Club (www.nmtrackclub.com); Albuquerque Fit (www.usafitalbuquerque.com); Fleet Feet Sports' No Boundaries Program; ABQ Running Shop's half marathon training programme, and Oxy-Gen Morons (oxy-genmorons.com).

Suitability for other sports

Albuquerque has a reasonable variety of mountain bike trails and some decent road cycling routes. Cycling and running options, together with access to a host of indoor and outdoor pools, mean that it is possible for triathletes to train here.

Cycling Once you get outside of the city, the roads around Albuquerque are relatively good for cycling. The NM-313 to Bernalillo (and on to Algodones and San Filipe Casino) is a relatively fast flat ride. Rio Grande Boulevard is a scenic ride through Los Ranchos and the scenic surrounding farming community. Route 66 leads to NM-14 through the Tijeras Pass, opening up more undulating and hilly rides. The flat Paseo del Bosque is suitable for the less serious cyclist. Mountain biking is popular in the Sandia Foothills, in Otero Canyon (off NM-14), at White Mesa, and along the Bosque flow trails (ideal for beginner mountain bikers). The summer sports section of the Sandia Peak website (www.sandiapeak.com) has details of technical downhill routes in the mountains. Information on bike hire and purchase can be found on *p. 96*.

Swimming There are a number of indoor and outdoor public pools with pay-as-you-go access. All pools can be rented for group use, subject to availability. Further information can be found under the recreation section of the City of Albuquerque website (www.cabq.gov).

Other sports With an abundance of sports facilities around the city, Albuquerque is a possible training venue for sports teams, and individuals in some other sports. Municipal facilities include basketball courts, tennis courts, golf courses and softball fields.

Quite, well-surfaced roads in the foothills provide excellent terrain for running (© Ryan McLeod, published with permission)

THINGS TO SEE AND DO BETWEEN TRAINING

With more than 300 art, music, literary, film, ethnic, dance and craft organisations, festivals, museums and associations, and a number of live performing arts and music venues, there is always something to do from a cultural perspective.

The Indian Pueblo Cultural Centre, the National Hispanic Cultural Centre and the Albuquerque Museum of Art and History offer an insight into the history of the area and its people, and National Museum of Nuclear Science and History is devoted to all things atomic. The American International Rattlesnake Museum, the New Mexico Museum of Natural History and Science and the Turquoise Museum in Old Town, and UNM's Maxwell Museum of Anthropology, Meteorite Museum, Geology Museum, and Art Museum are just some of the other museums on offer.

It's worth spending an afternoon exploring the narrow streets, specialty shops, informative museums, and hidden treasures of Old Town. San Felipe de Neri Church, on the north side of the central plaza, is the oldest building in Albuquerque. Albuquerque Museum operates guided tours of Old Town and there are also ghost tours though the area.

Albuquerque Biological Park contains a zoo, an aquarium, a botanic garden (with an emphasis on desert plants), and Tingley Beach where you can fish, rent a pedal boat, or relax in the cafe by the lake. A small train links the sites within the park.

Albuquerque's night sky features illuminated downtown hotels, banks and commercial buildings, bringing the city to light with bright shades of blue, green, yellow and red.

Petroglyph National Monument, located west of the city, is an important archaeological site which contains an estimated 23,000 ancient petroglyphs (rock engravings). The petroglyphs, carved into the black volcanic rocks of the area, provide an important record of the Spanish settlers and Native Americans who inhabited the area 400 to 700 years ago.

The Sandia Peak Tramway (www.sandiapeak.com) which runs from the north-eastern edge of the city to the crest of the Sandia Mountains (3,163 m above sea level) is the world's second-longest aerial passenger tramway. The tramway runs every 20–30 min daily, except in April and October when it is closed for maintenance. The trip to the top, which takes approximately 15 min, offers spectacular views of the city. There is a visitor centre and a restaurant at the summit.

The Albuquerque International Balloon Fiesta is the largest hot-air balloon event in the world, North America's largest annual international event and one of the world's most photographed events. The fiesta runs for nine days from the first Saturday in October. The public can walk among balloonists setting up, inflating, launching and landing their balloons at Balloon Fiesta Park. There are balloon races, mass ascensions, illuminations and displays of irregular shaped

Monument outside the Albuquerque Museum of Art and History

balloons during the fiesta which ends with a final farewell mass ascension.

Several companies operate year-round balloon rides. The Anderson-Abruzzo Albuquerque International Balloon Museum, located at Balloon Fiesta Park, has exhibits dedicated to the history and science of ballooning.

Other national and international festivals and celebrations include the Native American Gathering of Nations Pow-wow (Apr), the Festival Flamenco International de Albuquerque (Jun), the New Mexico State Fair (Sept) and the New Mexico Arts and Crafts Fair (Jun).

New Mexico Lobos (www.golobos.com) represent UNM in NCAA college sports and their basketball, American football and baseball teams are worth watching. Cheap tickets are often available for Albuquerque Isotopes minor-league baseball games. The Isotopes are an affiliate of the Los Angeles Dodgers. New Mexico Scorpions, who play at Santa Ana Star Centre in Rio Rancho, are the ice hockey team to watch. Albuquerque often hosts regional NCAA track and field competitions and the USATF Indoor Championships.

The Sandia and Manzano Mountains offer open spaces, trails and rock climbing for all ability levels. There is a city-owned shooting range near Double Eagle II Airport, 30 km west of downtown. Cliff's Amusement Park, located on Osuna Road NE, is a small amusement park with two roller coasters, and Outpost Ice Arena, located near the base terminal of Sandia Peak Tram, has four ice rinks.

REST DAY EXCURSIONS

Santa Fe, located approximately 100 km north of Albuquerque, is one of the best know and most interesting tourist destinations in New Mexico. It can be reached by road, via either the I-25 or the more scenic Turquoise Trail east of the Sandia Mountains, and by train (Rail Runner commuter service). Coronado State Monument, next to Bernalillo, various Native American pueblos, and the scenic Kasha-Katuwe Tent Rocks National Monument are just some of the sites and detours along the way.

Founded as the state capital in 1610, Santa Fe was the crossroads of two important trade routes, the Santa Fe Trail towards Missouri and the Camino Real route from Mexico. The Old Town, with its Native American, European and Mexican influences, flourished during the 1800s, and featured tavern-lined streets and a busy plaza. Today the area bustles with tourists, and is surrounded by blocks of narrow adobe building-lined streets, specialty shops, museums, cafes and restaurants. Nearby Canyon Road features approximately 80 art galleries showcasing the work of local artists.

Taos Pueblo, just north of Taos, Bandelier National Monument near Los Alamos, and Salinas Pueblo Missions National Monument near Mountainair, are the best examples of pueblo settlements and pueblo ruins in the vicinity.

HOT-AIR BALLOONS
From the blog, 8 May 2010

My dreams are somewhat bizarre at the best of times. Just like in my awake life, my sleep world is slightly on the eccentric side. I guess what I'm trying to say is that I'm just as weird when I'm asleep as I am when I'm awake. But bizarre and all as my dreams normally are, they get a lot worse when I'm at altitude. On a previous visit to Kenya I kept dreaming that I was pregnant, and the main topic of conversation at breakfast each morning was what strange and wacky dream I'd had the previous night.

Today though, I believe I reached the pinnacle of strange dreams. After waking from an afternoon nap (the joys of being a full-time athlete), I lay there wondering how on earth my subconscious had come up with my nap-time entertainment. I dreamt that while on a run in a park, I met a man running with a hot-air balloon attached to his body. I'm not sure of the purpose of the balloon, as his feet were still on the ground—perhaps it's the newest trend in performance enhancement, or injury prevention. I did try to get a photo, but had stupidly forgotten to put the battery in my camera. And then I woke up.

The hot-air balloon reference wasn't completely random. Albuquerque hosts an international balloon fiesta each October, and there are photos and paintings of hot-air balloons on the walls of nearly every hotel, restaurant and public building in the city. In fact, the lack of battery in my camera was not that strange either, and reminded me that my camera battery needed to be charged. But why would anyone ever run strapped to a hot-air balloon? And why don't I have better things to dream about?

A NOTE ON LIVING HERE LONG-TERM

Albuquerque may be one of the better venues to live and train in long-term. There are decent employment opportunities, though work visas are difficult for non-American citizens to obtain. The conveniently located airport makes it easy to get out for races at sea level. There are many indoor and outdoor track races in Albuquerque, and the altitude is not so high that racing there is impossible. If you get bored of the trails around the city, you can travel to Santa Fe or other surrounding cities. There is a large running community, the cost of living is relatively low, and the weather is suitable for training almost all year-round. The city isn't specifically built around tourism and it's possible to live a pretty normal life. Athletes have been moving to Albuquerque to study and train at UNM for decades, and many that did, never left. Life in a large city is not for everyone, and driving to trails every day can become tedious, expensive and time-consuming.

FURTHER INFORMATION

The Albuquerque Convention and Visitors Bureau has visitor information centres in the arrivals area of the Albuquerque International Sunport, and the Plaza Don Luis in Old Town.

It's a trip (www.itsatrip.org), the official website of the Albuquerque Convention and Visitors Bureau, has information on places to stay (including extended stay and rental options), things to do, and places to eat. The coupons and special deals section has advice on how to save money when travelling in Albuquerque. The site also has a visitor guide and vacation planner to download.

The official government website (www.cabq.gov) has information about getting around Albuquerque, a good map of the city's bicycle routes and trails, suggestions of things to see, and a list of all the city's parks.

OTHER ALTITUDE TRAINING SITES IN NEW MEXICO

Los Alamos, Santa Fe and Taos, all located in the high grounds between Albuquerque and the Colorado border, are other popular training venues within New Mexico. Winter temperatures are lower than in Albuquerque (partially due to the high altitude), and snowfall makes training difficult during the winter months. Accommodation prices tend to be higher than in Albuquerque. Trails are easier to get to and these options may be better for athletes looking to get away from the distractions of the big city. Albuquerque can still be used for quality sessions, particularly from Santa Fe.

Los Alamos (2,231 m)
www.visit.losalamos.com

The small town of Los Alamos, located at the end of the Jemez Mountains Scenic Byway and next to the Bandelier National Monument, the Valles Caldera National Preserve and the Jemez National Recreational Area, has excellent facilities and extensive open space. A number of events, across a range of endurance sports, are held in the town each year, and in addition to an urban trails system which links to the nearby National Forest trails, there is a golf course, an aquatic centre with 50 m swimming pool, a community skating rink, and a ski mountain.

The mesas and canyons within Los Alamos County's dramatic landscape are linked by almost 100 km of trails. Access to the Bayo and Pueblo canyons, large sections of wooded areas, is from the Kinnikinnick Park behind the aquatics centre. The Mitchell and Quemazon trailheads lead to the Santa Fe National Forest above the town. White Rock (1,940 m), 16 km east of the town, offers additional trail options, solitude and dramatic scenery.

The Los Alamos High Altitude Sports website (www.lahighaltitudesports.com) promotes skiing, cycling, triathlon, swimming and running events within the town, and has an event calendar, suggestions of places to stay, and other useful information on visiting the town. Information about races, including the ultra Jemez Mountain Trail Runs, can be found on www.highaltitudeathletics.org. The recreational section of the Los Alamos County website (www.losalamosnm.us) has details of open basketball, volleyball, table tennis and indoor football sessions which visitors can avail of, and information on use of facilities.

Los Alamos is located 150 km from Albuquerque, and 60 km from Santa Fe. The closest commercial airports are Santa Fe (flights to Dallas and Los Angeles only) and Albuquerque (less than 2 hr away). A car is the best way of getting into the town, though there are public transport options available, including New Mexico Park & Ride (www.dot.state.nm.us) connections from Santa Fe and Espanola; Roadrunner Shuttle and Charter (www.roadrunnershuttleandcharter.com) connections (by appointment) with Santa Fe airport, Lamy Amtrak train station or Albuquerque Airport; and free North Central Regional Transit

District (www.ncrtd.org) bus services from Taos, Santa Fe and Española (Mon to Fri only).

B&Bs and inns are the predominate type of accommodation, with some extended-stay and suite options available. Local property rental company Casa de Luz (www.casadeluz-losalamos.com) offers some short-term and furnished properties, which may be suitable for stays of a month or longer.

Santa Fe (2,134 m)
www.santafe.org

Santa Fe, the New Mexico state capital, is a popular altitude training base among American-based Kenyan athletes. Its higher altitude (2,134 m) means that athletes often travel from there to Albuquerque to do their faster runs and sessions. The city is steeped in history and culture, and there is plenty to see and do between training.

The Santa Fe Striders website (www.santafestriders.org) provides maps and descriptions of popular road and off-road runs in the area. The Striders organise weekly group runs from specialist running store The Running Hub (www.runsantafe.com).

Camp Marafiki (www.kenyausa.com) offers runners the chance to train the Kenyan way, with Kenyan athletes who are based in Santa Fe. Their annual camp provides transport to and from trails, meals, accommodation, talks and lectures, and social activities.

Swimming and gym facilities are available at the Genoveva Chavez Community Center (www.chavezcenter.com). Santa Fe Aquatic Club (www.sfaclub.com) arranges all-inclusive camps for groups of swimmers.

Santa Fe is located 100 km north of Albuquerque, and is linked to Albuquerque by the New Mexico Rail Runner Express commuter train. An Amtrak service passes through Lamy, just 32 km south of Santa Fe, and Lamy Transport provides shuttle transport from the train station to Santa Fe. American Eagle Airlines (Dallas-Fort Worth) and Great Lakes Airlines (Denver and Clovis) operate services to the municipal airport in Santa Fe (SAF).

Links to accommodation, which include a good choice of vacation rentals, can be found on the Santa Fe Convention and Visitors Bureau website (www.santafe.org).

Taos (2,124 m)
www.taos.org

The town of Taos, located in north central New Mexico, has become a popular travel destination in recent years. It is located just over 110 km north of Santa Fe, and 210 km from Albuquerque. The ancient Native American community of Taos Pueblo, a UNESCO World Heritage site, is located just north of the town. It is one of the oldest continually occupied settlements in North America. The nearby Taos Ski Valley receives the best snow in the state and the beautiful scenery attracts many artists to the region.

Trails in and around Taos tend to be hilly. Taos Ski Valley is a popular option. The 'Trails and Tracks' section of the Official Taos Vacation Guide (www.taos.org) and the Taos Hiking Trails website (www.taostrails.com) are good starting points for trail maps and descriptions.

The Taos vacation guide (www.taos.org) has information on sports arenas, golf courses, tennis courts and other sports facilities. The FIFA accredited Taos Eco Park (www.taosecopark.com), is a multi-sport training facility located close to the edge of town. Swimming is available at the Taos Youth and Family Centre (www.taosyouth.org). Running shoes can be purchased at Taos Running Company (www.goodsole.com).

Albuquerque and Santa Fe are the nearest commercial airports. A car is the best way of getting into the town, though there are public transport options available. The North Central Regional Transit District (www.ncrtd.org) provides free Monday to Friday bus services links with, Santa Fe, Los Alamos and Española. Taos Express (www.taosexpress.com) operates a weekend service between Taos and Santa Fe. Twin Hearts Express & Transportation (+1 575 751 1201) operates a shuttle service between Albuquerque International Airport and Taos.

Websites which list rental accommodations include Taos Luxury Property Rentals (www.taospropertyrentals.com), Taos Getaway LLC (www.taosgetaway.com) and Premier Properties (www.taosvacationhomes.com). Other properties, including B&B accommodation, hotels and suites, can be found on Taos Webb (www.taoswebb.com).

Useful information can be found on The City of Taos official website (www.taosgov.com) and on Taos Webb (www.taoswebb.com).

Flagstaff

Situated in the heart of Northern Arizona, the university city of Flagstaff is a popular altitude training destination among distance runners, triathletes and swimmers. The local trail system provides endless routes through, and within easy reach, of the town centre. Excellent facilities, plentiful accommodation, a relaxed atmosphere, and a thriving running community further add to the appeal of the area. Despite being central to a large number of national parks and other sites of significant natural and historical significance, Flagstaff is not particularly touristy.

Flagstaff, US (2,106 m)

Flagstaff is a small city located in Coconino County in the northern part of Arizona. It lies towards the south-western edge of the Colorado Plateau and along the western side of the largest ponderosa pine forest on mainland US. The San Francisco Peaks, the highest mountain range in Arizona, provide a dramatic backdrop to the city, and Humphreys Peak, the highest point in the state (3,850 m), is located just 16 km north of Flagstaff.

The city derives its name from a flagpole made from ponderosa pine by a scouting party from Boston to celebrate the US Centennial on 4th July 1876, the year of the first permanent settlement here. Growth during the 1880s saw Flagstaff grow to the largest city on the railway between the US west coast and Albuquerque by 1886. The town was chosen as the site for the Lowell Observatory, due to its altitude, in 1894, and the Northern Arizona Normal School, now called Northern Arizona University (NAU) was established here in 1899. During the 1890s, 80–100 trains a day travelled through Flagstaff and its importance in rail-related industry resulted in rapid growth of the city. The historic Route 66 was completed in 1926, and Flagstaff became an important stop along its journey across America. The city continued to prosper during the 1960s, and following some decline in the 1970s and 1980s, underwent some redevelopment in the 1990s.

Though technically a city, Flagstaff has a small-town America look and feel. The population, as of 2010, is just over 60,000, and the downtown area covers just a few blocks. Accommodations, training facilities, trailheads and amenities are all within easy reach of downtown and even the airport is close to the heart of the city.

With an economy traditionally built around the ranching, lumbar and railroad industries, Flagstaff today is an important distribution hub, a thriving medical device manufacturing centre, and a college town, with a strong tourism sector.

Author's verdict

I loved Flagstaff. It's big enough to have supermarkets, restaurants, shops and things to do, but small enough to be able get around on foot, and to be close to the trails, no matter where you're staying. There is a great running scene and I found the local runners incredibly friendly and helpful. The town was full of my type of trails (anything through pine forests usually does the job), and while my impressions may have been enhanced by the fact that I was starting to get fit for the first time in years, I really think Flagstaff has a lot to offer. I took a trip to the Grand Canyon on my rest day, but this was just one of the many excursions available. A car isn't essential, but would be useful for day-trips, and to get to Sedona for the occasional session at a lower altitude.

Running ★★★★☆ - Large variety of trails within easy reach of all accommodation; good facilities; often windy, making fast out-and-back runs difficult; 'train low' options available in Sedona.

Convenience ★★★★☆ - Flying from Europe typically takes 14-20 hr; most trails, facilities and amenities within walking distance of accommodation; car is not essential for training, but useful for excursions.

Safety ★★★★☆ - Low levels of violent crime; some risk of robberies in certain areas of town; no major disease or safety risk

Cost ★★★★☆ - Lower cost of living than other US venues; good choice of reasonably priced accommodation, restaurants and supermarkets; a car is not essential.

Cultural experience ★★★☆☆ - Ideal opportunity to sample Southwestern history and culture, visit national parks and monuments, see how Native Americans live and get to know local runners.

Things to do between training ★★★★★ - Area is second to none in terms of memorable day-trips; friendly student town with plentiful entertainment options.

Suitability for solo travellers ★★★★☆ Particularly suitable for solo travellers; trails easy to find; friendly running community; weekly opportunities to join local athletes on runs and social outings.

Must do Take a day-trip to the Grand Canyon; join the Northern Arizona Trail Runners Association on one of their runs; lose yourself on scenic trails in and around the town.

Ideal for Anybody that likes to run on forest trails, and appreciates not having to drive to trailheads.

> **Did you know?** Several of the running scenes in the classic film Forrest Gump were shot in and around Flagstaff! Nearby Sedona and Oak Creek Canyon were the shooting locations for more than a hundred 1940s and 1950s Western movies, and Flagstaff's Hotel Monte Vista hosted many film stars during that era, including John Wayne, Gary Cooper, Bing Crosby and Spencer Tracy.

ARIZONA
www.arizonaguide.com

People
The 23 Native American reservations within Arizona together make up approximately 27 percent of the state's total land. Nearly 300,000 indigenous people live in the state. The Navajo and Hopi peoples practise traditional crafts, and visitors can purchase their handcrafts from trading posts and shops across the state. They also have a tradition of running (see special feature). Approximately 20 percent of Arizona's total population are Hispanic, and Mexican cuisine, fiestas and Hispanic folk music and dance feature highly in Arizona's culture.

Places
Lush green forests, arid deserts, dramatic canyons, high mountain peaks, spectacular volcano craters and beautiful alpine meadows are all within easy reach of Flagstaff. The varied and spectacular landscape, weathered by wind, snow and water, features natural bridges, large underground caverns, petrified wood, pure white sand dunes and the world's most famous canyon. In the southern half of the state, spreading towards the border with Mexico, the saguaro cacti, with their spreading arms, characterise a landscape typical of Arizona's cowboy stereotype. Phoenix is the state capital.

Practicalities
Arizona operates on Mountain Standard Time throughout the year, though the Navajo Nation applies daylight saving, to be consistent with its New Mexico and Utah sections. Arizona is the only area of mainland US not to change its clocks. The maximum speed limit on rural freeways in Arizona is 75 miles per hour (120 kph). Other speed limits range between 15 miles per hour (24 kph) in residential areas, to 65 miles per hour (104 kph) on urban freeways and rural routes.

Possibilities
While small cities like Flagstaff appear to have little going on, a training trip to Arizona is anything but dull. In fact, the opposite is true—since you don't have to spend time travelling to trailheads or driving around congested streets to find somewhere to eat, you can spend more time soaking up the best that Arizona has to offer. A long training block can be broken up with trips to Arizona's most iconic sites, all of which are possible on a rest day from training. The friendliness of Arizona's running community means that you can make a few new friends along the way.

Special feature
RUNNING AMONG THE NAVAJO AND HOPI PEOPLE

The majority of Navajo, the largest tribe in the US, live in Navajo Nation, a semi-autonomous territory which occupies parts of north-east Arizona, north-west New Mexico, and south-east Utah. In 1864, the US government attempted to ethnic cleanse the country of Navajo people. Large groups of Navajo were forced to walk at gunpoint from their lands in Arizona to the east of New Mexico. Navajo Nation was established after they returned from imprisonment in 1868. The Hopi people live primarily on the Hopi Reservation, an area entirely surrounded by Navajo Nation.

Living in such close proximity has resulted in similar cultures and agriculture practices, but the Hopi and the Navajo are unrelated, speak different languages and follow different religions. The Hopi are a Pueblo tribe and traditionally lived in villages, while the Navajo, are semi-nomadic and reside in scattered camps of two to four families.

Historically, running is of significant spiritual value to some groups of Native Americans, in particular the Navajo and the Hopi. More recently running is being utilised as a tool to increase self-esteem, confidence, self-discipline and cultural identity among young Native Americans who may otherwise face a life of unemployment and substance abuse.

For centuries, Native Americans ran for hunting, communication and trade purposes. They also run because of their spiritual beliefs. Native Americans believe that a runner creates a link between the earth and the sky. In cultures where harmony between people and their surroundings is so highly valued, it is easy to see why running has an appeal. Navajo believe that the gods rise when the sun does, and they run east in the morning to meet them. They have long believed in the health benefits of running; that it increases energy levels, builds a strong body, and dispels unhappiness.

The running tradition declined as Native Americans adopted a sedentary lifestyle, and their health has suffered. Diabetes and childhood obesity are widespread. In an attempt to get back to their roots, initiatives are being set up across Navajo Nation and young people are encouraged to take up running, attain goals, and make something of their lives.

GETTING IN

By air
Flagstaff Pulliam Field Airport (FLG) is a small airport located 10–20 min by taxi from the centre of Flagstaff. Horizon Air operates non-stop flights from Los Angeles to Flagstaff, and the frequent US Airways flights from Phoenix link Flagstaff with the rest of the world. Flights from Europe typically take 14–20 hr, and often involve two connections.

Phoenix Sky Harbor International Airport is the closest major international airport. The 250 km journey to Flagstaff can take up to 3 hr by car, due to traffic jams in Phoenix.

By train
Amtrak's daily Southwest Chief service between Chicago and Los Angeles stops in downtown Flagstaff. Travelling west the train reaches Flagstaff in the late evening, and the eastbound train passes through in the early morning. The train journey between Flagstaff and Albuquerque is approximately 5 hr making it possible to combine two popular altitude venues in one trip (the flight between both would involve a change in Phoenix). Flagstaff is approximately 11 hr 30 min by train from LA and over 32 hr from Chicago.

By car
Flagstaff is located at the intersection of I-17, which runs north from Phoenix, and I-40 which travels east–west between New Mexico and California. Flagstaff is approximately 2 hr 30 min by car from Phoenix, 4 hr from Tucson; 4 hr from Las Vegas; 4 hr 30 min from Albuquerque and 7 hr from Los Angeles.

By bus
Greyhound operates direct services from Flagstaff to Albuquerque (approximately 5 hr) and Phoenix (approximately 3 hr), three times per day. The Greyhound station is on Butler Avenue near downtown.

Arizona Shuttle (www.arizonashuttle.com) operates a twice-daily seasonal (Mar–Oct) shuttle service between Sedona (uptown centre) and Flagstaff (Amtrak Train Station). Tickets must be booked in advance. The trip takes 40 min. Services also operate to/from Phoenix Sky Harbor Airport, Camp Verde, Phoenix Metrocentre, and the Grand Canyon.

OPPOSITE Flagstaff has numerous beautiful flat trails like this through forested areas in the south of the city. Some, but not all of the trails form part of the comprehensive Flagstaff Urban Trails System (FUTS)

GETTING AROUND

Flagstaff is relatively easy to get around on foot or by bicycle. The bus service connects the more dispersed areas of town.

By bike
Flagstaff is bicycle-friendly, and cycling is an excellent way to get around. There are many bike trails, and most major streets have cycle lanes. Mountain and road bikes can be rented from a number of shops, and second-hand bikes can be purchased from Flagstaff Bicycle Revolution on Mikes Pike.

By bus
The Mountain Line (www.mountainline.az.gov) is a seven-route local bus service linking most areas of the town. Services operate between 06:00 and 22:00 on weekdays, and between 07:00 and 20:00 at weekends and on holidays. Route maps and schedules can be picked up at information points and in hotels, or downloaded online. Monthly passes, purchased online or at Pass sales outlets around the city, are the cheapest option for frequent users, especially since only exact change is accepted when purchasing tickets on board. All buses are fitted with bike racks, and bikes travel free with a fee-paying passenger.

By car
Flagstaff is a relatively small city, and you can easily get around by car. While a car is not necessary to get to training facilities, it is useful to get to Sedona for training at lower altitude (essential during periods of snow), and to get to surrounding sites and National Parks. Cars can be hired from Alamo, Auto Europe, Avis, Budget, Hertz, Honk, Enterprise and National at Flagstaff Airport.

WEATHER AND WHEN TO VISIT

Flagstaff has a four-season dry continental climate with mild weather for most of the year. As with most places at altitude, temperatures drop sharply following sunset, and winter nights here can be particularly cold. Daily lows in December and January average approximately -8 °C and even in the summer can drop to an average of less than 10 °C. June, July and August are the warmest months with average daily highs of 26–28 °C. Average daily temperatures in December and January, the coldest months, are 6–7 °C.

Originating in the eastern Pacific Ocean, Flagstaff's winter weather patterns are frontal and cyclonic in nature. Flagstaff is among the US's snowiest cities, with an annual snowfall average of 255 cm. However, periodic snowfall in winter (almost all of the town's annual snow falls between November and April) is often followed by long spells of fine weather and prolonged snow cover is unusual. While visiting athletes may wish to avoid the cold winter months, athletes based in Flagstaff are able to train year-round by travelling to Sedona, an area which rarely experiences any more than an occasional snow shower.

Featuring an average of 276 precipitation-free days each year, Flagstaff's weather is normally stable. Afternoon downpours and thunderstorms, however, occur intermittently during July and August. The city can be windy, especially between March and June. The almost ever-present strong breeze can be frustrating when trying to complete fast out-and-back runs.

Accommodation

Due to its proximity to the Grand Canyon, Flagstaff boasts a large array of accommodation. There are more than 5,000 rooms available in and around the city. Hotels, motels, inns, hostels, suites and guesthouses provide accommodation to suit all tastes and budgets. Rental homes are available in easy reach of the trails. There is an RV Park on East Butler Avenue, and campsites and cabins within the surrounding forest.

Most hotels and motels are situated within easy reach of the trail network, and with large supermarkets throughout the city, accommodation can be chosen in any area. Older independent motels may be cheaper, but of lower quality, than discount chain motels and hotels. Proprietors of independent hotels and motels may be willing to lower prices outside the main season. Some hotels have extended stay options with studios and suites equipped for cooking. Hotels and motels are listed on www.flagstaffarizona.org and www.go-arizona.com.

A reasonable selection of serviced and furnished apartments and rental homes are listed on HomeAway (www.homeaway.co.uk), AlwaysOnVacation (www.alwaysonvacation.com) and TripAdvisor (www.tripadvisor.co.uk). Comfy Cottages (www.comfycottages.com) have a range of properties in downtown.

Arizona Snowbowl (www.arizonasnowbowl.com) and Flagstaff Nordic Centre (www.flagstaffnordiccenter.com) have rental cabins. Minimum stay for most properties is two nights, and reduced rates are offered for weekly and monthly stays.

Food

There are many good places at which to dine, with American restaurants and steakhouses, pizza and pasta restaurants, Southwestern and Mexican joints, and the occasional eclectic dining venue. Dining listings can be found on the Out West Food Review (www.outwestfoodreview.blogspot.com) and on Go-Arizona (www.go-arizona.com).

There are a number of large supermarkets, including branches of Safeway, Walmart and Target. Rental accommodations, and hotel suites and long-stay hotel rooms with cooking facilities are common, making self-catering a viable option. Groceries, like elsewhere in the US, are expensive, but self-catering is a much healthier option than eating out.

Shopping

There are a number of shopping malls, grocery megastores and department stores around the city. Flagstaff Mall and the Marketplace (www.flagstaffmall.com), on US-89 in the north-east of the city, is one of the most popular shopping areas. It has Sears, Dillard's, and JCPenney department stores, and there is a Safeway supermarket nearby. There are Safeway stores on Cedar Avenue and Plaza Way, a Walmart superstore with a grocery department on Huntington Drive, a smaller Walmart and some other stores on Woodlands Village Boulevard, and a Target store, with fresh groceries, on Milton Road, close to the NAU campus. A large Barnes and Noble bookshop is located just west of downtown. Old Town Shops (www.oldtownshops.net) is a collection of 10 independent shops and restaurants on the corner of Birch Street and Leroux Street, not far from the train station. Most of the craft and souvenir shops are located in downtown.

Run Flagstaff (www.runflagstaff.com), a specialist running shop located on Route 66, sells a wide range of running footwear and clothing, maps, magazines and other running essentials. Staff members are knowledgeable and helpful, and can suggest running routes and help with other running-related matters. The many outdoor, skiing and hiking shops around town may be able to help with your clothing and equipment needs in the unlikely event that Run Flagstaff falls short.

Communication

There is good mobile coverage with all the major mobile operators across Flagstaff.

The vast majority of hotels and rental accommodations have free Wi-Fi internet access.

There are post offices at the north-east corner of the NAU campus (1014 S Beaver Street) and in the heart of downtown (104 N Agassiz Street).

Health and Safety

The incidence of violent crime (murder, rape, etc.) is relatively low, though burglary and theft from properties is higher than the Arizona average, and high for a city of its size. Gang activity occurs in the centre of Sunnyside, a large neighbourhood to the east of the city. The area south of the railway and north of NAU, known locally as 'South Side', can become dangerous at times, and areas away from restaurants and bars should be avoided at night.

Located at 1200 N Beaver Street, Flagstaff Medical Centre (www.flagstaffmedicalcenter.com), is one of the best regional hospitals in the US. It has an emergency department.

Time

Arizona operates on Mountain Standard Time (MST; GMT-7) throughout the year, though the Navajo Nation applies daylight saving, to be consistent with its New Mexico and Utah sections.

There are approximately 10 hr of daylight in midwinter, and more than 14 hr 30 min in mid June. Because there is no daylight saving, sunset occurs relatively early, even in the summer.

	Mar	Jun	Sept	Dec
Sunrise	06.41	05.12	06.10	07.28
Sunset	18.32	19.43	18.33	17.16

Other Practicalities

Details on health and safety, language, communication, money, power, laundry, culture and respect can be found in the US general section *(pp. 68-69)*.

Opposite Views of the snow capped mountains from the trails in the south of the city
Following Trails, ponds, forests, blue skies; Flagstaff has it all

SPORTS FACILITIES AND SERVICES

With endless off-road running, Flagstaff is an ideal training venue for distance runners, triathletes and athletes in other endurance sports. There are hilly routes, undulating and technical trail routes, and long flat routes running through the NAU campus and into the surrounding Coconino National Forest. The locals use Buffalo Park, just north of the town centre, for tempo and threshold runs. Sedona, at 1,300 m and just a 40-minute drive away, is ideal for high intensity sessions. Facilities are plentiful within Flagstaff itself, with four Tartan tracks dotted around the town, and an indoor 300 m track on the NAU campus. The local runners are very friendly, and the Northern Arizona Trail Runners Association (NATRA) welcomes visitors on their regular Saturday morning runs. Other sports are also well catered for, and cross-training options are plentiful.

TRAINING CAMPS AND TOUR OPERATORS

Flagstaff's NAU was home to the Centre for High Altitude Training which was designated as an official US Olympic Training Site between 2004 and 2009. Despite the closure of the official training centre, the town is home to a number of elite athletes, and a host of national and international teams still carry out training camps in Flagstaff.

Hypo2 Sport (www.hypo2sport.com) organises logistics for international teams and groups of athletes. The training site management company is extremely experienced in providing training camp support to international athletes from across the world, and their list of past clients includes 152 London 2012 Olympians and Paralympians from 22 countries. Hypo2 Sport offers customised packages which can include accommodation, food, ground transport, training facility access, access to the Olympic weightlifting centre, blood profiling, lab testing, physiotherapy and massage treatments, excursions and team-building activities. Accommodation options include hotels, university dormitories and apartments, and vacation rentals. Groups can choose to cook their own food, or avail of the meal card option which provides access to the cafeteria and restaurant on the NAU campus. Hypo2 Sport also arranges camps for teams in other venues across the US.

The annual week-long Adidas McMillan Elite High School Camp (www.mcmillanelite.com) offers talented high school runners the opportunity to get a taste of training life in Flagstaff, meet Olympians, learn new training and strengthening techniques, and hear about post-high school running opportunities. Full board and day-camper options are available. McMillan Running (www.mcmillanrunning.com), the sister organisation of McMillan Elite, organises adult running camps during the summer months which are open to runners of all ages and abilities. Camps are normally four days long, and are a good way to get a taste of what Flagstaff has to offer, and to meet some of Flagstaff's elite athletes. The Run SMART Project (www.runsmartproject.com) also organises running retreats in Flagstaff every summer. The six-day Camps feature the normal group runs, advice sessions and social activities, a run at the Grand Canyon, and classroom discussions led by legendary distance running coach, Dr. Jack Daniels. Group camps work out more expensive than arranging a trip yourself, but the group atmosphere and added extras are the big attraction of this form of trip.

TRAILS AND RUNNING ROUTES

The Flagstaff Urban Trails System (FUTS; www.flagstaff.az.gov/futs) features more than 80 km of paved and unpaved trails that are maintained by the city for recreational and transportation purposes. These link to other trails and form the basis of the renowned Flagstaff trail network. No matter where you're staying, you're never too far away from a trail, and you should have access to one or more trails without having to drive to a trailhead.

Trail runners are very well catered for, with technical single-track trails in most of the forested areas surrounding the city. Mountain runners will find good options in the mountains north of Flagstaff. There are lots of flat routes for distance and marathon runners, and race walkers will find some of the paved sections of FUTS most suitable.

You should be able to find trails by simply stepping out the door and exploring. You'll quickly come across a FUTS trail, a single-track trail or a forest road almost anywhere outside of downtown. Alternatively, get yourself a map, join the local runners on their runs, take part in one of the Flagstaff summer series of trail races, or check out the trail suggestions and descriptions on the NATRA website (www.natra.org).

The Flagstaff Urban Trials and Bikeways Map can be downloaded from the FUTS section of the City of Flagstaff website, or picked up from City of Flagstaff offices and facilities. Detailed trail

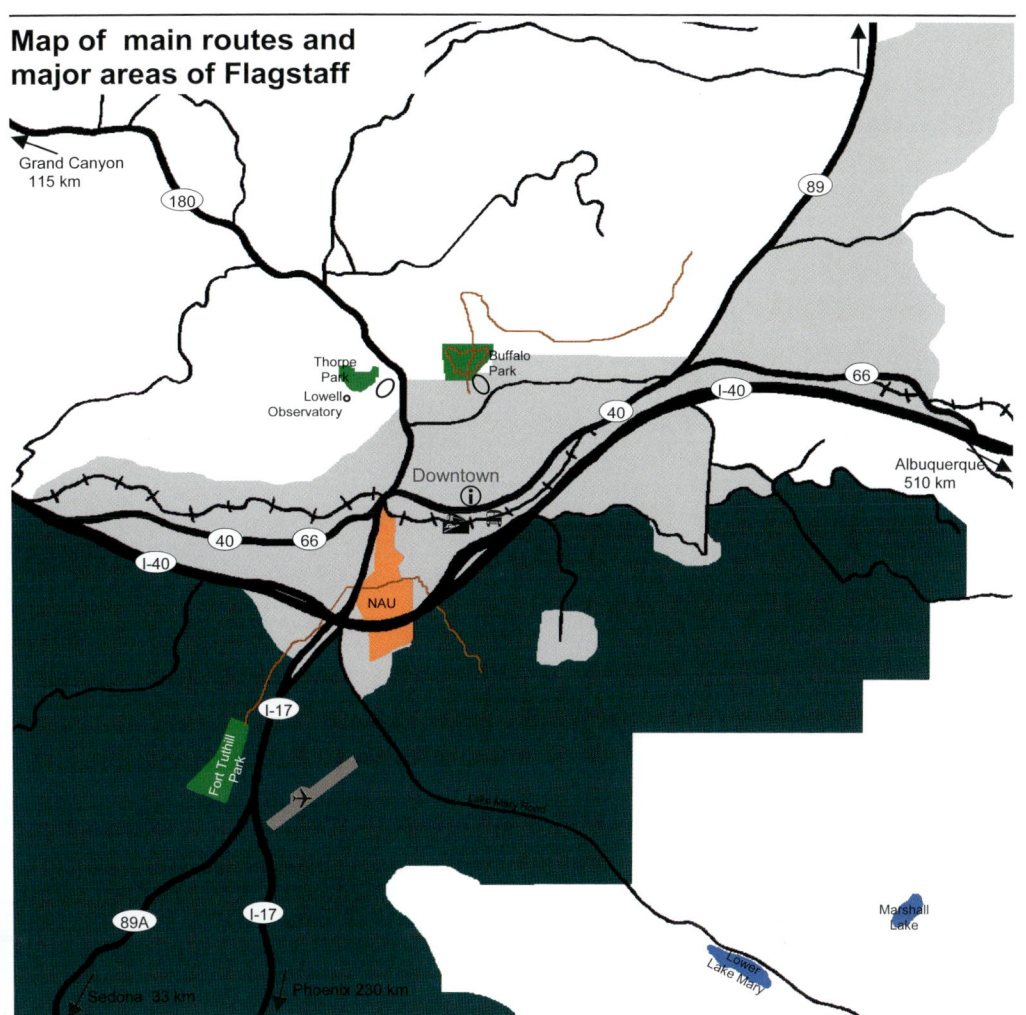

Map of main routes and major areas of Flagstaff

descriptions (including trail length, endpoints, elevation, grade, surface, trails it intersects and photos) are available on the FUTS website. Note that some of the FUTS trails are constructed of concrete or asphalt. The Parks and Recreation section of the Coconino County website (www.coconino.az.gov/parks) has information on other trails in the greater Coconino area, particularly those starting in Fort Tuthill Country Park just south of the city. Flagstaff Trails Map (Emmitt Barks Cartography), which covers hiking, biking and equestrian trails including single-track, forest roads, bikeways and FUTS trails, can be purchased from any outdoor shop. Emmitt Barks Cartography also produces a detailed Sedona Trails Map. Coconino National Forest Maps, which include the area around and to the south of Sedona, can be downloaded from the Red Rock Country website (www.redrockcountry.org) or obtained from any Coconino National Forest Information Centre (nearest one: Thompson Street, Flagstaff) or Ranger District Office. The interactive Flagstaff Recreation Atlas is available under the 'projects' section at www.grail.nau.edu.

South of the city

For those staying in the south of the city, Sinclair Wash, which has its trailheads in Fort Tuthill Country Park, can also be accessed from Walmart on Woodlands Village Boulevard, from NAU, or from Route 66. The trail is mostly flat, links to other trails at either end (including the Arizona Trail in the east), and is off-road apart from a small section between Walmart and NAU.

Cont. on p. 120

North of the city

The Thorpe Park and Buffalo Park trailheads provide good starting points for those staying north of the city. From the buffalo statue near the car park in Buffalo Park, a 3.2 km loop circles the park. The surface is crushed-cinder, and with an almost flat profile, it is popular among local athletes for tempo sessions. From the main loop, several single-track trails lead into the San Francisco Peaks. Thorpe Park is the starting point for the Mars Hill trail, a hilly route around the Lowell Observatory area. The Karen Cooper trail (formerly Rio North), with a starting point in downtown, runs through Thorpe Park.

Further afield

Schultz Creek, just north of the city limits, and Soldiers, which runs around Fort Tuthill Country Park, are good options slightly further afield.

TRACK FACILITIES

There are five tracks in the city. Members of the public can gain access to three of these (Coconino High School, Flagstaff High School and Sinagua Middle School) by purchasing a key card at the Flagstaff Unified School District (FUSD) office on Sparrow Avenue. Check out www.fusd1.org for further details and track open times.

GYM FACILITIES

Facilities at Aquaplex (www.flagstaffaquaplex.org) include a fitness centre with cardiovascular equipment, machine weights and free weights. Day passes are available, though there is a slightly higher rate for visitors from outside Flagstaff.

The well-equipped Flagstaff Athletic Club (www.flagstaffathleticclub.com) has facilities on Route 66 (west), and Country Club Road (east). Facilities include cardiovascular and weight training gyms.

CROSS-TRAINING OPTIONS

Mountain biking and road cycling are good cross-training options. Flagstaff is cycling friendly, and there are some good road routes out of town. The 95 km Mormon Lake Ride (along Lake Mary Road and around the lake) is particularly popular, and Snowbowl Road (off Fort Valley Road/US 180), climbing 900 m in the 24 km from the city to the summit, is perfect if you want a challenge. Mountain biking options are practically endless, with a large choice of flat and technical trails.

OPPOSITE McMillan Elite athletes running in Buffalo Park
PREVIOUS A sample of the trails in Buffalo Park and in the pine forests to the south of the city

Mountain bike rentals, sales and services are available at Flagstaff Bicycle and Fitness and Absolute Bikes (www.absolutebikes.net) on Route 66, Cosmic Cycles on Beaver Street, Single Track Bikes (www.singletrackbikes.com) on Riordan Road and Flagstaff Bicycle Revolution (www.flagbikerev.com) on Mikes Pike. Absolute Bikes also rent road bikes, and Flagstaff Bicycle Revolution sell second-hand bikes.

Swimming is available at Aquaplex (www.flagstaffaquaplex.org), the Wall Aquatics Centre (www.nau.edu) and Flagstaff Athletic Club (www.flagstaffathleticclub.com). Winter sports, including cross country and alpine skiing and snowshoeing are popular in and around Flagstaff during the winter months. The forests provide an extensive network of trails, and the ski resort at the Arizona Snowbowl, just 24 km north of the city, is a popular alpine resort. Open volleyball and basketball sessions are offered at the Aquaplex. Exercise classes are available at Aquaplex and Flagstaff Athletic Club, where there is also a climbing wall (east facility). Some trails in the FUTS network have concrete and asphalt surfaces and are suitable for inline skating.

SPORTS MEDICINE AND SPORTS SCIENCE SUPPORT

Sports massage for individuals, groups and races is available through Flagstaff Sports Massage (www.flagstaffsportsmassage.wordpress.com). They can provide support in hotel conference rooms, or wherever needed within the town, and are the sports massage service provider for Hypo2 Sport. Flagstaff Bone and Joint (www.flagstaffboneandjoint.com) offers sports injury care services. Oxygen consumption and lactate testing are available from Volt Sportlab (www.voltsportlab.com).

LOCAL RACES

Sedona Marathon (www.sedonamarathon.com), with accompanying 5 km, 10 km and half marathon races, is held on scenic Coconino National forest roads, Red Rock country trails and the streets of Sedona in early February. The Flagstaff Summer Series is a popular 6-race series of trail races in the town. Details of these and other trail races can be found on the NATRA website (www.natra.org). Flagstaff Marathon (www.flagstaffnordiccenter.com) is hosted by the Flagstaff Nordic Centre, and is completely off

road. Spaces are limited to 400 runners. For those looking for a real challenge, the Flagstaff Endurance Runs (www.aravaiparunning.com) are 50 mile and 50 km ultramarathon trail events held in the hills above the city.

RUNNING COMMUNITY

With a large population of runners of all abilities based in the town, it is unsurprising that there are a number of different clubs and groups to cater for their needs. McMillan Elite is the Greg McMillan-coached group of elite athletes which includes US internationals Brett Gotcher and Aaron Braun. Many of the McMillan Elite athletes are also part of Team USA Flagstaff, an organisation created to support post-collegiate runners. British Olympian Andrew Lemoncello, and ultramarathon runner Ian Torrence live and train here, and Ryan and Sarah Hall have spent time in Flagstaff. The Japanese female marathon team trained in the city prior to the 2012 Olympic Games and Oregon Track Club athletes sometimes train in Flagstaff. NAU has a competitive distance running squad, and a number of graduates remain in the area.

Team Run Flagstaff (www.teamrunflagstaff.com) is a community running club for athletes of all levels coached by the legendary Jack Daniels and Mike Smith. NATRA (www.natra.org) caters for the region's trail runners. They organise free Saturday morning runs on local trails which visitors can join. Flagstaff Trial Divas and Flagstaff Ultra-Running club also organise group runs (see Facebook). Flagstaff Footnotes (www.flagfootnotes.org) has news and information for the Flagstaff running community. The events page of the Run Flagstaff website (www.runflagstaff.com) details running-related events and social activities.

SUITABILITY FOR OTHER SPORTS

Flagstaff attracts mountain bikers and road cyclists, triathletes, swimmers, and increasingly, high-profile professional sports teams. Hypo2 Sport has hosted swimming, triathlon, Australian Rules football, and water polo athletes.

Cycling Flagstaff has good options for road cyclists; what the city lacks in variety, it more than makes up for in quality. In addition to the Mormon Lake and Snowbowl rides mentioned in the cross-training section, Wupatki National Monument/ Sunset Crater is both scenic and challenging. This 160 km loop is a popular ride among triathletes preparing for Ironman competitions. Cyclists who visit during the winter months, and who want to train away from the elements, can make use of the computraining facility at the Flagstaff Altitude Training Centre (www.flagstaffendurance.com). Flagstaff Biking (www.flagstaffbiking.org) is an excellent resource for cycling in the city and includes details of group rides which visitors can join. Flagstaff Bike Revolution (www.flagbikerev.com) also organises group rides during the summer months.

Swimming The Wall Aquatic Centre (see 'recreation' section of www.nau.edu), based at NAU, has hosted numerous national swimming teams from, among others, Australia, Germany, Italy, Japan, Norway and Denmark. Teams who wish to train at the centre are required to reserve pool time at least one month in advance. Contact the centre (wallaquaticcentre@nau.edu) for further details on scheduling a camp.

Sub-elite swimmers (and triathletes) have the opportunity to train with the masters' swimming programme based at NAU (Northern Arizona Masters). The group, which trains at the Wall Aquatic Centre, offers semester, annual and 'punch-card' membership options for visitors. Further details can be found on the Wall Aquatic Centre section of the NAU website.

Triathlon The running trails, cycling options and swimming facilities combine to make Flagstaff a good venue for triathletes. Open water swimming is available at Lake Mary from late April. Further afield, Lake Powell in Page, and Lake Saguaro, Bartlett Lake and Lake Pleasant near Phoenix provide winter alternatives. The water in these lakes is warm during the summer, and local air temperatures (as high as 45 ºC) are much higher than in Flagstaff. There are a number of triathletes based in the area, and the Flagstaff Altitude Training Centre (www.flagstaffendurance.com) is a good starting point for connecting with the city's triathlon community.

Team sports Sports teams can arrange training camps and facility access through Hypo2 Sport. In recent years, Hypo2 Sport has arranged logistics for high-profile international teams including Australian Rules football squads and the Canadian water polo team. Facilities in the city include outdoor grass and synthetic pitches, and an indoor field with artificial surface at NAU. Hypo2 Sport can arrange access to strength and conditioning facilities which have 10 lifting platforms; ideal for squad training.

OPPOSITE *View of Flagstaff from Mars Hill*

Fabulous Flagstaff
Adapted from the blog, 25 May 2010

This morning was the first morning that I woke up not wanting to leave my current destination. Not even the excitement of seeing a new place could get me over the sadness of leaving Flagstaff behind. Maybe it had something to do with my current trip nearing an end, or maybe it was the dread of repacking the suitcase yet again. Or maybe it was because I genuinely enjoyed my stay here. A trip to the Grand Canyon was the obvious highlight, I also enjoyed exploring a new network of trails, eating good food, and meeting some new people.

The 'unusual animal spotted in the wild count' has also gone up. I saw some elk in the Grand Canyon National Park, and then, when out for a run on Saturday evening, I saw a skunk. I'm just scared that sooner or later I'll come across a snake. I won't need to blog about that though, because I'm pretty sure that my scream will be heard right across the planet. And there definitely won't be time for photos!

I've always believed that a little bit of sunshine and a decent network of soft trails are the best motivators for training hard. Both were in good supply in Flagstaff. They say that no matter where you are in the city you are no more than three minutes from a trail (I prefer that statistic to the similar one about rats). I managed to clock up 120 kilometres in a week here, but after the ecstasy of such an impressive block of training (well by my standards), I was brought crashing down to earth yesterday. Literally! After tripping on a stone, I again managed to perform the face-plant manoeuvre almost perfectly. This time there was no grazing to my now perfectly tanned legs, but I did put a big gash in my hand, and got covered head to toe in dust and dirt. I should have been doing a little less looking at the beautiful scenery, and a little more looking at where I was going. Someday I will learn!

During a five-minute taxi ride to the airport this morning I got to hear about snakes (yes, those things again), Saint Patrick, and Catholicism, from a taxi driver who proclaimed to be Welsh, despite speaking with an American accent, and from what I could gather, never having visited Wales. I was told that there are more Irish in America than there are in Ireland, that the Irish hate the English, and that Clint Eastwood has Irish heritage. The $10 fare was a bargain given that I didn't have to pay for the history lesson!

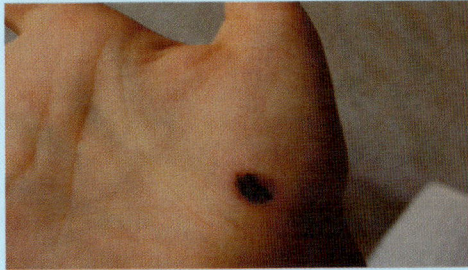

Another injury

The Grand Canyon, pictured from Grand Canyon Village on the South Rim

Things to see and do between training

Despite being a very small city, there is plenty to see and do in Flagstaff. City parks, forests and mountains combine to provide a popular destination for outdoor enthusiasts. Campers, climbers, mountain bikers, hikers and backpackers make use of the extensive trail network throughout the city. Thorpe Park is one of the largest of the city's parks, and among its facilities are tennis, softball, basketball and beach volleyball courts and softball fields. There are picnic areas in a number of the parks.

Flagstaff Extreme Adventure Course (www.flagstaffextreme.com), located at Fort Tuthill Country Park, offers elevated obstacle courses with rope swings, hanging nets, wobbly bridges and other suspended surprises. Skating is available at the Jay Lively Ice Arena (www.flagstaff.az.gov) on Turquoise Drive and there is a climbing wall at Aquaplex (www.flagstaffaquaplex.com). Several companies offer white-water rafting and kayaking tours along the Colorado River west of the city. There are cinemas, bowling alleys and other entertainment centres as you would expect in a university city.

The Lowell Observatory on Mars Hill to the west of downtown offers guided astronomy tours during daytime and in the evenings. It is from the observatory that the planet Pluto was discovered. The Museum of Northern Arizona on the north of the city records the region's natural history and Native American life. The 200-acre Arboretum at Flagstaff features a botanical garden, an environmental research station, and one of the largest collections of high country wildflowers in America. Riordan Mansion State Historic Park, built in 1904, is also worth a visit.

There are several traditional music festivals, classical music performances, open-air theatre productions and cultural events throughout the year. The Navajo and Hopi Festival of Arts and Crafts, the Flagstaff Festival of Science, the Flagstaff Mountain Film Festival and the Northern Arizona Book Festival are just some of the highlights.

Rest day excursions

As one of America's most diverse states, the countryside of Arizona offers incredible choice and variety to travellers interested in travelling beyond the bounds of Flagstaff. A disproportionate number of United States National Parks are located close to Flagstaff, and it is because of this that Flagstaff is often referred to as City of Seven Wonders. The Grand Canyon, Monument Valley, and other well known attractions make a suitable day excursion. Other natural and historical attractions, located within an hour of the town, are suitable trips to fill a spare morning or afternoon. Flagstaff offers the ultimate choice in things to see and do for those spending months, rather than weeks, at altitude.

The Grand Canyon

The Grand Canyon is undoubtedly Arizona's premier attraction and one of the world's most iconic natural wonders. The Canyon has been carved out by the Colorado River and uplifting of the Colorado Plateau, over millions of years, and the depth from rim to river is more than 1,600 m. It is 445 km long and ranges in width from 400 m to 29 km. The Grand Canyon isn't the longest, the widest or even the deepest canyon in the world, but it is by far the most famous and is witnessed by more than 4 million visitors per year. Set in a desert environment, a distinct lack of vegetation adds to the canyon's grandeur and its almost perfectly preserved layers of pink, red and yellow rock provide a view into almost two billion years of geological history.

The South Rim is much easier to access than the North Rim, and consequentially the most crowded. The journey from Flagstaff is approximately 130 km via either US-180 to Valle or I-40 to Williams, before joining AZ-64. Alternatively, the east entrance can be accessed by taking the US-89 north from Flagstaff towards the Navajo Indian Reservation and the Painted Desert and turning left onto AZ-64. Several tour companies operate guided tours from Flagstaff. A cheaper and more flexible option is the Arizona Shuttle Service which operates up to three times per day from Flagstaff Amtrak station to the park. A free shuttle service operates along the South Rim of the canyon. Mule rides, guided hikes, helicopter rides and white-water rafting excursions are all great ways to see the canyon.

Other excursions

In the north of Arizona, towards the border with Utah, there are a number of Native American reservations, national monuments and trading posts. The **Navajo Nation Reservation** *(p. 109)* occupies much of north-east Arizona; **Lake Powell**, America's largest man-made lake, straddles the state border; and **Monument Valley** begins in Navajo country close to the Utah border.

There are a number of Native American cliff dwellings to view at **Walnut Canyon National**

Monument, located just 16 km from Flagstaff. A trail approximately 1.4 km long descends into the canyon past 25 cliff dwellings constructed by the Sinagua cultural group. The Sinagua, who were experts with dealing with droughts and conserving water, left Walnut Canyon around 1250. The Canyon is an area of biodiversity which includes the Arizona black walnut and the prickly pear cactus and almost 400 other plant species. The 180 m deep canyon has been formed by the Walnut Creek which has cut through limestone and sandstone as it flows east to join the Little Colorado River on its way to the Grand Canyon. **Wupatki National Monument** contains one of the finest collections of Native American ruins outside of Colorado's Mesa Verde National Park. The ruins are scattered along a loop drive which also passes Sunset Crater, an extinct volcano. **Sunset Crater Volcano National Monument** is in itself an attraction. The spectacular crater was formed following a main eruption around 1064, and a final eruption in 1260. It is about 30 min drive from Flagstaff. **Barringer Meteor Crater** (www.meteorcrater.com), located just off I-40, approximately 70 km east of Flagstaff, is a well preserved meteor crater with an informative visitor centre. It is not the world's largest meteorite crater, as sometimes claimed, but it is impressive nonetheless. It has a diameter of approximately 1,200 m, is 170 m deep, and has a rim which rises 45 m above the surrounding plain. It is estimated to have been formed from the impact of a nickel–iron meteorite, travelling at about 46,080 kilometres per hour, around 50,000 years ago.

Petrified Forest National Park, situated in the southern extent of the Painted Desert, and accessible along I-40 near Holbrook, east of Flagstaff, contains a colourful landscape frozen in time. An estimated 225 million years ago, fallen trees were carried onto the plain by flood waters, and over time mineral deposits from the water replaced wood cell fibres. Quartz and jasper crystals now fill the spaces within the ancient timber, and preserve the giant trees in the spectacular environment. **The Painted Desert**, which draws its name from the multicoloured layers of sediment which make up the undulating mounds of silt and volcanic ash in this barren environment, stretches north from I-40 towards **Hopi Indian Reservation**. Little Painted Desert, just north of Winslow, offers views of some of the most colourful Painted Desert hills.

A trip to **Sedona**, 48 km south of Flagstaff (on AZ-89a) towards Phoenix, offers a particularly scenic trip through **Oak Creek Canyon**. Sedona itself, a town well known for its beauty, features a dramatic red rock backdrop, numerous art galleries, many shops specialising in Native American arts and crafts and a number of internationally acclaimed restaurants. Its real treasures, however, are in the outdoors and Sedona provides an excellent setting for hiking, mountain biking and off-roading.

The historic **Camp Verde**, cliff dwellings at **Montezuma Castle National Monument**, and **Arcosanti**, an experimental city in the desert, are just some of the attractions off I-17 between Flagstaff and Phoenix.

A NOTE OF LIVING HERE LONG-TERM

Flagstaff is a good place to live long-term and is the training home of many of the best distance runners in the US. The altitude is sufficient to stimulate a response, but low enough that acclimatisation can occur and with 'train low' options within easy reach of the city, it's possible to carry out quality training at any stage of the year. Sedona provides a winter training alternative when there is snow in Flagstaff. An athlete is unlikely to get bored of the trail options in and around the city. There is good sports medicine support and plenty of cross-training options for injured athletes. Getting out for races may be a little difficult, and flights to most destinations involve a connection in Phoenix. The variety of things to do, and places to see adds to Flagstaff's appeal, and the established running community makes it easy to make friends and settle into life in Flagstaff. There are employment opportunities for those who have the right to work in the US, and the cost of living isn't extortionate.

FURTHER INFORMATION

The Flagstaff Visitor centre is located by the Amtrak station on Route 66. Area maps, visitor guides and event calendars are available from the centre, which also contains a small gift shop. Useful information can be found on the Flagstaff Convention and Visitors Bureau website (www.flagstaffarizona.org), the City of Flagstaff website (www.flagstaff.az.gov), and Go-Arizona (www.go-arizona.com). Flagstaff 365 (www.flagstaff365.com) has listings for movies, stage productions, outdoor activities, sports events, live music concerts, art and photo exhibitions and other events. An interactive Discovery Map, which includes locations of attractions and services, can be accessed online at www.flagmap.com (paper copies of which can be picked up in hotels and visitor centres).

Boulder

Boulder is a small city located next to the eastern foothills of the Rocky Mountains. It boasts a huge variety of trails, excellent gym facilities, a comprehensive network of sports medicine support, and all the convenience of a hip university town. There is a good choice of food and accommodation to suit all tastes and budgets. The athlete-friendly city is home to BolderBoulder, one of America's most famous road races, and has become a top triathlon training base in recent years.

Boulder, US (1,655 m)

Boulder is located in Boulder County in the State of Colorado, just 40 km north-west of Denver. It sits in the Boulder Valley at the base of the Rocky Mountain foothills and on the edge of the Great Plains. Just west of the city, the distinctive Flatirons form an iconic backdrop. The city has a population of just under 100,000, and is famous for its colourful Western history, liberal views and laws, and high quality of life ratings.

The Boulder Valley, which was first inhabited by Native Americans, attracted gold seekers in the 19th century, and Boulder County's first non-native settlement was established near the entrance to Boulder Canyon in 1858. The Boulder City Town Company was formed the following year, and over 4,000 land lots were put on sale. Boulder City grew as a supply and entertainment base for the miners heading to the mountains in search of silver and gold.

A need for economic stability to continually attract residents and businesses saw the establishment of railroads, schools, hospitals and a town government. Bolder was incorporated as a town in 1871 when the city government was formalised. The University of Colorado was 'awarded' to Boulder in 1874, paving the way for further development, and by 1882 Boulder was incorporated as a city. Motorway links with Denver and development of a tourist industry saw continued growth and development, and today, the city is one of the most densely populated urban areas in Colorado,

Boulder Creek, the main body of water flowing through Boulder, was named after the large granite boulders which were washed into the creek over the years. The creek gave Boulder its name, rather than the other way round.

Author's verdict

Springtime in Boulder was good for the soul, and combining my trip with participation in the BolderBoulder made for a memorable stay. Located within easy reach of Denver, but close to the Rocky Mountain wilderness, Boulder provides the perfect link between urban conveniences and rural beauty and tranquillity. There is an excellent variety of trails, though I did need some help finding these, and access to a car (or bicycle) would have been useful. Boulder is quite a 'hip' city, and there are many trendy places to hang out in between training. Snow may be a minor inconvenience during the winter months, but the area becomes an endless playground for outdoor enthusiasts during the bright spring and mild summer. A week wasn't long enough to explore all that Boulder has to offer, and I would definitely consider returning.

Running ★★★★★ - Good variety of trails within easy reach of the town; car or bicycle required to get to most trailheads; mixture of terrains and surfaces; thriving running culture; good facilities and cross-training options.

Convenience ★★★★★ - Close to a major international airport; car or bicycle required to get to best trailheads; city somewhat spread out; some snow during the winter months.

Safety ★★★★★ - Low levels of violent crime, no major disease or safety risk

Cost ★★★★★ - Cost of living moderately high by US standards; good choice of flights and transport into the city; car useful but not essential.

Cultural experience ★★★★★ - Liberal, vibrant, active and youthful city, though there's less to see than in some other American destinations.

Things to do between training ★★★★★ - Many cool places to relax in between training, events and festivals to attend, and activities to get involved in; shopping opportunities in downtown Denver; outdoor activities and sightseeing in Rocky Mountain National Park.

Suitability for solo travellers ★★★★★ - Friendly, fitness-mad locals, and large running community, so solo travellers, who are willing to integrate, should have no problems.

Must do Take part in the BolderBoulder; run some of the trails in Chautauqua Park by the iconic flatirons; hang out at the Pearl Street Mall
Ideal for Young runners and triathletes who want to spend some time living in a trendy fitness-obsessed city.

BELOW and PREVIOUS Some of the beautiful scenery along the South Boulder Creek Trail

Colorado
www.colorado.com

People
Almost 4.5 million of Colorado's population of just over five million live along the Front Range Urban Corridor on the north-eastern edge of the Rocky Mountains. Hispanics and Latinos, mostly Mexican-Americans, make up more than 20 percent of the population, and it is estimated that approximately 14 percent of people aged five or over speak only Spanish in the home. Colorado, has the lowest rate of obesity in the US.

Places
Colorado encompasses the major part of the Southern Rocky Mountains, the western extent of the Great Plains and the north-eastern corner of the Colorado Plateau. It has four National Parks, seven National Monuments and a number of other protected federal lands. Colorado is the highest state in the US, with no point below 1,000 m and an average altitude of 2,070 m. Denver is the state capital.

Practicalities
Colorado operates on Mountain Standard Time (MST; GMT-7), with daylight saving between second Sunday of March and first Sunday of November. The main urban areas of Colorado form a line along the eastern edge of the Rocky Mountains (Front Range Urban Corridor), with easy drives between the main towns and cities along I-25. Travel to towns in the west and the south-west of the state is more difficult and cities outside of the state are usually accessed by air. Rural freeway maximum speed limits are between 65 and 75 miles per hour (104-120 kph) and as low as 25 miles per hour (40 kph) on residential streets.

Possibilities
People come to Colorado for the great outdoors. The Rocky Mountains provide a playground for skiers, hikers, cyclists, and runners. BolderBoulder and Leadville 100 are popular annual events. Boulder and Colorado Springs are easily accessible and emerging altitude training sites such as Estes Park and Mancos provide additional choice for those who want to sample the Rocky Mountains. With good transport links it's easy to get to sea-level races across the US.

Did you know? The popular 1980s sitcom *Mork & Mindy* was set and shot in Boulder. The New York Deli on Pearl Street and the house at 1619 Pine Street featured prominently.

Getting in
Boulder's proximity to, and excellent transport links with, Denver, make it particularly easy to get to. Denver is served by a major international airport, Greyhound bus services and Amtrak train connections.

By air
Denver International airport (DEN), often referred to as DIA, opened in 1995. It is the largest airport by area in the US, has the longest public-use runway in the country, and is one of the busiest airports in the world. It is situated 40 km north-east of downtown Denver, and 70 km from Boulder. It is United Airlines fourth-largest hub, and the main hub for the commuter airline Great Lakes Airlines, and the budget carrier Frontier Airlines. There are direct flights to Frankfurt, London, Tokyo, most US cities and many cities in Canada and Mexico.

Boulder is an easy drive from the airport via the E-470 (toll road) and US-36. The journey takes approximately 50 min. The E-470 is a cashless toll and you should check toll procedures with the car hire agency before making the journey. Most of the major companies operate car hire from the airport.

SkyRide, the Regional Transportation District's airport express bus service, operates frequent services throughout the Denver-Aurora and Boulder areas. Route AB serves Boulder, Louisville, Superior, Broomfield and Westminster. It stops at Table Mesa park-and-ride in south-east Boulder, and makes various stops along Broadway, before terminating at Boulder Transit Centre (14th Street and Walnut). SkyRide picks up and drops off passengers at both the east and west side of the Jeppesen Terminal. The journey between there and downtown Boulder takes approximately 1 hr during off-peak times, and anything up to 2 hr at peak times.

Taxis are available from the airport to Boulder, but are very expensive and should only be considered if you are travelling in a group.

Note that when flying out of Denver, it can take a considerable length of time to get through security and to your gate. Allow adequate time, even if you are only flying within America.

By car
Boulder is located north-west of Denver, and just west of I-25 which runs north to south through the state, and connects the cities of Denver (where I-

25 intersects I-70 running east to west through the state), Colorado Springs and Pueblo. Unless driving south from Wyoming, travel to Boulder by road is likely to be via Denver.

Travel by road from Denver is via US-36 (Denver–Boulder Turnpike). Despite being called the Denver–Boulder Turnpike, this section of the US-36 no longer has a toll. The journey takes approximately 40 min.

Colorado Springs is 160 km (90 min) from Boulder; Pueblo, at 230 km, is just over 2 hr away; and the journey from Grand Junction, 410 km away, takes over 4 hr. Flying tends to be more convenient than driving from anywhere outside of Colorado.

By bus

The nearest Greyhound stop is on 19th Street (near Union Station) in Denver. Denver is well connected with other cities within the Greyhound network. Services to and from Mexico are operated by Autobuses Americanos, which links with the wider Greyhound network. Autobuses Americanos services stop at both Denver Station and Denver AAU Broadway (2147 N Broadway).

The Regional Transportation District (RTD) 'B' Route buses (B, BF, BMX, BV, BX) connect Denver with Boulder. Journey time is in the region of 50 min for express services (BX) and 60–65 min for other services. Buses leave from Market Street Station (near Union Station), and Chestnut Place and 17th Street (convenient for light rail transfers within Denver). Buses stop at Table Mesa Park-n-Ride (which may be more convenient for accommodation south-east of downtown) and other stops along Broadway on the way to Boulder Transit Centre (14th Street and Walnut).

By train

There is currently no passenger railway serving Boulder though a commuter rail service is planned to connect Denver, Boulder and Longmont from 2014. Amtrak's California Zephyr service stops in Denver once a day on its journey between Emeryville in the San Francisco Bay Area of California, and Chicago. Major cities along the route include Sacramento, Reno, Salt Lake City and Omaha. The service also stops in Fraser and Granby in the Rocky Mountains just west of Boulder, though connecting services from there are more difficult than from Denver. At the time of publishing, Denver's main train station, Union Station (1701 Wynkoop Street), is closed for major renovations, and is due to reopen as a major transport hub in summer 2014. Trains currently arrive at a temporary station at 1800 21st Street, just behind Union Station.

GETTING AROUND

While Boulder is not a big city, getting around is not always possible on foot. Many shops, restaurants and businesses are centred around Pearl Street, the 29th Street Mall, and the Hill area west of the University of Colorado (CU) main campus. The larger supermarkets, many of the sports facilities, and the best trailheads are located away from downtown. Free maps of the city are available from hotels and other businesses. The Boulder Chamber of Commerce map, which covers the entire city, is particularly detailed.

By bus

The Regional Transportation District (RTD) is a mass transit system which operates across Boulder, Denver and the surrounding towns. Express routes, referred to as 'HOP', 'SKIP', 'JUMP', 'BOUND', 'DASH' and 'STAMPEDE', run frequently (up to every 10 min during peak times), and other routes operate every 15–30 min. Regional routes connect Boulder to the nearby cities of Denver (B/BX/DM/HX/S/T), Longmont (J/BOLT) and Golden (GS). Fare, route and schedule information can be obtained on the RTD website (www.rtd-denver.com)

By car

While a car is useful for getting to trailheads, driving in downtown can be frustrating due to heavy traffic, large numbers of cyclists and pedestrians, and difficulty finding parking. Car hire is available through AVIS, Enterprise, Budget and Hertz in Boulder, or from any of the main companies at Denver International Airport.

By bicycle

Boulder is a renowned bicycle-friendly city and many locals commute by bicycle. Hundreds of kilometres of lanes, paths and routes form a network with year-round access, and dozens of bike underpasses facilitate safe travel throughout the city. Personalised bike routes can be mapped on the Go Bike Boulder website (www.gobikeboulder.net).

Bikes (comfort, road and mountain) can be hired from Full Cycle (www.fullcyclebikes.com) which has premises on Pearl Street and on 13th Street, and other bike shops around the city. For those looking to cycle purely as a means of transport, Boulder B-cycle (www.boulder.bcycle.com)

operates a bike hire system similar to those operated in other cities around the world. Select a bike from one of the many stations around the city, cycle to where you need to get to, and return the bike to a station. Bikes are free for up to 60 min use.

Weather and when to visit

Boulder has a relatively dry climate, classified as semi-arid, and experiences many sunny days each year. The mountains in the west have a drying effect on the air and protect the city from precipitation during the winters, which are cold. Occasional snowfall does occur (total average of 220 cm per year; mostly between Nov and Apr), but strong sunshine often melts the shallow snow during the day. January and December are the coldest months with average daily highs less than 8° C and average lows of -6 to -7° C. May, with an average of 12 rain days, is the wettest month. June to August is the warmest phase of the year (monthly average daily highs 28-31° C) and May and October are relatively warm.

The late spring, summer and early autumn months are the best times to visit. A large number of fitness facilities can support training at any time of the year, but runners visiting the city will want to enjoy the many fabulous trails on offer, and this is best done when there is no snow on the ground. Many runners have BolderBoulder on their bucket-list of races. Participation in the Memorial-Day race can easily be combined with a training stint in

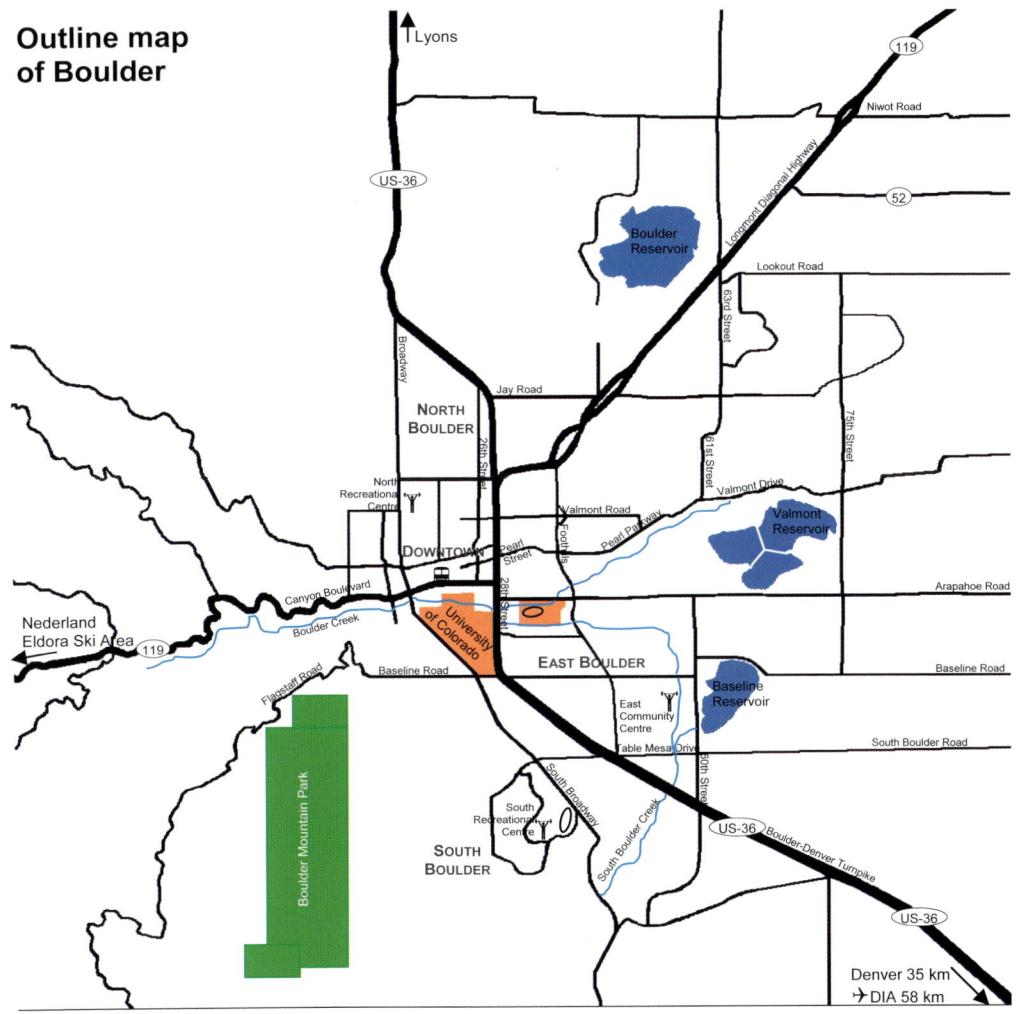

the city. There is a special buzz around town on race weekend, and with many extra visitors in the city at that time, booking accommodation well in advance is advised.

Accommodation

There are a number of good hotels, inns, guesthouses and motels, many of them located close to the downtown and university areas. Accommodations are listed on the Boulder Convention and Visitors Bureau website (www.bouldercoloradousa.com) and the Boulder Hotel/Motel Association website (www.boulderlodging.com). A number of the hotels offer suites and extended stay options and many offer rooms with kitchens or kitchenettes (see www.boulderlodging.com for list of hotels with cooking facilities).

HomeAway (www.homeaway.co.uk) lists more than 150 rental accommodations in Boulder. There is a good variety of 1–4 bedroom properties, including houses, condominiums and apartments. Many properties are located in the downtown area, though there is also a good choice of properties in the foothills to the east of the city, where the altitude is higher and trails closer. There are many advantages to staying outside of the city, so long as you have access to your own transport to get to shops and other amenities. Many properties offer nightly, weekly and monthly rates.

Food

Boulder boasts an eclectic mix of restaurants including those that serve contemporary American, Mexican and Asian cuisines, pasta and pizza, and sushi and Japanese foods. Restaurants are plentiful along the Pearl Street Mall in downtown, in the Twenty Ninth Street Retail District and in the Hill District around the university. There are also restaurants in both North and South Boulder. Plentiful cafes, breakfast bars, bakeries, and sandwich shops, provide delicious treats, and a great environment to relax in between training. Many restaurants endeavour to source ingredients locally, ensuring that food comes straight from farm to table. Local, fresh and organic foods typify Boulder dining.

Restaurant listing can be found in the Downtown Boulder guidebook (www.boulderdowntown.com) and on the Boulder Convention and Visitors Bureau website (www.bouldercoloradousa.com). More than 600 Boulder restaurants and eateries are listed on www.menupix.com, with restaurants categorised by area and by cuisine, and menus included in many cases.

Among Colorado's best produce are melons, cherries, sweetcorn, chilli peppers and peaches. Buffalo, freshwater trout, and lamb are all deeply associated with Colorado, and fresh game, including quail, rabbit, moose, elk and venison are common. Rocky Mountain oysters have nothing to do with seafood, and are in fact bull and sheep testicles, battered and pan-fried.

Eating in is a great option for those with cooking facilities. Supermarkets tend to be found south and east of downtown. Fresh produce can be purchased at the farmers' market which is held every Wednesday evening and Saturday morning (Apr–Oct) on 13th Street in downtown, and in various speciality seafood, oriental and vegetable shops around the city.

Shopping

Pearl Street Mall, a pedestrian area which stretches four blocks in downtown, is a social hotspot. It has a variety of restaurants and specialty shops, and, at the weekends and during summer, features a number of street performers. Beyond the mall, Pearl Street's charming East End (between 15th Street and 21st Street) has an array of restaurants, unique boutiques, bookstores and art and gift shops. The street's West End, located between 8th Street and 11th Street, also has a range of shops and restaurants. There are few grocery or department stores in downtown.

The Hill, next to the university, is a historic shopping area which features some the city's landmark stores. A retail area known as Twenty Ninth Street (www.twentyninthstreet.com) opened east of downtown in October 2006. It features a range of shops and services, including a branch of Macy's department store. Listings of shops, services and businesses can be found at www.shopinboulder.com.

There are many running shops, outdoor stores and general sports shops. Boulder Running Company (www.boulderrunningcompany.com), located on Pearl Street, stocks a broad range of running footwear, clothing and accessories. Fleet Feet Sports (www.fleetfeetboulder.com), on Broadway Street, sells running, cycling, swimming and triathlon kit, footwear and accessories, and offers bike case, wetsuit and snowshoe rentals. Newton Running (www.newtonrunning.com), a Boulder-based running shoe manufacturer, has a laboratory and retail outlet on Walnut Street.

Other sports shops in the area include REI Boulder (www.rei.com), an outdoor and sport store on 28th Street; Colorado Multisport (www.coloradomultisport.com), located on Canyon Boulevard and specialising in high-performance cycling and triathlon bikes, components and clothing; Pro Peloton (www.propeloton.com), an elite road bike and racing shop on 13th Street; and High Point Swim (www.highpointswim.com), which sells swimwear and wetsuits, is located on Pearl Street.

COMMUNICATION

Mobile phone access is good in the city, though signal is generally weak in Boulder Canyon.

Practically every hotel and inn offers free Wi-Fi access. Wi-Fi access is also available in some of the city's leisure centres, and in a number of cafes including Brewing Market Coffee at various locations around the city and Red Rock Coffeehouse in North Boulder

There is a post office on 15th Street, just south of the Pearl Street Mall. Other post offices are located in North Broadway Shopping Centre, at the junction between Broadway and College Avenue, at the junction between Valmont Road and 55th Street, and on Moorhead Avenue near Table Mesa Drive.

HEALTH AND SAFETY

Boulder has a low crime rate, and no particularly seedy neighbourhoods. Common sense should be used and females are advised not to walk alone on University Hill or near Pearl Street Mall after midnight. University Hill and downtown Boulder can become rowdy at night.

There is a slight chance of encountering a mountain lion (cougar), black bear or rattlesnake when running. Fatal attacks on humans are very rare, and cougars in particular are reclusive and avoid people. However, it is advised to remain vigilant, keep to designated trails, and never approach a wild animal.

Rattlesnakes tend to hide in long grass. Avoid grass verges and never leave designated trails. Rattlesnakes rarely bite unless provoked, and any snakes spotted should be given a wide berth. Rattlesnake bites are venomous but are rarely fatal if treated promptly. If bitten by a snake, take note of its colour, patterning and any other defining features, so that the correct anti-venom can be administered promptly.

Severe floods, due to extreme rainfall, hit Boulder and surrounding towns in September 2013, and thousands of people had to be evacuated from the area. Such heavy rain is unusual, and flooding is uncommon. In the case of such natural disasters, it is important to heed warnings, and to evacuate early where possible.

Boulder Community Hospital is the city's main hospital, and has facilities at the junction between North Broadway and Balsam (main hospital), and at the junction between Arapahoe Avenue and Foothills Parkway (Boulder Community Foothills Hospital). Both have 24-hour accident and emergency departments.

TIME

Boulder operates on Mountain Standard Time (MST; GMT-7), with daylight saving between the second Sunday of March and the first Sunday of November. Daylight hours range from 9 hr 20 min in mid December, to 15 hr in mid June.

	Mar	Jun	Sept	Dec
Sunrise	07:13	05:31	06:42	07:16
Sunset	19:07	20:31	19:11	16:36

OTHER PRACTICALITIES

Details on health and safety, language, communication, money, power, laundry, culture and respect can be found in the US general section *(pp. 68-69)*.

BELOW View of the iconic Flatirons
FOLLOWING Beautiful scenery just off South Boulder Creek Trail

SPORTS FACILITIES AND SERVICES

In addition to the excellent training facilities and spectacular trails and running routes on offer, Boulder is welcoming to athletes. There are sports shops, physiotherapists, and gym facilities. Access to a major international airport makes it easy to get out for competitions. For those looking to race at altitude, BolderBoulder is one of the most famous road races in the world, and the Leadville 100, held in the nearby Rocky Mountains, is one of the world's best trail ultras. Many athletes and triathletes are based in the city throughout the year. The altitude, at just 1,655 m, is slightly on the low side.

The Boulder Parks and Recreation Department's recreation guide, which can be downloaded from www.boulderparks-rec.org or picked up from the Parks and Recreation Administrative Office on Broadway Street, is a useful starting point for locating facilities and sporting activities. The City of Boulder's Parks and Recreation Department has three sports complexes, each with a swimming pool, fitness equipment, a weight training area and sports facilities.

TRAINING CAMPS AND TOUR OPERATORS

Boulder Wave (www.boulderwave.com) has been organising training camp logistics in Boulder since 1993. They provide training and management support to elite athletes, and runners of all levels, who are looking to make the most of their time in Boulder.

Mark Allen online (www.markallenonline.com) hosts three-day triathlon training camps and Boulder Performance Network (www.boulderperformance.net) includes training-camp hosting, seminars and workshops among its extensive list of services.

TRAILS AND RUNNING ROUTES

Some 150 square kilometres of recreational open space, nature reserves and conservation land surrounds the city. Well-kept hiking and running trails transverse those open spaces, and provide an almost unlimited variety or trails and running routes.

Boulder Book Store (Pearl Street) and Gallery Map Store (Broadway Street) sell maps and guides for the local area. The Boulder Open Space and Mountain Parks (www.osmp.org), Boulder County Open Space (www.bouldercounty.org), Boulder Trail Runners (www.bouldertrailrunners.org), Pro Trails (www.protrails.com) and Colorado Runner (www.runcolo.com) websites have detailed maps and trail descriptions. All Open Space and Mountain Parks trailheads have bike racks, so it's possible to cycle to the trailheads and park your bike while you run.

There is a good mix of surfaces and terrains for track and road runners. Trail runners will be at home among the trails around the Flatirons, and further into the Rocky Mountains. Mountain runners will find many hills within easy reach of the city, but will have to drive deeper into the mountains to get race-specific terrain. Race walkers have lots of flat options including Boulder Creek Path, South Boulder Creek Trail, and along the East Boulder Trail, but should note that the surface of these trails is mostly crushed dirt. Coaches who want to cycle alongside their athletes should be able to do so along the East Boulder Trail, the streets of North Boulder and most of the 'up Canyon' trails. Bikes are not allowed on the South Boulder Creek Trail, and some other trails.

In September 2013, just prior to publication, heavy floods in the area caused severe damage to the trails. Every effort is being made to repair and reopen the trails as quickly as possible, but it may take some time for all the trails to recover fully. Trail status can be found on the Boulder County Open Space and Boulder Open Space and Mountain Parks websites.

Boulder Creek Path
Boulder Creek Path runs along the banks of Boulder Creek through the centre of the city, and is popular among walkers, runners and cyclists. From downtown, the path can be accessed at Civic Park on Broadway Street, just between Arapaho Avenue and Canyon Avenue. Part of the path is concrete, and it can become crowded.

South Boulder Creek Trail and Buffalo Ranch
The South Boulder Creek Trail offers a flat running route into the countryside. The trail runs south from the intersection between Baseline Road and Cherryvale Road (Bobolink trailhead), across South Boulder Road, and on towards Marshall Road. There is also an access point from the East Boulder Community centre. The trail is just over 5 km long. There are some gates to be opened and closed along the trail, making it unsuitable for long repetitions or hard tempo runs, but the flat terrain and well-maintained surface make a pleasant change from the usually rocky and undulating trails of the foothills.

From the Marshall Road end of the trail you can turn right, run a couple of minutes down the road and join the Buffalo Ranch cross country course and trail system. The Buffalo Ranch entrance, marked 'Rich's Tennis School', is located close to the Table Mesa exit of US-36, though entry can also be gained via the trails that link to the course. The area can be used for off-road sessions, for warm-up and cool-down when training at Fairview High School track, or for a short recovery run. There is a challenging hill on the course, and the trail is rocky in places.

Chautauqua Park trailhead

Chautauqua Park is situated at the base of the Flatirons rock formations at Baseline Avenue and 8th Street. Interconnecting trails that start here include Flatirons Loop, Bluebell Road, Enchanted Mesa, Baseline Trail and Chautauqua Trail. The trails are undulating and sometimes technical, and offer spectacular views of both the city and the Flatirons.

Also offering spectacular scenery a little further south is the extensive network of trails starting at the Marshall Mesa, Greenbelt Plateau and Flatirons Vista trailheads (access off South Foothills Highway).

Up Canyon

Canyon Boulevard (CO-119), which runs east–west through the city just north of the CU campus, becomes Boulder Canyon Drive as it winds up the foothills to the west of Boulder. A number of trailheads, including Switzerland and Magnolia, lie just off this section of road, and these trails are referred to as 'up Canyon'.

Switzerland is a non-technical dirt-road route, with some climbs. It starts from the parking area at the base of Sugarloaf Mountain. To get to the trailhead, take Boulder Canyon Drive west for 8 km, and turn right on Sugarloaf road (very sharp right turn, almost heading back the direction you came). Climb along Sugarloaf Mountain Road for approximately 8 km, turn right, and continue approximately 1.5 km uphill to the parking area. From the car park, you can run out-and-back routes along either the north or south section of the Switzerland Trail, or do a complete lap by linking via Pennsylvania Gulch Road.

Magnolia Road is one of Boulder's iconic routes, immortalised in *Running with the Buffaloes* (Lear, 2003). From the city, take Boulder Canyon Drive and after approximately 8 km, turn left onto Magnolia Road (opposite Sugarloaf Mountain Road). Continue along Magnolia Road, until the paved road turns to dirt. Parking is available at this point. The section of the road which follows, features rolling hills, and a substantial gain in elevation. The road is approximately 12 km long to the highway just south of Nederland, and is run in an out-and-back fashion. Those who are doing a long run can cross the highway, and continue along what is the flattest section of the road.

Teller Farm/East Boulder Trail

On the east of the city, Teller Farm trailheads provide access to the East Boulder Trail. From Teller Farm South Trailhead (off Arapahoe Road between 75th and 95th Streets), head north through farmland along a very slightly downhill crushed dirt trail. After approximately 3 km, you will reach Teller Farm North Trailhead. Turn left, run through the trailhead car park, across Valmont Drive, and join the remainder of the trail. Just over 5.5 km into the run, the trail narrows and begins to climb. The trail continues for a further 4 km, climbing all the way to Gunbarrel Farm Trailhead. This trail is good for long runs, and the first part is ideal for tempo runs and sessions with just one gate, approximately 3 km in, to negotiate.

North Boulder

Boulder Reservoir Park in North Boulder is a popular area for recreation. There is a trail around both the reservoir and the nearby Coot Lake, though the best option in North Boulder is the network of dirt roads which criss-cross farmland in the area. Tom Watson Park, located off 63rd Street, has toilets, showers and water fountains, and is a good starting point, though you could park on the side of the road and start anywhere. There are some small hills and a general elevation gain as you head north. From the Park, turn right onto 63rd Street, and explore the roads in the area. Niwot Road and 63rd Street are paved, but most of the other roads are not.

TRACK FACILITIES

There are synthetic tracks at CU's Frank Potts Field (north of Colorado Avenue between Foothills Parkway and 30th Street), which has limited early morning and late afternoon open public access (www.cubuffs.com for further details), and at Fairview High School (on Greenbriar Boulevard near South Boulder Recreational Centre).

FOLLOWING Various trails in South Boulder

GYM FACILITIES

Many of the city's excellent gym and fitness facilities offer guest access or punch-card memberships suitable for visitors to the city.

Each of the City of Boulder's Parks and Recreation Department's three sports complexes (North Recreational Centre at 3170 Broadway Street, South Recreational Centre at 1360 Gillaspie Drive and East Community Centre at 5660 Sioux Drive) have excellent fitness and weight training facilities. Cardiovascular equipment includes treadmills, arc-trainers, steppers, rowing machines and spin bikes and weight training rooms have machine and free weights, exercise balls, foam rollers, and balance discs. The centres offer annual, monthly and off-peak memberships, 10, 20 and 40 punch passes and daily drop-in access. A variety of exercise classes are offered, including a specialised Pilates workshop for runners, cyclists and triathletes.

Colorado Athletic Club-Flatirons (www.flatironathleticclub.com), formerly known as Flatiron Athletic Club, is located on Thunderbird Drive in South Boulder, and within easy access to the trails in the south of the city. Dave Scott, a six-time Hawaiian Ironman champion, coaches out of the club, which is the centre of Boulder's triathlon community. Fitness facilities include cardiovascular equipment (treadmills, stationary bikes, cross-trainers and elliptical machines, steppers, versa-climbers, rowing machines and a Vasa swim bench), a large weight training room, a 20-piece Precor circuit, designated core and stretching rooms, a swimming pool, courts for racquet sports, sports halls and a 1/8 mile (approximately 200 m) jogging track. Daily fee, punch card and extended period guest passes are available for non-members.

Body Dynamics (www.bodydynamics.net), on Canyon Boulevard, offers a wide range of studio-based fitness classes, including Pilates, TRX and Kangoo, and Rally Sport Health and Fitness Club (www.rallysportboulder.com), located on 29th Street, offers facilities, fitness classes, and other services.

CROSS-TRAINING OPTIONS

It's not surprising to learn that there are many cross-training opportunities available in a city so popular among triathletes. Cycling is popular and there are excellent mountain bike and road cycling routes from the town. Bikes can be hired from Full Cycle (www.fullcyclebikes.com) at their Pearl Street or Hill (13th Street) branches, and from University Bicycles (www.ubikes.com) on Pearl Street. Swimming is available at any of the three city-owned indoor pools located at the sports complexes, at the outdoor Scott Carpenter (50 m; 30th Street), and Spruce (25 yards; Spruce Street) pools, at Colorado Athletic Club-Flatirons (25 m heated outdoor pool), and at Elks Club (25 m; off 28th Street). The City of Boulder's three sports complexes have cardiovascular training equipment, run a large variety of exercise classes and offer drop-in basketball and volleyball sessions. There are racquetball courts at the North and South centres, an indoor climbing and bouldering wall at the East facility, beach volleyball, disc golf and inline hockey facilities at the South centre and softball, baseball and multi-use grass fields around the city. There are public tennis courts at 14 different locations. To book one of these, or any of the many city owned sports facilities, contact the City of Boulder's Parks and Recreation Department. Valmont Bike Park is also city-owned, and is free to access. Colorado Athletic Club-Flatirons offers tennis, squash and racquetball courts, and many other fitness and leisure clubs provide similar cross-training opportunities.

SPORTS MEDICINE AND SPORTS SCIENCE SUPPORT

Boulder Centre for Sports Medicine (www.bouldersportsmedicine.org), located on Mapleton Avenue, offers physical therapy, sports massage, sports medicine, nutrition, physiological testing, running gait analysis, 3D bike fittings, coaching, and alter G and supplemental oxygen training. Endurance Sports Therapy (www.sportsmassageboulder.com), located within Body Dynamics on Canyon Boulevard, and Massage Boulder (www.massageboulder.com), located at Marine Street Wellness Centre on Marine Street, offer therapeutic and sports massage. Body Dynamics also offers physical therapy services. Facilitated Wellness (www.facilitatedwellness.com), based at Colorado Athletic Club-Flatirons, and Massage Specialists (www.massagespecialists.com) on Broadway Street, provide massage, acupuncture and other muscular treatments. Chiropractic services are available through North Boulder Chiropractic (www.northboulderchiropractic.com).

Boulder's many sports centres and clubs offer sport-specific classes which can be used in injury prevention and management. Dave Scott runs a strength and injury prevention class for endurance athletes, and City of Boulder's recreation centres run Pilates classes for endurance athletes.

Fuelary (www.fuelary.com), a walk-in sports recovery service on 29th Street, provides compression boots, ice baths, massages, chiropractic treatments and other recovery and injury prevention services. Nutrition advice and support is available through Forbes-Grayson (www.forbesnutrition.com) and Julie Emmerman (www.julieemmerman.com) is a clinical psychologist who specialises in providing support to athletes.

Of all the venues included in this book, Boulder has by far the best choice of sports medicine and sports science services. A range of practitioners, including nutritionists, psychologists, biomechanists and physiotherapists, operate in the city, and a quick internet search will help locate any specialist that you require.

LOCAL RACES

Colorado has an extensive race calendar, catering for athletes of all levels. While BolderBoulder is the annual race highlight, there are many other races in which visitors can participate.

BolderBoulder (www.bolderboulder.com) is probably the most famous race at altitude in the world. The annual 10 km has been held on Memorial Day every year since 1979. With over 50,000 participants, it is one of the largest road races in the world, and the international race, which follows the mass-participation event, has one of the largest non-marathon prize funds in road racing. Three competitors from each participating nation run for the lowest accumulated time, and a share of the jackpot. All races finish in Folsom Field, CU's main stadium. The route is relatively flat, and congestion is avoided as waves of time-matched runners are started at two-minute intervals.

Ultra and trail runners have access to a great choice of races. Held at altitudes of between 2,800 m and 3,850 m in the Rocky Mountains, 180 km south-west of Boulder, Leadville 100 Trail (www.leadvilleraceseries.com), is the ultimate challenge. Most of the 100 mile out-and-back course is on forest trails.

Other races in the city and surrounding areas, which include everything from the mile to ultramarathons, can be found on the Colorado Runner (www.coloradorunnermag.com) and Run Colo (www.runcolo.com) websites. Boulder Road Runners (www.boulderroadrunners.org) organises a series of evening open track and field meets (Summer All-comers Track Meets) at CU's Frank Potts Field. Races are hand-timed and include everything from 100 m to 10,000 m. Events are held fortnightly during the summer.

RUNNING COMMUNITY

Frank Shorter trained in Boulder prior to winning the marathon at the Munich Olympics, and during the 1980s, the town was home to distance-running legends Ingrid Kristiansen, Steve Jones, and Pricilla Welch, among others. The distance runners were later joined by cyclists, and in turn triathletes, and today Boulder is one of the world's most popular triathlon training bases. Chrissie Wellington, four-times Ironman triathlon world champion, was based here during the second half of her illustrious career. Australian World Cross Country champion Benita Willis lives here and Olympians Coleen De Reuck and Kathy Butler can be found coaching athletes in Boulder. A number of US distance runners also train in the city.

There are a number of training groups that visitors can join. Boulder Trail Runners organise regular trail runs via their Yahoo! Group (BoulderTrailRunners-subscribe@YahooGroups.com).
Fleet Feet Sports organises free fun runs every Monday for runners and walkers of all levels. Boulder Track Club (www.bouldertrackclub.com) caters for track, cross country, road, mountain, trail and ultra runners of all ages and abilities. Coaches and groups offering fee-based training programmes and coaching to runners and triathletes of all levels include Boulder Striders (www.boulderstriders.com), a group led by Colleen De Reuck, Revolution Running (www.revolution-running.com), Ric Rojas (www.ricrojasrunning.com), Jay Johnson's Athletics Boulder (www.athleticsboulder.org) and Bobby McGee (www.bobbymcgee.com).

Newton Running Elite (www.newtonrunningelite.com) is a professional running group supported by the Boulder-based running shoe manufacturers Newton Running. Athletes based in Boulder who compete regularly, hold down a full-time job, and train and race in Newton Running shoes can apply to become part of the team.

SUITABILITY FOR OTHER SPORTS

Boulder is a very popular destination among triathletes, and has been voted the Top Triathlon Town by popular triathlon magazine *Inside Triathlon*. The city is also suitable for road cyclists, swimmers, and other sportspeople. High-profile teams such as St Kilda FC (Australian Rules football) have used Boulder for altitude training. Boulder is home to USA Ultimate and the headquarters of USA Rugby. Valmont Bike Park hosts national cyclocross events.

Cycling Boulder's location results in a variety of hilly routes in the Rocky Mountain foothills and flat roads across the nearby Eastern Plains. Morgul-Bismark route, between Boulder and Denver, is one of the most famous rides in the area. Full Cycle (www.fullcyclebikes.com) has cycling route suggestions and maps on their website. Full Cycle, University Bicycles (www.ubikes.com) and Vecchio's Bicicletteria (www.vecchios.com), all located on Pearl Street, offer bicycle sales and services. Both Boulder Centre for Sports Medicine (www.bouldersportsmedicine.org) and Rally Sport Health and Fitness Club (www.rallysportboulder.com) organise indoor cycling training sessions during the winter months. Colorado Athletic Club-Flatirons organises group no-drop rides from the athletic club, and indoor and spin bike sessions during the winter.

There are numerous single-track mountain bike routes around Boulder. Boulder Mountain Bike Alliance (www.bouldermountainbike.org) and Colorado Mountain Bike (www.comtb.com) have mountain bike trail maps on their websites. Mountain bikes are not allowed on some of the city's trails.

The Boulder Valley Velodrome (www.bouldervalleyvelodrome.com) opened in Erie, 22 km east of Boulder, in 2013. While track time is allocated predominately to the teams that are based there, there are some open sessions, particularly between November and March, and non-members can purchase an Open Track Card. Bike hire is included.

Swimming There are many swimming pools around the city, most of them city owned. There are indoor pools at North Recreational Centre (8-lane, 25 yard pool in separate room from recreational pool); East Community Centre (8 lanes, 25 yards); South Recreational Centre (6 lanes; 25 yards). Scott Carpenter Pool, the only 50 m pool in Boulder, is a 6-lane facility on 30th Street, and Spruce Pool, located just north of Pearl Street, is an 8-lane, 25 yard outdoor pool. Elks Club, at Elks Lodge off 28th, north of Palo Parkway is an outdoor 25 m pool with six lanes. Colorado Athletic Club-Flatirons (505 Thunderbird Drive) boasts a heated 6-lane 25 m outdoor pool which is used for training by the city's best triathletes throughout the year. For those looking to swim with a club, Boulder Aquatic Masters (www.bamswimteam.org) offer annual, quarterly, monthly, summer and punch pass memberships which include access to the city recreational centres and a host of other benefits.

Triathlon Cycling, swimming and running facilities and opportunities mentioned previously combine to make an ideal training environment for triathletes. Drop-in and punch card access is available for open water swimming at Boulder Reservoir (www.boulderrez.org). Swimmers and triathletes can join Boulder Aquatic Masters (www.bamswimteam.org) on their Tuesday and Thursday morning open water swims at the reservoir without becoming a member. Squads and teams can also make reservations for group swims at the reservoir. Colorado Athletic Club-Flatirons (www.flatironathleticclub.com) is the centre of triathlon in Boulder. Six-times Hawaiian Ironman champion Dave Smith (www.davescottinc.com) coaches from there and many of the world's best triathletes swim at the club. Many of the city's cycle shops deal in triathlon and road bikes. Wet suits can be hired at Fleet Feet Sports (www.fleetfeetboulder.com).

Team sports The City of Boulder's Parks and Recreation Department manages a range of grass fields suitable for football and other team sports. University of Colorado's Bubble, a state-of-the-art indoor American football pitch, has been used by teams such as Australian Rules football club, St Kilda FC. Those looking to access CU or City of Boulder facilities for team training camps or events should contact the Sports and Events Sales Manager at Boulder Convention and Visitors Bureau (www.bouldercoloradousa.com).

Other sports Boulder offers great climbing routes for ice climbers and rock climbers of all abilities. The iconic Flatirons above the city, Eldorado Canyon to the south and Boulder Canyon to the west, provide a host of technical climbing options, and there are a number of indoor climbing walls suitable for competitive and recreational climbers. Rowing is possible on Boulder reservoir (www.boulderrez.org). There are facilities for tennis and squash around the city.

OPPOSITE Scenes from the international men's race at the 2010 BolderBoulder (CLOCKWISE FROM TOP LEFT) Paraglider entering Folsam Field as part of the Memorial Day celebrations; start of the men's race with the East Africans already running away from the field; the chasing pack; some of the athletes entering the packed stadium at the end of 10 gruelling kilometres

THINGS TO SEE AND DO BETWEEN TRAINING

The open space of Boulder city and county provides an endless playground for outdoor enthusiasts. Popular hikes in the area include the Anne U White hiking trail, Boulder Creek, Green Mountain, Eagle Trail, Walker Ranch and the trails starting at Chautauqua Park, White Rocks and Dowdy Draw. Some of the shorter summit hikes include Mount Sanitas and Flagstaff just to the west of the city. Fly-fishing is a popular leisure activity, and boating and kayaking are available on Boulder Reservoir. Rollerblading is possible along Boulder Creek Path and the ice rink at One Boulder Plaza (www.bouldericerink.com) is open between November and February. Tubing down Boulder Creek is a popular activity during summertime. Students raft down the creek in inflated inner tubes purchased from a local service station.

Rock climbing opportunities for skilled climbers include routes in Eldorado Canyon, 10 km south of Boulder, in Boulder Canyon west of downtown, and on the Flatirons. There are indoor climbing walls at Boulder Rock Club and School (www.boulderrockclub.com) and The Spot Bouldering Gym (www.thespotgym.com). The closest ski resort is Eldora (www.eldora.com), near Nederland, a 45–60 min drive from downtown. Flatirons Golf Course, a city owned facility, offers reasonable daily rates.

Mile High Gliding (www.milehighgliding.com) operates gliding experiences and Life Cycle Balloon Adventures (www.lifecycleballoons.com) offers tours over the city for those with plenty of money to spend.

University of Colorado Museum of Natural History, with exhibits of Rocky Mountain region animals, fossils, and ancient Southwestern cultures, is one of the best university-based natural history museums in the US. Celestial Seasonings, the US's largest specialist tea company, offers free tours of their facility on Sleepytime Drive. There are also free tours of the National Centre for Atmospheric Research, Leanin' Tree Museum and Sculpture Garden of Western Art, the Boulder Beer Company and Redstone Meadery.

TOP LEFT *Squirrels and other wildlife can be spotted along Boulder Creek Path near downtown.*
LEFT *Students tubing down Boulder Creek, a popular activity on sunny summer afternoons*

Major festivals include Boulder International Film Festival, Shoot Out 24 Hour Filmmaking Festival, Colorado Music Festival (a six-week long classical music event), Colorado Shakespeare Festival, the week-long Conference on World Affairs, and Boulder Creek Festival, a Memorial Day Weekend event which coincides with BolderBoulder.

REST DAY EXCURSIONS

Denver, just 30 min from Boulder, has many museums, beautiful parks and a diverse collection of interesting neighbourhoods to explore. Tours are available around Colorado State Capitol Building where the big tourist attraction is the 'One Mile Above Sea Level' engraving on the front steps. Denver Zoo, Denver Botanic Gardens, Washington Park and Confluence Park are all popular places to spend an afternoon. There are amusement parks, festivals, comedy clubs, and performing arts performances across the city. Among the city's National League teams are Denver Broncos (American football), Colorado Avalanche (ice hockey), Colorado Rapids (football), and Colorado Mammoth (lacrosse). Frisbee golf (frolf or disc golf) is a popular activity. Cherry Creek Shopping District, 16th Street Mall, LoDo (Lower Downtown), Larimer Square and Capitol Hill are the main shopping areas.

Red Rocks Amphitheatre in Morrison, on the outskirts of Denver, is an outdoor concert venue set against a backdrop of red sandstone. It offers great views of Denver, and is situated next to the interesting Rock and Roll Museum. Nearby there are a number of hiking trailheads which meander through scrub oak and the red sandstone.

Estes Park, 75 km from Boulder, provides a gateway to Rocky Mountain National Park. Trail Ridge Road, the highest continuous stretch of highway in the US, runs west from Estes Park through the park, and offers great views of the Rocky Mountain peaks. Glacier-formed valleys, rushing streams, tranquil lakes, and beautiful alpine meadows provide spectacular scenery, and deer, elk, porcupines, coyotes and chipmunks can be spotted in the area. Hiking is popular along the park's many beautiful trails. The park offers a great out-of-town training venue for those looking for additional variety, though the extreme altitude (2,400–3,700 m) can be a challenge. Mountain biking and road cycling are also popular.

A NOTE ON TRAINING HERE LONG-TERM

Though training may be interrupted by snow during the winter, it is possible to live and train in Boulder year-round. The city contains all the amenities that you need for training, and to live a normal life. Cost of living is higher than other training venues in the US, but, for those that are eligible to work, there are some employment opportunities. Suitable training groups are easy to find. There is a choice of things to do between training both in Boulder and in nearby Denver, and a good supply of comfortable apartment accommodation. Denver International Airport provides a quick and convenient way to get out for competitions. There are some opportunities for sponsorship for high performance athletes based in Boulder and many of the main sports shops support teams of elite athletes. With everything you need in a small city, it's not surprising that many elite athletes and keen recreational runners make Boulder their home.

FURTHER INFORMATION

The Boulder Convention and Visitors Bureau website (www.bouldercoloradousa.com) provides hotel and restaurant listings, information on getting to and around Boulder, maps of trails, a visitor guide, and suggestions of things to do. The Convention and Visitors Bureau is located at 2440 Pearl Street and has a visitor kiosk, stacked with maps and brochures, by the courthouse on Pearl Street Mall.

The City of Boulder website (www.bouldercolorado.gov) provides additional useful information including a bike route finder, the history of Boulder, and a link to the city's Parks and Recreation Department (www.boulderparks-rec.org). Recreational guides can be downloaded from the website or picked up from the Parks and Recreation administrative office at 3198 Broadway. The Downtown Boulder website (www.boulderdowntown.com) and the interactive Boulder Discovery Map (www.discoverymap.com/boulder) are useful for locating essential services, things to do, and places to eat, shop and stay.

OTHER ALTITUDE TRAINING SITES IN COLORADO

Colorado is the highest state in the US both in terms of mean elevation (2,070 m), and low point (1,011 m). With the Rocky Mountains and the High Plains making up most of the state, Colorado isn't short of altitude training sites. Even the sprawling mass of Denver is located 1,600 m above sea level. Boulder, Colorado Springs, Estes Park and Mancos are all very different places, and are likely, between them, to suit the tastes and requirements of any athlete.

Colorado Springs (1,832 m)
www.visitcos.com

Colorado Springs, Colorado's second largest city, is home to the United States Olympic Committee (USOC) headquarters, and their flagship training centre. The city is located in the foothills of the southern edge of the Rocky Mountains, approximately 115 km south of Denver.

There are numerous running options in the Pike National Forest and within the city's many parks. The Barr Trail accent to the summit of Pikes Peak, about 16 km west of the city, is both challenging and rewarding.

Travellers to Colorado Springs can fly to Denver International Airport (DEN) and get a transfer from there, or get a connection to Colorado Springs Municipal Airport (COS), located less than 20 km east of downtown. There are direct flights to Colorado Springs from Denver, Houston, Dallas, Phoenix, Chicago, Los Angeles, Atlanta, Washington and San Francisco, among others. Downtown Colorado Springs Greyhound bus terminal is located on Weber Street. A bus links the Amtrak train station in Denver with Colorado Springs. I-25 runs through Colorado Springs linking it to Denver in the north and Albuquerque in the south.

Rental properties, which include a particularly good choice of cottages and houses, can be found via TripAdvisor (www.tripadvisor.co.uk) or HomeAway (www.homeaway.co.uk).

There are free daily tours of the US Olympic Training Centre, many museums and places of interest to visit, and plentiful opportunities for rock climbing, horse riding, mountain biking and white-water rafting. Garden of the Gods, with its dramatic sandstone formations, is a particularly popular attraction.

Estes Park (2,293 m)
www.estesparkcvb.com

Estes Park is located in Larimer County on the eastern edge of the Rocky Mountain National Park, 110 km north-west of Denver. Most of the three million visitors to the park travel through, or stop in Estes Park, and during the key tourist season (Jul–Sept) the population of just under six thousand, almost triples.

The Rocky Mountain National Park website (www.rockymountainnationalpark.com) provides comprehensive details on the park's 150 trails, including trail descriptions, three-dimensional views of the trails, and instructions on how to get to the trailheads.

Active at Altitude (www.activeataltitude.com) organises camps for trail runners, female runners and triathletes and provides self-catering accommodation and coaching for groups looking to train in the area. PRS FIT (www.prsfit.com) also organises all-inclusive four-day trail running camps.

Hiking, fishing, mountain climbing, camping, horse riding, rafting and bird spotting are popular and cross country skiing and snowshoeing are possible during the winter months when there are considerably fewer tourists.

The town is located 120 km north-west of Denver International Airport (DEN), and Estes Park Shuttle (www.estesparkshuttle.com) operates a scheduled shuttle service from the airport to the town via Lyons, Boulder and Longmont. A free shuttle bus system operates between the Visitor Centre and Rocky Mountain National Park. Restaurants and tourist amenities are plentiful.

Chain hotels, motels, campsites, cabins, bungalows and holiday apartments provide good choice, though accommodation can fill up during July and August, and on most holiday weekends. Estes Park Condos (www.estescondos.com) offers cottages and suites on three sites on the western edge of the town next to the forest, and YMCA of the Rockies (www.ymcarockies.org) has over 200 fully equipped cabins. The Estes Park website (www.estes-park.com) links to a comprehensive collection of all accommodation types and other rentals can be found via TripAdvisor (www.tripadvisor.co.uk) and HomeAway (www.homeaway.co.uk).

Mancos (2,137 m)
www.mancoscolorado.com

Mancos is a small town of just under 1,500 people located close to the Four Corners border with Utah, Arizona and New Mexico. It is the gateway to the Mesa Verde National Park and UNESCO World Heritage site, a location of well-preserved cliff dwellings and notable desert landscapes. Located at 2,137 m of altitude, and surrounded by mountains, forests and range land, Mancos is a great place for running.

Run Mancos, part of the Mancos Project (www.themancosproject.org), is a running group which provides affordable altitude training camps.

Bolder Boulder
Adapted from the blog, 4 June 2010

Well it has been a crazy week. The jet lag which I've been dreading ever since I planned this leg of the adventure, didn't take a hold of me. I simply haven't had time to let it!

The American leg of the travels concluded with a big race in Boulder on Monday. BolderBoulder is one of the best road races, in terms of quality, outside of Africa, and more than 50,000 people participate. With some 400 people breaking 40 minutes (at altitude!) for the 10-kilometre distance each year, I was hoping to get close to my PB from 2005. One good week's training and I thought I could take on the world! I guess 42 minutes wasn't too bad, and two months ago, I would have been ecstatic with just being able to complete 10 km. After all, I did finish in the top three percent of finishers.

After the main race, I managed to watch the elite men from the media truck. The three Ethiopian athletes who ran away from the rest of the high-quality field did so with such ease that they could control the second half of the race, and slow to cross the finishing line together in the University of Colorado American football stadium, which by that time was packed to the rafters with finishers from the citizens' race. The whole event has given me the inspiration and motivation to train even harder, and to one day go back and try again to break 40 minutes.

So, after 64 days of living out of a suitcase; thousands of kilometres of air travel; 12 different airports; 13 different hotel rooms, 10 time zone changes, and far more tacos than I care to count, the first leg of my adventure has come to an end. A 7-hour overnight flight back to Birmingham, was followed by the completion of a 3,000 word assignment; some birthday cake (yes I turned 31 yesterday); endless rummaging through bags and boxes to find belongings, and some manic rushing across the city to reach the Frankly Services in time to catch my lift to Cardiff for some races tomorrow. Finally, I can take a deep, oxygen-rich, breath, and think about where I'm going to hit next.

The facility can cater for up to 10 athletes at a time, and groups and individuals are welcome. Included in the package are room, food, airport transfers, and training partners. Local nutritionists, physiotherapists and massage therapists offer reduced rates to those based at the camp which is set up for distance runners, but equally suitable for cyclists, triathletes and cross country skiers.

Though there are no public transport services to Mancos, the town is not far from two small airports. Durango-La Plata County Airport (DRO), has daily flights from Denver, Phoenix and Dallas, and is 65 km east of Mancos. Great Lakes Airlines operates flights from Denver to Cortez-Municipal Airport (CEZ), just 36 km west of the town. There are car hire companies based at both airports. Durango, 45 km east of Mancos, has a Greyhound bus station.

Other options
The Montrose-based Snow Shadow Gymnastics (www.snowshadowgymnastics.com) runs altitude training camps for gymnastics, karate and judo, among other sports. Montrose is located in south-west Colorado, 100 km south of Grand Junction. There are also has campuses in nearby Timberline and Tomahawk. They provide all-inclusive camps that combine traditional training methods with exciting forms of cross-training including canoeing and kayaking for building upper body strength and horse riding for lower body conditioning. The centre is not specifically designed for endurance sports.

The High Altitude Training Centre in Alamosa (www.blogs.adams.edu/hatc) offers the opportunity for University-level students to undertake a human performance and physical education class through Adams State University. Students have the opportunity to learn about the physiological benefits of training at altitude, and how to structure training when at altitude. Students undertaking the class live in on-campus apartments and have plenty of time to train with classmates. Runners of all levels are welcome. Alamosa is a historical college town in the south of Colorado, approximately half-way between Denver and Albuquerque. It sits in a valley at 2,300 m and is surrounded by 4,000-m high mountains. Alamosa hosted the US Olympic marathon trials for the 1968 Mexico City Games.

Breckenridge (www.townofbreckenridge.com; www.breckenridge.com) is a ski resort, situated at 2,926 m, 130 km west of Denver, and close to Leadville. The hilly terrain provides an excellent base for road cycling, and mountain bike trails are plentiful. The Breckenridge Recreation Centre offers day-pass access to its 25 m swimming pool, gym and other indoor and outdoor facilities.

Font Romeu

It doesn't take long to work out why the picturesque town of Font Romeu is Europe's premier altitude training destination. Sitting in the Pyrenees, the laid-back town offers splendid views of the surrounding countryside. Budget flights to nearby airports, and a splendid choice of self-catering accommodation, make Font Romeu an accessible option. Many of the trails around the town are hilly and rough underfoot, but just 20 min drive away, the flat routes around Lac de Matemale, at only 1,530 m above sea level, are perfect for quality runs and sessions. There is a track, gym facilities, and several alternative activities available, should some cross-training be required.

Font Romeu, France (1,850 m)

The French ski resort town of Font Romeu forms part of the Font-Romeu-Odeillo-Via commune in the Pyrenees-Orientales region of southern France. Nestled into the mountainside in the Pyrenees Catalanes Natural Park, the town sits at an altitude of 1,850 m above sea level. It has long been an altitude training base for athletes in a variety of sports. World marathon record holder Paula Radcliffe has regularly trained in the town, and the British Athletics team use it as one of their altitude training bases.

Pyrenees-Orientales stretches from the Mediterranean Sea westwards to the Pyrenees and the border with Andorra. The drive from Perpignan, the region's capital, to Font Romeu features dramatic scenery as the road rises from sea level to over 1,800 m and winds through the mountainside, first past fabulous gardens, vineyards and olive orchards and then by forests, through medieval villages and across spectacular bridges and aqueducts. The region is essentially one big open-air museum filled with medieval castles and palaces, Vauban-designed royal fortifications, and a stunning collection of Romanesque, Gothic and baroque churches, abbeys and priories.

Font Romeu boasts in excess of 300 days of sunshine a year and the way of life of southern France, typified by friendly, down-to-earth people enjoying fine food, markets, festivals, outdoor activities, in the pleasant climate and the beautiful surroundings, is very much evident. At times, it appears that everyone in the town is on a permanent holiday.

Author's verdict

I liked Font Romeu, but struggled communicating without adequate French. The town, and its surroundings, are beautiful, and after some experimentation, I managed to find a variety of trails within reach of my accommodation. Font Romeu has everything that an endurance runner needs—choice of trails, track, gym facilities, self-catering accommodation, access to training at lower altitudes and cross-training options. A car is useful for getting to flatter trails, getting in, excursions and picking up groceries from the larger supermarkets outside Font Romeu. There is an excellent choice of holiday apartments in both Font Romeu and nearby Pyrenees 2000, and many relaxed cafes in which to treat yourself between hard workouts. The weather can be slightly temperamental, and considerable snowfall is possible as late as April.

Running ★★★☆☆ - Reasonable variety of trails within easy reach of all accommodations, though many are hilly or tricky underfoot; better trails, at a lower altitude, a short drive from town; track in town; range of cross-training options.

Convenience ★★★☆☆ - Many airports within driving distance; car useful for getting to/from airport; some trails accessible from town, though travel required for quality off-road sessions; good choice of accommodation; English not widely spoken.

Safety ★★★★★ - Low levels of crime; no major disease or safety risk.

Cost ★★☆☆☆ - Accommodation prices high during the peak winter and summer seasons; budget flights from most European cities affordable; car required.

Cultural experience ★★★☆☆ - Opportunity to enjoy relaxed, outdoor lifestyle of the South of France, or nip across the Spanish border and explore the culturally-rich Catalan region.

Things to do between training ★★★☆☆ - Variety of activities in town, though these usually involve exerting energy; castles, abbeys, palaces and other sites of historical interest within driving distance of the town; historic cities of Girona, Barcelona and Carcassonne only a day-trip away.

Suitability for solo travellers ★★☆☆☆ - Solo travellers who don't speak good French will find their time in Font Romeu difficult. Occasionally you'll find an English-speaking athlete or two to befriend, but athletes who train here often do so in groups or teams.

Must do Take a ride on the Petit Train Jaune through the Pyrenees towards Perpignan; enjoy a feast of crêpes in one of the local cafes or crêperies; feel good doing a tempo session around Lac de Matemale.

Ideal for Athletes who want to live at altitude within easy reach of races on the European track circuit.

FRANCE QUICK FACTS

Capital/largest city Paris
Official language French
Currency Euro (€; EUR), divided into 100 cents
Public holidays New Year's Day (Jan 1), Good Friday*, Easter Monday*, May Day (May 1), Victory in Europe Day (May 8), Ascension Thursday*, Whit Monday*, Bastille Day (Jul 14), Assumption Day (Aug 15), All Saints' Day (Nov 1), Veterans Day (Nov 11), Christmas Day (Dec 25), St Stephen's Day (Dec 26).
Time zone Central European Time (GMT+1); daylight saving (last Sun Mar–last Sun Oct)
International dialling code +33
Outgoing access code 00
Emergency contact 112
Power 400 V; 50 Hz supply; Type E (CEE 7/5) Europlug-compatible plugs and sockets with two small round pins (and a round male pin permanently mounted to the socket)
Driving Right side
Measurement Metric

* vary according to Christian calendar

BACKGROUND *A small lake at the Sentier Sportif Ticou just east of Super Bolquére*
OPPOSITE *A trail through the beautiful open countryside below the town*
PREVIOUS *The town of Font Romeu, from the trails below the town*

Getting In

The nearest city is Perpignan (87 km away), though Font Romeu is also easily accessible from Montpellier, Girona, Barcelona, Toulouse and Carcassonne. While car is the quickest way to get to Font Romeu from any of the local airports or cities, travel by public transport is also possible. Flying to a French airport may not always be the most convenient option, and many of those travelling here will come via Spain. Flight choice and price are often the best determinants of the route to take.

By air

Perpignan Airport, located 93 km away, is the closest airport. It offers a limited choice of flights to European destinations, while Girona (165 km) and Barcelona (175 km) offer flights to a host of European cities. Carcassonne (128 km), Toulouse (195 km) and Montpellier (245 km) are also within driving distance, but have limited public transport links. Barcelona offers the best options for international connections from outside of Europe. Budget airlines often make Girona, Perpignan and Carcassonne the cheapest options.

Perpignan–Rivesaltes Airport (PGF) is located on the northern side of Perpignan, less than 8 km from Perpignan city centre, and 93 km (1 hr 30 min by car) from Font Romeu. There are a small number of flights from international destinations, including Amsterdam, Birmingham, Brussels-Charleroi, Dublin, London and Southampton, and domestic flights from Paris and Nantes. Flights are operated by Air France, Aer Lingus, Iberia, and budget airlines Ryanair, Flybe and Volotea. Car hire is available through Advantage, Avis, Budget, National Citer, Europcar, Hertz and Sixt. Line 7 of the CTPM town bus service (www.ctpmperpignan.com) links the airport and Perpignan city centre, and the train and bus station can be reached by changing to Line 2 at 'Place de Catalogne'. Services are limited on Sundays and public holidays. Continue the journey from Perpignan to Font Romeu by car, bus, or train.

Girona–Costa Brava Airport (GRO) is located 12.5 km south-west of the Spanish city of Girona. Ryanair, by far the airport's biggest airline, offers year-round services to Manchester, Turin, Dortmund, Eindhoven, Frankfurt-Hahn, Pisa and Marrakech, among others, and a range of seasonal flights (Mar–Nov) from a range of other European cities. Car hire is available through Hertz, Europcar, Avis, Auriga Crown, Atesa, Budget and Economy. The E-15/AP-7 toll road links the airport to Perpignan, while the N-11 provides toll-free access. The journey to Font Romeu is approximately 190 km (2 hr 20 min). Frogbus (www.frogbus.com) operates a coach service six times per day between Girona and Perpignan train/bus station. The journey takes approximately 2 hr (plus the 2 hr 30 min journey by train from Perpignan to Font Romeu).

Montpellier–Méditerranée Airport (MPL) is served by major international airlines such as Alitalia, Lufthansa and Air France and is a better option than Perpignan or Girona for long-haul connections. Montpellier Airport is located 245 km (2 hr 45 min by car) from Font Romeu.

Barcelona–El Prat Airport (BCN), located 14 km from the centre of Barcelona, serves approximately 30 million passengers each year. It is connected to the centre of Barcelona by train (R2 of the Rodalies Barcelona commuter train line, from Terminal 2) and bus (line 46 of the TMB public bus network). It is a 175 km, (2 hr 20 min) drive from the airport north to Font Romeu via the C16/A-9. Most national European carriers, and budget airlines such as EasyJet, Ryanair and Wizz Air, offer flights to El Prat from cities right across Europe. The airport is the main hub for Spain's second airline Vueling. There are also flights from North Africa and the Middle East, seasonal flights from Montreal and Toronto, and year-round services from Atlanta, Miami, Newark, New York, Sao Paulo, Buenos Aires, and Singapore.

Carcassonne Airport (CCF) is a small airport located 3 km from Carcassonne city centre, and 128 km north of Font Romeu. Ryanair operates year-round flights to Brussels Charleroi, Dublin, Liverpool and London Stansted, and seasonal flights to other airports in Western Europe. By car, you can travel south via minor, toll-free roads (D118) to Font Romeu, a journey which takes approximately 2 hr 20 min, or travel via Perpignan on a journey which is 85 km longer, but which takes approximately the same time. Car hire is available through Avis, Budget, Enterprise, Hertz, Sixt, and Thrifty.

Toulouse–Blagnac Airport (TLS) is just 7 km west of Toulouse city centre, and 195 km from Font Romeu. Air France, Alitalia, British Airways, Iberia, KLM, Lufthansa, Turkish Airways and some smaller and budget airlines provide flights to many European and North African cities. There is a regular 20 min shuttle bus service (Flybus Airport Shuttle) to Toulouse, from where you can take the train to Latour-de-Carol-Enveitg and the Petit Train Jaune to Font Romeu. The total journey by train takes approximately 6 hr. Cars can be hired from Avis, Budget, Europcar, Hertz, National/Citer and Sixt. The journey takes approximately 2 hr 30 min via the N20 toll road, or just over 3 hr via toll free roads.

Reus–Costa Daurada Airport (REU) is located south-west of Barcelona, 240 km (2 hr 45 min) from Font Romeu, and may offer an additional option for those who are driving. Reus is one of Ryanair's main hubs with seasonal and year-round flights from UK and Western European cities.

By car
Driving is the quickest way to get to Font Romeu from any of the surrounding cities or airports. Font Romeu is linked directly to the coast via the N116, a regional road which climbs from Perpignan into the mountains. There are a few steep climbs and some sharp bends requiring caution, but the road is direct, and the drive scenic. Travelling from Girona and Marseilles will require driving towards Perpignan, and connecting to the N116 on the western outskirts of the city. The A9/E-9, travelling north from Barcelona and south from Montpellier, Lyons, Marseilles and Paris, has toll sections, but offers more direct access than the alternative regional roads.

Map of airports, cities and main roads linking to Font Romeu

In general, roads in France are in excellent condition, and outside of Paris, there is little congestion. Large sections of motorway (autoroute) have tolls, and though these can be avoided in some instances, the additional distance costs more in petrol than the tolls would have. Autoroutes are usually indicated by an autoroute 'A' number and a Euroroute 'E' number. Fuel in autoroute service stations is considerable more expensive than in urban areas away from the main routes, and diesel tends to be considerably cheaper than petrol.

The normal speed limit on motorways is 130 kph, or 110 kph in rain. Duel carriageways have a speed limit of 110 kph and the limit on main roads, outside of built-up areas, is 90 kph. In built-up areas, the limit is 50 kph, unless otherwise indicated. Built-up areas are generally signified by the name-boards entering villages and towns, rather than speed limit signs.

By train
There are direct services to Perpignan train station, from cities throughout southern France and north-east Spain. Train Tickets for services starting in France can be booked through SNCF (www.voyages-sncf.com) and services starting in Spain are booked through RENFE (www.renfe.com). From Perpignan, take the train to Villefranche-de-Conflent and the historic Petit Train Jaune (little yellow train) to Font-Romeu-Odeillo-Via station, 3 km south of the centre of Font Romeu. The total journey from Perpignan is approximately 2 hr 30 min and there are approximately five services per day. Shuttle buses connect the station in Odeillo-Via to the centre of Font Romeu (pick up outside the station). Taxis can also be ordered from the station. The journey from the station to the town centre is completely uphill, and not suitable for transporting heavy suitcases on foot.

By bus
The regional council, Conseil Général Pyrenees-Orientales (www.cg66.fr), operates a regional bus service (Le bus à €1) which includes a route (Route 260) linking Perpignan and Latour de Carol, via Font Romeu. There are four services per day from Monday to Friday, with limited services at the weekend. The journey from the train station in Perpignan to the tourist office in Font Romeu takes approximately 2 hr 30 min. Routes and timetables ('*plan et horaires*') can be found on the Conseil Général website.

Frogbus (www.frogbus.com) operates a ski transfer service from Perpignan train station to Pyrenees 2000, three days per week (Wed, Sat, Sun) and from Perpignan airport to Pyrenees 2000 and Font Romeu, also three days per week (Fri, Sat, Sun), during the ski season.

By taxi and private transfer
For larger groups, who don't wish to hire a car, Altitude Taxi Christian Salvat provides transfers from all the region's airports and train stations. Cathie et Jean-Claude Leber (+33 (0)68 689 9982) and Taxis des Cimes (+33 (0)67 134 8564) also operate airport pick-up services.

Visa requirements
Visas are not required for citizens of any EU or EFTA country, Andorra or Monaco. Citizens of Australia, Canada, and the US, among others, do not require a visa for stays of up to 90 days. Schengen visas are also valid. Citizens of other countries, including South Africa, must apply for a visa in advance of travel.

GETTING AROUND

A car is useful to get to and from some of the trails, particularly the flat ones around the lake. A car is also useful to pick up shopping from the larger supermarkets just outside the town, and for sightseeing. Cars can be hired from any of the airports, or from the Europcar base in Font Romeu itself.

The town itself can easily be navigated on foot, though the hillside location means that there are lots of steep steps. The main shops, restaurants and businesses are located on Avenue Emmanuel Brousse and Avenue du Maréchal Joffre. Most of the accommodation is located close to the town centre. Good maps of the town can be picked up from the tourist information centre.

BELOW The Petit Train Jaune which operates between Villefranche-de-Conflent and Latour-de-Carol
OPPOSITE The road from Lac de Matemale to Font Romeu

Weather and when to visit

Font Romeu has a pleasant climate, and with approximately 300 sunshine days per year is the sunniest ski resort in France.

From a weather perspective, July and August are the best months to train in Font Romeu. They are the hottest and driest months, with average daily highs between 20 and 25 ºC, and on average 2-3 rain days per month. These are also peak summer season months, and accommodation may be limited and more expensive. Book well in advance, and be prepared to share the trails with numerous other users. The advantage of visiting during peak season is a greater variety of restaurants open, and more things to do between training.

The months between November and February are the coldest and snowiest, though snow showers are possible as late as April. If you choose to train in Font Romeu in April, you should be prepared for all weather conditions, and be willing to travel towards Perpignan for training if it does snow. The track at CNEA is usually cleared during prolonged periods of snow cover, but the trails may be more difficult. Late spring might be a good time of year to combine running with some cross country skiing.

Accommodation

Rental accommodation is plentiful, though demand can be high during the main ski season (Dec–Feb), and the main hiking season (Jul–Aug). Rental options include studios, apartments, houses, gîtes and chalets. Most charge per week (Sat–Sat), though some also offer weekend rates. The Font-Romeu Tourism Office produces a list of private rentals ('*liste des loueurs particuliers*') which can be requested via their website (www.font-romeu.fr). Accommodations can also be booked via holiday rental websites such as Homelidays (www.homelidays.co.uk) and HomeAway (www.homeaway.co.uk). Linen (sheets and towels) isn't always included. There are also camping options, and a few small hotels.

Font Romeu is built on a hillside, and not all accommodations are at the same altitude. Odeillo (~1,600 m) and Via (~1,700 m) areas, though close to Font Romeu, are at much lower altitude. Pyrenees 2000, a ski resort adjacent to Font Romeu, is at a similar altitude, and is a good alternative. It has a supermarket, is linked to the better trails within the area, and may have a better selection of accommodation than Font Romeu outside of the ski season. There isn't the same choice of restaurants and cafes, but this isn't a problem if you have a car. Pyrenees 2000 is located on D618, the road out of Font Romeu towards Mont-Louis and the Lac de Matemale turn-off.

Food

There are a number of restaurants, though most are basic tourist-focused restaurants serving bog-standard pizzas, pasta and burgers. Fine dining, available in a few of the local hotels, is expensive. Preparing your own food is preferable, particularly for athletes looking to meet the nutritional demands of their sport. Where Font Romeu does succeed on the food-front is in its bakeries (*boulangeries*), specialist pastry bakeries (*pâtisserie*), cafes and crêperies with plenty of options for the occasional treat.

Most accommodations are self-catering, and cooking your own food, made with fresh local produce, is not difficult. The medium-sized supermarket (Shopi) on avenue du Maréchal Joffre sells a good selection of food, including

fresh fruit and vegetables. There are larger supermarkets just outside of town—a Lidl in Odeillo, close to the Four Solaire, and a large supermarket (Casino) in Pyrenees 2000. There are also bakeries, cheese shops, and greengrocers. A small local market, held on Saturdays, provides additional opportunity to purchase fresh produce.

Shopping

The supermarkets in and around the town cater for most needs, and, in addition to food, sell holiday and domestic essentials, guidebooks and toys. There is a well-stocked newsagent and a relatively large pharmacy on the main street. Other shops include small boutiques, sport and outdoor shops, and shops selling crafts and gifts. Prices are often high. Many shops close at lunchtime, and not all open on Sundays.

There are a number of sports shops and outdoor stores, with practically every second shop along the main street selling or renting some form of sports equipment or gear. While there are no specialist running shops, Intersport on Avenue Emmanuel Brousse, and some of the other outdoor shops, sell running shoes and training kit.

Language

French is the official language of France, and the only one spoken by the majority of French people. Some Font Romeu residents speak Catalan, and only a small handful, usually those working in the tourism sector, speak English. The French, like the British, make little effort to speak any language other than their own. At least greeting a person in French and asking if they speak English, ('*parlez-vous anglais?*') will reap better results than making no effort at all.

Few menus are available in English, and signs, maps and tourist information leaflets are rarely published in any language other than French. The Pyrenees-Orientales official tourism website, and the website of the Pyrenees-Orientales cultural network do have English versions.

There are some useful words and phrases to help you get by in appendix 1.

Communication

There is good mobile reception in and around Font Romeu. Orange, SFR/Simpleo, Virgin Mobile and Bouygues Telecom are the main mobile providers. Those who have a phone capable of receiving 900/1800 MHz GMS (2G) or 900/2100 MHz UMTS (3G) services should have no problem getting reception. Recent changes to roaming charges within the EU greatly reduce bills while abroad, but those from outside the EU, or who will be using their phone a lot while in France should consider purchasing a French SIM. US residents can purchase a bill pay SIM online in English in advance of travel (www.rebelfone.com). SIM cards can also be purchased in France for unlocked GSM phones. There is an Orange shop selling mobile and internet devices and access on avenue Emmanuel Brousse.

A number of dial-around services (e.g. www.allo2556.fr) allow international calls from landlines at a local rate. Public payphones are relatively common in France, and there are phones at various locations around town, including outside the post office. Payphones are usually card operated, and use either credit card, or prepaid calling cards which can be purchased from newsagents or post offices.

Wi-Fi internet access doesn't come as standard in rental properties. Some of the cafes and restaurants offer free Wi-Fi access to customers, while Burofax (Avenue du Maréchal Joffre), and Webhouse (Rue Maillol) provide internet access to those who don't have their own computer. Burofax also provides printing, fax, photocopying and laminating services. There is also internet access at Bibliothèque Municipale (avenue Emmanuel Brousse). Mobile Wi-Fi hotspots can be rented from www.frenchconnection.fr. These hotspots, which can be used with up to five devices, are ordered through an English-language website in advance, and sent to your accommodation. They can simply be returned by pre-paid post following use. Internet Max, a short-term SIM for smartphones and tablets, from Orange offers a nearly unlimited month-long internet package.

The French postal system (La Poste) is efficient. There is a post office on Rue du Docteur Capelle.

Health and safety

There are no major health concerns, and few personal safety issues in Font Romeu. The town is very peaceful, and crime is rare.

Health care in France is of a very high standard. European Union residents are covered by the French social insurance system and are entitled to a 70 percent deduction or reimbursement on medical expenses incurred. Visitors from outside the EU are not covered, and should obtain travel insurance with medical cover. A list of medical practitioners operating in the town can be found under the '*Santé*' menu on the Font Romeu website (www.font-romeu.fr).

Tap water is drinkable, unless clearly signposted '*eau non potable*'. Water may be heavily chlorinated, and bottled water, if preferred, is widely available.

Money

France and Spain, through which many visitors travel, are both in the eurozone. There are a few ATMs and small banks, and debit and credit cards are widely accepted.

Power

France uses Europlug-compatible Type E (CEE 7/5) plugs and sockets (2 small round pins; with a round male pin permanently mounted to the socket), and operates on 400 V; 50 Hz supply.

Time

France operates on Central European Time (CET; GMT+1). Summer time operates between the last weekend of March and the last weekend of October.

Daylight hours range from 15 hr 20 min in mid June to just over 9 hr in mid December. Take note of the early sunset, and short days if training here in the winter.

	Mar	Jun	Sept	Dec
Sunrise	07:04	06:14	07:32	08:14
Sunset	18:58	21:31	20:02	17:20

Laundry

Most rental accommodations have a washing machine. There is a self-service launderette (*lavomatic*), with token-operated washers and dryers, beside Hotel Pyrenees.

Culture and Respect

Restaurant bills in France always include a 15 percent service charge ('*service compris*'), as, under French law, all tips must be assessed for income tax purposes. The service charge is included in the menu price, and is itemised on the bill. You are not expected to leave an additional tip, though a small tip is always appreciated. Taxi-drivers also appreciate a small tip, but this is not expected.

BELOW The gondola from Font Romeu to Les Airelles
FOLLOWING View of the valley from the forest above Font Romeu

Sports facilities and services

The National Centre for Altitude Training (CNEA) at Font Romeu was set up as a French training base prior to the 1968 Olympic Games in Mexico City, and since then athletes in many sports, but in particular athletics, have come to the town to train. Many athletes who train here are regulars, and have been coming back year-on-year, testament to the merits of the town as a training base. There are good training facilities at the centre, gym facilities at Espace Sportif Colette Besson, and trails both in the town, and at a lower altitude by Lac de Matemale.

Training camps and tour operators

The National Centre for Altitude Training (CNEA) provides accommodation, food and training facilities for teams and squads in a variety of sports. Unlike other venues which have established all-inclusive camps, the CNEA doesn't form the basis of what Font Romeu has to offer athletes training here and most runners visiting the town arrange their own accommodation and food. They are likely to use only the track at the centre.

Trails and running routes

A map detailing all hiking trails in Font Romeu can be purchased for just a few euro from the tourist information office on avenue Emmanuel Brousse. Take note of altitude deferential and route description. For those who wish to venture beyond the immediate surroundings of the town, outdoor shops, newsagents and supermarkets sell detailed maps of the area which include all trails in 1:25 000 and 1:50 000 scale. On the trails themselves, there are markers indicating trail numbers, distances to points of interest and trail direction.

Font Romeu sits on the side of a mountain, and there are many technical single-track trails. Some of the routes marked on the aforementioned maps are only suitable for mountain-biking, hiking or for runners who have complete confidence in their ankle stability and robustness, and most are not suitable for anything faster than steady running. There are three main routes from the town, each with multiple add-on options, and trail and mountain runners will have plenty of variety. For those looking for something a little flatter, and more solid underfoot, and for those wishing to follow a 'live high, train low' routine, then it's worth making the trip to Lac de Matemale, about 15 km (20 min by car) from the town. There you will find plenty of options and loops, up to 16 km long, which cover soft forest paths, quiet tarred roads and mildly undulating gravel paths. This is also where race walkers staying in Font Romeu do their training. Some relatively flat, firm trails and roads can be found closer to the town, once you know where to look.

Here are just some of the options available.

Pyrenees 2000

For the flattest option from town, head along the Mont-Louis road. Just after the campsite, take the next right turn (Boulevard Campredon), and almost immediately there will be a single-track trail on your left. Follow this up a slight incline until you reach the Mont-Louis road. Just across the road, there is a double-track forest road. Follow this straight until it reaches a gate into the forest on your left, leaving Pyrenees 2000 on your right. Follow the path through the forest. The path continues gradually uphill, and eventually reaches the main road at the Paula Radcliffe circuit between the les Airelles and Col del Pam chairlifts. Choose to continue on, return the way you came, or take the road back to Font Romeu (turn left onto the road, and turn right when you reach the small roundabout). The surfaced road past les Airelles and towards La Calme is mildly undulating, and other trails, varying in terrain and difficulty, meander around the various peaks and from La Calme.

Collette Besson/CNEA

A number of trails, mostly single-track dirt trails which lead through the forest above the town, start just east of the Collette Besson Sports Centre and tennis courts. From here, follow the main trail towards the CNEA, turn left and follow the perimeter of the centre up the hill. Turn left, cross under the main chairlift, and follow the track through the forest. Continue around the hill, across the road, and around the golf course until you return past the Grand Hotel to the starting point. This route is not suitable for fast running, but at approximately 7 km is good for light recovery runs. There are some add-on options, but these are quite hilly.

Les Estanyols

A number of trails, some of which are used for cross country skiing during the winter months, start at les Estanyols, beyond Pyrenees 2000, approximately halfway between Font Romeu and Mont-Louis. Most of these trails start just north of the road, though there are some shorter ones to the south of the road which pass the Sentier Sportif Ticou (outdoor circuit). These trails are

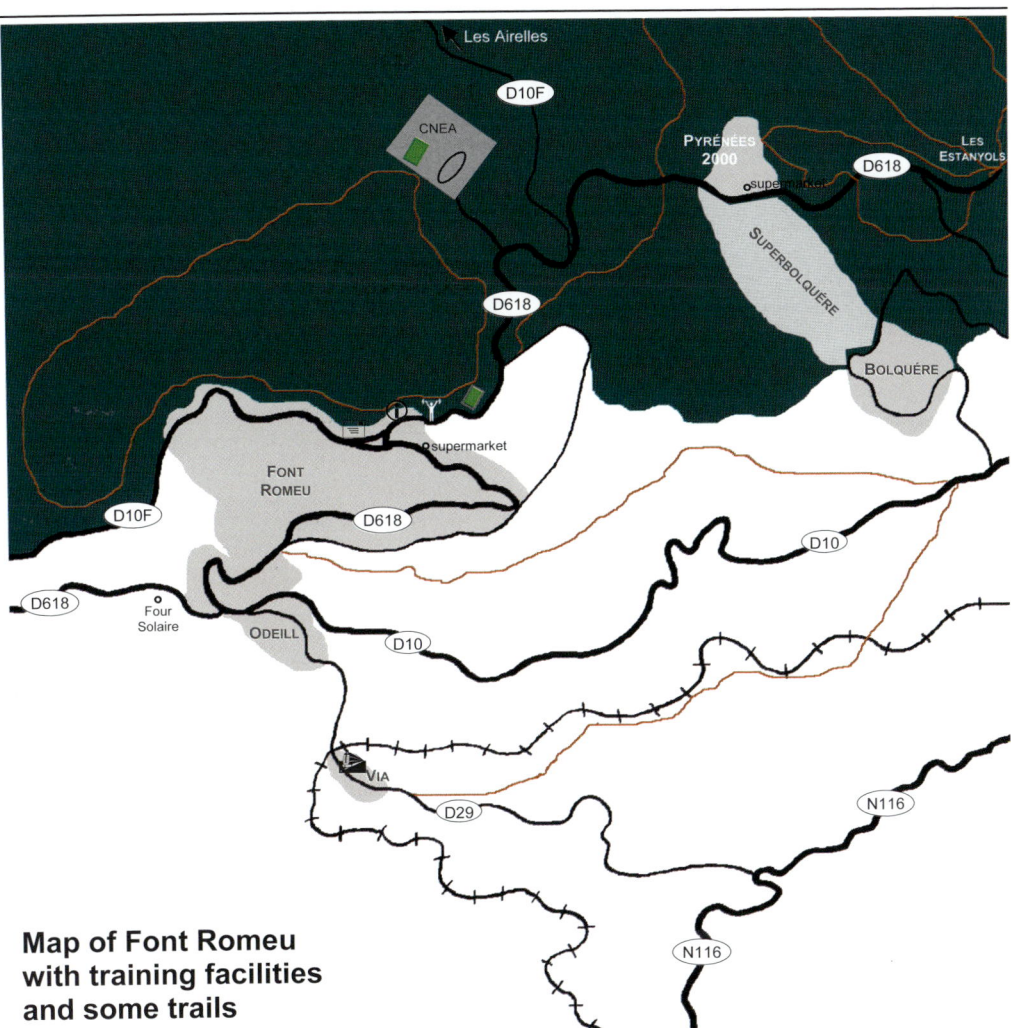

Map of Font Romeu with training facilities and some trails

flatter and less technical than those close to the town, and are a mix of single and double tracks.

Odeillo/below the town

There are other trail options below the town towards Odeillo. A rocky, single track leads through the scenic countryside east towards Bolquère. Just before Bolquère, you reach the road, and a junction. Cross the road, and take the next road almost immediately to your right. Follow this to the railway line, cross the railway line, turn right and follow in the direction of the railway line back to Via, and then up the hill to Font Romeu. This route is challenging, but the open countryside makes a change from all the forest trails, and the views of the town are spectacular.

Lac de Matemale

The area around the lake is the most popular place for training. The lower altitude (the lake's altitude is 1,540 m) and the flat terrain make it possible to carry out quality sessions and tempo runs. To get to the lake, drive towards Mont-Louis, take the first exit at the roundabout before Mont-Louis and continue along the D118 until the lake appears on your left. There is a small car park just by the corner of the lake, and a larger one along the road towards les Angles (next left). A trail, approximately 10 km long and consisting of a mixture of tarmac, gravel paths, and a small area of concrete, leads right around the lake. There are add-on options through the forest to the north of the lake.

TRACK FACILITIES

There is a 6-lane, 400 m track at the National Centre for Altitude Training (CNEA). There is a small fee for each use. A short trail (approximately 1 km), suitable for warm-up and cool-down jogs, runs around the perimeter of the centre.

The Stade Municipal, on the corner of Avenue Jean Paul and Route de l'Ermitage, is a small football field with a level grass surface. This is a good place to do drills, barefoot running, and strides. Respect the fact though that the field is primarily for football, and keep to the perimeter where possible.

GYM FACILITIES

Espace Sportif Colette Besson, a sports centre located above the town next to the Grand Hotel, provides pay-as-you-go gym access for visitors. You can pay per session, or purchase 5-session and 10-session multi-activity cards which offer slightly better value. Facilities include free weights and machine weights areas, cardiovascular training equipment, a sauna, a mini-golf course, fitness classes and tennis, squash and badminton facilities.

For those who don't want the expense of gym facilities, or who just want to maintain basic strength, the Sentier Sportif Paula Radcliffe (near les Airelles) and the Sentier Sportif Ticou (near les Estanyols) offer outdoor circuit stations along forest trails. Used cleverly, these circuits can add a novel element to your training.

CROSS-TRAINING OPTIONS

Cycling and swimming are the obvious choices for cross-training. Mountain bikes can be rented in the town. Swimming is available at CNEA. The gym facilities at Colette Besson facilitate stationary biking, exercising on a cross-trainer, and other forms of low impact exercise. Cross country skiing and snowshoeing are also good cross-training options during the winter and spring months.

For those just looking to add some variety to training, tennis, squash and badminton are available at Collette Besson, and football is available at the Stade Municipal. A variety of exercise classes are available at Colette Besson. Biathlon, climbing and archery are just some of the other activities offered which may be suitable as cross-training.

SPORTS MEDICINE AND SPORTS SCIENCE SUPPORT

Sports medicine and physiotherapy services are available at CNEA. Field and laboratory physiological testing is also available. Doctors, physiotherapists and massage practitioners travelling with teams training at the CNEA can hire treatment rooms within the centre.

RUNNING COMMUNITY

Paula Radcliffe is one of the best known athletes to have trained regularly in Font Romeu. In recent years, British Athletics have based regular training camps here, and most top British distance runners will have trained in Font Romeu at some stage in their career. It is estimated that some 10,000 elite athletes, including at least 100 Olympic medallists, have trained in the town over the years. Team Altitude (www.teamaltitude-fontromeu.com) is a multi-sport team of athletes based in Font Romeu, who represent the town's philosophy of well being and appreciation of life. The website, in French, has interesting updates on sport in the town.

SUITABILITY FOR OTHER SPORTS

Font Romeu has terrain and facilities to suit a host of different sports. Cycling and other endurance sports are particularly well catered for, and the facilities at CNEA and Espace Sportif Colette Besson are suitable for a number of team and racquet sports.

Cycling Good road surfaces, hilly terrain and reasonable variety make Font Romeu a great base for road cyclists. Cyclists have the option to leave via the top of the town, and head towards Mont-Louis, where they can either head north along the D118 past Lac de Matemale and Lac de Puyvalador, or join the N116 and continue towards Perpignan. This road is twisty, and has some sharp switchbacks. It is also the busiest road traffic-wise, and it is almost all downhill on the way out, and uphill on the way back. If leaving through the bottom of town, cyclists can take the D618 west (turn right before you reach the Four Solaire), or continue down through Odeillo and Via, past the train station, and turn right on the N116. These two routes run west across the valley floor, and are relatively flat to begin with, before branching off in various directions.

Mountain biking ('VTT' in French) is also very popular, with the Pyrenees 2000 and Font Romeu ski-slopes providing ideal terrain for experienced downhill mountain bikers. There are numerous technical routes for bikers of all levels. Font

Romeu-Pyrenees 2000 Bike Park (open Apr–Oct) has three tracks (dirt track, downhill board cross track and downhill cross country track) for experienced riders. There is also a bike park at les Angles (www.lesangles-vtt.com). Mountain bike maps can be obtained from the tourist information centre.

Swimming There are indoor 25 m and 50 m swimming pools at the CNEA. There is public, pay-as-you-go access to the 25 m pool.

Triathlon With good running, cycling, swimming and gym facilities, Font Romeu has everything that a triathlete needs.

Team sports There are football pitches at the Sade Municipal and the CNEA has two grass pitches. There is also indoor hall space at CNEA for a range of team sports.

Other sports Speed skaters can use the 300 m roller-skating circuit at the CNEA for dry-land training. There are good tennis facilities, both at Colette Besson and at the CNEA, and there are badminton courts and squash courts at Colette Besson. Wrestlers and other indoor sports athletes can train at CNEA. The town's surroundings are perfect for orienteering. With equestrian, fencing and shooting facilities at CNEA, Font Romeu is even a potential base for modern pentathlon training.

BELOW *The author enjoying a run at Lac de Matemale*
RIGHT *The accommodation block at CNEA*
PREVIOUS *Some of the trails that are accessible from Font Romeu*

Altitude training camp
CENTRE NATIONAL D'ENTRAINEMENT EN ALTITUDE (CNEA)

Following disappointing results at the 1964 Tokyo Olympics, and the announcement that the 1968 Games were to be held at altitude in Mexico City, the French authorities set about building an altitude training base in Font Romeu. The centre is open year-round and any athlete or sportsperson with a competition licence or NGB membership card is welcome.

Facilities
- 6-lane 400 m Tartan track
- 25 m and 50 m swimming pools
- 44 x 24 m sports hall with wooden floor
- 30 x 24 m sports hall with Taraflex surface
- 60 x 30 m skating rink
- Wrestling room
- Shooting range
- Fencing room
- Weightlifting and fitness room
- Specialist swimming weights room
- 300 m tarmac roller track
- Equestrian centre
- 2 grass football fields
- Outdoor handball, basketball & tennis areas

Contact
Website www.cnea-fontromeu.com
Postal address CREPS de Font-Romeu. BP 88, 66123, Font Romeu

Things to see and do between training

Font Romeu is a great place for those who love the outdoors. Road cycling and mountain biking (p. 166), hiking, horse riding, climbing and fishing are popular activities. QBX quad bikes can be rented in Pyrenees 2000 and there is an archery range by les Airelles ski slopes. A zip wire park, located at l'Ermitage (www.rando-pyrenees.com), offers circuits of various difficulties. Many of the ski lifts operate during the summer months taking mountain bikers, hikers and sightseers to the top of the various mountain peaks. The cinema at the casino on avenue Emmanuel Brousse shows films three times per week and bowling and paintballing are available in Pyrenees 2000.

A number of companies organise outdoor pursuit activities. Aventure Pyrénéenne (www.aventure-pyreneenne.com) organises sledging, biathlon, and snowshoeing in winter, and canyoning, climbing and Nordic walking in summer.

There are few cultural sites or places of interest in Font Romeu itself, though the solar furnace (Four Solaire d'Odeillo), may be of interest to some visitors. Les Angles Animal Park features 10 species of wildlife native to the Pyrenees, including wolves, wild boar, bison and brown bears. Dorres Roman granite baths and granite museum are located just 13 km south of the town. The fortifications of Mont-Louis are also worth a visit.

Rest day excursions

The Andorran border lies just 45 km east of Font Romeu. On clear days, the drive is a very scenic one. Andorra is a tax haven, and has numerous duty-free shops and cheap petrol. The principality is a popular ski destination, regularly hosts stages of the Tour de France, and has some churches and shrines of note. Tourism accounts for around 80 percent of Andorran GDP, and the country attracts close to 10 million visitors each year. Make sure that you take your passport with you, and visitors from outside the EU should note that Andorra is not a Schengen Agreement country.

Villefranche-de-Conflent is a beautiful medieval town located approximately 40 km from Font Romeu on the road to Perpignan. Within the walls lies a well-preserved 11th century town, which hosts souvenir and craft shops, cafes and restaurants. On the hill overlooking the town sits Fort Libéria (www.fort-liberia.com), a military fort built in 1681. Details of abbeys, castles, palaces, art museums and historical sites within Pyrenees-Orientales, can be found on the region's cultural network website (www.reseauculturel.fr).

Perpignan (www.perpignantourisme.com) is 90 km, and approximately a 1 hr 30 min drive north-east of the town. Perpignan has lots of small boutiques, and a few larger department stores. Spectator sports are popular, and USA Perpignan (rugby union) and Catalans Dragons (rugby league) both play in French top-flight competitions. The Cathedral of Saint John the Baptist and the Palace of the Kings of Majorca are the main historical sites. Just 15 km east of Perpignan, Mediterranean beaches stretch along the French coastline.

Special feature
Solar furnaces

The space-age looking structure in Odeillo is in fact a solar furnace. A solar furnace harnesses the sun's rays, through the use of curved mirrors, to produce extremely high temperatures, usually to generate electricity or melt steel. The mirrors reflect and concentrate the light onto a focal point which can reach a temperature of 3,500 °C. The same principles on which the solar furnace is based are being used to create solar-powered barbeques and inexpensive solar cookers. The furnace at Odeillo (**Le Grand Four Solaire d'Odeillo**; www.foursolaire-fontromeu.fr) is the largest in the world, and utilises a series of plane mirrors which reflect the sun's light onto a larger curved mirror which in turn focuses the rays onto an area the size of a kettle. The 300 plus days of sunlight a year, no doubt make this area a prime location for such technology. The world's first ever solar furnace (**Four Solaire de Mont-Louis**; www.four-solaire.fr) stands, not far away, in Mont-Louis. This 1420-mirror furnace was built in 1949, and the whistle for the Petit Train Jaune was one of the first objects produced there.

Le Grand Four Solaire d'Odeillo

Girona is one of Catalonia's main cities, and a major day-trip destination from Barcelona. Among its main sites are the cathedral, the old fortifications, the Collegiate Church of Saint Feliu and the Plaça de la Independència. The historic Carcassonne city centre, with its well-preserved medieval complex, is a UNESCO World Heritage site. Barcelona is one of the most visited cities in Europe, and its many architectural delights, beaches, museums, churches, and outdoor markets, together with the shops, cafes and restaurants along La Rambla, an iconic street through the heart of the old town, ensures that it has something to offer everyone. Toulouse has some sites of historical interest, but is best known for aviation and spaceflight. Airbus offers tours, in English and in French, of its aerospace assembly facilities. The historic centre of Montpellier has many interesting sites, and is located just 10 km from the Mediterranean coast.

A NOTE ON LIVING HERE LONG-TERM

English is not widely spoken, and good spoken French would greatly add to the enjoyment of any long-term stay in Font Romeu. Cost of living is relatively high, and a job may be required to fund a prolonged stay. France is in the EU and therefore all EU citizens have the right to work there without a visa. Any available employment is likely to be in the leisure and tourism sectors, and fluent French would be essential. Font Romeu is snow-covered for the winter months, so unless you were willing to combine cross country skiing with running, living there year-round may not be appealing. The good quality of life and laid-back atmosphere are definitely a draw. The ability to carry out quality sessions at a lower altitude means that it's possible to train here during the competition season.

FURTHER INFORMATION

A range of brochures, including accommodation listings, visitor guides, and maps, can be downloaded or ordered from the Font Romeu tourism office website (www.font-romeu.fr) or picked up from their office at the base of the main ski lift on Avenue Emmanuel Brousse. There is also useful information on the Font-Romeu-Odeillo-Via municipal website (www.mairie-fontromeu.fr), in French only, and the Pyrenees-Orientales tourism website (www.tourisme-pyreneesorientales.com), in French, English and other European languages.

RIGHT and ABOVE RIGHT The medieval town of Villefranche-de-Conflent

Sierra Nevada

World-class facilities and hotel-style accommodation at the CAR Sierra Nevada High Altitude Training Centre are major draws for athletes in a variety of sports, though the town's mountainside location makes it less attractive for runners. Spanish endurance runners and race walkers train here, but for those with a low boredom threshold, the lack of variety can be a major drawback. There is a synthetic track, and just 30 minutes down the mountain in Granada, there are options for almost sea-level track and off-road training. Sierra Nevada has a longer and warmer summer than any of the European altitude training alternatives, and at 2,430 m, is also one of the highest options on the continent.

Sierra Nevada, Spain (2,320 m)

Spain's national altitude high performance training centre, the Centro de Alto Rendimiento (CAR) Sierra Nevada, is based in Pradollano, on the slopes of Veleta, Sierra Nevada's second highest peak. Built in the early 1990s, and best known as a training venue for swimmers and alpine skiers, the centre is sometimes used by race walkers, and has some potential for athletes in other endurance sports.

Located approximately 30 km south of Granada, Pradollano is also the location of Sierra Nevada Ski Station, Europe's most westerly ski resort. The resort has hosted numerous alpine skiing, freestyle skiing and snowboard world cup events and the 1996 Alpine World Ski Championships. Sierra Nevada ('snowy range') is the dominant mountain range of mainland Spain, and Mulhacen, its highest peak, reaches 3,478 m.

Granada and the surrounding area has been populated by Iberians since the 8th century BC, and has experienced Phoenician, Greek and Roman influences, among others. The city itself was founded in the 11th century in the aftermath of civil wars which ended the Caliphate. The Emirate of Granada became the Iberian Peninsula's longest surviving Muslim dynasty, and finally surrendered to the Catholic monarchs after the last battles of the Granada War. A period of persecution, execution and expulsion of large Jewish and Muslim populations followed. Many of the mosques which were not destroyed, were converted to Christian churches, and the Jewish quarter was destroyed to make way for Catholic buildings and Castilian institutions. The Alhambra, a palace and fortress complex overlooking Granada, is the leading product of the city's Moorish history. It is this turbulent history, and diversity of cultural influences that make Andalucía one of the most vibrant and interesting regions in Spain; culture, as well as beaches, make the region a popular tourist destination.

AUTHOR'S VERDICT

Sierra Nevada isn't top of my recommendations. The accommodation and facilities at CAR Sierra Nevada are excellent, and the centre may be particularly appealing to teams wishing to train away from the media and distractions. However, the variety of trails is poor, and there is not much to do between training sessions. A car, to get away from the mountain every now and again, would be ideal. With nearby Granada just 700 m above sea level there is scope to 'live high, train low', but high temperatures in the city may make training difficult during the summer months (average daily highs for July and August are in excess of 33 ºC). Prolonged stays at the CAR Sierra Nevada would work out expensive, and given the great variety of other venues available for distance runners, I would suggest Sierra Nevada only for track runners or athletes in other sports.

Running ★★★★★ - Poor choice of trails; track for sessions; good gym facilities and support at the CAR Sierra Nevada; opportunity to 'live high, train low'; one of the few European destination greater than 2,000 m.

Convenience ★★★★★ - Though there is an airport in Granada, connections via Madrid are usually required; feels a little isolated; car required to get to civilization and flat training routes; higher temperatures and longer snow-free season than St. Moritz or Font Romeu.

Safety ★★★★★ - Very low levels of violent crime, no major disease or safety risk.

Cost ★★★★★ - Cheap flights to Malaga from many European destinations; cost of staying at CAR Sierra Nevada is high; car essential.

Cultural experience ★★★★★ - Opportunity to experience Andalucían culture and history in nearby Granada; Pradollano itself offers nothing in terms of cultural experience.

Things to do between training ★★★★★ - Pradollano is practically devoid of things to do between training; a few worthwhile sites in Granada, most notable the Alhambra, but spending time in Granada during the warm summer months can be exhausting.

Suitability for solo travellers ★★★★★ - Little to do between training; many guests don't speak English; car required to get off mountain; athletes training at camp are often in groups or teams; no running community.

Must do Visit the Alhambra in Granada; run or cycle at least part of the road up to CAR Sierra Nevada; have your breath taken away by beautiful sunsets.

Ideal for Athletes looking to 'live-high; train-low'.

Did you know? The access road which passes behind CAR Sierra Nevada, and within about 10 m of the summit of the Veleta, is the highest paved road in Europe. Because of its altitude, the road is used by major European car manufacturers to test new vehicles.

OPPOSITE Some of the accommodation in Pradollano
PREVIOUS Sunset viewed from the CAR Sierra Nevada

SPAIN QUICK FACTS

Capital/largest city Madrid
Official language Spanish
Currency Euro (€; EUR), divided into 100 cents
Public holidays New Year's Day (Jan 1), Epiphany (Jan 6), Día de Andalucía Easter (Feb 28)‡, Maundy Thursday*, Good Friday*, Labour Day (May 1); Assumption (Aug 15); Fiesta Nacional de España (Oct 12), All Saints' Day (Nov 1), Constitution Day (Dec 6), Immaculate Conception (Dec 8), Christmas Day (Dec 25)
Time zone Central European Time (CET; GMT+1); daylight saving (last Sun Mar–last Sun Oct)
International dialling code +34
Outgoing access code 00
Emergency contact 112
Power 230 V; 50 Hz supply; Type F, German-style (CEE 7/4) Europlug-compatible plugs and sockets, with 2 small round pins, and two earthing clips on the inside of the socket.
Driving Right side
Measurement Metric

* Varies according to Christian calendar
‡ Andalucían regional holiday

GETTING IN

The small Federico Garcia Lorca Granada-Jaen Airport (GRX) is just under 20 km from the centre of Granada, and 55 km from the camp. The airport has daily flights to a number of Spanish airports including Madrid and Barcelona. Budget airline Vueling (www.vueling.com) operates flights between Granada and Barcelona. The bus service connecting Granada Airport and Granada City Centre takes approximately 40 min.

Malaga-Costa Del Sol Airport (AGP) is located just 135 km away, and is easily accessible by road. It is the main international airport in Andalucía, and offers daily links to 27 Spanish cities, and over 100 cities across Europe. During the summer season there are also direct links to African, Middle Eastern and North American cities. A number of budget airlines operate from Malaga. A bus links Malaga Airport to Malaga city centre, with bus connections from there to Granada. The entire journey takes approximately 2 hr 40 min.

Almería Airport (LEI), 2 hr 15 min by car from Sierra Nevada, is also a viable option, with budget and charter flights from the UK, Brussels, and various Spanish airports.

Buses arrive at Granada bus station on the edge of the city. The journey between the bus station and the city (linked by Bus 3 and Bus 33) takes approximately 15 min. ALSA (www.alsa.es), the main intercity bus operator, runs buses to Granada from many of Spain's major cities. Granada is also linked to the rest of Spain by train. Services take approximately 11 hr from Barcelona, just over 3 hr from Seville, and approximately 4 hr 30 min from Madrid. Tickets booked online (www.renfe.es) at least 15 days in advance, can be up to 60 percent cheaper than those booked in the ticket office on the day of travel.

A scheduled shuttle bus service (Autocares Bonal) operates between Granada and Sierra Nevada, during the winter months (Nov–Apr). The journey takes approximately 1 hr, and buses leave from the bus station in Granada (Avenida de Juan Pablo II).

Apart from transfer services available through CAR, the only ways to get between Granada and Sierra Nevada during summer are by car or taxi, the latter which is expensive.

Visa requirements

Visas are not required for EU or EFTA citizens, or for stays of up to 90 days for citizens from Australia, Canada, the US and New Zealand, among others. Spain is part of the Schengen agreement, and holders of a valid Schengen visa can also gain entry. Others will need to apply for a Schengen visa in advance of travel. Visas normally take up to 15 days to process, but may take up to 60 days in some special cases.

Getting around

The resort itself is small enough to get around on foot, and if living and training solely at CAR, a car may not be required. Transport is useful for getting to flatter trails, for picking up supplies and for exploring the area. There is not much to do in the resort, so getting to Granada for entertainment is important. Cars can be hired from the airports in Granada and Malaga, and from the railway station in Granada.

Weather

Sierra Nevada's climate is classified as Mediterranean Subarctic. Average maximum daily temperatures in Pradollano for July and August are in the region of 20 °C. Cloud cover during the summer months is rare. Snow is normal between late November and late April.

Accommodation

Most athletes who train in Sierra Nevada stay at CAR Sierra Nevada. The centre, with its excellent facilities and comfortable full board accommodation, is the main attraction of the area. It is possible to stay outside of the centre and still use some of its facilities (for a daily fee), though priority will always be given to residents at the camp. Some apartment accommodation is available in Pradollano outside of the ski season and self-catering accommodation may work out cheaper for small groups and prolonged stays. Apartments are not always adequately equipped for self-catering. Accommodation can be booked through: www.go-sierra-nevada.com. Check when booking that your accommodation is actually in Pradollano, as other areas (e.g. Monachil) are just a short drive from the resort, but situated at a much lower altitude (Monachil is at 792 m). Accommodations in Zona Alto and Zona Media will be higher than those in Zona Baja/Centro. There are a few restaurants in the resort, but most are closed outside of the ski season. Apart from one small shop with basic items, a trip to Granada will be required to pick up food supplies. Many of the self-catering accommodations come with Wi-Fi access and laundry facilities.

Language

There are usually a few people who speak basic English at CAR, but some proficiency in Spanish is definitely an advantage. Andalucíans speak their own dialect of Spanish, with the final syllable less pronounced than in other areas of Spain (e.g. *buenos días* is pronounced as if it were *bueno día*). While locals will understand standard Spanish, they may be difficult to understand.

Health and safety

Pradollano is a very quiet town, and there are no serious health or safety risks.

Time

Spain operates on Central European Time (CET; GMT+1) with daylight saving between the last weekend of March and the last weekend of October.

Daylight hours range from just over 9 hr 30 min in mid December, to 14 hr 45 min in mid June.

	Mar	Jun	Sept	Dec
Sunrise	07:25	06:54	07:56	08:20
Sunset	19:22	21:36	20:22	17:58

Map of Granada, Pradollano and surrounding area

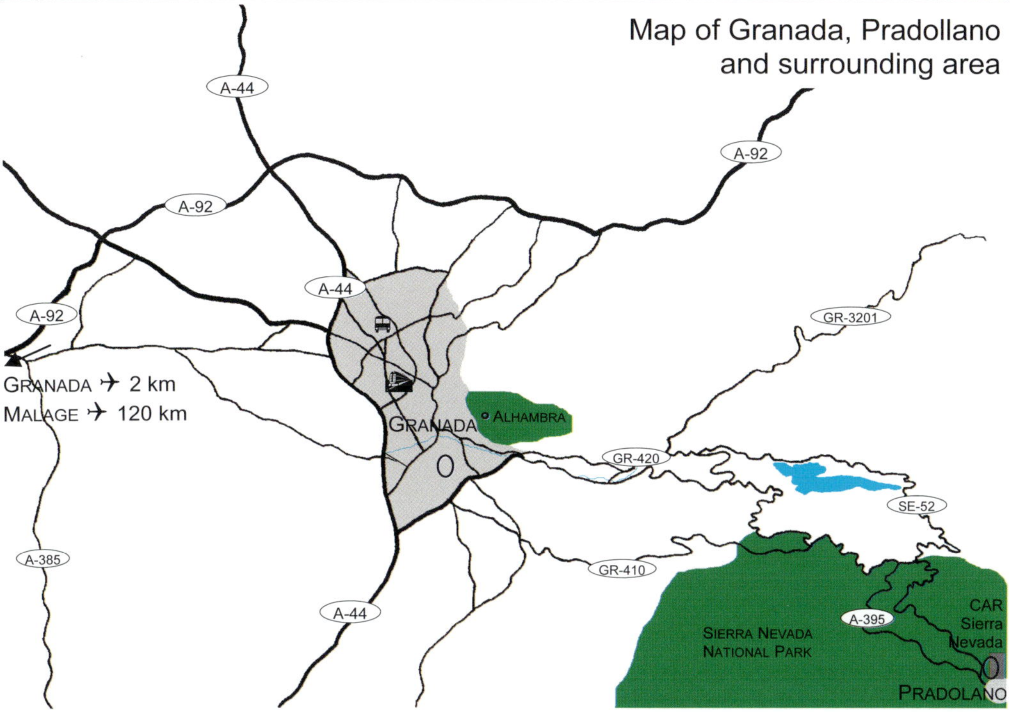

The ski resort of Pradollano

Training Camp
CENTRO DE ALTO RENDIMIENTO (CAR) SIERRA NEVADA

The Spanish High Performance Training Centres (Centro de Alto Rendimiento; CARs) were set up in the early 1990s to improve Spanish sporting success in the run-up to the 1992 Barcelona Olympic Games. While priority is given to Spanish teams, athletes from across the world have benefited from the excellent facilities and the hotel-style accommodation at CAR Sierra Nevada. Located at 2,320 m of altitude, and just 35 min by car from Granada (738 m) the location is perfect for a 'live high, train low' approach to training.

With fantastic jumping facilities, both indoor and outdoor, the centre has attracted elite level decathletes, long jumpers and triple jumpers. It is also a popular training base for Spanish and Portuguese endurance athletes including race-walkers and marathon runners. World-class triathletes have also trained from the centre.

Accommodation

The standard package includes accommodation, three meals per day, access to sport specific training facilities, basic health care, and transfers to and from Granada. Athletes stay in single or twin rooms equipped with phone, TV and Wi-Fi internet access. The accommodation block forms part of the same building that houses the canteen, the swimming pool, and the rest of the indoor facilities and is built around the 400 m outdoor Mondo athletics track. There is a coin-operated laundry facility within the residence building. A games room, TV lounge, library computer room and teaching classrooms are among the other facilities within the accommodation block. Any additional food and snacks required can be purchased at the coffee shop in the centre or at the small shop in the ski resort. A trip to Granada is required for any more than the very basic supplies.

As with other all-inclusive packages, staying at CAR Sierra Nevada is a more expensive approach to altitude training, though for some athletes, particularly for large teams, the convenience and comfort make it worthwhile.

Training facilities
The facilities at the centre include:
- 8-lane, 400 m Mondo athletics track with excellent high, long and triple jumping and pole vaulting facilities
- 6-lane indoor 130 m sprint straight with separate high jump and pole vault facilities
- 3G artificial football field (100 m x 53 m) in centre of athletics track
- An outdoor basketball court
- 6-lane 50 m Olympic swimming pool with facilities for underwater filming
- Two well-equipped weight-training rooms with free and fixed weights and gymnastics training facilities. One of the rooms opens out onto the track

- Indoor sports hall for basketball, handball, futsal, indoor hockey, tennis, volleyball and badminton
- Facilities for boxing, wrestling and martial arts
- Saunas, hydrotherapy pools
- Meeting rooms and conference room with capacity for 150 people and facilities for simultaneous translation into three languages, library, internet lounge, TV lounge, classroom

Additional services
A number of add-on services are available for an additional cost. Any medical or performance analysis services should be requested well in advance to ensure that adequate staffing is available, and that support fully meets your needs.
Transport Groups can avail of mini-bus transport to and from off-site training venues (e.g. athletics track in Granada).
Medical support Physiotherapy, sports massage, diagnostic testing in the event of injury (radiology, ultrasound, etc.) and blood screening (biochemical, haematological, lactate response) are available.
Performance analysis There is excellent biomechanical support for swimmers, and the pool is fully equipped with three-dimensional underwater video cameras to give poolside video feedback. Qualitative and video analysis of technique is also available for other sports.
Fitness assessments Speed, strength, agility and endurance capacity can be tested.
Nutrition Body composition assessments and nutritional advice are also available.

When to visit
The camp is usually very busy in the run-up to major European and World Swimming championships, when a number of national teams carry out the final phases of their preparation at altitude, and away from the media. Additionally, the centre is closed to non-skiers when FIS World Cup or other major skiing events are hosted by the Sierra Nevada Ski Resort (almost annually). Spanish athletes always have priority, and since the majority of the clientele are large national teams and groups, the centre's 87 rooms quickly fill up. You are advised to book early to avoid disappointment.

Contact
Website www.carsierranevada.com
Postal address Centro de Alto Rendimiento, Sierra Nevada, Monachil C.P. 18196, Granada

OPPOSITE Track with accommodation block in the background
RIGHT (TOP to BOTTOM) pool, indoor track, track and gym at CAR Sierra Nevada

SPORT FACILITIES AND SERVICES

In addition to the facilities at CAR Sierra Nevada, there are other training options in the area. The 8-lane 400 m Mondo track in Granada (Estadio Zaidín) is situated on Calle Torre Pedro de Morales at an altitude of approximately 700 m and is ideal for quality sessions. Reservations for the track can be made at CAR Sierra Nevada. There is a small per-session fee.

The limited trails and running routes from the camp are mostly hilly road or off-road routes. Approximately halfway down the mountain, 11 km from the centre, there is an almost flat gravel road which winds around the mountain at an altitude of approximately 1,700 m. This road is just over 2 km one-way. At the bottom of the mountain there is a flat path alongside the banks of Río Genil as it flows towards Granada. The river runs close to the A-395, and the path starts just beyond the link road between the A-395 and the GR-420. The altitude of this path is approximately 700 m.

Athletes in a variety of sports train at CAR Sierra Nevada. The area is particularly suitable for cyclists, and though there is only one main road off the mountain, there are plenty of good options in the region. Just remember to keep enough energy for the climb back up the mountain at the end of the ride.

Trail Run Spain (www.trailrunspain.com), organises trail running holidays in Granada province which include runs at altitude.

THINGS TO SEE AND DO BETWEEN TRAINING

The Sierra Nevada National Park and the city of Granada both offer sites and activities for those looking to be entertained during their down time. Overall, entertainment is limited, and athletes are advised to bring their own entertainment, or to have some study to do while on camp.

For those looking to ski, Sierra Nevada Ski Station (www.sierranevada.es) has a season which can last from late November until early May. Hiking is a popular activity, and while the summits of Veleta and Mulhacen are easy to reach, others offer more of a challenge for hikers. Mountain biking is also popular.

The national park, in which the resort is located, is ideal for those with an interest in flora and fauna. The Botanic Garden of Cortijuela houses many of the area's endemic plant species. Birdwatching is popular, and the Sierra Nevada Observatory is situated on the northern slopes of the range. There is a thriving population of Spanish ibex, some of which can be spotted around the ski resort, as well as wild boar, wildcats, and badgers. More information on the park can be found on www.juntadeandalucia.es.

Granada is known the world over for the splendid architecture reminiscent of its Arabic history. Alhambra (www.alhambragranada.com), a palace and fortress complex located on the Sabika Hill on the edge of the city, is one of the most visited sites in Spain. Constructed during the mid 14th century by the Moorish rulers and later used by the Catholic monarchs, this UNESCO World Heritage site combines Islamic architecture with 16th century and later Christian building and garden interventions, and is a must visit during your stay in the region. There is limited access to the site, and tickets should be booked in advance.

Other places of interest in Granada include the historic district of Albaicín which was awarded UNESCO World Heritage status in 1984; the cathedral, which is thought to be the first Renaissance church in Spain; the Royal Chapel; the Cartuja Monastery; Sacromonte Abbey; and Alcázar Genil, a 13th century Almohad palace.

A NOTE ON LIVING HERE LONG-TERM

While the 'live high, train low' possibilities make quality training possible almost year-round, Sierra Nevada offers little as a semi-permanent training home. Away from Granada, there is little to do between training, few employment opportunities outside of the ski season, and no established running group or club to get involved with. Granada can become very warm during the summer months, making training there difficult, though the city is reasonably well located for getting to races across Europe. Though cost of living in Spain is lower than many other European countries, living in a ski resort is not so cheap. The poor choice of trails would become unbearably monotonous over time. Apart from the lack of trails, Sierra Nevada is well equipped for short training stints, but not advised as a long-term training base.

FURTHER INFORMATION

Further information on travelling to and within Andalucía can be found on www.andalucia.org. The website www.turgranada.es provides details on sites in Granada and practical information in Spanish, English and other major European languages.

A flat trail approximately 11 km from the centre

Iten

Home to more world-class distance runners than anywhere else on earth, endless kilometres of undulating dirt tracks, beautiful views of the Great Rift Valley, a local diet perfect for endurance performance, a laid-back atmosphere with few distractions from training, and a cultural experience to cherish for life; Iten really is the ultimate running holiday destination. With an altitude of almost 2,400 m, track and gym facilities, and basic but comfortable accommodation, elite athletes looking to train with the best distance runners in the world are well catered for. Solo travellers can expect to make life-long friends, and runners of all levels will be inspired to be the best they can be.

Iten, Kenya (2,380 m)

Sitting on the edge of the Rift Valley, Iten is a distance-running mecca that provides the ideal training environment for endurance athletes. Some 2,400 m of altitude, an abundance of off-road running trails, and a history of distance running success (sprouting from Saint Patrick's High School, and Sing'ore Girls' School) makes Iten the most successful running town in the world. Runners from across Kenya flock to Iten to have a shot at running stardom and to hopefully gain financial security for themselves and their families. Iten is where Kenyan dreams come true.

Iten is to marathon running what Silicon Valley is to computer technology, and what Hollywood is to film production. More than a quarter of the town's 4,000 people are distance runners. Your status here is not determined by how much you earn, how big your house is, or how old your car is. Rather, the digits that really matter are those which represent your personal best for the 42.2 km marathon distance. Though best known for dominating steeplechase and cross country races at world level, it is the marathon which has truly caught the imagination of the Kenyan people. No country comes close to matching the Kenyans for their strength-in-depth over the distance. In 2012, 97 different Kenyans, many of whom train in Iten, ran faster than 2:10 for the marathon, including 58 of the top 100 times in the world.

A visit to Iten is the ultimate laid-back running experience. Kenyan athletes are incredibly friendly, and even without any special arrangements it is possible to find groups of Kenyan athletes happy for you to join in their runs and sessions, that is if you can manage to keep up. It's not unusual to spot world record holders like David Rudisha (800 m), or Saif Saaeed Shaheen (steeplechase) before him, blazing a trail around Iten or Eldoret, and it's possible to befriend elite-level athletes like nowhere else on earth. Even if you don't get to know world or Olympic champions, you're sure to be joined on your runs by a fleet of future champions, and by the time you leave, you'll no doubt have formed your own theory on why the Kenyans are so good.

Kenya is not for everyone. If you like your home-comforts, have a severe objection to hand-washing your own clothes, or find it difficult to switch-off, Kenya will either completely mellow you, or make you wish you'd never left home. Power supply can be patchy, at best; nothing is done with a sense of urgency; and the brown dust gets just about everywhere.

Author's verdict

Kenya is my number one destination and always the first place I suggest to people when they ask for advice. I've made numerous friends there, and get a fresh perspective each time I visit. I can't pick too many other destinations where I could spend ten consecutive weeks of my life and still be sorry to leave. Places like Iten demonstrate that there is more to training at altitude than hypoxic air. The town is beautiful, and the locals love athletics. Athletes of all levels come here to be inspired, and ever-improving facilities are making it a popular training destination for elite athletes from all over the world. Lornah Kiplagat's High Altitude Training Centre (HATC) offers warm showers, satellite TV, excellent food, and other Western comforts, while still affording guests an authentic Kenyan experience. If you want to see how the best in the world train, go to Iten!

Running ★★★★☆ - Dirt roads suitable for running everywhere; most routes are hilly, and become dusty when dry and muddy when it rains; dirt and Tartan tracks for sessions; all-inclusive camps meet needs of high performance athletes.

Convenience ★★★☆☆ - Getting in may take some time if connecting flights from Nairobi are not timed right; good weather most of the year; English widely spoken.

Safety ★★★☆☆ - Slight malaria risk; some risk of civil unrest; most crime is avoided by bypassing Nairobi and exercising common sense; poor health care; travel insurance with medical cover and repatriation in event of illness is essential.

Cost ★★★☆☆ - Low cost of living; flights are the major expense; some hidden costs including visa and vaccines; car not required (or recommended).

Cultural experience ★★★★★ - This is the real Kenya, the Kenya that you miss on safari; everyday opportunities to experience the laid-back rural life, to meet locals and to learn about Kenyan culture and life.

Things to do between training ★★★☆☆ - Ideal for those who are happy to chill out between training and get to know new people while drinking tea on the edge of the Rift Valley; not so stimulating for those who find it difficult to switch off and lead a laid-back lifestyle.

Suitability for solo travellers ★★★★★ - Plentiful opportunities to meet local athletes and other running tourists; locals are very friendly; safe for females, though white females will attract attention of local men.

Ideal for Any jogger, runner or international athlete who wants a running holiday to remember.

A BIT ABOUT KENYA

Kenya, named after Mount Kenya ('White Mountain'), Africa's second highest peak, straddles the equator, and has a diverse landscape consisting of desert, rolling plateaus, tropical forest and wildlife-rich savannah grasslands. The country's economy is largely dependent on tourism and agriculture, and almost half of its 43 million people live in poverty.

The Rift Valley, which runs through the centre of Kenya, is believed to be the birthplace of mankind. The boundaries of present-day Kenya, and neighbouring Uganda, were set by the British Prime Minister and the German Chancellor prior to colonisation in 1886. Kenya achieved independence from British colonial rule in 1963.

Kenya's diverse population includes the majority of linguistic and ethno-racial groups found in Africa. The estimated 42 different communities or groups are largely either Bantu or Nilotic in origin, with Cushitic groups, Indians, Arabs and Europeans forming small ethnic minorities. The decorative nomadic herders (Maasai, Samburu and Turkana people) are the most famous of Kenya's people, and are, in themselves, a tourist attraction.

KENYA QUICK FACTS

Capital/largest city Nairobi
Official language English (business), Swahili (conversational)
Currency Kenyan shilling (KSh; KES), divided into 100 cents
National holidays New Year's Day (Jan 1), Good Friday*, Easter Monday*, Labour Day (May 1), Madaraka Day (Jun 1), Mashujaa Day (Oct 20); Jamhuri Day (Dec 12), Christmas Day (Dec 25), Boxing Day (Dec 26), Eid ul-Fitr[†] and Eid ul-Adha[†]
Time zone East African Time (EAT; GMT+3); no daylight saving
International dialling code +254
Outgoing access code 000
Emergency contact 999
Power 240 V; 50 Hz supply; Type G British (BS 1363) plug and sockets with three rectangular prongs
Driving Left side
Measurement Metric

* varies according to Christian calendar
† varies according to Muslim calendar

BELOW Kenyan children taking a break from supervising their cows grazing at Kamariny Stadium
PREVIOUS The fertile land of the Rift Valley

This is Kenya
Adapted from the blog, 2 November 2010

Yesterday, for the first time, I heard a Kenyan child cry. The reason for the toddler's tears were not that he had fallen and grazed his pride, not that he had no shoes on his feet, not that he had been denied a fist full of hyperactivity-inducing sweets, nor that his parents had refused to buy for him the latest games console. The reason for his tears were that he just couldn't keep up with me running, no matter how hard he tried to make his little legs run... and this in Kenya, even for the youngest of the Kalenjin tribe, is classed as failure. I have no doubt that soon this child will be keeping up with the *wazungu* visitors to Iten, and who knows, maybe one day he will join the long list of Olympic and world champions that this tiny Rift Valley town produces; for running in Iten is everything.

Just a normal Tuesday morning at the track

Nowhere else in the world is your '42 km' (marathon) personal best so valuable, yet a sub 2:10 clocking potentially so insignificant. Last weekend a Kenyan won the Venice Marathon, another won the Dublin Marathon, and just yesterday the Frankfurt, Athens and, not surprisingly, the Nairobi marathons were won by Kenyans. Figures of 2:05, which wouldn't even guarantee you a place in a Kenyan championship team, would put you top of the European or American rankings.

The question I feel is not why are the Kenyans so good, but rather why is running success so important here? Why do young men from all over the country leave their homes and families to travel to Iten, and other similar training venues, to pursue running success? Why, with no guarantee of ever getting a trip to Europe, do they put everything into training for those 42 km of cardiovascular endeavour?

It seems that in Kenya, more than anywhere else in the athletics world, role models are a major player in the running success of the nation. In a town the size of Iten, Joe Jogger (by Kenyan standards), has the opportunity to train among world record holders. Everyone knows the ordinary guy next door who has reached international stardom. Athletes view those who are successful as being just like them, and rather than thinking of their more illustrious peers as being genetically gifted, they truly believe that if they too train hard enough, they can be the next Kenyan success story.

Tree to honour one of Iten's most famous stars

Just this morning I was training in the gym alongside recent world 800 m record-breaker David Rudisha. Conscious of not distracting him from his training, I failed to pluck up the courage to ask him to pose for a photo with me. Later I found that he was not only a celebrity among us *wazungu*, but a star attraction among the Kenyans who are very proud of their athletics stars. Like everywhere in the world, football in Kenya is big business, but it is here that athletics comes closest to rivalling 'the beautiful game' for popularity.

Kenyans, like most Africans, are very laid-back people. *Hakuna Matata* (no worries), is very much the order of the day. That is, of course, with two exceptions: driving and running. Then, almost like as if they have transformed into different people, Kenyans are suddenly in a hurry. Kenyan roads have no street lights. In fact, most of them are not surfaced, and having arrived at Eldoret airport after dark on Tuesday 5 October, I was reminded of how crazy the roads are. As we drove from the airport, in some heavy rain, the headlights of the taxi showed locals cycling along the side of the road without any form of lighting that either illuminated the road ahead or indicated their presence to other road users. And I'm not talking about one or two cyclists, I mean hundreds of them.

The trusty matatu

Matatus—crammed full Toyota Hiace vans—are the usual form of transport in Kenya. The drivers communicate with other road users, friends, and potential customers in a complicated series of horn beeps. Indistinguishable to the untrained ear, the relevant beeps can mean 'howaya', 'get the hell out of the way', or 'matatu approaching, climb on in with your chickens, sack of corn and empty buckets; we're full, but there is always room for more'. And these machines know nothing of road safety, common road courtesy, or patience on the roads. Totally mad! On the up side though, they are cheap, and you usually don't have to wait for very long to be picked up by one.

How are you mzungu?

In Iten, the children are either very cute or very annoying, depending on what mood you're in, how fast you're trying to run, or how many days you've been there. '*Mzungu*, how are you?' is the common cry of the local young (and sometimes not so young), as they attempt to high-five you, or run alongside you, on their way to school. The special skills of the Kenyan child means that he can spot you from miles off, and often you can hear the distant cry 'how-are-you-mzungu?' without actually being able to see anyone. One morning earlier this week, I was 'how-are-youed' by a small child squatting in his front garden—the Kenyan child is never too busy with the task at hand to greet a foreigner!

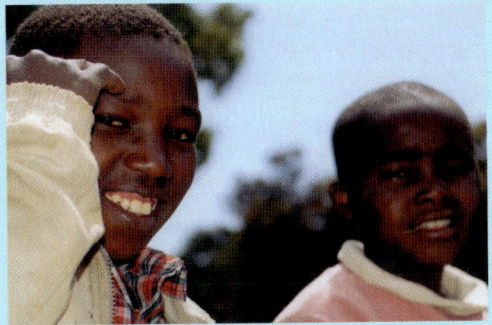

Future champions?

This is my sixth visit to Kenya, and I never tire of this very different way of life. It is a privilege to witness the best in the world training, but also to live for a short while among Kenya's very laid-back and friendly people. Part of me is sad when, over the five years that I have been visiting the country, I see how little change and development is occurring; how far behind the West the country still is; and how poor so many of its people still are. Part of me is happy that things are not changing; that the Kenyans remain true to their simple and happy existence. But the largest part of me is angry, when, just like the rest of the world, people think that money will give them a better life. In the past, I have seen the children cheekily asking for money. This time the popular request was 'mzungu, give me my sweets'. They may rot away their teeth, but maybe they won't rot away their souls.

Kenyan children do love to be photographed

Getting in

In most cases, travel will incorporate a flight into Nairobi, followed by an internal flight or bus connection to Eldoret and a taxi to Iten. Though well connected, travelling to Iten from Europe can take some time. Getting there from the US, Asia or Australia could take up to two days.

By air

Jomo Kenyatta International Airport (NBO) is a busy, three-terminal airport located approximately 15 km from central Nairobi. Terminal 1 and Terminal 2 are used mainly for international flights and Terminal 3 for domestic flights.

There are direct flights to Nairobi from Paris Charles de Gaulle (Air France), London Heathrow (British Airways), Zurich (Swiss Air), Amsterdam (KLM/Kenyan Airways), Brussels (Brussels Airlines), Istanbul (Turkish Airlines), Dubai (Emirates), Doha (Qatar) and Abu Dhabi (Etihad). Direct flights from mainland Europe take 8–9 hr, and from the Middle East approximately 5 hr. In addition to connecting through these cities, indirect routes from Europe or the UK could include an Ethiopian Airways connection through Addis Ababa, in which case you will need a valid yellow fever certificate to enter Kenya.

Flights from east coast North America, with one stop (Europe or Middle East), take from 19 hr, while one or two-stop flights from the west coast take 25 hr or more. Flights from Sydney, with stops in Johannesburg or the Middle East take just over 20 hr. Kenyan Airlines and their partners operate direct flights from Mumbai and Bangkok, which take approximately 6 hr and 10 hr respectively. There are direct flights to Nairobi from most of Africa's major cities, and to and from most of the major tourist attractions within East Africa.

Food outlets are scarce in the airport. Immigration and baggage collection can take some time. Check-in queues can be long and slow, so allow plenty of time for check-in on the return journey.

Since 2012, when Kenyan Airways started operating two flights per day, six days per week (not on Sunday) between Nairobi and Eldoret (ELD), it's possible to book flights right the way through to Eldoret. Budget operator Fly540 also operates flights between Nairobi and Eldoret, though these need to be booked separately through their website (www.fly540.com). When booking flights, check the departure times of connection from Nairobi to Eldoret. Arriving in Nairobi in the late afternoon will usually necessitate an overnight wait for a connection to Eldoret. There are no affordable hotels at the airport. Flights between Nairobi and Eldoret take approximately 50 min. From Eldoret take a taxi to Iten. Most accommodations will arrange for a reliable driver to collect you, and the journey will take approximately 1 hr.

By bus

Travel by bus is the cheapest way to get from Nairobi to Eldoret, but travel by road in Kenya is notoriously dangerous. The journey is long (at least 6 hr for the 330 km journey between the two cities) and dusty, though the views along the Rift Valley route are amazing. Keep an eye out for the equator crossing, baboons and zebra in the more rural areas, and the pink mass of flamingos feeding on Lake Nakuru.

Some services don't have a timetable (they simply depart when full), and those that do, rarely run to it. The Great Rift Express operates a shuttle minibus service between the two cities. This can be a particularly uncomfortable way to travel, though a seat in the front will give you a spectacular view. Easy Coach (www.easycoach.co.ke) is among the coach companies that operate between Nairobi and Eldoret. Their day service leaves Nairobi at 08:30. If travelling by bus arrange for a taxi to pick you up at the airport and drop you to the coach station (your accommodation provider in Iten may be able to recommend a reliable taxi driver in Nairobi). Be particularly vigilant, and keep your luggage close in the coach station. Where possible choose services that will start and complete their journey during daylight.

From Eldoret, take either a *matatu* or a taxi to Iten. Your accommodation provider may be able to arrange taxi pickup. A matatu is not recommended for those with a lot of luggage, but you may be able to hire an entire matatu at a more reasonable price than a taxi.

By car

Driving in Kenya, as in most African countries, is not recommended. The roads are treacherous, and navigating them is best left to the locals. In any case, a car is hardly needed, and flying between cities is much cheaper than hiring a car. If you do decide to drive, avoid travelling at night at all costs, as many vehicles do not have lights, animals may wander onto the road, there is a high risk of hitting a pedestrian or cyclist, and if you do break down, a recovery service is unlikely to come rescue you.

Visa requirements

Visitors from the EU, the US, Canada, Australia and New Zealand require a visa, which can be purchased on entry into the country. Visitors from a small number of countries (currently Afghanistan, Armenia, Azerbaijan, Cameroon, Iraq, Jordan, Lebanon, Mali, Nigeria, North Korea, Senegal, Somalia, Syria, and Tajikistan), must apply in advance for a visa. At time of publishing visas are not required for nationals of a number of African nations, including South Africa, and a small number of other countries.

Visitors are required to have six months validity on their passport from the date of entry into the country, and at least one blank page for visa and entry and exit stamps. Cash, in US dollars, euro or British pounds, is required to purchase the visa.

Working in Kenya, including voluntary work, requires a work permit. There can be significant delays in obtaining work permits. To avoid complications at immigration, do not state on your immigration form that you are a professional athlete in the country to train (as technically that's work).

GETTING AROUND

Getting around Iten and Eldoret is easy, although the trip between the two can sometimes take longer than expected due to overcrowded transport. Indeed, even a short walk to the shops can take a little longer than anticipated, as locals stop to greet you, and ask 'how are you?'

Most of the town is situated along the main Eldoret–Tambach road. The High Altitude Training Centre (HATC), Kerio View, and the police station are located close to the 'gates' of the town on the Eldoret side (west) of the town. The market, matatu station, some small supermarkets and most of the shops are located at the Rift Valley (east) end. The area between is mostly residential. The hospital and St Patrick's church and school are located just off the main road to the left as you head towards the valley (take the road just after the playing field). The

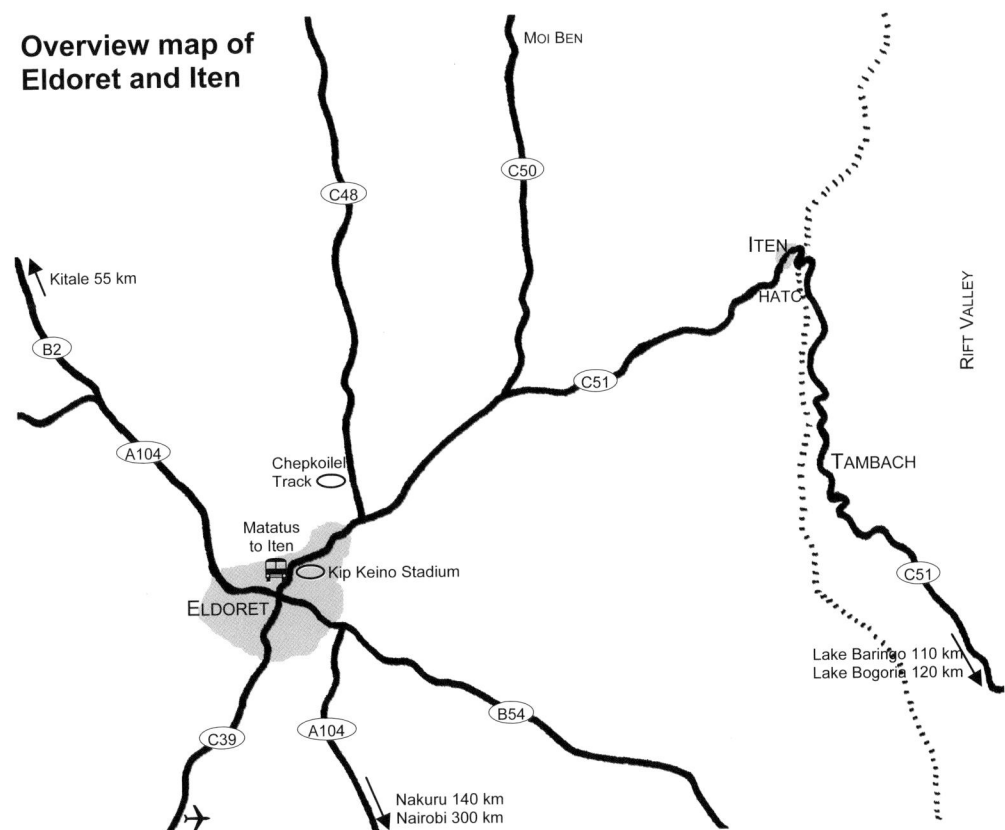

Overview map of Eldoret and Iten

distance between HATC and the Kerio Valley end of town is approximately 2 km.

By public transport
Matatus (public or line taxis), in the form of white and yellow minibuses, are the cheapest way to get to Eldoret. They operate fixed rates and run standard routes. Most run the whole way between Iten and Eldoret. To catch one of these, stand on the roadside, anywhere it would be possible for the bus to stop, and hail as approaching. At some stage during the journey, the conductor will indicate that he wants payment, at which point you pass the money to him. To get out, simply attract the conductor's attention when you reach your destination (though it's likely that they will remember where you're going if you told them when you got in).

Allow plenty of time for your trip. While Kenyans generally ignore laws restricting the number of passengers in a vehicle, you may be left waiting some time for a matatu with space if trying to board at an intermediate point along the route. Vehicles tend to wait until they are full or near full before departing their first stop, so it may be easier to get a seat if boarding at the station in Iten, or in Eldoret, than along the main road.

The buses are not the most comfortable form of transport, and occasionally experience delays due to punctures (spare wheels, if available, tend to be under everyone else's luggage and take some time to retrieve), or running out of fuel. Matatus make many trips each day, are usually in poor order, rarely have a full set of working seatbelts, and have a poor road safety record. That said, they are getting better, and, unless you have your own car, are the only way to get around. Matatu journeys can be somewhat enjoyable if you remember to take your sense of humour, your traveller's curiosity, and a lot of patience with you. After all, there's usually not much to rush for in Kenya.

The journey between Iten and Eldoret by matatu usually takes 35–45 min. Sometimes smaller vans operate direct services (with no stops) between the two, and while these charge a little more, and will only leave once they are full, they are slightly quicker, and slightly more comfortable. It may also be possible to hire a minibus if you are willing to pay the fare of a full bus, but generally Kenyans don't like to leave others waiting on the roadside. The smaller square vans, usually seen with people hanging off the back, are deathtraps, and should be avoided. These are becoming less and less common.

Taxis are also available. These are useful for making journeys that would normally involve changing matatu, if you have a lot of shopping or luggage, or if you are travelling in a large group. Negotiate a fair price (drivers usually hike up prices for wazungu) before hiring, and ensure that the car is in good condition. Minibuses can also be hired by the hour, or for a trip (e.g. if you want to take a trip to one of the nature reserves). Again, don't be afraid to negotiate a fair price.

Bodabodas are bicycle (or motorcycle) taxis which operate in areas where matatus and other forms of transport don't run, particularly on some of the rougher dirt roads near Eldoret, and around the city itself. You simply sit on the back of the bicycle and the 'driver' takes you where you need to go.

WEATHER AND WHEN TO VISIT

The Rift Valley's high altitude ensures a moderate temperate climate, much cooler than other parts of Kenya. There are two rainy seasons—a period of heavy rains between March and May, and a short rainy season between October and December. Rainfall, which can be heavy at times, usually occurs in the late evening and at night. Temperatures vary little during the year, and even when it rains there are usually periods of bright sunshine.

If you are coming to Iten to see the local stars training, consider that track athletes will be racing in Europe during the summer months, and that they spend a considerable amount of time at home with their families at the end of the season, before returning to Iten to train for the following season. Cross country races are the most exciting to watch, and you may want to time your trip to coincide with the Kenyan trials, which are normally held in Nairobi in mid to late February. District and regional championships take place closer to Iten, and there is usually at least one other large cross country race, featuring Kenyan international stars, in Eldoret during the cross country season. As many top athletes compete for the defence forces and the prison services, the annual championships of these services are also competitive affairs. A schedule of races can be found on the Athletics Kenya website (www.athleticskenya.or.ke).

Given its relatively high altitude, the lack of facility to 'live high, train low', and the abundance of hills, Iten is probably best suited for early season base training. Additionally, it takes approximately 24 hr to get from Europe to Iten (door to door), and the considerable travel involved should be considered when choosing Iten as a training destination in the run-up to an important race.

ACCOMMODATION

The main accommodations in Iten, particularly for first-time visitors, are Lornah Kiplagat's renowned High Altitude Training Centre (HATC; *pp. 200-201*), and the nearby Kerio View hotel and cottages. The HATC, in particular, is specifically designed to meet the needs of performance athletes, and charges an all-inclusive price which covers accommodation, three meals a day, and access to the gym.

Kerio View (www.kerioview.com), a well-known restaurant and bar on the edge of the Rift Valley, offers limited accommodation in cottages on the secure restaurant grounds. Rooms are more expensive than at HATC, but athletes, agents and other running-related visitors regularly stay there. B&B, half board and full board options are available.

For many years, these were the only two Western-standard accommodations available. Recently, Dutch athlete Koen Raymaekers opened a guesthouse (www.koenraymaekers.nl) which has luxury circular rooms on the edge of the valley and in 2012 Wilson Kipsang opened the Keellu Resort (www.keelluresort.com), which has self-contained single, double and deluxe rooms, each equipped with a telephone and satellite TV.

There are other cheaper forms of accommodation, including Jumbo Hotel near the Rift Valley end of the town, and a number of rooms, with outdoor showers and toilets, which can be rented by the month. For first time visitors, one of the more established accommodations is recommended, at least until you find a suitable alternative. Do not rent a room without viewing it first, and consider the difficulties of cooking your own meals, without modern kitchen appliances, before considering self-catering.

FOOD

Eating out in Iten and Eldoret is generally cheap, though away from the cafes and fast-food restaurants, choice can be poor, and service notoriously slow. Kerio View, the HATC and Keellu Resort have restaurants which are open to non-guests, and which sell traditional and Western foods, beverages and desserts. The views of the Rift Valley make the walk to Kerio View particularly worth the effort.

If you are staying in rented accommodation, sourcing and cooking food with basic equipment may be difficult. Consider hiring a cook and cleaner to prepare your meals and carry out basic domestic duties. If the cost is shared between a group, hired help will still work out cheaper than staying at one of the established camps.

BELOW Kerio View Restaurant overlooks the Rift Valley

Ugali is the Kenyan staple, and a diet of ugali is one of the many things attributed to Kenya's running success. Made from corn (maize) flour mixed with hot water until it becomes stiff like bread, ugali is traditionally served with boiled *sukuma wiki*, a strong-tasting kale-like vegetable. 'Sukuma wiki' means 'see-you-through-the-week'.

A typical lunch in Iten consists of kidney beans served with corn (*githeri*), or rice. *Uji* is a sweet, brown porridge made from maize flour, and is popular among athletes after a hard training session. Chapattis are a tasty flatbread served with beef or chicken stew and beans or peas. When eating out, snack foods include samosas (a version of the Indian classic usually filled with minced beef and chilli), *mishaki* or kebabs (lamb on a skewer, grilled until almost burnt), *mandazi* (a deep-fried dough), and roasted cobs of corn. Mangos and passion fruit are grown locally, and much cheaper and tastier than those available in Western supermarkets. Fruit juices are widely available and usually cheap, as are sodas and fizzy soft drinks such as Coca Cola, Sprite, Fanta, Krest (a bitter lemon drink) and Stoney ginger beer. Tea (*chai*) is the national drink and is usually made by boiling water, tea leaves, milk, large amounts of sugar, and sometimes ginger, together in a kettle.

SHOPPING

The small shops and supermarkets of Iten sell basic foods and biscuits, cooking fat, soap, plastic buckets and basins, and mattresses. Phone credit and Coca-cola is available at just about every food stall, shop and supermarket. There are also corn (maize) mills and butchers shops. There is a fruit market just beyond the Matatu rank. The general market, which operates on Saturdays, is on the hill opposite the fruit market. Stalls sell an interesting array of plastic buckets and water containers, second-hand clothes and footwear, and other household and hardware items. If you are looking for something specific, you may have to ask around, or more likely, take a trip to Eldoret.

There are a number of medium-sized supermarkets in Eldoret. Nakumatt (Oginga Odinga Street) and Tuskers Mattresses Supermarket (Komora Centre, Kimalel Street) are particularly good for food products, hardware, and Western toiletry brands. The market opposite the Komora Centre is a good place to buy fruit and vegetables, though this end of town tends to have more beggars and petty-thieves. The majority of businesses and shops are located in the blocks between Nairobi Road and Nandi Road and between Oloo Street and Oginga Odinga Street/Eldoret–Kitale road.

Though only a small percentage of Kenyans are Muslim, Muslim Indians (who observe Islamic holidays, that are not national holidays) run most of the shops. You may find that a large number of shops in Eldoret are closed on certain days, outside of normal Kenyan holidays, particularly during the holy month of Ramadan. Apart from a few small stalls in Iten, and a few of the larger supermarkets in Eldoret, shops and businesses are closed on Sundays. Some shops close for lunchtime, and you'll rarely find a shop open after dark.

Many Kenyan athletes get their running footwear and training kit either from sponsors, or second-hand from other athletes. Finding good-quality running shoes may be difficult, if not impossible, to find in Iten or Eldoret.

LANGUAGE

English is the official language of business and of the government, and school is taught through English. Most people speak good English, albeit with a strong African accent. All signs and official documents are in English, and most of the main newspapers, including *Daily Nation* and *The Standard* are in English. Kenyans also speak a basic form of Swahili, the official conversational language of the country, along with their own tribal language. The tribal language of the Kalenjin people is Kalenjin, also referred to as Nandi. Kenyans will take great pleasure in teaching you Swahili and Kalenjin phrases and greetings. Swahili is easy to pick up. The language is written phonetically, with each letter pronounced fully apart from 'sh' and 'ch', which are pronounced as in English.

Tea is known as *chai*, *safari* refers to any journey, and a *shamba* is a field or smallholding. White people are referred to as *mzungu* (singular) or *wazungu* (plural), a *matatu* is the common form of transport, and a small restaurant is sometimes called a *hoteli*. When the Kenyans say that they are running *polepole*, it means that they are jogging slowly, something which they do surprisingly often. When all else fails, '*hakuna matata*' (no worries) is the order of the day.

COMMUNICATION

There is good mobile coverage in Iten. Kenya operates on the same 900/1800 MHz GSM

Special feature
WHAT'S IN A NAME?

Just as O'Connor, O'Connell, and O'Brien are all common Irish surnames, and surnames beginning with Mac and Mc are commonplace in Scotland, Kenyan Kalenjins have their own set of common names. Names like Kiplagat, Kipkirui, Kipkoech and Kipkemboi repeatedly appear when Kenyan athletes are being mentioned. The shortened version of these names (e.g. Lagat, Kirui, Koech) also feature heavily, and first, middle and family names are often interchangeable. Recently there have been three different athletes by the name Robert Cheruiyot competing on the world marathon circuit, causing great confusion among journalists and commentators.

Although just 10 percent of the Kenyan population are Kalenjin, they account for approximately three-quarters of Kenya's elite distance runners. Kalenjin names, both birth names and surnames, are usually derived from a collection of just a few dozen. A Kenyan's first name (birth name), relates to the circumstances of his (or her) birth, with a boy's name typically, but not always, starting with the prefix 'Kip', and a girl's name usually starting with 'Che' or 'Chep'. A few months after a child's birth, they are given an ancestral name, usually only used by close relatives, and a biblical name. Following circumcision, a boy takes the shortened version of his father's birth name (i.e. without the Kip), or one of his other forenames as his surname. As brothers attempt to distinguish themselves they choose to take different components of their father's name, and blood brothers can often have different surnames. More recently, young men and women have begun to adopt their father's surnames in a similar way to Western tradition (e.g. Kipchoge Keino's sons have taken the surname Keino, rather than Choge, as would have been the traditional choice). Schools and the armed forces often drop the surname, and refer to a young boy by his biblical name and birth name. Don't be surprised if Kenyan athletes introduce themselves by a different name (usually their biblical name) than the one which they are referred to by their friends or family.

Some of the common Kalenjin birth names and their meanings:

Cheruiyot – born when everyone was asleep
Kibet – born at midday
Kigen – a long awaited son
Kimutai – born in mid-morning
Kipchoge – born near the grain store
Kipkeino – born when goats or sheep are being milked
Kipkemboi – born at night
Kipkoech – born at dawn
Kipketer – born on the veranda
Kipkorir – born shortly before dawn
Kiplagat – born at sunset
Kiprotich – born when cattle are brought home for evening milking
Kiptanui—failed to cry or breath at birth
Kiptoo – born when there was visitors
Komen – born when beer is being drunk or brewed

If you spend long enough with Kenyans, you're likely to be given your own Kenyan name. You'll feel like a world-class athlete almost instantly!

network as Europe and much of the rest of the world outside of North and Central America. Mobile roaming charges are very high, and visitors are advised to purchase a SIM card for one of the local providers (Safaricom or Zain). These can be purchased from one of the mobile phone retailers in Iten or Eldoret. Almost all shops and Kiosks in Iten sell top-up credit which the locals call 'scratch-cards'. International calling cards are also widely available.

While there have been internet cafes in Iten in the past, you are more likely to find working computers in Eldoret. Internet is cheap, but the connection is slow. Kerio View and HATC provide Wi-Fi internet connection for guests, but even this is slow, and uploading video footage or images

Some useful Swahili phrases
hello *jambo/salama*
how are you? *habari?*
very well *mzuri sana*
yes *ndiyo*
no *hapana*
please *tafadhali*
thank you (very much) *asante (sana)*
goodbye *kwaheri*
my name is… *jina langu ni…*
sir *bwana*
madam *mama*
how much? *bei gani?*
sorry *pole*
welcome *karibu*
me/you *mimi/wewe*

can take some time. A third option is to buy mobile internet connection. Internet dongles are sold in the Safaricom shops in Iten (though not always in stock), and Eldoret, and credit 'scratch-cards' can be purchased throughout Iten.

Kenya has a relatively efficient postal service, and international letters posted from Kenya can reach their destination in Europe in as little as two days. Incoming mail is not delivered to Kenyan addresses, and must be picked up from a post office box in the local town or village. Post office box numbers are therefore a crucial part of Kenyan postal addresses. Note that some businesses in Iten may have an Eldoret post office box number.

HEALTH AND SAFETY

Though safer than many African countries, there are some important health and safety issues to consider. Malaria and cholera are widespread, and a number of vaccines are required before you travel. It is not advisable to drink tap water. Bottled water is inexpensive and is available in most shops in Iten. Personal safety is also a concern, particularly if spending time in Nairobi, and the roads of Kenya are particularly dangerous.

Temperatures at altitude are generally insufficient for the parasite which causes malaria to develop in live mosquitoes, and malaria-carrying mosquitoes are generally not prevalent in the Rift Valley. However, some cases of malaria have been reported in recent years, and it is important that you follow the most up-to-date medical advice. Other species of mosquitoes, which can carry and transmit other diseases, are common around Iten and precautions should always be taken to avoid mosquito bites. Wear long sleeved clothing during and after dusk, sleep under a mosquito net, and use insect repellent when mosquitoes are around. You may need prophylactics if you plan to travel outside of Iten/Eldoret during your trip. Coastal areas, and the Maasai Mara, are among the many high-risk areas. There is a low risk of malaria in Nairobi.

Cholera, an acute diarrhoeal disease, is common in Kenya, and without medical assistance, may be fatal. To avoid the disease drink only boiled or bottled water, and eat only foods that you can peel or cook. Always wash hands before eating.

If you are travelling through Ethiopia, Uganda, or any other yellow fever risk area (mostly African and South American countries; www.who.int for further details), you will be required to show a valid yellow fever vaccination certificate to gain entry. Note that immunity starts 10 days after vaccinations. Other vaccines or boosters (including diphtheria, hepatitis A, hepatitis B, polio, tetanus and typhoid) are likely to be recommended for those who have not had vaccination in the last 10 years. Recommendations will be made based on the areas that you plan to visit, the time of year, and the activities that you will be undertaking.

You may notice that Kenyans refer to pretty much any illness as malaria, from the common cold to much more serious illnesses, sometimes including HIV. Malaria is the leading cause of morbidity and mortality in Kenya and approximately one in five deaths in children under the age of five are malaria related. HIV and AIDS are epidemic, and while rates have dropped in recent years, it is estimated that more than six percent of the Kenyan population are HIV-positive.

The Rift Valley region is normally peaceful, but following the disputed 2007 Presidential election, violence between tribes broke out across much of the area and Eldoret was particularly badly affected. More than 1,000 people were killed across the country in the disturbances. Presidential elections, which occur approximately every five years, are always likely to cause tension, and extra vigilance should be exercised if you plan to visit around election time.

Some parts of Kenya should be avoided, notably the Mount Elgon area near the Ugandan border, where there have been armed clashes since 2006, the roads in the north of the country where bandits abound, and the area around the border with Somalia, which has been closed since 2007.

Nairobi's reputation for theft and other street-crime has earned it the nickname 'ni-robbery'. Do not carry valuables such as jewellery, cameras and laptops, keep money in a safe place, do not walk around on your own, and avoid walking around at night. Avoid Eastleigh, Kibera, and all other slum and low-income areas of the city. Terrorist attacks have also occurred in Nairobi, the most recent in October 2013. The city is best avoided where possible.

Similar precautions and common sense should be exercised in Eldoret, especially around the matatu stations and the market area. Petty theft is the most common crime, though even this is relatively rare, and in general, the locals wish you no harm. Iten is usually a relatively safe place to be, and the aforementioned 2007 disturbances were a rare exception.

Money

The Kenyan shilling (sign: KSh; code: KES) is the local currency. Prices are sometimes listed in US dollars, particularly in the airport, and foreign currency is sometimes accepted. Like most African currency, the shilling is not widely available abroad. Foreign currency, is not restricted, and can be easily exchanged for shillings within the country.

Ensure that you have enough foreign currency (euro, dollar or British pound), to pay for your visa on entry. There are a number of currency exchange services and ATMs in Nairobi airport before immigration.

While most bank and credit cards work in the ATMs of the larger international banks (Barclays, Standard Chartered), not all are accepted at the small bank and ATM in Iten. Eldoret is a better option for withdrawing money, and even if your card doesn't work in the ATM, cash can usually be withdrawn, on production of your passport, within the bank itself. Only use an ATM outside an open bank branch, in case there are any issues. Both Barclays and Standard Chartered banks have branches at the Nairobi Road end of Kenyatta Street in Eldoret.

Power

Kenya operates on a 240 V; 50 Hz supply and uses Type G British (BS 1363) plugs and sockets with three rectangular prongs. Power supply in rural areas is notoriously unpredictable, and power cuts can occur daily. Don't become overly dependent on electrical equipment and charge laptops and phones when there is power. Power cuts rarely last much longer than an hour or two, so be patient. Pack a torch, or have candles and matches within easy reach in the likely event that the lights go out.

Time

Kenya operates on East African Time (GMT+3) and does not operate daylight saving, so, during British Summer Time, there is just a 2 hr difference between Kenya and the UK.

Due to its location close to the equator, there is roughly 12 hr daylight throughout the year. Sunrise starts between 06:30 and 07:00, and sunset at 18:30 and 19:00. Again, because of its equatorial location, the sun sets quickly in Kenya. There are no street lights in rural areas, including around Iten, so be sure to have your training finished before sunset.

BELOW Small stalls like this are common along all surfaced roads in Kenya

LAUNDRY

There are no laundry facilities in Iten. Individuals will need to wash their clothes outdoors by hand in basins of cold water. Bearing this, and the fact that the brown dust of the dirt roads gets everywhere, in mind, you should pack dark coloured, easy-to-clean clothing with which you are not too emotionally connected. On the plus side, the warm midday sun dries clothes quickly.

Older clothes blend in well around Iten, and the local aspiring athletes will be appreciative of any clothing that you wish to leave behind. Kenyans are particularly good with scrubbing and washing, and can give even the grubbiest pair of training shoes a new lease of life. Indeed, many of them clean their shoes daily.

CULTURE AND RESPECT

Kenyans shake hands when introduced to somebody new, and each time they meet an old friend. After just a few days in the country, you will find yourself giving firm, friendly handshakes to everyone you meet. It is not unusual for a Kenyan to invite you into their humble home where you will be offered chai, ugali, or even chapattis. Kenyans are proud of the little they've got, and like to show off their homes.

Though the locals find it strange that wazungu wear shorts when they are wearing heavy overcoats (anything below 25 °C is considered cold), they are used to athletes running around town in shorts and vests, and are not overly offended by scant clothing. However, a Kenyan would never run around topless. Away from the track, as a matter of respect, men should not run topless, and girls should wear more than a crop top. Walking around town in excessively revealing clothing will certainly draw unwanted attention, and may even offend.

It is illegal to destroy Kenyan currency, though paper notes may become so worn that they fall apart. Do not deface money in any way. It is also illegal to photograph or video any official building, including embassies.

Service charges are normally included in restaurant bills and tips are optional. You are not expected to tip a minibus or taxi driver. Hairdressers, porters, tour guides and bar staff do expect to be tipped. Any tip you do give should reflect your satisfaction with the service provided.

Service in restaurants, shops, banks and other businesses tends to be slow, and queues and delays are common. In some instances, wazungu will be fast-tracked, but don't depend on this. Allow plenty of time to do your business, take a good book to read, and either try to remain calm, or talk with your feet and leave. Getting stressed or irate usually tends to get you nowhere.

BELOW A beautiful sunset in Iten
OPPOSITE There is always a group or two of athletes causing a dust up on the dirt trails around the town

Special feature
SOME OF THE KEY PLAYERS IN KENYAN DISTANCE-RUNNING HISTORY

Kipchoge ('Kip') Keino was the first black African to have sustained success on the European and American racing circuits. At the Mexico Olympics Keino won silver in the 5,000 m before taking the 1500 m in an Olympic record 3:34.9. His achievements were spectacular given that he'd already raced in the 10,000 m and had a gallbladder infection, which prevented him from eating solids, for the entirety of the games. Four years later, Keino was pipped for gold in the 1500 m final in Munich, before taking the steeplechase title in his first serious attempt at the distance. Keino's success in the face of adversity in Mexico, together with his post-athletics endeavours (including building schools and helping support orphans), have made him the 'father' of all Kenyan running legends.

Sammy Wanjiru won Kenya's first and, to date, only Olympic marathon title in Beijing in 2008, thanks to the extraordinary front-running tactics that defined his short career. Wanjiru broke the world junior 10,000 m record, held the world half marathon record on two separate occasions, and his run in Beijing knocked almost three minutes from the previous Olympic record. Despite his undoubted athletic prowess, Sammy was a somewhat controversial figure, who, like some other successful Kenyan athletes, appeared to struggle to remain grounded following fame. He had children with multiple wives, was reported to be drinking heavily, was involved in a serious car accident, and was accused of illegal possession of a firearm and threatening assault on his wife in the months prior to his death. Wanjiru died following a fall from the roof of his Nyahururu home in 2011.

Kenyans are best known for their successes in long-distance races, but they have also had considerable success in the 800 m. As an African, world and Olympic champion, a former world junior champion, a world and Olympic record holder, an IAAF Athlete of the Year and a Kenyan Sportsman of the Year, there's nothing that **David Rudisha** hasn't achieved in the sport. His front-running tactics have brought a new dimension to championship 800 m running, and his gun-to-tape world record-breaking victory at the 2012 Olympics will go down in history as one of the highlights of the London Games. Over a distance which is notoriously unpredictable at major championship level (in London Rudisha became the first ever reigning world champion to win Olympic gold over 800 m), Rudisha has become peerless. Unlike most Kenyan athletes, Rudisha is a member of the Maasai tribe. He started out as a decathlete, and then a 400 m runner, before being prompted to try the 800 m. He became the world junior champion in 2006, and the rest is history.

When Rudisha first broke the world 800 m record in 2010, it was the 13-year-old record of former compatriot **Wilson Kipketer** that he broke. Kipketer was not only born in Kenya, but like Rudisha, was coached, too, by Brother Colm. During his illustrious career, Kipketer, competing for Denmark, won three world 800 m titles, a world indoor title, and a European title, and set a number of world records. His indoor 800 m and 1,000 m records still stand.

Paul Tergat, one of the greatest Kenyan athletes, is featured elsewhere *(p. 210)*.

BELOW *Trees dedicated to Yusuf Biwott, Augustine Choge and Isiah Kosgei on the grounds of St Patrick's High School in Iten*
OPPOSITE *The Jubilee Gardens in front of the classrooms at St. Patricks*
OPPOSITE (INSET) *Entrance to St. Patricks High School*

Tegla Loroupe is a three-times world half marathon champion, a former world marathon record holder, and the reigning holder of three long-distance track records (20,000 m 25,000 m and 30,000 m). She was the first African woman to win the New York Marathon, and added London, Boston, Rotterdam and Berlin marathon titles during her long and successful career. Loroupe is a global spokesperson for peace, education and women's rights, and founded a series of Peace Marathons which are run through the Tegla Loroupe Peace Foundation.

Kenyan-born, Dutch citizen **Lornah Kiplagat** is, like Loroupe, a three times world half marathon/world road race champion. She previously held the 20 km and half marathon world records, and won the world cross country title in Mombasa in 2007. Lornah continues to invest in the country of her birth and the HATC co-owner has been instrumental in putting Iten on the map.

One of the most famous people in Kenyan distance running is actually an Irish man. **Brother Colm O'Connell**, a retired Patrician Brother from County Cork, went to Iten in 1976 to teach geography for three months, and has lived there ever since. He had no coaching experience when he started teaching at St Patrick's High School, but he quickly learned the ropes, and today is one of the most respected coaches in the world.

Brother Colm has coached more than 25 world champions, including Rudisha and Kipketer, and his annual training camps attract budding distance runners from across the country.

A tree is planted on the grounds of **Saint Patrick's High School** in Iten to commemorate each world champion who studied there and a hall of fame details the exploits of the alumni of this, the greatest running school in the world.

Sing'ore Girls' School, located 6 km from the centre of Iten, has also produced numerous world-class distance runners. Among the school's alumni are double world champion Vivian Cheruiyot, Olympic 1500 m champion Janeth Jepkosgei and world championship medallists Silvia Kibet, Sally Barsosio, Lydia Cheromei and Jeruto Kiptum.

SPORTS FACILITIES AND SERVICES

Some of the best athletes in the world train in Iten, so you would expect to find everything you need for world-class training in the town. While that is the case, the facilities are surprisingly basic; evidence that you don't need shiny facilities or equipment to be the best in the world.

TRAINING CAMPS AND TOUR OPERATORS

Iten's most famous camp is the HATC *(pp. 200-201)*. It offers all-inclusive camps with accommodation, food and gym access for all guests. Kerio View also offers accommodation, food and gym access packages for athletes. A number of international organisations organise complete running safaris to Kenya for athletes of all levels. Trips last between one and two weeks and itineraries incorporate organised training runs, talks from local athletes, excursions, and safari trips. Accommodation, during the time in Iten, tends to be at either HATC or Kerio View. While these trips are more expensive than going it alone, they do have additional benefits, and may be attractive to recreational runners who want to sample all that Kenya has to offer. The Kenya Experience (www.traininkenya.com); Run With Kenyans (www.runwithkenyans.org), with trips which incorporate the Lewa Marathon and visits to other Kenyan training sites; Sports Tours Kenya (www.sportstourskenya.com); and Run Kenya (www.runkenya.com), which organises tailor-made trips with a variety of accommodation options, transport, trips and excursions, training programmes, physiotherapy and massage, are just some of the options available. Strive (www.strivetrips.org) organise three-week trips which incorporate volunteering and a trip to Maasai Mara for US students (age 14–19).

TRAILS AND RUNNING ROUTES

It is easy to find off-road running routes around Iten. With the exception of the main road to Eldoret, all the roads in the area are constructed of either compacted dirt or a mixture of rock and dirt. Even the asphalt Eldoret–Tambach road has a clay path running alongside it the whole way to Eldoret. As soon as you step from your accommodation, you are almost certain to be standing on a dirt track, perfect for running. If it's early morning, you're likely to have hundreds of training partners too.

The dirt roads have a few drawbacks. They become very dusty after dry spells, and if you're not careful, you can get a lung-full of dust each time a truck or car drives past. Following heavy rain, the dust turns to a thick red mud which clings to shoes and makes running very difficult. Luckily the sun dries the ground quickly, and normally your run will just have to be delayed an hour or two.

The area around Iten is hilly, and most routes will have at least one long climb. Running uphill at 2,300 m of altitude is not easy, and the hills may aggravate Achilles tendon or calf injuries. On the plus side, the area is hilly rather than mountainous, so you're unlikely to have to spend the first half of your run going uphill and the second half running down. Of course, if you do want to do a lot of climbing, take a matatu down the escarpment to Tambach, and run the 16 km back uphill to Iten.

If the hills are too much for you, especially as you acclimatise to the altitude, run at Kamariny Stadium. Running lots of laps will be tedious, but this is the only flat ground in Iten. The Eldoret road is undulating, and has some long climbs, but no steep hills. As Eldoret is approximately 200 m lower than Iten, there is a net drop on the way out, and a net rise on the way back. The path is slightly bumpy in places, but it's fine to run on. The asphalt is popular among marathon runners, especially on Sunday mornings when there's little traffic. Some people choose to run all the way to Eldoret (approximately 36 km from Iten), and take a matatu back to Iten.

Trail and mountain runners aren't particularly well catered for—the forests are probably the best option—and race walkers are confined to the track area, and the tarmac road to Eldoret.

While the running routes are easy to find, you quickly reach isolated rural farmland where it is easy to lose your sense of direction. One of the few landmarks in Iten that can be seen from the surrounding land is the telecommunication mast by the police station. Use this to find your way home, and remember that if you come to an asphalt road, it's probably the Eldoret–Tambach road. Keep a track of the turns you take in case you have to retrace your steps, and if you do find yourself really lost, don't panic; the locals will usually be able to direct you back to Iten. Getting seriously lost is rare, but going astray can be problematic if you're running in the midday heat and have no fluid with you, or if it is getting dark.

The fear of getting lost shouldn't stop you from exploring the best that Iten has to offer. The route suggestions *(p. 202)* will get you started.

European athletes of all levels have the opportunity to train on the same track as the best athletes in the world

Altitude training camp
HIGH ALTITUDE TRAINING CENTRE (HATC)

In 1999, Lornah Kiplagat and her husband Pieter Langerhorst set up the High Altitude Training Centre (HATC) in Iten. Today, it is one of the best known altitude training camps in the world. It has been used by Dutch athletes of all levels since it opened, and became one of Britain's official altitude training bases in 2010.

As a former world champion and world record holder, Lornah understands the requirements of elite athletes. Though her work means that she is often outside of Kenya, she ensures that the camp is left in safe hands while she's away. When she is in Iten, Lornah makes every effort to get to know the guests at the camp, and to ensure that all their needs are being met.

Buffet-style meals, which include European and Kenyan dishes, are served three times a day in the camp restaurant. Approximately 90 percent of the food served comes from the HATC organic farm, and is harvested on the day of cooking. All food is prepared with the nutritional needs of athletes in mind. In addition to the food provided as part of camp package, a restaurant (Iten Club) which serves traditional and Western food including pizzas, burgers, chapattis and pastries throughout the day, was opened on the camp grounds in 2013. Iten Club is also open to the public.

Guests are accommodated in basic but comfortable standard twin and deluxe en suite rooms. The showers are solar powered ensuring that hot water, a commodity in rural Kenya, is available even when there are power cuts.

The gym within the camp is well equipped by Kenyan standards. Use of the gym is free for those staying at the camp, and other athletes and visitors to Iten can use it for a small daily, weekly or monthly fee. Equipment includes free weights and benches, a squat rack, a cable machine, other machine weights, some cardiovascular equipment and saunas. Gym instructors at the camp run core/circuit sessions three times per week which are also free for guests at the camp. Some of the local athletes take part in these sessions. A map of the local running routes is displayed in the centre, and training advice and schedules, for athletes of all levels, are available for a fee.

Physiotherapists based at the camp provide massage and treatments. Physiotherapists working at the camp have been trained by world-renowned physical therapist Gerard Hartman, and treatments are charged per session. Groups travelling with their own physiotherapist can hire a treatment room within the gym complex.

An outdoor swimming pool, with a new solar heating system, provides the perfect environment for cross-training, and aqua jogging belts are available to borrow at the camp. Mountain bikes can also be rented for a small daily fee. Guests will also have access to the 400 m Tartan track at the Lornah Kiplagat Sports Academy, 2 km from the track, once it opens in 2014.

There are table tennis tables, and a lounge with satellite TV and free Wi-Fi internet access, and other entertainment at the camp. There is 24-hour security at the camp and its location next to the police station makes it the safest place in Iten.

Camp prices include accommodation, three meals per day, and use of gym and pool. Transfers to and from Eldoret airport can also be arranged. The camp is located on the Eldoret side of Iten close to the track. Though large groups are more frequent in the last couple of years, the HATC is still one of the best camps to stay at as a solo traveller and there is a great opportunity to meet like-minded runners from around the world.

When to visit
The HATC is busier at certain times of year, with the Christmas holiday period particularly popular. With national teams like Great Britain now using the camp on a regular basis, spaces may be limited from time to time. Book early if you have your heart set on a certain time of year.

Contact
Website www.lornah.com
Postal address PO Box 6943, Eldoret, Kenya

OPPOSITE The main reception area at HATC
RIGHT (TOP to BOTTOM) The dining area, swimming pool, chill-out area and one of the accommodation blocks at the centre

Pond Loop (approximately 8 km)
Starting on the dirt track alongside the main asphalt road opposite the HATC entrance/Kaptagat road, head towards Eldoret for approximately 3 km. This first section is mostly gentle downhill. After approximately 3 km you will pass a lake on the left and come to an area with a few houses and shops. There is a road to the right (Kipsoen Road), and directly opposite there is a small road beside a corn mill which is not clearly visible from the main road. Beware of traffic when crossing the main road. Follow this road sharply downhill for approximately 100 m, leaving the lake to your left, and then take the steep uphill that follows. At the top of the hill the road levels out, and winds past a few small homes before reaching the Kaptagat road. At the junction (approximately 5.5 km into the run) take a left turn, and continue on this road, up a few smaller hills, until you return to the starting point.

The Kaptagat Road, known locally as the all-weather road, has a stone base, and doesn't get as muddy as other roads after rain. It is a popular out-and-back route, and also has other turn-off points that connect back to the main Eldoret–Tambach road.

Helen's Hill Loop (approximately 4.5 km)
From HATC head downhill towards Iten. At the bottom of the hill, which is a popular meeting point for athletes, take a left turn along the Kiptabus Road. The road will continue flat for approximately 1.5 km, curve to the right, and then go slightly downhill. Take the next left up a big hill. This hill is often used for hill repetitions. At the top of the hill you join another road. Turn left and continue up the gradual climb until you reach the Eldoret–Tambach road. Turn left and head towards the starting point. The simple instruction for this route is to take the first left all the way around.

To make this route longer don't take the left up the hill off the Kiptabus road, but take the left turn, almost immediately after it. Continue past a school on the left, take the next left turn, and the turn left when you reach a T-junction. You will now be on the road which eventually rejoins the Eldoret–Tambach road.

For some of the more ambitious routes, get somebody to lead the way, but take note of any turns that you take, and any signposts or landmarks. This may sound obvious, but in Kenyan countryside, where homes are either mud huts or timber shacks, things can look surprisingly similar.

Iten Playing Fields (Location Field), the area of grass on the left as you reach Iten, is where local cross country races are held. The fields here, together with the grass area in the centre of the track, are used for 'diagonals'. Sing'ore Forest, approximately 5 km from Iten, is popular for long runs, though some of the routes within the forest can be very hilly. There is also a steep hill in the forest near Kamariny which is ideal for killer hill repetitions.

You are likely to be joined on your run by schoolchildren asking 'how are you?' If you find this distracting, try to avoid running in the evenings when the children are making their way home from school.

TRACK FACILITIES

Renovated in 2010, Kamariny Stadium is located approximately 3 km from the centre of Iten (1.5 km from HATC). It is a dirt track that is just slightly longer than 400 m (nobody appears to know the exact distance, but it is somewhere between 404 and 410 m). There is no fee to use the track, but beware that at certain times, Tuesday mornings in particular, you may have to share with up to 200 other athletes, and sometimes sheep or cows may be grazing on the infield. The track becomes almost unusable after rain, so be prepared to defer your session to another day, or to take the trip to Chepkoilel track.

In January 2013, work began on a synthetic track at the Lornah Kiplagat Sports Academy, a new state-of-the-art girls' academy due to open soon.

Chepkoilel track on Chepkoilel University College Campus, like Kamariny, is a dirt track approximately 400 m around. To get to the track from Iten, take a matatu towards Eldoret, as far as Kimumu, the large built-up area before Eldoret (approximately 28 km from Iten) where there are a number of small furniture 'factories'. From there, take a matatu down the road to the right towards Chepkoilel University College (Moi University). Get off at the first gate and follow the road straight into the campus until the track appears on your right after approximately 800 m. The road from Kimumu to the track is also perfect for a warm-up.

There is a track on the Iten side of Eldoret at Kip Keino Stadium. This is where most local track meets including the provincial championships, are held each May and June.

OPPOSITE The dirt roads and forest trails of Iten make ideal running surfaces

Map of Iten and suggested trails

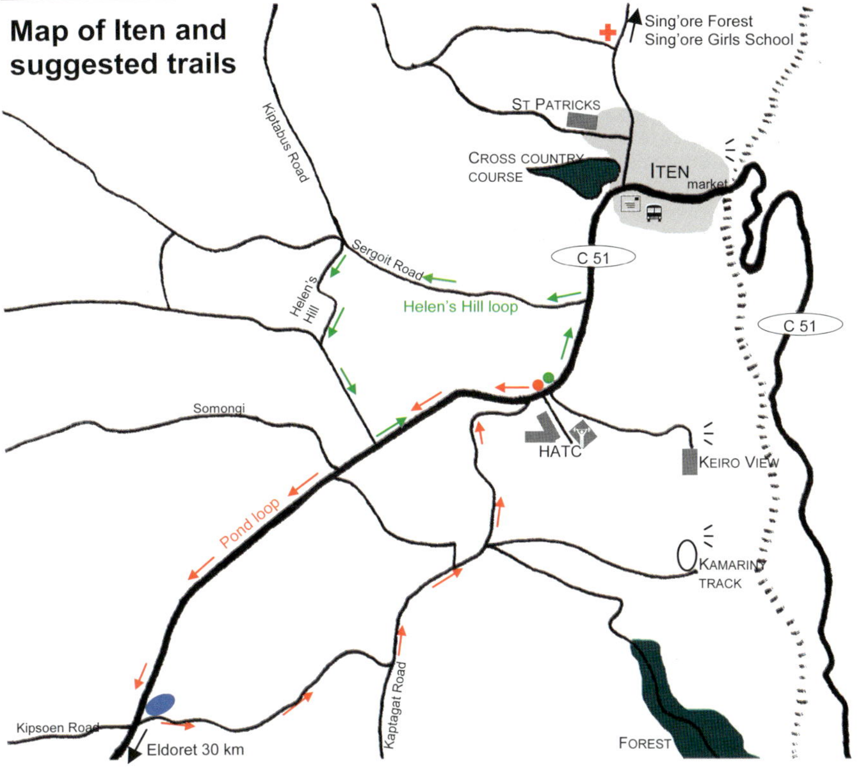

Gym facilities

The medium-sized gym at HATC is free for guests, and open to non-guests for a small daily, weekly or monthly fee. Core and strengthen sessions, specific to runners, are run three evenings a week at the camp. There is also a gym in the accommodation block at Kerio View.

Cross-training options

Most cross-training opportunities in Iten are through the HATC, and include mountain biking, swimming, aqua jogging, and gym work. The trails are great for mountain biking, and guests can hire bikes from the HATC.

Sports medicine and sports science support

There are physiotherapists based at HATC who can provide physiotherapy and massage treatment for a fee to guests at the camp and non-guests. There are usually a couple of other massage therapists based in the town who offer various standards of service. Ask local athletes for their recommendations.

Local races

You can nearly always find a local cross country or road race to participate in around Iten or Eldoret, but race details are often spread by word of mouth and often change at the last minute. Start times are certainly a misnomer. If you are taking part in a local race, be sure that you have realistic expectations. Not only will you be battling 2,400 m of altitude, but you will also be racing against the best running population in the world. Any mzungu who places any higher than the back of the field has done quite well.

Further afield, the Nairobi Marathon, and the Lewa Marathon, an off-road race held on Lewa Wildlife Conservancy, are popular among foreigners. Both Nairobi and Lewa are at approximately 1,700 m above sea level.

Running community

Iten is the training base of hundreds of Kenyan athletes, including 800 m world record holder and Olympic champion David Rudisha, World Half Marathon champion Mary Keitany, 2011 World Marathon champion Edna Kiplagat, Florence Kiplagat, Linet Masai and Wilson Kipsang, to name but a few. Since 2010, the British athletics squad have been using it as a winter training base, and double Olympic champion Mo Farah regularly trains here. Members of the Qatar team, many of them born in Kenya, train in the town. A number of Dutch athletes also use Iten as a training base, and athletes from over 40 countries have stayed at HATC.

Suitability for other sports

Iten is a running town, and you will rarely see athletes from other sports training here. Swimming is possible in the 25 m pool at HATC, and recently there has been a group of Kenyan road cyclists training in the town. With only one asphalt road in the area, road cycling may become monotonous, though the road for Tambach will provide a suitable challenge. Bike parts will also be very difficult to find.

BELOW Kenyan athletes perform 'diagonals' on the infield at Kamariny Stadium
OPPOSITE The gym at HATC provides a range of equipment for high performance training

Kenya: the ultimate experience

A visit to Iten is as much about the experience as it is about the altitude. Anyone with any interest in running will be aware of the depth of Kenyan distance running talent, and no town in the world has produced distance-running champions like Iten has. These are some suggestions on how to get the full Kenyan experience:

Sit on the edge of the Rift Valley. It's inconceivable that anyone could tire of the view across the valley, a wonderful sight that changes with season and the time of day. Marvel at the beautiful patchwork of fields in the Kerio Valley, or try to spot the lakes of Baringo and Bogoria in the steamy Rift Valley floor beyond. There are views of the valley from the view point (end of the road through Iten), from Kerio View, and from Kamariny Stadium.

Run with the Kenyans. The Kenyans love to welcome wazungu of all levels into their group. They run surprisingly slow on their recovery runs and keeping up is not always a problem, but beware! Morning runs usually start at a pace that is barely faster than walking, and gradually get faster and faster. Know which direction home is, because if they wish, Kenyans can drop you in an instant. Thursday morning fartlek sessions bring together many of the town's runners, and are a great way of experiencing the training environment. Just don't expect to be at the front of the pack.

Watch a track session. The wildebeest are not the only ones that cause a dustup in Kenya. Colourful, beautiful, dusty and very fast is the best way to describe the weekly group sessions at Kamariny Stadium.

Have tea with a world champion. World, Olympic, and major city marathon champions are in plentiful supply around Iten and don't be surprised if you find yourself having tea in the home of an accomplished athlete. Kenyans love to welcome visitors into their homes and the successful athletes are no different. In Iten, everybody is equal.

If really brave, enter a race. Prepare to be humbled. While the Kenyans may show some compassion during a training run, it's every man for himself come race day. Kenyans use every opportunity they get to impress agents and potential managers, and racing can be a humbling experience for any mzungu athlete.

THINGS TO SEE AND DO BETWEEN TRAINING

When not running with the Kenyans, or watching them train, the local way-of-life is to drink tea and relax. If relaxing is not for you, there are just a few options. The HATC offers table tennis for its guests, and you can hire a bike and search for monkeys in the forest. Locals are more than willing to teach you how to grind corn, and how to make your own ugali. It may be possible to visit St Patrick's High School, but you should bear in mind that it is a working school. Card and board games are common forms of entertainment at the camp. African crafts and other souvenirs are sold in Eldoret–once you've managed to find where the traders are based (they move around a bit) you can practise your haggling skills and get your hands on some wooden giraffes, colourful jewellery and beautiful batiks. And of course there's always the dreaded hand washing to be done!

BELOW Monkeys can be spotted in the forest
OPPOSITE The track at Kamariny is the flattest place in Iten to run or race walk

REST DAY EXCURSIONS

Thousands of tourists flock to Kenya each year for the wildlife, and the country certainly has one of the most diverse collections of mammals and birds in the world. Lake Nakuru National Park, on the road between Eldoret and Nairobi, and approximately 200 km (3 hr 30 min by car) from Iten, is one of the most famous national parks in the country. The lesser-visited Lake Baringo and Lake Bogoria nature reserves, situated near the Tugen Hills in the Rift Valley, 115 km (2 hr) east of Iten, also offer a wide selection of wildlife. The easiest way to get to the parks is to group up with other visitors and hire a vehicle and a driver for the trip. Most drivers around Iten will have done the trip before, and will happily act as a guide. The park restaurants are expensive, and it is recommended that you take your own food.

Lake Nakuru National Park is famous for the massive flocks of lesser and greater flamingos that gather around the water. They can number as many as two million at some stages during the year! While there are no elephants in the park, you are guaranteed to spot rhinos, buffalo, giraffe, impala, zebra, baboons, monkeys, pelicans, and storks. Hyenas, hippopotamus, jackals and pythons are common, and if you are lucky, you will see lions and leopards. The park boasts one of the world's largest black rhino populations. The landscape in itself is an attraction and varies from dense forests to grasslands.

Hippopotamuses, crocodiles and more than 400 species of bird, including Goliath heron, the largest of the heron species, can be spotted at Lake Baringo. Lake Bogoria, 30 km south of Baringo, has geysers and hot springs and its colourful waters are particularly beautiful. Large populations of lesser flamingos can be seen here at certain times of the year.

Even if you can't afford the time to go on safari, you are likely to spot some wildlife during your trip. If you choose to take the bus between Nairobi and Eldoret, you are almost certain to pass groups of baboons and zebra along the way. Keep an eye out for the distinctive pink hue of the flamingos around the lake as you pass through Nakuru. Just 40 min from Iten, along the scenic road to Kabarnet, the Rimoi Game Reserve is home to some wild elephants and buffalo, and crocodiles can be spotted in the nearby Cheploch Gorge. Herds of giraffe can be spotted around Moiben, the distinctive peak to the north about halfway between Eldoret and Iten, and there are baboons and monkeys in the forests around Iten.

A NOTE ON LIVING HERE LONG-TERM

A number of Western athletes move to Kenya to train long-term, or base themselves there for a considerable length of time. The cost of living is very low, particularly if you rent one of the basic rooms in the locality, and even if you choose to hire a cleaner and cook. Individuals may choose to volunteer at the hospital in Iten, or in Eldoret, or in one of the local schools, but finding paid work is virtually impossible. Any work, including voluntary work, requires a work permit. Tourist visas are valid for up to three months. Racing may be a problem, as getting to sea level competition would involve travelling outside of Kenya. It's difficult to buy sports clothing and training shoes, so ensure that you take all the kit you need with you. Not everyone will adapt to living in Kenya; many miss their home comforts, and become irritated with constant delays and the laidback, non-progressive attitude. For those that want to escape the stress of life in the West, there is no better destination than Kenya.

FURTHER INFORMATION

Kenya is a major tourist destination, though Eldoret and Iten rarely feature in travel guides. The North Rift Valley Tourism website (www.northrifttourism.com) has useful information and a good map of Eldoret. Good general Kenyan tourist websites include the Ministry of tourism website (www.tourism.go.ke), Magical Kenya (www.magicalkenya.com), and the website of the Kenyan Tourism Federation (www.ktf.co.ke). The website of the Kenyan embassy or high commission in your country should be a good resource for up-to-date travel and safety information. There are a number of travel agents and tour operators based in Eldoret. Ian Chaney, an athlete representative who has spent a considerable length of time in Kenya, has published an e-book entitled *Travel Kenya: The Essential Guide*. The book, available through Lulu (www.lulu.com), provides lots of useful information on running-related travel within Nairobi, Eldoret and Iten.

OTHER ALTITUDE TRAINING SITES IN KENYA

While Iten is the best known Kenyan training base, Eldoret, Kaptagat and Nandi Hills are also popular. Though a large number of athletes train in Eldoret, it is a lot more polluted than Iten, spending time there can be draining, and there are added distractions from training. Eldoret is at a slightly lower altitude than Iten, and consequently, becomes warmer during the day. Unless you are working or volunteering in Eldoret, the city is best avoided. Wazungu do use Kaptagat (approximately 30 km south of Iten) and Nandi Hills from time to time, but trips there are easier to arrange if you know a local athlete.

Run2gether (www.run2gether.com) is a running organisation born out of a partnership formed between sports clubs in Austria and Kenya. The organisation welcomes visitors to their sites in Austria *(p. 339)*, and in Kiambogo, a village 80 km north-west of Nairobi. Accommodation and food is provided as part of the package, and guests have the opportunity to visit a number of sites and national parks, including Hell's Gate National Park and Lake Nakuru, within an hour of the centre.

BELOW Another beautiful Iten sunset
OPPOSITE The Rift Valley

Extra Special Feature
RIFT VALLEY RIVALS: KENYA V ETHIOPIA

The rivalry between the Kenyan and Ethiopian distance-running communities is epitomised in about 15 seconds of Olympic history. The final 100 m of the 10,000 m final at the Sydney Olympics in 2000 saw the tall Kenyan Paul Tergat, and the barrel-chested Ethiopian Haile Gebrselassie do battle for the coveted Olympic gold medal. Gebrselassie was the reigning Olympic and world champion, and the current world record holder over the distance, but was carrying an injury. Tergat had five consecutive world cross country titles to his name, and had finished runner-up to Gebrselassie at world-level over the distance on three previous occasions. They both wanted that title, and neither gave an inch. The race grew and grew in momentum over the course of the 25 laps, and reached one of the greatest crescendos in the history of sport down the home straight in Stadium Australia on Friday 22 September 2000.

Kenyan and Ethiopian rivalry began long before the duels between Tergat and Gebrselassie. The East African neighbours have surprisingly little in common culturally or historically, apart from their successes in athletics, and the national importance that distance-running holds. The Melbourne Olympics in 1956 saw the first appearance of both countries. Just four years later Ethiopia won their first Olympic title courtesy of Abebe Bikila. Kenya had to wait a further Olympic cycle until they made it onto the medal table, but by 1968 Kenya had the slight upper hand winning nine medals. It was in the 10,000 m at these Games, when Kenya's Naftali Temu outsprinted Mamo Wolde of Ethiopia for the title, that the seeds of this great rivalry finally germinated, and set the tone for Olympic finals to follow.

This rivalry isn't just among the men. Epic duels between Ethiopia's Tirunesh Dibaba and Kenya's Vivian Cheruiyot in recent years have put female East African distance runners well and truly in the spotlight. The Kenyan women have won the World Cross Country team title 11 times; the Ethiopian women are just behind on 10. Only once since 1990 (Portugal 1994), has the title gone outside of East Africa. Since its first running in 1989, no other country has won the junior women's team title.

Incidentally, Gebrselassie came out on top in the Olympic final in Sydney. He came from behind to cross the line just 0.09 seconds ahead of Tergat, the smallest ever winning margin in an Olympic 10,000 m final.

Ethiopians have won 45 Olympic medals, all in the sport of athletics, and 79 of Kenya's 86 Olympic medals come in the sport of track and field (as of 2012). Athletes from Kenya currently hold the 800 m, 3,000 m, 10 km and marathon records, while Ethiopian athletes hold the 5,000 m and 10,000 m records. Kenya and Ethiopia have dominated world cross country championships since the early 1980s. All nine senior men's individual and team titles have been won by either Kenya or Ethiopia, and no other country has won a senior men's long course team title since 1980.

- The twenty fastest times ever run for 5,000 m belong to twelve athletes from the two countries (six Ethiopians; six Kenyans).
- World record holder Zersenay Tadese (Eritrea) is the only athlete not from Kenya or Ethiopia in the all-time top 20 for the half marathon.
- The seven fastest athletes ever over 10,000 m come from the two countries, four from Kenya, and three from Ethiopia.

Tergat and Gebrselassie were two of the greatest athletes the world has ever seen. The fact that both graced the tracks, roads and fields during the same era, is the great privilege of the world of athletics. While the two are friends off the track—Gebrselassie even apologised to Tergat after he broke his marathon world record—their rivalry on the track and roads excited and enthralled for almost a decade.

Tergat's five consecutive world cross country titles, and the eight team titles which he won with Kenya, make him one of the most successful athletes ever on grass, but he is also an accomplished athlete on the track and on the roads. He held the world 10,000 m record from 22 August 1997 until 1 June 1998. He has run under the 60 minute mark for the half marathon more times than any other athlete, twice won the World Half Marathon Championship, and in 1998 he set a new world record over the distance which stood until 2005. In 2003 Tergat broke the then world marathon record, only to see it broken in 2007 by, none other than his long-time rival, Gebrselassie. Tergat, nicknamed 'The Gentleman', is goodwill ambassador for the United Nations' World Food Programme.

Gebrselassie, known as 'the Emperor', has broken 27 world records over distances from 2,000 m (indoor), up to and including the marathon. He won two Olympic titles, four world athletics titles, four world indoor titles, and a world half marathon title, and has won nine major international marathons. Often referred to as the world's greatest distance runner, Gebrselassie has won every honour the sport has to offer. Having first competed on the world stage in 1992 when he won silver in the junior race at the World Cross Country Championships, he made a valiant, but unsuccessful, attempt to make the Ethiopian Olympic team 30 years later! Gebrselassie has done much for Ethiopian development outside of athletics. He owns businesses and enterprises across the city of Addis Ababa, is the joint owner of Yaya Village, featured elsewhere in this book, and opened a resort hotel in Hawassa in the south of the country in 2010.

The Great Rift Valley

The Great Rift Valley is a massive geographic trench which runs through East Africa. It was originally thought to be part of a rift valley which ran for approximately 6,000 km from Syria in the Middle East down through East Africa to central Mozambique. It is now believed that this rift is actually a group of related, but separate rifts. The rift valleys that run through Kenya and Ethiopia are part of the East African Rift system, caused by tectonic forces which are trying to split a plate into two separate plates and subsequent pressure caused by heat under the surface. Relatively recent volcanic activity has resulted in fertile soil in the valley floor. Lakes and volcanoes are also common along the valley.

BELOW The Great Rift Valley
OPPOSITE Kenyan and Ethiopian athletes battle for honours at the 2010 BolderBoulder, as they do at road races across the world

Features of Kenyan running

- Kenyan men have won the last 8 Olympic Steeplechase titles, and 10 in total.
- Kenya has won 24 senior men's long-course world cross country team titles.
- To rank in the Kenyan annual top 100 for the marathon you'd need to run 2:10:00 or faster.
- The majority of Kenyan distance runners come from the Kalenjin tribe, based in the Rift Valley area of the country.
- Athletes looking to make it big-time move to rural towns such as Iten, Kaptagat, and Eldoret, high in the Rift Valley to train.
- Kenyan athletes are famous for training three-times per day (though this is normally only during camps before major competitions), fartlek training, diagonals (running figure of eights on the track infield where they sprint the diagonal and jog the curve), and running *polepole* (very easy) on their recovery runs.
- Ugali is the food of choice of Kenyan athletes.

Suggested reading and watching

Kenya
Toby Tanser (2008) *More Fire: How to Run the Kenyan Way*
Adharanand Finn (2012) *Running with the Kenyans*
Bale & Sang (1996) *Kenyan Running: Movement, Culture, Geography and Global Change*
Fudge & Potsiladis (2009) *Elite Kenyan Endurance running: Diet, Hydration, Lifestyle and Training Practices*

Ethiopia
Jerry Rothwell (2012) *Town of Runners* (DVD)
Paul Rambali (2008) *Barefoot Runner*
Jim Denison (2007) *The Greatest: The Haile Gebrselassie Story*

BELOW A Tuesday morning at the track in Kenya
OPPOSITE Ethiopian athletes show their dominance on the roads

NATIONAL RECORDS OF KENYA AND ETHIOPIA

	Male			Female		
	WR	Kenya	Ethiopia	WR	Kenya	Ethiopia
800 m	1:40.91	**1:40.91** David Rudisha 9/8/12, London	1:42.53 Mohammed Aman 6/9/13, Brussels	1:53.28	1:54.01 Pamela Jelimo 29/8/08, Zurich	1:57.48 Fantu Magiso 9/6/12, New York
1500 m	3:26.00	3:26.34 Bernard Lagat 24/8/01, Brussels	3:31.13 Mulugeta Wondimu 31/7/12, Heusden-Zolder	3:50.46	3:56.98 Faith Kipyegon 10/5/13, Doha	3:56.54 Abeba Aregawi 31/5/12, Rome
1 mile	3:43.13	3:43.40 Noah Ngeny 7/7/99, Rome	3:48.95 Deresse Mekonnen 3/7/09, Oslo	4:12.56	4:24.00 Jackline Maranga 25/8/98, Lausanne	4:18.23 Geleta Burka 7/9/08, Rieti
3,000 m	7:20.67	7:20.67 Daniel Komen 1/9/96, Rieti	7:25.09 Haile Gebrselassie 28/8/98 Brussels	8:06.11	8:23.23 Edith Masai 19/7/02, Fontvieille	8:24.51 Meseret Defar 14/9/07, Brussels
3,000 m s'chase	7:53.63*	7:53.64 Brimin Kipruto 22/7/11, Fontvieille	8:06.16 Roba Gari 11/5/12, Doha	8:58.81	9:07.14 Milcah Chemos 7/6/12, Oslo	9:09.00 Sofia Assefa 7/6/12, Oslo
5,000 m	12:37.35	12:39.74 Daniel Komen 22/8/97, Brussels	**12:37.35** Kenenisa Bekele 31/5/04, Hengelo	14.11.15	14:20.87 Vivian Cheruiyot 29/7/11, Stockholm	**14:11.15** Tirunesh Dibaba 6/6/08, Oslo
10,000 m	26:17.53	26:27.85 Paul Tergat 22/8/97, Brussels	**26:17.53** Kenenisa Bekele 26/8/05, Brussels	29:31.78	30:11.53 Florence Kiplagat 14/6/09, Utrecht	29:53.80 Meselech Melkamu 14/6/09, Utrecht
10 km	26:44	**26:44** Leonard P Komen 26/9/10, Utrecht	27:02 Haile Gebrselassie 11/12/02, Doha	30:21	30:27 Isabella Ochichi 26/3/05, New Orleans	30:30 Tirunesh Dibaba 1/9/13, Tilburg
Half marathon		58.33 Samuel Wanjiru 17/3/07, The Hague	57:47 Atsedu Tsegay 31/3/12, Prague	1:05.50	**1:05:50** Mary Keitany 18/2/11, Ras Al-Khaimah	1:06:56 Meseret Hailu 13/2/13, Ras Al-Khaimah
Marathon	2:03:38	**2:03:23** Wilson Kipsang 29/9/13, Berlin	2:03:59 Haile Gebrselassie 28/9/08, Berlin	2:15:25	2:18:37 Mary Keitany 22/4/12, London	2:18:58 Tiki Gelana 15/4/12, Rotterdam

The faster of the two national records in each event is indicated by the darker shaded box.
National records that are also world records are indicated in bold.
Records correct as of 1/10/13.

Features of Ethiopia running

- The majority of Ethiopian Olympic titles have been in the 10,000 m (5 men's titles and 4 women's).
- The Ethiopians have also won six Olympic marathon titles, (4 men's; 2 women's). By contrast, Kenya has only produced one Olympic marathon champion to date.
- A large proportion of Ethiopia's most successful athletes come from the Oromo tribes.
- Athletes looking to make it big-time head to the capital Addis Ababa.
- Ethiopian athletes are famous for zigzag running, perfectly synchronised running drills, and beautiful running form.
- Injera is the food of choice of Ethiopian athletes.

'The dirt here is gray rather than red like in Kenya, and the fields are full of wheat and teff, unlike the maize-dominated landscape of Iten. While everything is transported by bicycle in Kenya, here the donkey makes transportation of goods possible. While the kids cry '*mzungu*' in Kenya, here '*farangi*' is what you can expect to be called. The people though are still friendly, the skies are still blue and the roads are still dusty! And the people are also running like their lives depend on it' *(Extract from the blog, 9 October 2010)*

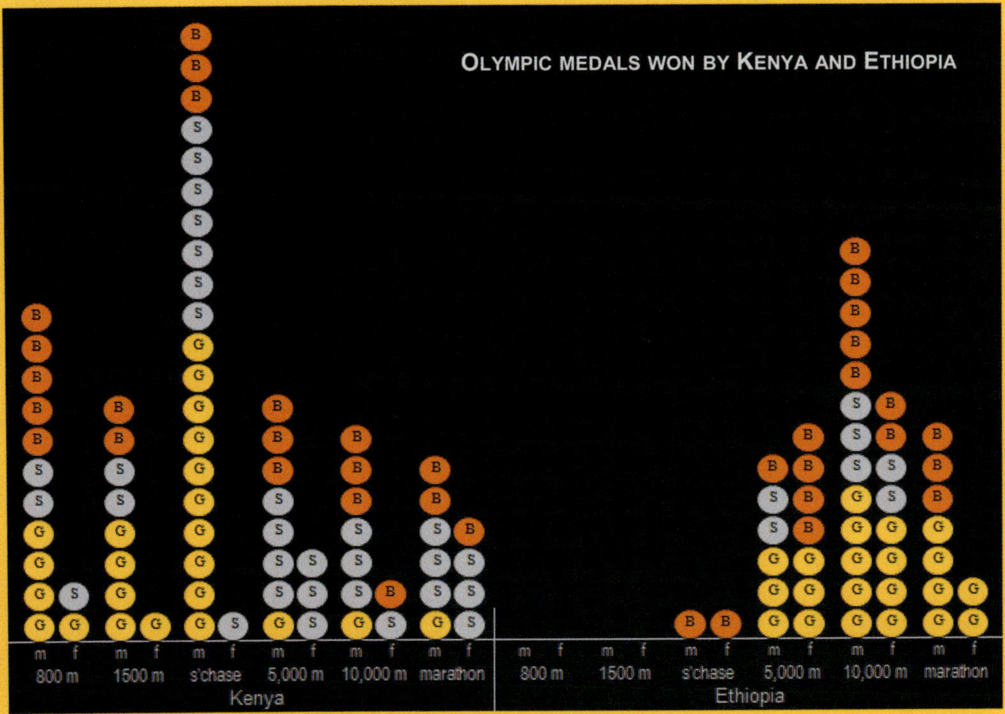

OLYMPIC MEDALS WON BY KENYA AND ETHIOPIA

m: male; f: female
Kenya has also won medals in 400 m and 400 x 400 m relay not included above

Addis Ababa

The beautiful people of Ethiopia, and the beautiful hills and countryside surrounding the city, combine to make Addis Ababa a welcoming and enjoyable place to train. Despite its difficult past, Ethiopia is developing fast, and modern facilities, funded by some of Ethiopia's most successful athletes, are sprouting up across the capital. Ethiopians flock to the city to train, and more and more Western athletes are making the trip to one of Africa's great running centres. Addis Ababa is steeped in running lore and has much to offer serious and recreational athletes alike. Camps such as Yaya Village provide a suitable environment for training, and Running Across Borders provides running excursions for those who wish to travel beyond the capital.

Addis Ababa, Ethiopia (2,200-2,650 m)

A trip to Addis Ababa, the Ethiopian capital, is essential for those who want to experience the East African running culture. While most of Ethiopia's athletes are not from the capital, wannabe champions flock here in their hundreds to have a shot at success like their great heroes. Local athletes will happily show you the routes, which usually involve infamous zigzagging over a relatively small area of land. Taking part in the Great Ethiopian Run will make you fully appreciate the difficulties of running at altitude. The locals are friendly, and English is now widely spoken. While Addis makes an ideal running holiday for recreational athletes, it is also a great venue for serious athletes looking to train with some of the world's greatest distance runners. Yaya Village and Kenenisa Resort welcome Westerners.

Addis Ababa, or Addis as it is known locally, had a population of just under 3.5 million in 2007, and at the recent rate of increase, the 2013 population is estimated to be over 4 million. As with all other developing countries, people flock to the city to make their fortune. The city's inhabitants cover every ethnic group from within Ethiopia, and many from outside. Addis is where the African Union is based, and is often referred to as the Capital of Africa. Addis is built on a series of hills and the altitude varies between 2,200 m and 2,650 m depending on where you are in the city.

Author's verdict

Of all the venues I visited, Addis Ababa surprised me the most. The city was more beautiful and a lot safer than I expected and I was delighted to find that English was widely spoken. The Ethiopians have a number of idiosyncrasies in their training, and joining some local athletes on a training run is highly recommended. As long as you avoid the heavy rains during the summer months, the weather is ideal for training, and once you've made the trip, living costs are extremely low. The new camps just north of the city add to the comfort of your stay, and mean that the crowds and pollution of the city can largely be avoided.

Running ★★★★☆ - Off-road routes are plentiful, though many are uneven and rocky; dirt and all-weather tracks; all-inclusive camps available with gym facilities and medical support; very high altitude; some pollution around city.
Convenience ★★★★★ - Easily accessible from Europe; good weather most of the year; English widely spoken; all-inclusive options.
Safety ★★★☆☆ - Safe by African standards; some petty crime in the city; relatively low health risks.
Cost ★★★☆☆ - Low cost of living; flights are main expense; minimal travel expense once in Addis Ababa; some hidden costs including visa and vaccines; car not required (or recommended).
Cultural experience ★★★★★ - Top cultural experience; opportunity to experience Ethiopian culture and the East African running phenomenon.
Things to do between training ★★★☆☆ - There are some sights and points of interest in Addis; most time between training is spent relaxing and socialising.
Suitability for solo travellers ★★★★★ - Excellent place to meet local athletes and other running tourists, particularly if staying at one of the camps; locals are very friendly; fine for females travelling on own once suitably planned.

Ideal for Distance-running lovers who would like to experience the Ethiopian way of training.

Ethiopia quick facts

Capital/largest city Addis Ababa
Official language Amharic
Currency Ethiopian birr (sign: Br; code: ETB), divided into 100 santim
National holidays Ethiopian Christmas (Jan 7), Epiphany (Jan 19‡), Victory at Adwa Day (Mar 2), Good Friday*, Easter Day*, Labour Day (May 1), Patriots' Day (May 5), Derg Downfall Day/National Day (May 28), New Year's Day (Sept 11‡), Finding of the True Cross (Sept 27‡); Mawlid†, Eid al-Fitr†, Eid al-Adha†
Time zone East African Time (EAT; GMT+3); no daylight saving
International dialling code +251
Outgoing access code 00
Emergency contact 112
Power 220 V; 50 Hz supply; Type C (CEE 7/16) and Type F (CEE 7/4) Europlug-compatible plugs and sockets with two round prongs
Driving Right side
Measurement Metric

* Varies according to Christian calendar
† Varies according to Muslim calendar
‡ One day later in leap years

PREVIOUS *The teff fields on the edge of Addis Ababa*
OPPOSITE *Construction sites in farmland around Addis Ababa*

THIS IS ETHIOPIA
Adapted from the blog, 20 November 2010

Before I came to Ethiopia, all that I knew about the country was that it borders Kenya, that it had a famine about 20 years ago, and that it produces a multitude of world-class distance runners. I've done a little research and what follows should give you a better insight into Ethiopia and its people.

Ethiopia has more than 80 different ethnic groups and tribes, and a different language to go with each. The country's official language is Amharic (with its own crazy squiggly alphabet, called Fidel), though English is becoming more widely spoken, and is even used by the government. The 2010 census estimates the population of Ethiopia to be just over 85 million people, making it the second most populous country in Africa. Ethiopia is divided into nine ethnically-based administrative countries and two chartered cities.

A poster in the Ethiopian Tourist Office in Meskel Square reads 'Ethiopia - 13 months of sunshine!' At first, we were unsure if that was a genuine mistake, or an exaggerated comment to emphasise just how much sunshine there is in the country. Later I learned that it was neither. I was aware that Ethiopia does not operate on the Gregorian calendar like we do, and that it is actually some years behind the rest of the world—seven years to be precise—but what I didn't realise is that its months are actually different too. In Ethiopia each month is exactly four weeks, and the remaining five days (6 in leap years) are bundled into the 13th month (called Pagumen). The Ethiopian New Year is on 11th September (or 12th September in leap years) and today's date is actually Hidar 11, 2003. The daily clock is different too. Time starts at about sunrise (06:00), and lunchtime is six daylight hours in Ethiopian time. The locals are aware that we operate on a different time system, and will usually quote times and dates according to Western practices. Like elsewhere in Africa, time matters little either way.

Ethiopia is a land of natural contrasts, with spectacular waterfalls and volcanic hot springs, some of Africa's highest mountains and some of the lowest points below sea level. The largest cave in Africa is located in Ethiopia at Sof Omar, and the country's northernmost area at Dallol is one of the hottest places year-round anywhere in the world (an average annual temperature of 34 ° C was recorded between 1960 and 1966). The country is also famous for its rock-hewn churches and as the place where the coffee bean originated.

Ethiopia is the source of over 85 percent of the total Nile water flow and contains rich soils. Despite this, it suffered a series of famines in the 1980s. Exacerbated by civil wars and debilitating geopolitics, these famines resulted in the death of hundreds of thousands of Ethiopians. Slowly, the country has recovered, and today Ethiopia has the biggest economy (GDP) in East Africa, and one of the fastest growing economies in the world. This development was evident and there was extensive road and building construction in the suburbs of Addis where I was staying.

Ethiopia has close historical ties to all three of the world's major Abrahamic religions (faiths tracing their origin to Abraham; Judaism, Christianity, and Islam). It was one of the world's first Christian countries, and though it still has a Christian majority, a third of the population is Muslim. Ethiopia is the site of the oldest Muslim settlement in Africa at Negash. Until the 1980s, a substantial population of Ethiopian Jews resided in Ethiopia. The country is also the spiritual homeland of the Rastafari religious movement, and I saw many Rastafarians around Addis during my stay. Rastafarians claim that Haile Selassie I, who was the Emperor of Ethiopia from 1930 to 1974, is the resurrected manifestation of Jesus Christ and that he will lead the righteous into creating a perfect world, which they call 'Zion'.

When Africa was divided by European powers at the Berlin Conference, Ethiopia was one of only two countries to retain its independence (the other being Liberia, founded with the support of the US for returned slaves). Knowing this, I wrongly assumed that Ethiopia hadn't had much contact with the Western world. This contributed further to my surprise at the progressive nature of the country and the widespread influence of Western life in modern-day Addis.

From my experiences, Ethiopia is definitely a country of contrasts; a place of cultural diversity; and a land of hope and opportunity. I look forward to returning in the future, not only to see what progress has been made, but also to travel beyond Addis and to delve further into Ethiopia's rich history and culture.

Addis Ababa by picture
Adapted from the blog, 26 November 2010

Check out www.altitudetrainingcamps.com/blog2.htm for photo descriptions

Getting in

With direct flights, lasting 7–8 hr, available from a number of European cities, little delay through Ethiopian immigration, and the main camps located within an hour of the airport, it's possible to escape the northern hemisphere winter and be sitting in a modern Ethiopian training camp in less than half a day. Air travel is the recommended mode of transport to get to Addis from both within and outside of Africa.

By air

Bole International Airport (ADD) is the busiest airport in East Africa. It is the hub for Ethiopian Airlines, Africa's most successful airline. In 2013, a new runway and a modern new terminal (T2) were opened at the airport which is located in the Bole region, 6 km south-east of the city centre.

There are two terminals. The smaller Terminal 1 deals with all domestic flights, and services to all neighbouring countries except Kenya. All other international flights arrive at, and depart from Terminal 2. Access to the terminals is restricted, and pick-ups and taxis have to go to the car park. Many of the larger hotels have a booth inside the arrivals area where transfers can be arranged.

There are daily direct flights to Addis from Europe, North America, Asia, and a number of major African cities including Cairo, Dakar, Dar es Salaam, Harare, Johannesburg, Khartoum and Nairobi. Ethiopian Airlines operate services to Beijing, Brussels, Dubai, London Heathrow, Rome, Stockholm, Toronto and Washington, among others. Lufthansa operate a service to Frankfurt, and Istanbul is served by Turkish Airlines.

The fast expanding Bole International Airport is close to capacity, and there are current plans to build a new airport on the Hawassa Road between the towns of Modjo and Meki (approximately 100 km south of Addis). The new airport will deal with long-haul international flights.

If not getting picked-up at the airport, the easiest way to get into Addis Ababa is by taxi. There are also hire cars available at the airport. Hiring a car with a driver is recommended for trips outside the city.

By car

It is not advisable to travel into Ethiopia by car from any of its neighboring countries.

Visa requirements

Visitors from all countries except Kenya and Djibouti must obtain an entry visa. Tourists from more than 30 countries, including Australia, Canada, UK, Ireland, US and South Africa can purchase an entry visa upon arrival at Bole International Airport. The price for tourist, business and transit visas are the same, and the process is relatively quick. Visas can be purchased on entry at Addis Ababa and Dire Dawa airports, but those entering overland will have more difficulty. Visas are valid for three months, and extending a visa in Addis can be a

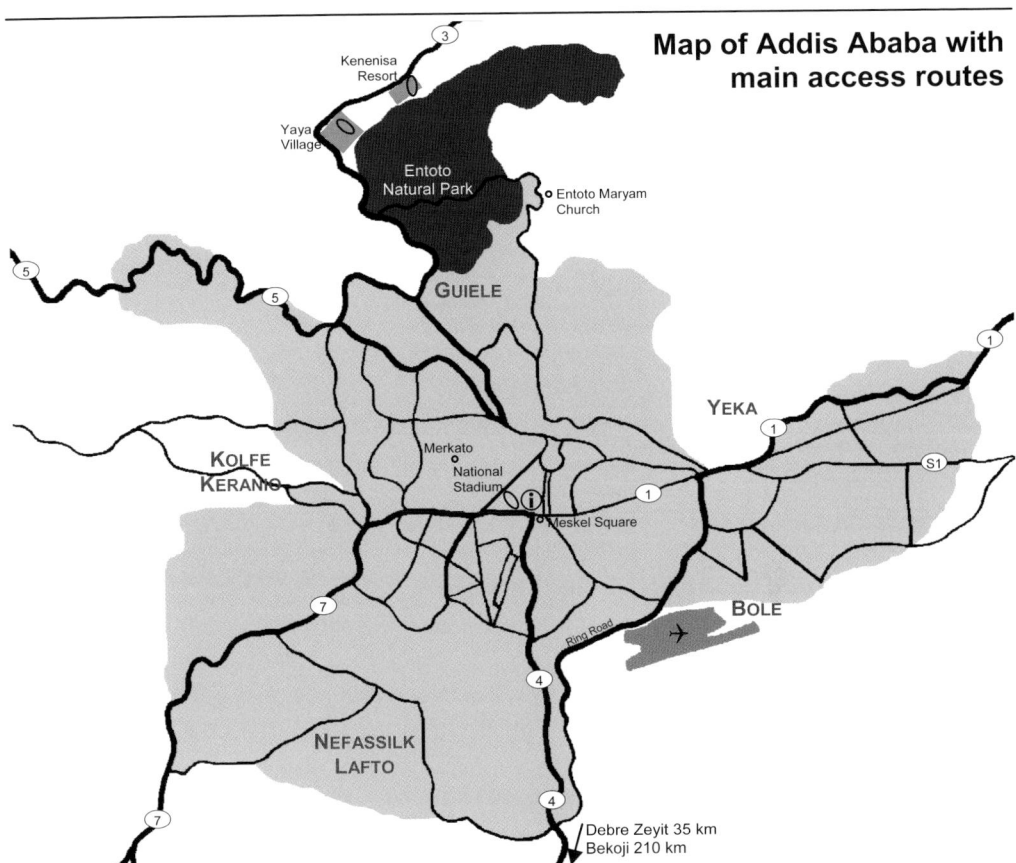

tedious, day-long process. Cash (in euro or dollars) is required to purchase the visa on arrival.

GETTING AROUND

Getting around the city can sometimes be difficult. Few of the streets have names, and those that do often conflict with those on a map. The best way to navigate the city is to use landmarks. Churchill Avenue is the main thoroughfare running north–south through the city centre from the Piazza area to the main train station area near Meskel Square. Route 1 (S1), known by various names, including Ras Mekonnen Street, Haile Gebrselassie Street, Equatorial Guinea Street and Asmara Road, as it runs from the west of the city, through the centre past Meskel Square, and through the eastern suburbs, is the main artery through the city. Bole Road runs from Meskel square south-east to Bole International Airport.

OPPOSITE A public line taxi, and a bus, the main forms of public transport in Ethiopia

There can be many traffic jams, and getting around can take some time. The minibuses are often busy, and fill quickly, especially when travelling from the city. Over-filling of buses is illegal, and passenger limits are sometimes adhered to in parts of the city. Allow plenty of time for your trip, and try not to get stressed; the Ethiopians definitely won't!

By public transport

Blue and white minibuses, which are public/line taxis, are the cheapest way to get around town. They operate fixed rates, and run standard routes. To catch one of these, stand on the roadside anywhere that it would be possible for the bus to stop, and hail as approaching. The conductor will call out the final destination, and if that's where you want to go, climb in. At some stage during the journey the conductor will indicate that he wants payment. This won't normally be at the start of the journey. To get out, simply say '*woraj alle*' or '*woraj*', or make eye-contact with the conductor.

It is useful to have an Ethiopian guide with you the first time you use these buses. It can sometimes be difficult to work out which minibuses go where, and where they depart from. Despite their chaotic nature, the minibuses are a great way to experience Ethiopian life.

There are also larger buses which run similar routes to the minibuses, but which have fewer stops and run more infrequently.

Bajajis (auto-rickshaws also known as tuk-tuks) and horse-drawn carts operate where minibuses can't get to, particularly around housing estates in the suburbs. You will generally find them at the end of minibus lines, or at popular stops along the way. These are useful if you have lots of shopping to transport, or are covering a short distance.

By taxi

Lada taxis, also painted blue, are more expensive, but more convenient if you are making a trip that would require changing minibus more than once, or during busy times that would involve a long wait for a minibus. It is advisable to negotiate. It is difficult for a foreigner to get a reasonable price, but don't be afraid to bargain with the driver. Taxis can be contracted for a single trip, by the hour, or for a full day. Rates go up at night.

There are also yellow and green taxis, which hover around the large hotels including the Sheraton. While they are more expensive, the cars are more modern, comfortable, and in better condition.

By foot and bike

Walking in Addis Ababa is easier than in other African cities. The locals will greet you, and will try to help with directions, though they don't always know where you're looking for. Cycling around Addis takes considerable skill, and is not recommended.

By car

Driving within Addis can be a challenge for those not accustomed to driving in African cities. Additionally, drivers from outside Ethiopia must obtain a temporary Ethiopian driving licence, even if they possess an international driving licence. In order to do this, licences have to be authorised at the embassy of the country in which they were issued, authorised at the Ministry of Foreign Affairs, and then exchanged for an Ethiopian licence at the Transport and Communications Office. The process can be costly in terms of both time and money.

Renting a car with a driver may be an easier, and cheaper, option.

WEATHER AND WHEN TO VISIT

Addis Ababa's high altitude ensures a moderate temperate climate, much cooler than other countries this close to the equator. Rainfall, rather than temperatures, which remain relatively stable throughout the year, defines the seasons. A light rainy season between March and May is followed by a season of heavy rains between the months of June and September. Even during the worst of the rainy season, there are usually several hours of bright sunshine on most days. Average daily maximum temperatures are in the region of 20–25 °C, and overnight lows average 5–10 °C.

Many people who come to Ethiopia as sports tourists choose to time their trip around Africa's largest race. The Great Ethiopian Run is held annually in late November, and in addition to a mass participation race, features an elite race renowned for springboarding Ethiopian talent onto the world stage.

Because of the high altitude (up to 2,750 m if staying in Sululta), and the relative lack of 'train low' options (it's not possible to train lower than 2,300 m), Addis Ababa may be best suited to preseason base-building training. Addis Ababa is at a higher altitude than any of the other venues featured in this book.

ACCOMMODATION

There is a wide range of accommodation in Ethiopia, including a number of cheap and moderately priced hotels, though staying at one of the specialised training centres will help greatly with meeting your specific needs as an athlete and getting to the best trails to train. Yaya Village and Kenenisa Resort offer accommodation and food suitable for endurance athletes.

The Sheraton and Hilton hotels in central Addis come with swimming pools, good restaurants, travel agents, and other amenities within a secure compound, and a very steep price tag. This is where NGO officials and foreign diplomats spend their time in Addis.

There is a greater choice of accommodation in the tourist areas (e.g. Piazza area in central Addis, and around Bole Airport). Hotel owners tend to charge 'farangi' (foreigner) prices, sometimes as much as twenty times the local rate. It is therefore

THE CARB QUEEN IS DEAD AND GONE
Adapted from the blog, 11 November 2010

Enjoying massive portions of pasta at least twice a day; not thinking twice about devouring a full loaf of bread in one sitting; and happily eatting bowls of cereal between meals, I have long considered myself to be the carb queen. Having spent a week in Ethiopia without seeing anything resembling a cake, a sweet or a biscuit, I'm reconsidering that title. In fact, I'm not sure I can cope with this much pure carbohydrate in my diet. 'I just want a big juicy stake' I sometimes hear myself cry, but all we get is bread, pasta, potatoes and rice.

On my first day at the camp, I was greeted with a breakfast of bread (not of the sliced variety, just a big massive chunk of it) and a bowl of porridge. As my mother well knows, I hate porridge, but given that it was made with water rather than milk, I was willing to give it one last try. I managed to force down half of it, just so that I didn't seem rude.

Lunch consisted of a massive bowl of spaghetti, which even I struggled with, and a small portion of tomato and onion sauce. But the best bit was dinner—rice with potato. Yes just rice and potato! I'm by no means against double carbs. In fact, I applaud it. But when all you have to add some taste to it is a small bit of butter that the potatoes have been cooked in and a slice or two of carrot to give it some colour, even I'm going to struggle.

No wonder these people run so fast. Their muscles must be so loaded with glycogen that sitting still for two minutes is a chore.

Just a little bit of bread to see me through until rice and potatoes at lunch

acceptable to bargain, particularly if you are staying for a prolonged period. Bargaining is not possible in the more upmarket chain hotels which have a fixed price for foreigners, including the government-run Ghion chain (www.ghionhotel.com.et). Hot water and reasonable levels of cleanliness are common, but not standard, particularly at the cheapest hotels.

FOOD

To say that Ethiopian athletes eat a diet high in carbohydrates would be an understatement. Rice, pasta, potatoes, bread, porridge and injera, the local staple, all feature highly at mealtimes, and, with the exception of injera, are served with minimal sauce or meat. Protein tends to come from eggs, and lentils. Traditionally, the Ethiopians eat little sugar and enjoy a lower rate of diabetes than world average, though this is changing with increased sugar and processed food consumption among the younger generations.

Visitors staying at Yaya Village will benefit from all-inclusive packages, but even guests there may wish to eat out from time-to-time. Eating out in Addis is generally cheap, and there is a large variety of restaurants in Addis featuring African, Asian and European cuisine, and fast foods. Thanks to the brief Italian occupation, spaghetti bolognese and lasagne is served in many restaurants. Pizzas freshly prepared in some of the bakeries and served with very little cheese, are actually a reasonably healthy option.

Injera, a large flatbread eaten with meals, is made from the flour of teff, a grain indigenous to Ethiopia, and similar to, but smaller than, quinoa or millet. The teff grain, which is gluten free, is rich in iron, calcium and protein. Injera is eaten with *wot*, stews made with meat (lamb, fish or chicken) or legumes and other vegetables and spices, and forms the main part of the Ethiopian diet. Injera tastes very different to other breads and carbohydrate foods. It is eaten with the right hand.

Fir-fir is a dish of fired, shredded injera served with vegetables and sometimes meat. *Tibbs* is spicy beef fried in butter and *kitfo* is minced meat spiced with chilli. Ethiopians prefer meat, so vegetarians may find it difficult to get food that doesn't come with meat. *Shiro wot* is a vegetable stew served with injera.

There are thousands of cake and coffee shops in Addis Ababa, and the cafes around the Piazza area and along Bole Road are relatively inexpensive and of a high standard. A common drink is 'sprice juice', layers of fruit pulp served in a glass and eaten with a spoon. Fruit juices are also good value and wonderfully fresh. In addition to pizzas, bakeries serve wonderfully fresh and cheap bread and cakes.

Shopping

Addis Mercato (market), is not only a great place to experience Ethiopian life and a tourist attraction in itself, but is also a great place to shop. The area does attract petty-thieves, and you should be very careful with your valuables. Mercato is the largest outdoor market in the world, and you can expect to find handcrafted goods, and other useful items. Be prepared to haggle, and don't be bullied. If you can, bring a local guide or friend with you. Shiro Meda Market, between Mount Entoto and Sidist Kilo, is a calmer alternative to the Mercato.

Friendship Supermarket, at the airport end of Bole Road is a well-stocked Western-style supermarket. There are other supermarkets and shopping centres around the city, and most items can be purchased cheaply somewhere in the city. Fruit and vegetables, fresh eggs and other basic groceries can be bought at the small stalls which line the streets in both the centre and suburbs of the city.

Sports shops, particularly ones that sell running-specific clothing and footwear, are difficult to find. The best chance of finding one is to head to the large, modern shopping malls.

Most shops are open from 09:00 until 18:00, Monday to Friday, with many closing for a lunch break between 13:00 and 15:00. Some shops close early on Saturdays, and only a few small multi-purpose shops open on Sunday mornings.

Language

Amharic is the first official language of Ethiopia, though getting by with just English is possible. English is now the primary foreign language taught in schools and most people under the age of 40, speak reasonably good English, albeit with a strong accent.

Amharic is a Semitic language written in the Ge'ez script and related to Arabic and Hebrew. All Ethiopians speak Amharic to some extent, irrespective of their first language. Tigrinya and Oromo are other widely spoken languages. Ethiopians will happily teach you some basic phrases and words in Amharic, and will greatly appreciate any effort, no matter how basic, to speak their national language.

Communication

Mobile coverage is good in and around Addis Ababa and operates on a 900 MHz GSM network. Mobile roaming charges are high, and the best option is to buy an Ethiopian SIM card from any one of the many mobile phone retailers around the city. You will need two passport sized photos and a photocopy of your passport to purchase a SIM. Check that the SIM works in your phone before handing over the money. Almost all local stores sell international calling cards.

Ethiopian phone numbers were extended to 7 digits, and city codes to 3 digits, in 2005, though numbers have not all been updated on websites and in other information sources.

Internet cafes are plentiful in and around the city and any young local will be able to direct you to the nearest one. While some cafes still use dial-up connections, broadband use is widespread. Internet access is cheap, but the international high-speed connection is unstable and not always working. Electricity blackouts can also affect the availability of internet services. There are 3G services in some parts of the city, and many of the big hotels provide free Wi-Fi.

Ethiopia has a very efficient postal service, though mail is not delivered to your address, and must be picked up from a post office box which you need to buy if expecting incoming post.

Health and safety

Addis Ababa is much safer than other African capitals. Violent crime, especially against tourists, is rare. Petty-theft is, however, not uncommon and visitors should exercise caution and use common sense in a city where it's estimated that half of the population live below the poverty line. Pickpockets and con-artists are the most common form of criminals, especially in Bole Airport, in and around the Mercato and Piazza area. Be sensible, pay attention to your surroundings, and keep your belongings close. Criminals are usually unarmed, and tend to be young boys who get intimidated and go away when they realise that you are suspicious of their intentions. While the major streets are generally safe at night, normal

Opposite Ethiopian children are incredibly photogenic

common sense should be applied. Being accompanied by an Ethiopian can usually deter any potential criminals.

There are low to moderate rates of corruption among authorities, though security guards may be rude. Unlike in other African cities, police in Addis Ababa never approach foreigners to ask for ID or legal papers. You should not expect to be approached by a police officer looking to extract bribes, or be questioned about who you are and what your purpose is in Addis Ababa.

Locals may stare at you, approach you for money, or ask questions about you and where you come from. In most cases, they are being either curious or friendly. Once you get used to this, you won't see it as harassment, and can simply choose to say to those that are begging that you don't have anything to give.

All visitors to Ethiopia are required to have a valid yellow fever vaccination certificate. Cholera vaccination may also be required for any person who has transited through or visited an infected area (India, Brazil, Kenya, Peru and numerous other African and South American countries) in the six days prior to arriving in Ethiopia. Hepatitis A, polio and typhoid vaccines are also recommended. Malaria is endemic in Ethiopia, though the risk is low in Addis and the highlands. Prophylactics should be taken, as prescribed, if you are planning to travel outside the capital during your visit, particularly if going to the lake regions and lowlands. Bilharzia is common throughout the country, but avoided by drinking bottled water, and by avoiding swimming in lakes and rivers. There are lower incidences of HIV and AIDS than in other countries in Africa, with an estimated rate of approximately 3 percent among adults. Beware of stray dogs, and avoid running too close to farm enclosures where there may be a dog. If you are bitten, seek immediate medical attention, as rabies is prevalent in Ethiopia.

It is not advisable to drink tap water. Bottled water is extremely cheap and is available in most shops.

Medical facilities, which have a poor reputation, are fast improving, and both private and public medical centres are growing in number. If you do get sick, or need medical assistance, go to one of the large private hospitals (Hayat, Korean or St Gabriel). Travel insurance, with medical cover is essential, and should include cover for emergency air evacuation.

At the time of publishing, there are no incidences of civil disturbances in or around Addis Ababa or in any of the main tourist sites in Ethiopia. Gambela in western Ethiopia, and Ethiopia's border area with Somalia should be avoided. Ethiopia experienced a number of crippling famines in the 1980s, and some areas of the country are susceptible to food shortages during times of adverse weather. Addis Ababa suffers less from such disasters.

MONEY

The birr (sign: Br; code: ETB), is the currency of Ethiopia. Tourists are not permitted to import or export more than 100 birr. There are many ATMs around the city, and if you are having difficulty obtaining cash from a machine, you may be able to withdraw cash from a cashier inside a bank (you will need your passport to do so). Dashen Bank accepts most foreign bankcards.

Major foreign currencies (euro, dollar, British pound) can also be exchanged for local currency in the airport or at any bank. Exchange rates are standard. It is illegal to exchange money on the black market, and the rates are not usually much better than those offered by the banks. There are numerous commercial banks, including in the baggage claim hall in Bole International Airport, and in the Hilton and Sheraton hotels. Traveller's cheques are difficult to cash. Most hotels accept payments in US dollars, and US dollars can be used in the airport.

It is important to have some euro or US dollars with you so that you can purchase a visa when entering the country. Though VISA cards are sometimes accepted, a number of services only accept cash payments.

POWER

Ethiopia operates on a 220 V; 50 Hz electricity supply and uses Type C (CEE 7/16) and Type F (CEE 7/4) Europlug-compatible plugs and sockets with two round prongs. Adaptors and transformers may be difficult to purchase in the city, and if required, should be brought from abroad. Power cuts are common.

TIME

Ethiopia operates on East African Time (EAT; GMT+3) and does not operate daylight saving. In the Ethiopian clock, 06:00, roughly equal to sunrise, is 12 a.m., and 18:00 is 12 p.m. on the Ethiopian clock.

Due to its location close to the equator, there are roughly 12 hr of daylight throughout the year. Sunrise starts between 06:15 and 06:30, and sunset occurs between 18:00 and 18:45. With sunset occurring early, it is advisable to get your training done early.

Laundry

Unless you are staying at one of the luxury hotels, it is likely that you will have to do your own washing by hand. The city is also relatively dusty. Synthetic clothes are easier to clean than heavy cotton or denim ones. Older clothes blend in well around Addis Ababa, and the local aspiring athletes will be appreciative of any clothing that you wish to leave behind. Ethiopians, like Kenyans, are particularly good at scrubbing and washing, and can give even the grubbiest pair of training shoes a new lease of life. Indeed, many of them clean their shoes daily. Laundry facilities are available for guests staying at Yaya Village.

Culture and respect

Ethiopians are incredibly proud of their country, and take criticism of their culture, especially their religion, very badly. Avoid arguing about religion, and instead ask Ethiopians to explain their culture and beliefs.

If you are a woman travelling with men, it will be normal for Ethiopian men to avoid eye contact, and to address questions to your male travel companions. This is a form of respect in Ethiopia, so don't be offended, and is normal on public transport, and in restaurants.

It is a special honour to be invited into an Ethiopian's home for the coffee ceremony, a ritual involving drinking at least three cups of coffee and eating bread and popcorn. Coffee is served black and with lots of sugar. You should remove your shoes when entering an Ethiopian home. Eating food with your left hand is considered a sign of disrespect.

Tips of up to 10 percent are appreciated. It is common to tip a guard who watches your car outside a restaurant at night. You are not expected to tip street parking boys during the day if their service was unsolicited. Minibus drivers don't require a tip, though you can tip a taxi driver if the service has been particularly good.

BELOW Tradition combines with development where new apartment blocks are being build on farmland on the edge of the city

Sports facilities and services

Ethiopian athletes flock to Addis Ababa from the surrounding towns and villages because of the potential it offers aspiring superstars. While the facilities are by no means luxurious, high performance athletes have everything they need.

Training camps and tour operators

In recent years altitude training camps, suitable for foreign visitors, have been opening in Addis Ababa and surrounds. Yaya Village, located 11 km north of Addis Ababa near Sululta, and Kenenisa Bekele's resort facilities and hotel in Sululta, are the most recent additions to Ethiopia's altitude training offer. Both offer all-inclusive packages, excellent training facilities, and the opportunity to train with Ethiopian athletes. Olympia Altitude Training Centre (www.olympia-atc.com), located on the east of the city, is an option for those who want to stay in the city. Run Africa (www.runafrica.co) organises a range of trips to Ethiopia, and other African destinations. The not-for-profit organisation Running Across Borders (www.runningacrossborders.org) arranges trips to Bekoji, the birthplace of Kenenisa Bekele, Tirunesh Dibaba, and Derartu Tulu among others *(p. 238)*.

Trails and running routes

As a large city, Addis Ababa offers a range of running surfaces, terrains and locations around the city. The city is growing fast, and the unfinished roads on the east of the city provide ideal off-road training for steady and tempo runs. The roads which have been tarred, but which are not yet in full use, are great for road sessions. The downside of the development is that farmland is being taken over by residential buildings, and what is a scenic rural road one year, is a busy highway the next.

Yaya Village and Kenenisa Resort are located away from the city, and surrounded by numerous running options in the countryside. There are surfaced and dirt roads, forest trails and grass areas on which to run. Yaya has a dirt track and trail within the compound itself. Olympia Altitude Training Centre is located on the eastern edge of the city, not far from rural farmland. The city is expanding at this point, and getting to the best trails involves crossing some construction sites.

Off-road routes tend to be unlevel and rocky. If you run with Ethiopians you will notice that they use hand signals to indicate upcoming obstructions. While these surfaces are fine for recovery runs, which even the Ethiopians do at a very relaxed pace, the dirt and surfaced roads are better for faster tempo runs and sessions. Ethiopians will often run on uneven surfaces, over rocks and tree roots, but normally only when they are doing relaxed recovery runs.

Mount Entoto

The forests of Mount Entoto Natural Park is a popular place to run, and one of the few areas of the capital immune to the spread of the city. Eucalyptus trees cover the hills and the area is known as the 'lung of Addis Ababa'. The high altitude—up to 3,200 m on Mount Entoto—makes this area considerably cooler than the surrounding city. The dirt roads, asphalt roads and grass areas within the national park are all good for running on, and incorporate hilly and relatively flat terrain. Beware of the additional altitude and the cooler temperatures. The height difference between the city and the hills will be noticeable, and outer layers will be required when running here in the early mornings.

Sululta

Just north of Entoto Natural Park the Sululta area provides an ideal environment for training. Most Ethiopian athletes train here at least twice per week, and since Kenenisa Bekele has just finished building a synthetic track in the town, it is likely to become even more popular. From dirt trails through the forests, to grass tracks through nearby farmland, Sululta has everything to offer in terms of off-road running routes away from the pollution of Addis Ababa. The town is situated at 2,750 m above sea level and the additional altitude should be taken into consideration, especially for those that are staying in central Addis Ababa.

Meskel Square

Meskel Square, also known as Abiot or Revolution Square, is a popular venue for public gatherings, and was a popular venue for propaganda demonstrations during the reign of Derg leader Mengistu Haile Mariam. The steps bordering the square make for a unique training environment. Hundreds of Ethiopians of all ages and abilities come here every morning to carry out a fitness routine, or to train to be the next international star. Runners start on the bottom row, run to the end, and then run in the opposite direction across the next row, and so on and so on until they have reached the top. Running at Meskel Square is part of the Ethiopian running experience, though the pollution means that it isn't the best environment to run in.

TRACK FACILITIES

The track at the National Stadium (Ydnekachew Tesema Stadium) in central Addis Ababa had, until recently, a reputation for being hard, and not suitable for endurance training. Indeed, the injuries incurred by Kenenisa Bekele following training on it, were the main reason for him building his own track in Sululta. The National Stadium, which was re-laid in 2013, is located off Ras Mekonnen Street, west of Meskel Square.

There are a number of dirt and cinder tracks around the city, and in the surrounding towns. The cinder track at Addis Ababa University is popular among local athletes. There is a dirt track on the campus of Yaya Village near Sululta, and Bekele's personal track is open to guests at Kenenisa Resort, in Sululta.

GYM FACILITIES

Both Yaya Village and Kenenisa Resort have modern gym facilities suitable for cross-training and strength work. For athletes staying in Addis Ababa, Alem Fitness Centre, the gym facility owned by Haile Gebrselassie, is the best option. The facility is located in the Alem Building on Bole Road, close to the airport. The building also houses Haile's office, the Ethiopian Airways office, a cinema, a cafe, and the headquarters of the Great Ethiopian Run. The major hotels within Addis Ababa also have gyms.

CROSS-TRAINING OPTIONS

Apart from the gym facilities mentioned above, there are few options for cross-training within Addis Ababa. Yaya Village does offer horse riding, and there are swimming pools in some of the major hotels. Cycling is not advised within the city, though mountain biking may be possible in Sululta and other more rural areas.

SPORTS MEDICINE AND SPORTS SCIENCE SUPPORT

Both Yaya Village and Kenenisa Resort provide massage and sports injury treatments. Yaya Village also provides sports science support for guests and local athletes.

LOCAL RACES

The Great Ethiopian Run (www.ethiopianrun.org), a 10 km through the streets of central Addis Ababa, was set up in 2001 and quickly grew to be the biggest race in Africa. In 2012, more than 35,000 runners took part, and the race usually attracts more than 500 participants from overseas. Everyone in the mass start is issued with a race tee shirt, which makes for a colourful scene, but race numbers or timing chips are not used unless you preregister and pay an additional fee. The Great Ethiopian Run organisers also run other races in Addis and around Ethiopia. International half marathon and marathon events start from Haile Gebrselassie's resort in Hawassa in the south of the country.

RUNNING COMMUNITY

Most of Ethiopia's international athletes train in and around Addis Ababa. The number of foreign athletes training in the city is always increasing. In recent years, a number of British athletes, including Julia Bleasdale who finished 8th in both the 5,000 m and 10,000 m at the London Olympic Games, have spent time training in the area.

SUITABILITY FOR OTHER SPORTS

Ethiopia is a country of runners, and you will rarely see athletes from other sports training here. Swimming is possible in some of the city's pools, and at Kenenisa Resort in Sululta. Cycling is not recommended. Apart from the city-owned Arat Kilo, Ras Hailu and Hanmeda sport and education centres, details of which can be found on the Addis Ababa sport Commission website (www.aasc.gov.et), there is a lack of facilities for other sports. That said, Addis Ababa is developing fast, and the potential of sports tourism is widely recognised. As successful athletes continue to invest their winnings in the city, it is likely that other facilities will be built. Kenenisa Beleke's resort (p. 231) is set to feature state-of-the art training facilities for a number of sports and a golf course. Plans are in place to replace the National Stadium with a modern 60,000-seat stadium and athletics track, an aquatic centre, sports halls and arenas, and a residential village.

BELOW Dirt roads make ideal running trails

Training Camp
YAYA VILLAGE

Located 11 km from the centre of Addis Ababa, Yaya Village is a four-star resort which opened its doors in 2011. Situated at 2,700 m altitude, on the north-western edge of Entoto Natural Park, Yaya Village welcomes athletes from all around the world to train at their wonderful facility. Yaya Village has attracted a host of European athletes to Ethiopia, and is the premier training facility in the Addis Ababa area. The centre is co-owned by Ethiopian distance-running legend Haile Gebrselassie.

Facilities at the camp include a 400 m dirt track and a 1 km dirt trail within the camp compound, a large gymnasium with modern cardiovascular and weight training equipment, a sauna and steam room, a beach volleyball court, a football field, a horse-riding trail and a conference room. Training programmes and advice are available on request, and running guides are available to pace runs and show you the best trails.

The camp's physiotherapy and massage clinic has experienced professionals to help with injury treatment and prevention, and has contrast baths for recovery.

The village hotel has capacity for 30 guests accommodated in twin rooms, and is surrounded by a garden with views of the mountains. The package includes breakfast, lunch and dinner prepared to the specific needs of endurance athletes and served in the restaurant. Meals are ordered from a menu, providing better choice than camps which serve buffet-style meals. Wi-Fi internet connection is available and airport transfers can be arranged.

Yaya's location outside of the city means that the best trails are within easy reach of the compound. Entoto Natural Park, utilised by Ethiopia's best athletes, provides endless trails in eucalyptus forests, while the surrounding rural farmland provides scenic running routes on a variety of surfaces.

Like many training camps, Yaya was set up to support aspiring young Ethiopians. It provides 4 month scholarships, with English tuition, job skills training and access to a high performance training environment, to promising young female athletes through the Girls Gotta Run Foundation. The camp's long-term goal is to produce an Olympian.

Contact
Website www.yayavillage.com

Training Camp
KENENISA ATHLETIC RESORT

Multiple Olympic and world champion Kenenisa Bekele is following Haile Gebrselassie's footsteps in investing his winnings in Ethiopia. He already owns a successful resort hotel in the Bole area of the city, and in 2013 finished construction of a synthetic track, hotel and training facility in Sululta.

The camp provides a high-performance training environment for Ethiopian athletes, but athletes from around the world are also welcome. The track was built by Bekele as an alternative to the National Stadium in central Addis Ababa, which was causing injuries prior to resurfacing in 2013.

Kenenisa Resort provides quality accommodation, meals designed for the endurance athlete, a modern gymnasium, a swimming pool, and coaching and injury consultations. Guests will have the opportunity to train with Kenenisa during their stay, and will be provided with suitable male and female training partners. Airport transfers and transport to training venues are also included in the package. Conference and meeting facilities are also available and emergency medical services provided.

Training routes are provided in Sululta, on Mount Entoto, within Entoto Natural Park, and at 2,300 m in Sebeta.

Further expansion and development of the resort is planned and Bekele has indicated that his facility will soon include facilities for other sports, and eventually a golf course.

Contact
Address Sululta, Ethiopia
Website www.kenenisaathleticresort.com

Author's note: As mentioned elsewhere, Addis Ababa is developing fast, and Ethiopia's tourism potential is finally being realised. Since I visited Addis Ababa in November 2010 Yaya Village and Kenenisa Bekele's track and resort have opened in Sululta, just a few kilometres north-east of Addis Ababa. In other chapters, I've avoided featuring camps that I have not visited, but in this incidence, I've made an exception. The presence of these camps greatly affects Addis Ababa's suitability for altitude training. Every effort has been made to provide the most up-to-date objective information.

OPPOSITE The outdoor area at Yaya Village
RIGHT (TOP to BOTTOM) Haile Gebrselassie running with a group of visitors, the accommodation block, a group running on the dirt trail, and the gym, all at Yaya Village.
Photos courtesy of Yaya Village

Special feature
SOME OF THE KEY PLAYERS IN ETHIOPIAN DISTANCE-RUNNING HISTORY

Abebe Bikila was the first of the great African runners, and his efforts in winning the Rome Marathon, while running barefoot, heralded the start of the golden age of African distance runners. How Bikila came to be competing at an Olympic Games in the first place involves more than a couple of cases of good luck, and getting to a second Olympics was an even greater miracle.

Born on 7 August 1932, the day on which the Los Angeles Olympic marathon was held, Bikila, it would seem, was born to run. Bikila, the son of a shepherd, decided to join the Imperial Bodyguard and walked the considerable distance to Addis Ababa where he enlisted as a private. Around the same time, a Finnish-born Swede by the name of Onni Niskanen was hired by the government of Ethiopia to train potential athletes. Onni spotted Bikila, and became his coach.

Bikila was only called up as a replacement for the injured Wami Biratu for the 1960 Olympics as the plane was about to leave for Rome. Just hours before the marathon he decided to run barefoot rather than wear the ill-fitting shoes which he had been given. He went on to win the race and became the first person from sub-Saharan Africa to win an Olympic title. Four years later, Bikila defended his Olympic marathon title, just 40 days after collapsing with pain, due to appendicitis, during a training run. He had his appendix removed, and started jogging, in preparation for the Olympics, before being discharged from hospital.

Bikila started the marathon at the 1968 Olympics, but was unable to finish due to a knee injury. His friend and long-time training partner Mamo Wolde went on to win, and brought the title back to Ethiopia for the third consecutive Games. Bikila was paralysed in a car accident in 1969. He died four years later from a cerebral hemorrhage, a complication from the accident. Such was Bikila's status in Ethiopia that 75,000 people attended his funeral.

Affectionately known as 'Yifter the Shifter', **Miruts Yifter** won gold in the 5,000 m and 10,000 m at the 1980 Olympic Games. Yifter's ability to change speed over the final lap, something which we now associate with Ethiopian athletes, won him both those medals, as well as many more championship titles. Like many Africans, much debate existed over his true age, and when he won his Olympic double, he could have been anything between 33 and 42.

Haile Gebrselassie, perhaps Ethiopia's most famous athlete, is featured elsewhere *(p. 210).*

Three Olympics Gold medals; 11 World Senior Cross Country titles (including five long/short course doubles); five World Athletics titles, a World Indoor title, two African Games titles, and an All-African Games make **Kenenisa Bekele** one of the most decorated athletes in the history of athletics. He is the current world and Olympic record holder over both the 5,000 m and 10,000 m. His four consecutive 10,000 m titles between 2003 and 2009 matched the accomplishment of compatriot Haile Gebrselassie, and he was unbeaten over the distance between his debut in 2003 and his failure to finish the World Championship final in 2011. His 2009 World Championship double over 5,000 and 10,000 m was the first in history, and his Olympic double, over the same distances in 2008, was the first such double since fellow Ethiopian Miruts Yifter in 1980. Combining junior and senior titles and team medals, Bekele has won an impressive 27 medals at the World Cross Country Championships. It took the heat and humidity of the 2007 World Cross Country Championships in Mombasa to bring to an end his 27-race winning streak over the cross, a non-beaten record that stretched back to December 2001.

Tirunesh Dibaba is probably the best known, and best loved, of Ethiopia's female athletes. With the 2008 Olympic 10,000 m silver medallist Sileshi Sihine as husband, 2000 Olympic champion Derartu Tulu as a cousin, and Ejegayehu Dibaba and Genzebe Dibaba, both themselves champions at world level, as sisters, Dibaba comes from a successful family. Tirunesh herself is a three-time Olympic champion, winning the 5,000/10,000 m double in 2008, and the 10,000 m in 2012; a five-time World Athletics Champion; and a four-time senior World Cross Country winner. She is the current 5,000 m world record holder, and famous for her on-track rivalry with compatriot Meseret Defar.

OPPOSITE *The tiered levels in Meskel Square*
BELOW *and* BELOW INSET *Some of Ethiopia's heroes watch over aspiring athletes and keep fit enthusiasts in Meskel Square, Addis Ababa's most famous running ground*

Eliz's Great Ethiopian Run experience
Adapted from the blog, 21 November 2010

It's Sunday 21 November 2010 and I have been up since the crack of dawn to take my place alongside 35,000 others on the starting line of the Great Ethiopian Run. In its 10th year of running, the elite race boasts Haile Gebrselassie, Gebregziabeher Gebremariam, and Sileshi Sihine among its past winners. I'm not quite good enough to make it among the elites who start in the main stadium, and must instead make my way to the mass start in Meskel Square. Having pushed my way close to the head of the field, I'm still concerned about what might happen once the gun goes, and many of those in front of me look far from serious runners. Even in Ethiopia, there are fat people, and I'm not sure there should be this many of them in front of me on a 10 km starting line. The sun is scorching down on me, and as we stand there in anticipation for almost 30 minutes (nothing in Africa starts on time, not even the biggest 10 km on the continent), I wonder how long I can cope with my individually tailored race tee shirt (the sleeves of my oversized cotton tee shirt have been shortened to allow for some air circulation and the collar has been removed to prevent me from choking). I try to remain calm. Myself and Jacob (a Brit who, like me, has also spent the last two weeks at the Running Across Borders camp on the edge of Addis) decide to run together at least until the last few kilometres, and then it will be every man for himself.

Finally the gun goes. We don't move. I push through some people in front of me. Nobody seems to be in a hurry to go anywhere. Everybody is in a carnival mood. I feel trapped. I've been looking forward to this for months. My legs are fired up to race (that's what a diet of pure carbohydrates does for you), but they can't get a clear run at it. It seems like I'm going to have to push and shove my way through this one. That's the last I see of Jacob until after the finishing line. I have a habit of going off too fast in distance races, but there isn't much chance of that today. Still, I know I'm wasting too much energy. The people in front have decided to get into the spirit of things and run along shoulder to shoulder. My spirit is racing. I barge through, but only to be hindered in my progress again a few metres later. I spot a slight gap to the left of the field close to the footpath and choose to take that, but I know that there's a right-hand turn coming up. I pass a few hundred people. I thought that we were only about 20 people back from the front at the start but there are still thousands stretched out in front of me. While I was struggling to get through the starting line it seems that thousands of people on either side of the wide line stormed through. I reach the first kilometre marker in about five and a half minutes, and my lungs are already burning. People who have started too aggressively keep stopping to walk right in front of me. I keep having to adjust my stride. This is going to be hell!

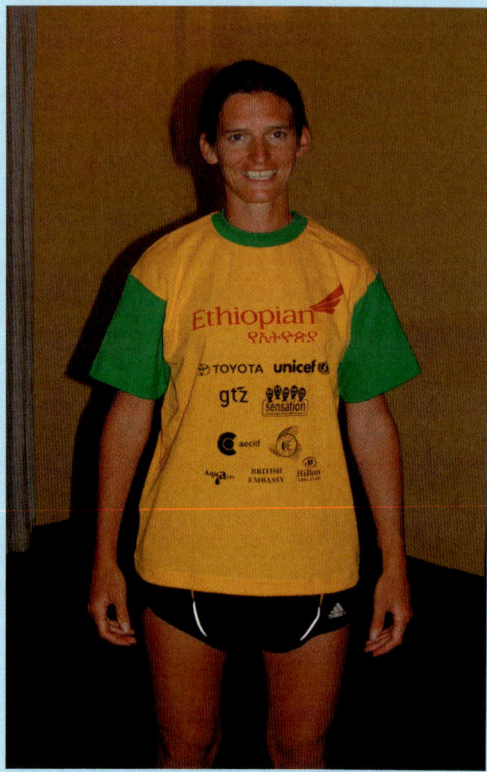

Me with my tanned legs, my panda eyes and my Great Ethiopian Run teeshirt, before I attacked it with a scissors

After two kilometres in something over 11 minutes, I remove the tee shirt. Forget about decency; this is crop top weather! At what must be the three-kilometre point I run straight into two 'civilians' stupidly choosing to cross the road amid the 35,000-person stampede. I'm not sure if they escape uninjured, but I battle on. I haven't seen the four-kilometre marker yet and the time on my watch is approaching 25 minutes. There's a marker ahead. To my relief it's the five-kilometre marker. Crossing the halfway point has never felt so much like finishing a race before. The revised finishing time of 50 minutes is still possible. There

Already a champion; because race preparation should always involve a bit of wishful thinking!

are still hundreds of people obstructing the way though. And people in front who shouldn't be. I pass people who are walking and haven't even worked up a sweat yet. I wonder if they started at a later point. No time to ponder though; there are still plenty of obstructions to pass. After six kilometres, I see a sign for a shower. That's a huge relief. A splattering of water is exactly what I need at this point. More obstructions though—half a dozen people have stopped to make the most of the shower. I barge through. Not far after the drinks station at seven kilometres I pass a guy with a walking stick—surely he didn't get here quicker than me? Did he? I battle on. I pass eight kilometres and I'm still in one piece. Just 2.2 kilometres to go! My mind has obviously gone dead—how can a 10 kilometre race be 10.2 kilometres? What am I thinking? I battle on. The nine-kilometre mark. I up the pace. Finally, finally, there is space to run freely. And a downhill stretch. Time to make up time. I break into a canter. What's this? Meskel Square? The finishing line? I'm closer than I think. One last effort. I cross the line. I'm glad just to have finished. I swear 'never again'. Jacob crosses soon after and we congratulate each other on making it around in one piece. A guy with a microphone grabs me and asks some silly questions. I mention something about it being the hardest thing I have ever done. Someone else wants to interview me. I try to follow her questions and put on some sort of strained smile for the cameras. I just want to get out of there and puke my guts up. I pick up my finishers medallion and free water. I take a sip. My mood changes and something strange happens. I feel like I haven't raced at all. I want to do it all over again...

Note: By paying a small additional fee and preregistering, I could have received a special start number in advance of the race, started from a different starting line and had a clear run at it.

For more blogging build-up to the race, check out www.altitudetrainingcamps.com/blog2.htm, 18 Nov 2010.

Ethiopia: the ultimate experience

Ethiopia is one of the most successful distance-running countries in the world, and the vast majority of its world class athletes live and train in Addis Ababa. Experience East Africa and take the opportunity to live and train like an Ethiopian champion.

Run in Meskel Square. Join hundreds of locals who come to Meskel Square every morning to run over and back the semicircular paths along the tiered steps that surround the old square in central Addis. Famous for their zigzag running routes, the Ethiopians make good use of small spaces, and here is no different.

Visit Mount Entoto. The Eucalyptus forests of Mount Entoto are a popular training venue for Ethiopia's elite athletes, and Mount Entoto is a particularly important spiritual site. Situated on the northern edge of the city, the summit of Mount Entoto reaches 3,200 m above sea level. The spectacular views of the city, and the beauty of the surrounding hillside, make the hair-raising trip to the top well worth the effort.

Take part in the Great Ethiopian Run. If you time your trip so that you are in Addis in late November, you can take part in Africa's biggest mass participation road race. While the race itself is a challenge, with altitude, heat and hills to deal with, it's encouraging to see that not all Ethiopians are distance-running superstars. You're unlikely to be last, and though you'll have crowds to negotiate if you don't get a position at the front, you will get to run alongside thousands of Ethiopians in carnival mood.

Hang out with some local runners. Ethiopians are very friendly, and local runners like to chat to foreigners, no matter what standard a runner you are. It's a great way for them to practise their English, and to show off the country of which they are so proud. If you're lucky, you'll get to share some tea and injera with them, or to join them on an Ethiopian-style run.

Try injera. While injera is not for everyone, the favourite dish of Ethiopia should be sampled at least once. To feel like a local, tear off strips, and use to 'scoop up' mouthfuls of the tasty stews with which it's served. Use only your right hand when eating.

THINGS TO SEE AND DO BETWEEN TRAINING

As a large city, Addis Ababa offers a number of things to do between training, though spending time in the city can be draining. Getting to and from the centre can take time, and the smog in the centre doesn't provide the best environment for recovery. That said, short trips provide a great opportunity to experience Ethiopian life first-hand. In addition to Meskel Square, the Mercato, and the National Stadium mentioned elsewhere, there are a few sites of note within the city. The National Museum of Ethiopia, which houses pieces of the skeleton of one of the oldest humanoids ever discovered, is located near Arat Kilo, north of the city centre. The Ethnological Museum is located in the former palace of Emperor Haile Selassie, where much of the former emperor's living quarters remain untouched.

There are cinemas around the city. DSTV houses (pubs that have a room at the back showing satellite TV) are popular places for watching sport, particularly English Premier League football games, and international races featuring Ethiopian stars.

BELOW Athletes relax between training
OPPOSITE Remains of 'Lucy', the oldest humanoid ever discovered

REST DAY EXCURSIONS

There are a number of beautiful and interesting sites in Ethiopia, though many of them are more than a day trip from Addis. Among Ethiopia's highlights are the astonishing rock-hewn churches in Lalibela; the ancient tombs in Axum; rare Ethiopian castles in Gonder; the ancient walled city of Harar located near Ethiopia's second city, Dire Dawa; the unusual mountain peaks of Simien Mountains National Park; the spectacular waterfalls, hot springs and palm tree groves of Awash National Park; and the Blue Nile Falls and the monasteries on the islands of Lake Tana near Bahir Dar. Tribal region safari tours through the Lower Omo Valley are also popular. Flights are available between Addis Ababa and Bahar Dar, Dire Dawa, Gambella, Gondar, Jimma, Lilibella, and Makale.

Debre Zeyit (also known as Bishoftu), just 50 km from the capital, is a common weekend getaway for foreign residents of Addis Ababa. It has a pleasant climate, and seven beautiful Rift Valley lakes, which are popular for water sports, birdwatching and relaxing at the luxury resorts. Green Crater Lake and Babogaya are the most scenic of the lakes.

A NOTE ON LIVING HERE LONG-TERM

Africa is not for everyone, and you would be advised to spend some time in Addis before deciding to move there for a prolonged period. It's a great place to sample life of an athlete, but surviving without Western comforts may be a challenge. The climate is suitable for training between October and May. 'Live high, train low' is not possible, and the ability to perform quality training may be limited. Travel to sea-level races may also be difficult, but with Europe just an 8-hr trip away, it rates higher than Iten in that regard.

The cost of living is very low, and those with savings can survive for months without having to work. There are many opportunities to volunteer, including teaching English, assisting with healthcare, and caring for children. Addis is one of the fastest developing cities in Africa, and has one of the lowest reported unemployment rates. There is a demand for IT professionals, and many of the city's start-up companies seek individuals with computer networking experience. Many NGOs, who also provide employment opportunities, have their African headquarters in Addis. Work permits may be difficult to obtain, and impossible if you're planning on doing casual or unskilled work. Tourist visas are valid for up to three months.

While the high carbohydrates diet is ideal for endurance performance, good quality meat is hard to find. Iron is of paramount importance at altitude, and extra care should be taken if meat is restricted over a prolonged period. Have your iron levels monitored, and take iron supplements if required. Ethiopian athletes are friendly, and will happily accept you into their training group. Most young Ethiopians speak good English. As cultural experiences go, there are few places where a long-term training stint can be so rewarding. Combine it with a volunteering placement, and it will be an experience to cherish forever.

FURTHER INFORMATION

The office of the Ethiopian Tourism Commission (www.tourismethiopia.org) in Meskel Square is a good place to pick up information on sites and attractions across Ethiopia. What's Out! Addis (www.whatsoutaddis.com), a monthly English language newsletter, listing arts and cultural activities, galleries, cinemas and restaurants, is available in galleries, hotels and restaurants around the city. The official tourism portal (www.tourismethiopia.gov.et) and the city website (www.addisababacity.gov.et) may also be useful.

OTHER ALTITUDE TRAINING SITES IN ETHIOPIA

Bekoji (2,810 m)

Similar to Kenya, most of Ethiopia's best athletes come from a small area of the country. In the case of Ethiopia, the Oromia region is the main 'athlete producer'. While athletes in Kenya flock to small towns along the Rift Valley to train, in Ethiopia the runners move to the big city to train and, if all goes well, to be picked up by a manager or agent. It is in the big city that Ethiopian athletes make their break.

Ethiopian athletes often come from poor farming backgrounds in small rural towns and villages. One of the more famous of these places is Bekoji, a town in the Arsi Zone of the Oromia Region in central Ethiopia, which has produced athletes who between them have won 10 Olympic Gold Medals, broken 10 world records, and won a staggering 32 world championship titles. These would be exceptional statistics for any country, let alone a town of less than 17,000. Among Bekoji's illustrious athletes are Derartu Tulu, Kenenisa and Tariku Bekele, Ejegayehu, Tirunesh and Genzebe Dibaba, Fatuma Roba and Tiki Gelana.

The town has been immortalised in the 2010 feature-length film, *Town of Runners*. The Total Film documentary follows two Bekoji friends over a period of three years as they try to succeed as athletes. The film tracks the highs and lows of the life of an aspiring athlete in rural Ethiopia, and provides a unique insight into Ethiopian tradition life, the advance of the modern world, and the beauty of this African nation.

The not-for-profit organisation Running Across Borders (www.runningacrossborders.org) have teamed up with Town of Runners (www.townofrunners.com) to provide a 'Visit and Train' opportunity to Bekoji for Westerners. The programme offers access to running tracks and trails, pacesetters, coaching if required, and opportunities to run in domestic races. Guests stay in Wabe Hotel which was opened in November 2011 and has en-suite rooms, hot showers and cable TV. Running Reborn (www.runningreborn.co.uk) will also be organising trips to Bekoji from 2014.

Bekoji is situated at an altitude of 2,810 m, 220 km south of the capital. The journey between Addis Ababa and Bekoji takes approximately 4 hr (approximately 3 hr 30 min by bus to Assela, via Nazret, and 35 min from Assela to Bekoji). The Tartan track in Assela is the only one in Ethiopia outside of the capital. Assela is the hometown of Haile Gebrselassie.

Bekoji is more a destination of special interest than it is an altitude training venue for high performance athletes. Trips to the town can be organised alongside a stay at Yaya Village in Addis Ababa. Running Across Borders can arrange transport from Addis, and other logistics.

BACKGROUND Sunset over Addis Ababa viewed from Mount Entoto
OPPOSITE TOP (LEFT and RIGHT) Wabe Hotel, the accommodation used by Running Across Borders in Bekoji
OPPOSITE BOTTOM (LEFT and RIGHT) Training in the forests of Bekoji

Falls Creek

The beautiful ski resort of Falls Creek is one of the most peaceful altitude training destinations. The small village offers the ultimate retreat from stresses and distractions, and the laid-back atmosphere, and friendly locals make it a very pleasant place to be. Though there is no track, or any fancy training facilities, there are plenty of scenic running options both on and off-road. The plateau, at the top of the mountainside on which the village is located, provides almost flat trails, while there are plenty of more challenging options in the surrounding valleys.

Falls Creek, Australia (1,530 m)

Falls Creek is a small ski resort situated in the Victorian Alps National Park, about 2 hr 30 min drive from Albury/Wodonga. Mount McKay, situated at 1842 m, is a short hike from the village and close by is Mount Bogong which, at 1,986 m, is Victoria's highest mountain.

The area in and around Falls Creek was, until the mid twentieth century, used solely for summer cattle grazing. After the Second World War, a hydroelectric power station was built in the nearby Kiewa River Valley, and the first ski lodge was built by workers in the hydroelectric scheme in 1948. A rope tow was constructed in 1951, and in 1957, Australia's first chairlift was build in Falls Creek. Cattleman's huts survive in the area, and are part of the summer tourist offer, providing refuge to hikers travelling through the national park.

The village has remained small, and while it's potential as a summer resort and altitude training destination is not yet fully realised, runners can benefit from the un-spoilt environment, and kilometres of quiet trails surrounding the village.

Author's verdict

Despite its isolation, I found Falls Creek an extremely beautiful place to train. Even though the village is located on the side of a mountain, there was a good variety of flat and mildly undulating trails. The locals are extremely friendly and laid-back, and solo travellers should never feel lonely. There was an excellent variety of cheap apartment accommodation available when I visited, but because it was between seasons, many of the shops and restaurants were closed. Falls Creek was difficult to get to without a car, though the trailheads are easily accessible on foot. There wasn't a lot to do between training, but I didn't mind because I could always sit in a cafe drinking tea and reading. After two weeks training in Falls, I felt suitably rejuvenated.

Running ★★★★☆ - Good variety of trails; many flat routes despite the village's mountain-side location; no track; relatively low altitude; some opportunity for 'live-high; train-low'.

Convenience ★★☆☆☆ - Long way from Europe and some way from nearest international airport; car is required to get there, to pick up supplies, and to get to a track; village easily navigated on foot; not many shops or restaurants; plentiful self-catering accommodation.

Safety ★★★★★ - Very low crime; no major disease risk; some risk of forest fires.

Cost ★★★☆☆ - Expensive to get to; accommodation cheap outside of ski season; good deals may be negotiated for longer stays; car required; relative strength of Australian dollar ultimately determines value for money.

Cultural experience ★☆☆☆☆ - Not much to see from a cultural perspective; get to experience laid-back Australian lifestyle.

Things to do between training ★☆☆☆☆ - Not much to do here between training; ideal for those who have study or work to do and don't want distractions; cycling, hiking, horse riding and hanging out in local cafes are popular activities.

Suitability for solo travellers ★★★☆☆ - Decent option for solo travellers willing to interact with the locals, despite the lack of entertainment and sightseeing options.

Must do Run or hike to the peak of Mt McKay; hike the route by Falls Creek Falls at the bottom of the village; pass an afternoon in one of the cafes looking out at the beautiful countryside.

Ideal for Anybody who values peace and tranquillity while on a training holiday and European athletes looking to combine altitude training with the southern hemisphere track season.

Australia quick facts

Capital Canberra
Largest city Sydney
National language English
Currency Australian dollar ($; AUD), divided into 100 cents
Public holidays (Victoria): New Year's Day (Jan 1), Australia Day (Jan 26), Labour Day (second Mon in Mar), Good Friday*, Easter Saturday*, Easter Monday*, Anzac Day (Apr 25), Queen's Birthday (second Mon in Jun), Melbourne Cup Day (first Tue Nov)‡, Christmas Day (Dec 25), Boxing Day (Dec 26).
Time zone (Victoria) Eastern Standard Time (EST; GMT+10), with daylight saving October–April.
International dialling code +61
Outgoing access code 0011
Emergency contact 000
Power 220-240 V; 50 Hz supply; Type I (AS_3112) Australian plugs and sockets with one flat vertical pin, and two flat slanted pins
Driving Left side
Measurements Metric

* Varies according to Christian calendar
‡ Observed in most of the state

AUSTRALIA IN A NUTSHELL
Adapted from the blog, 16 November 2011

Australia is a strange country. In many ways it is very American, so much so that it's difficult sometimes to remember its distinctly British past, and continued, yet complicated, connection with the monarchy and Commonwealth. Indeed, British and American 'cultures' collide in a seemingly bazaar way. The money has the Queen's head on it, and looks very British, but is called dollars. Everyone drives an SUV or four-wheel drive, the trucks look American, and the streets and avenues are distinctly American. The traffic lights and street signs are just like what you'd expect to find in America, but they drive on the left like in Britain. The TV channels show infomercials to outrival the Americans themselves, but they also seem to have a distinct affinity with British programmes. The country is a mishmash of cultures all rolled into one, but their pronunciation of vowel sounds is their own. Nobody can take blame for that.

Being here has made me realise how little I know about the country/island/continent of Australia. Well I've done a bit of research, and here are some of my more interesting findings.

1. It is very, very, very big! It's only since I came to Australia that I realise just how big it is. On the map, Melbourne, Canberra and Sydney look very close together, just like Liverpool, Chester and Manchester. The reality is a whole lot different. If you had an afternoon to spare, cycling between these three English cities wouldn't be out of the question. It would take more like a week just to cycle from Melbourne to Canberra. Australia is the 6th biggest country in the world (behind Russia, Canada, China, the US and Brazil). It is the largest borderless country in the world, and the largest country wholly in the southern hemisphere.

2. There are very few people here! Well, 22.8 million may not sound like very few, but that's only about three people per square kilometre, and given the disproportionate number of people who live in the main cities in the south and east, there are large parts of the country with nobody at all. This is probably why beautiful villages like Falls Creek, can be practically isolated from civilisation at this time of year.

3. It is the flattest continent. Only six percent of the Australian land mass rises above 600 m. The highest point is Mt Kosciuszko in New South Wales at 2,228 m. By contrast the average altitude of the whole of the north-west of Kenya is more than 2,000 m. It makes me wonder why I've bothered coming here for altitude training—oh yes, the beautiful, quiet isolated village of Falls Creek perhaps!

4. Australians are very good at sport. Relative to their population, Australians are among the most successful sportspeople in sport. At the 1996 Olympics, for example, Australians won 3.78 medals per million of population, two and a half times more than Germany, the next best performer, and despite being only the 52nd largest country by population, finished 5th on the medal table. What makes this even more impressive is the fact that Australia's top sports are listed as footy (Australian Rules), cricket, rugby league, horse racing and surfing, none of which are Olympic sports. Australians excel in almost every sport imaginable and there are even three dozen Australians playing baseball in the US.

5. It is a dangerous place. Three-quarters of the world's most venomous snakes can be found in Australia. However, only a small number of people live in prime snake habitats, and India has thousands more snake-related fatalities each year (remind me to scratch India off my list of places to visit). Australia is also home to many more of the world's deadliest creatures, including crocodiles, at least two types of spider with potentially fatal bites, and the highly venomous box jellyfish which can practically kill you with a look (not really, but apparently it could paralyse your heart muscle in an instant). On the upside, (I think) you are apparently more likely to be killed by a bee sting, or drown while surfing, than be killed by shark attack in Australia. Still, take care out there boys and girls.

BELOW *A flat trail from Falls Creek*
PREVIOUS *Rocky Valley Lake*

Getting in

Falls Creek is not served by public transport outside of the ski season and private transfers work out very expensive if you're not travelling in a large group. While many of the trails are reachable on foot from the village, a car is useful to get a break from the village, and to pop down to Mount Beauty for additional supplies. Mount Beauty is the closest town, and the twin cities of Albury and Wodonga which straddle the Victoria/New South Wales border are the closest cities. Visitors can hire a car from Melbourne or Sydney, or travel by air, train or bus to Albury, and hire a car from there.

By air

The nearest major international airport is Melbourne Airport (MEL), also known as Tullamarine Airport, though Albury Airport (ABX), just 5 km from Albury offers connections to and from Melbourne (Regional Express) and Sydney (Regional Express, Qantas, Virgin Blue). Car hire is available from Albury Airport and Albury downtown (Thrifty, and others).

Melbourne Airport is the second busiest airport in Australia, and located 23 km from central Melbourne. There are direct flights from Beijing, Dubai, Doha, Hong Kong, Kuala Lumpur, Los Angeles, Shanghai, and Singapore, among other major international airports, Auckland, Christchurch and Wellington in New Zealand, and most major Australian cities. Qantas also operates a flight from London Heathrow which has a fuel stopover, but no aircraft change, in Dubai. The quickest flights between London and Melbourne take 21–22 hr. Melbourne Airport has four terminals, so on the return leg of your journey ensure that you know which terminal your flight leaves from, and allow enough time to get to the correct terminal.

The Skybus Super Shuttle operates between the airport and Melbourne's Southern Cross Station (www.skybus.com.au) and takes approximately 20 min. Most major international car hire companies operate from the airport.

Australia has very strict quarantine requirements regarding the import of plant and animal derived products, including food products, seeds, and wooden products among others. Such items must be declared, and baggage is scanned and examined by dogs to ensure that it does not contain plant or animal products. Chocolate, biscuits and other commercially processed and sealed foods are often permitted but should still be declared. Items made from a protected species, including coral and some shells, are also prohibited. The Australian Government Department of Agriculture, Fisheries and Forestry website (www.daff.gov.au) has information on what plant and animal products must be declared when entering the country. In order to minimise stress, and to avoid spending time in customs try

to avoid bringing any plant or animal products into the country. Bring plastic handled hairbrushes rather than wooden ones, and make sure that training shoes are clean (or new).

The Australian Government's travel security website (travelsecure.infrastructure.gov.uk) provides useful information on security measures in place in Australian airports.

By train
Twice daily Countrylink (www.countrylink.info) services between Melbourne and Sydney stop at Albury Station. The journey between Melbourne Southern Cross station and Wodonga takes approximately 3 hr 30 min, and the journey from Sydney Central takes just over 7 hr 30 min.

V-Line trains (www.vline.com.au) operate three daily train services and one coach/train service (Mon to Fri only; train to Seymour and coach from Seymour) between Melbourne Southern Cross Station and both Albury and Wodonga stations. The journey by train takes approximately 4 hr 30 min.

By bus
Greyhound (www.greyhound.com.au) operate services to Albury from Melbourne (1/day; 3 hr 40 min); Canberra (2/day; 4 hr 25 min to 5 hr 20 min); and Sydney (2/day; 8 hr 20 min and 10 hr 20 min). Buses are also operated by Firefly Express (www.fireflyexpress.com.au) from Melbourne (2/day), Sydney (2/day) and Canberra (1/day).

By car
The 30 km drive from Mount Beauty to Falls Creek is spectacular. The road winds up the mountain switching over and back through the forest. If not driving, watch out for spectacular waterfalls, and wildlife within the forests. Falls Creek is approximately 360 km (3 hr 30 min) from Melbourne. Sydney is 690 km away, and Canberra 506 km. Albury is 120 km from Falls Creek.

From Melbourne, take the Hume Highway (M31) towards Sydney as far as Wangaratta; take the Great Alpine Road (B500) to Bright; after Bright take the C536 to Mount Beauty and from there take the twisting Bogong High Plains Road (C531) up the mountain to Falls Creek.

From Sydney, take the Hume Motorway/Highway/Freeway (Route 31) towards Canberra, Melbourne, Wollongong) as far as Albury; from Albury, follow the B400 to Wodonga and take the Kiewa Valley Highway (C531) through Mount Beauty and on to Falls Creek.

Note that there is no petrol station in Falls Creek. The 24-hour Caltex service station (next to the Falls Creek Coach Service depot) in Mount Beauty is the nearest available option, so make sure that you have adequate fuel before heading up the mountain.

Driving in Australia

All distances are in kilometres and speeds in kilometres per hour.

Australians drive on the left side of the road.

Foreign licences in English are valid for driving in Australia for up to three months. Drivers with licences not in English should apply for an International Driving Permit in their home country before arriving in Australia.

The default speed limit in urban areas is 50 kph.

Maximum speed limits, which vary from state to state, are normally signposted on open road. The default speed limit in Victoria is 100 kph. In New South Wales, maximum speed limits on motorways away from built-up areas, and other high quality roads in low traffic volume areas, are normally 110 kph, and 100 kph in other areas.

School buses in New South Wales have flashing lights when children are boarding or disembarking. When passing a bus with flashing lights, it is illegal to exceed 40 kph.

An increasing number of toll roads collect tolls via transponders fitted inside the vehicle. Ensure that your hire car is fitted with a transponder, or that you pay toll charges incurred within the required timeframe (usually 24-72 hr).

Drivers from the US, or other countries which don't have many roundabouts, should familiarise themselves with how to negotiate them.

Animals wandering onto roads are a common sight in Australia. Be prepared for kangaroos, emus, horses, wombats, cattle and other animals wandering onto roads away from the main highways, particularly at dawn and at dusk.

OPPOSITE *Falls Creek and surrounding mountainside*

Hitchhiking

Though legal in some states, hitchhiking is illegal in Victoria, and in Queensland.

By private transfer

Outside of the ski season, Falls Creek Coach Service (www.fallscreekcoachservice.com.au) offers private transfers from Melbourne, Albury and Mount Beauty. While a private transfer is expensive for an individual, it may be the most convenient way for groups to get to Falls Creek. Transfers should be booked well in advance.

Visa requirements

Citizens of all countries require a tourist visa to enter Australia, though NZ citizens can apply on arrival, and have the right of abode. Citizens of EU and EFTA countries can apply, free of charge, for an eVisitor (subclass 651) visa in advance of travel. Citizens of Canada, US, Brunei, Hong Kong, Japan, Malaysia, Singapore, and South Korea can apply for Electronic Travel Authority (ETA; subclass 976) visas, for a small fee. Most eVisitor and ETA visa applications are approved instantly, and visas are valid for holidays of up to three months. Passport holders of all eVisitor and ETA eligible countries, together with citizens of Argentina, Bahrain, Brazil, Chile, Croatia, Kuwait, Maldives, Oman, Qatar, Saudi Arabia and the United Arab Emirates, can apply online for a Tourist Visa (subclass 676). These tourist visas are issued for up to three months by default, but are eligible for extension for up to 12 months. Citizens of all other countries need to apply for a Tourist Visa (subclass 676) and must do so by paper form, which may involve a visit to an Embassy. Further information is available on the Australian Government Department of Immigration and Citizenship website (www.immi.gov.au).

GETTING AROUND

Falls Creek is small enough to get around on foot. Indeed, because of its situation on a mountainside it's sometimes quicker to get from one street to another walking than driving. Many of the trails are accessible from the village. Good maps, with every building in the village marked, are available from the tourist information office, and online at www.fallscreek.com.au.

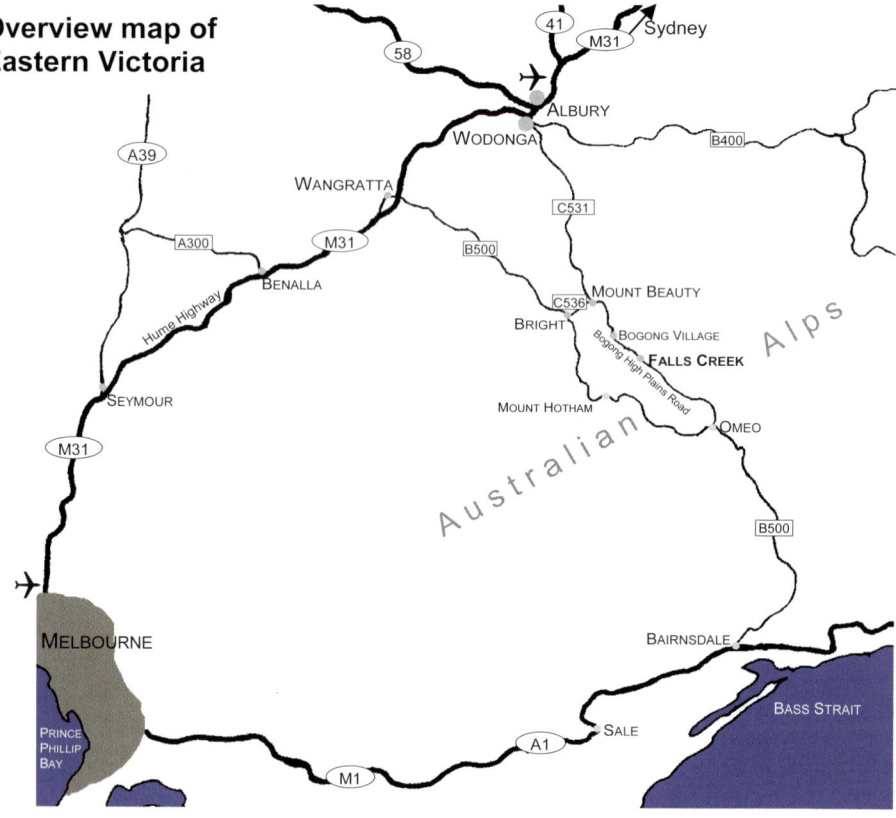

Overview map of Eastern Victoria

WEATHER AND WHEN TO VISIT

Falls Creek's climate is typified by cold snowy winters and mild summers. January and February are the warmest months, with monthly average daily highs of 17–18 °C, and maximum daily highs above 28°C. November, March and April have monthly average daily highs in the region of 12 to 15 °C. June, July and August are the coldest months, with monthly average daily highs below 3 °C, average lows of approximately -3 °C, and maximum lows of around -6 °C.

Precipitation is regular throughout the year, with an annual average of more than 120 rain or snow days. November tends to have particularly high rainfall, and more than 12 rain days on average, but even then heavy rain days are interspersed with warm sunny days.

Falls Creek's main season is the winter ski season (early Jun–late Sept), and though its summer resort potential is being developed, there are definite off seasons. The months of October and November and the period between Easter (Mar or Apr) and the start of the ski season are very quiet and many businesses may be closed. While the weather may be temperamental during late October and early November, the snow has melted and it is warm enough to train. If you can get over the solitude, there is the bonus that rental accommodation is both cheap and plentiful during these months.

Outside of the main ski season, a number of the village's accommodations, shops, restaurants and services are closed, or have limited opening hours. A list of services that are open, and their opening days and hours, is available from the visitor information centre. The Falls Creek & Mount Beauty 'This Week' newsletter (www.alpinehighcountry.com) is also a good source of local information, and details services that are open at various times of the year. Copies can be picked up from restaurants.

January and February are the best months to visit, and in addition to warmer and drier conditions, there is more to do, and a training trip here can be combined with the Australian track and field season with the Australian National Athletics Series running from February through to April *(p. 256)*. There is some risk of forest fires during the summer *(p. 249)*.

ACCOMMODATION

Rental properties are listed on the Falls Creek (www.fallscreek.com.au) and Falls Creek Central Reservations (www.fallscreekreservations.com.au) websites. There is a good choice of studios, apartments, lodges (most with shared kitchen facilities and common rooms) and hotels.

Frueauf Village (www.fvfalls.com.au) is particularly suited to sports people. There is a small gym created especially for triathletes, a carpeted stretch area, and secure bicycle storage. Apartments come with free Wi-Fi access, their own kitchens, and private balcony hot tubs, and cater for various group sizes.

BELOW Rocky Valley Lake

Food

Outside of the ski season, there are only a few restaurants and eateries open and eating out has the potential to become boring. Most rental properties have kitchen facilities, and a mix between preparing your own food and eating out a couple times a week is probably ideal. Details of which restaurants are open during the summer, which days they open, and what time they serve food, are available on the Falls Creek website (www.fallscreek.com.au). The supermarket is small, so consider this when preparing to cater for yourself. It does stock some fresh fruit and vegetables, but consider picking up additional supplies from Mount Beauty, Bright, or Wodonga before heading up the mountain.

Shopping

There is a small, but reasonably well stocked FoodWorks supermarket at 17 Bogong High Plains Road. Opening hours vary according to the season, but always closes early in the evening outside of the ski season. There are few other shops open outside of the ski season, only a few small ski and snowboard rental and retail shops during the winter, and nowhere selling souvenirs.

Mount Beauty has some additional small shopping and grocery stores, and Bright, just over 60 km from Falls Creek, also has some supermarkets. Farm gates around Mount Beauty are also good for stocking up on locally grown fresh produce. You may be required to travel to Wodonga or Albury for anything other than basic items.

There are no running shops in Falls Creek. The nearest specialist store is The Athlete's Foot (www.theathletesfoot.com.au) in Albury.

An 11 percent sales tax, known as Goods and Services Tax (GST) is included in the price of all goods and services in Australia, with the exception of medical and educational services and unprocessed foods. If you spend more than $300 on goods in one shop, and take those goods out of the country within 30 days, you can obtain a refund of the GST on those items. Pack the items in your hand luggage, and present along with the sales receipt at the tax refund desk after clearing immigration and security in your departure airport.

Language

English is the official language of Australia, and the first language of all but a very small number of Aboriginal elders, who may not be fluent in the language. There are more than a hundred Aboriginal languages still spoken by Aboriginal people, though they are all very different from each other, and there is no predominant native language. Visitors who do not speak at least basic English will struggle to communicate in Australia, especially in rural areas such as Falls Creek.

Communication

Mobile phone coverage is good. Telstra, Optus and Vodafone are Australia's three nationwide mobile phone operators. All three operate on standard 900/1800 MHz GSM network similar to Europe. Networks also operate 3G (UTMS) services. Most European phone users will be able to pick up signal, but should be aware of roaming charges.

You can buy a prepaid SIM card for your existing phone, or a cheap handset and SIM, with prepaid cards available in all supermarkets and newsagents, and even at some ATMs. If you are considering this option, buy the phone and SIM before heading to Falls Creek, as you won't be able to buy a phone in the village. Calltime packages and bundles can be good value, but become expensive if you exceed your cap minutes. There are a number of options available so try to get the deal that suits your needs best. A passport may be required as identification to purchase a SIM, but there is no restriction to individuals from overseas purchasing an Australian prepaid SIM.

There is a public payphone in the village. Numbers commencing with 13 are charged at a local rate, numbers starting in 18 are free from landlines or payphones, and are often used for tourist information or hotel reservations, and numbers with 19 at the beginning are premium rate calls and incur hefty charges.

There may not be any cafe or restaurant offering Wi-Fi or other internet access during the summer months and only about half the accommodations provide Wi-Fi internet connection. Some prepaid mobile phone options also include internet access, and UBS modems and Wi-Fi dongles can be purchased for contract-free prepaid access. You should look into options before heading to Falls Creek, and ensure that you will have access for the network and service that you choose once you get to the village.

There is a post office just in front of FoodWorks supermarket on Bogong High Plains Road. Falls Creek collection times fall outside the normal timeframes, and outgoing post may take longer to be delivered than from elsewhere in Australia.

HEALTH AND SAFETY

Falls Creek is a very quiet mountain village, and violent crime is unheard of. The main dangers come not from humans, but from nature.

The forests around the village were destroyed in three major fires in the past decade and the Upper Kiewa Valley, including Falls Creek Village, has an 'Extreme' bushfire risk. Fire spreads quickly uphill, and it is the visitor's responsibility to be adequately prepared. Be aware of the current Fire Danger Rating (www.cfa.vic.gov.au), and take action if the rating is 'Severe', 'Extreme' or 'Code Red'. There is currently no designated 'Neighbourhood Safer Place' in Falls Creek. Leaving early is always the safest option, and is crucial when the danger rating is 'Code Red'. You can find refuge in Mount Beauty (30 km north), or Omeo (77 km south), depending on the direction the fire is spreading. The Falls Creek bushfire information guide is available on the Falls Creek website (www.fallscreek.com.au).

If you are running alone, ensure that you have a reasonable sense of direction and that you let someone know where you are heading and how long you plan to be. At certain times of the year, particularly outside of the main seasons, you are unlikely to encounter many other people. If you do get lost, or get into any form of trouble, you could have a long wait for a passer-by to assist you or to direct you back to the village.

Australia has the highest rate of skin cancer in the world. This is partially due to the effects of the hole in the ozone layer above the continent. Take extra care to protect your skin and eyes from the sun.

The Falls Creek Medical Centre, staffed by Mount Beauty Medical Centre (www.mbmc.com.au), is only open during the ski season. The closest medical services available are at Mount Beauty Medical Centre, and Mount Beauty Hospital (+6 (0)35 754 3500).

Travellers from some countries, including Finland, Ireland, Italy, Malta, Netherlands, Norway, New Zealand, Sweden and United Kingdom, are entitled to free reciprocal health treatments. In some instances (e.g. New Zealand and Ireland), this only applies to hospital treatments. Private hospitals are not covered in any reciprocal agreements. Travel insurance, with good medical cover, is highly recommended.

There is no rabies in Australia and no endemic communicable disease which requires non-routine vaccination. Like most other countries, a valid yellow fever vaccination certification is required for entry if you have been in or travelled through an effected country at any point in the six days prior to arrival in Australia. Tap water is safe to drink, unless otherwise indicated, though the taste and hardness can vary considerably. If preferred, bottled water is available.

You are unlikely to encounter snakes or venomous spiders, but if you do get bitten by either, seek medical assistance as quickly as possible, identify the creature that bit you (size, colour, any patterns or other features), and in the case of snakebites, wrap the affected area tightly with cloth to prevent the venom spreading. Do not clean the wound as venom residues can be used to identify the snake and determine the anti-venom required for treatment. The poison information hotline (131 126) is a useful resource, and will give advice on treatment necessary for spider, snake and insect bites.

MONEY

Australia uses the Australian dollar, with the symbol $, and usually written as AUS or A$. The value of the Australian dollar against other major currencies is highly variable, and variations of up to 2 percent in a single day are not unusual.

Airports and major tourist centres should generally be avoided for currency exchange. Fees are inconsistent and shopping around is advised.

There is no bank and no currency exchange in Falls Creek, though there are a few ATMs. Taking money from an ATM in Australia is possible with any Cirrus or Maestro bank card or MasterCard or Visa credit card, but will incur an ATM fee (approximately $2 but varies depending on the bank) in addition to any fee imposed by your bank.

Debit and credit cards are widely accepted in Australia and in almost all restaurants and shops in Falls Creek, though there may be a minimum purchase amount. Cash may be required for payment of accommodation.

POWER

Australia operates on a 220–240 volt; 50 Hz power supply. Type I (AS_3112) Australian plugs have three flat pins—a single vertical one below two slanted at 30 degrees to vertical. Some smaller, double insulated appliances have unearthed plugs with just the two slanted pins. Most worldwide or all-in-one travel adaptors fit into Australian sockets.

Time

Victoria operates on Australian Eastern Standard Time (EST; GMT+10) with daylight saving operating between the first Sunday in October and the first Sunday in April.

Hours of daylight range from just over 9 hr 30 min in mid June to 14 hr 40 min in December.

	Mar	Jun	Sept	Dec
Sunrise	07:09	07:22	06:11	05:46
Sunset	19:30	17:01	18:02	20:26

Laundry

Most rental properties either have a washing machine or have access to coin operated laundry facilities within apartment complexes.

Opposite Trail leading to, and part-way around, Rocky Valley Lake
Following Aqueduct Trail

Culture and respect

Australians are incredibly friendly and easy-going people, and those in rural areas like Falls Creek are particularly laid-back. It is difficult to insult an Australian unless you are specifically trying to do so, and offending through cultural ignorance is unlikely. Australia has a very multicultural society, with approximately a quarter of the population born outside of the country, and a mix of cultures and traditions is normal.

Australian modes of address tend to be familiar, and it is both normal and acceptable to use first names in all situations. Australians regularly use and give nicknames, even to people they have only recently befriended, and nicknames are rarely condescending.

Tipping is not compulsory in any situation in Australia, and is generally not expected. If a tip is given, it is usually the small change from a cash payment rather than a percentage of a bill. Tips are not expected in country restaurants, though 5 or 10 percent will be appreciated in restaurants where table service is provided. Tipping is not expected in taxis, though it is common for passengers to round up to the next whole dollar.

I'm in heaven
From the blog, 5 November 2011

I'm not sure if it's the clear blue sky, knowing that winter is setting in back home, the peace and the tranquillity of this hillside village, the novelty of my own company, or the sheer and utter freedom that comes with being on the road again, but right now, as I sit on a rock in the warm sunshine on the edge of Rocky Valley Lake, I could be a thousand kilometres from the hustle and bustle of London. In fact, I'm many thousand kilometres away, but that's not important. I could well be on a different planet. I know it's only my first day in Falls Creek, and that two more weeks of my own company could well change my mood, but for now, all that could break the euphoria is if a snake crawled from under this rock that I'm sitting on.

It would have been easy for me to skip Falls Creek. I could have justified omitting it from my travels by saying that Australia is so far from anywhere else in the world and that the readers of my book are likely to either live a few too many time zones away, or already know of the magic of Falls Creek. As recently as Thursday, when sorting out a transfer from Albury was proving difficult, I came close to giving up on getting here. In fact, when I arrived in Albury yesterday and thought that I'd missed my connection, I was pondering what other ways I could fill two weeks in Australia. As we drove to the village yesterday evening, I had accepted that I was doing this purely to tick a box and to ensure that Australia featured in the book. Arriving after dark, I failed to find an open supermarket and struggled to find a restaurant open at this time of year. I sensed that this could be a very long two weeks.

But each dawn brings a new day, and after an incredibly enjoyable morning run, I had a relaxing breakfast and green tea in a restaurant around the corner, did some reading and bought some groceries in one of the small local supermarkets. Now I'm out on an afternoon walk to get some photographs and I find myself sitting and smiling. The true wonder of the world lies in the beauty of the unexpected.

Today, life is very good.

PS Two weeks of isolation didn't kill me; in fact, in the beautiful surroundings of Falls Creek, it was very enjoyable indeed.

Sports facilities and services

Though there are limited sports facilities, the good variety of trails and terrain make Falls Creek suitable for a broad range of athletes. There is some opportunity to 'live high/train low', and while the moderate altitude shouldn't hinder quality training sessions too much, some might argue that the altitude isn't high enough to maximise the response.

Trails and running routes

Despite being situated on the side of a mountain, the trails in and around Falls Creek are relatively flat. Trails run across the mountain alongside aqueducts, and the landscape reaches a plateau above the village. There are hilly routes too, but you don't have to worry about running up and down a mountain every day. The general rule is to head up from the village.

Aqueduct
A soft flat trail runs along the mountainside just above the village (the ski slopes will lead you up to the trail) towards Bogong High Plains Road. Cross the road, follow the trail towards Rocky Valley Lake, take the road across the dam wall and turn left onto Ropers Lookout track. This trail is almost entirely flat, and mostly off-road. Though not very long, sections of it may be suitable for short efforts or strides, and it is particularly suitable for light recovery runs.

Rocky Valley Lake/Sun-Valley
Turn right at Rocky Valley (i.e. don't cross the dam) and follow a slightly undulating gravel access road around part of the lake. Again, the road isn't very long, but is accessible from the village, relatively easy, and adds variety.

Mt McKay
Approximately 300 m along Bogong High Plains Road there is a right turn for Mt McKay (McKay Road). This gravel-surfaced road leads up the mountain above Falls Creek. After an approximately 2 km climb, the road becomes relatively flat. You can choose to do an out-and-back route, add a loop around Ruined Castle (the hill before Mt McKay) before returning the way you came, add in an additional climb to the summit of Mt McKay (1,842 m), take the road down the hill towards the power station and continue downhill to join Bogong High Plains Road below the village, or continue on a large loop (up to 36 km) around the lake and through Pretty Valley. For the latter, turn left before Mt McKay onto Pretty Valley Road, continue to Pretty Valley Hut and take a left after the creek following a dirt trail past Mt Cope until you reach Bogong High Plains road again. From here, you can choose to follow the road back to Falls Creek, or to take the Langford West Aqueduct from just after Cope Hut back to Langford Gap and rejoin the Bogong High Road from there.

Big River Fire
Big River Fire trail leads from Watchbed Creek into surrounding hillside. Choose to do an out-and-back run, or follow a single track to the right until it joins the Langford East Aqueduct.

Langford's Gap
Langford's Gap is located along Bogong High Road approximately 6 km from the village. There are two aqueducts, Langford East Aqueduct and Langford West Aqueduct from Langford's Gap, both of which are flat and have trails running alongside them. There are also a number of add-on options, across rougher and hillier trails.

Track facilities

There is no track in Falls Creek. Alexandra Park in Albury has a 400 m synthetic athletics track which is available for public hire through the Lauren Jackson Sports Centre (www.laurenjacksonsportscentre.com.au), and Wodonga Athletics Complex on Pearce Street in Wodonga has a 400 m grass track, with all-weather areas for jumps and throws.

Gym facilities

There is a small community gym, located at the QT Falls Creek complex, close to the supermarket. The gym, which is open seven days per week, has free weights, spin bikes, treadmills and rowing machines, and while the facilities are far from extensive, they are adequate for endurance athletes. Single-visit, week, season and annual memberships are available to purchase at the visitor information centre.

Cross-training options

Road cycling and mountain biking are good forms of cross training in and around Falls Creek. Mountain bikes can be rented from the visitor information centre. Rocky Valley Bikes & Snow Sports in Mount Beauty sells, rents, services and repairs bikes. They are located on the Kiewa Valley Highway in Tawonga South, next to the Mount Beauty Holiday Centre and Caravan Park. There is some cardiovascular training equipment in the Falls Creek Gym. There are two grass

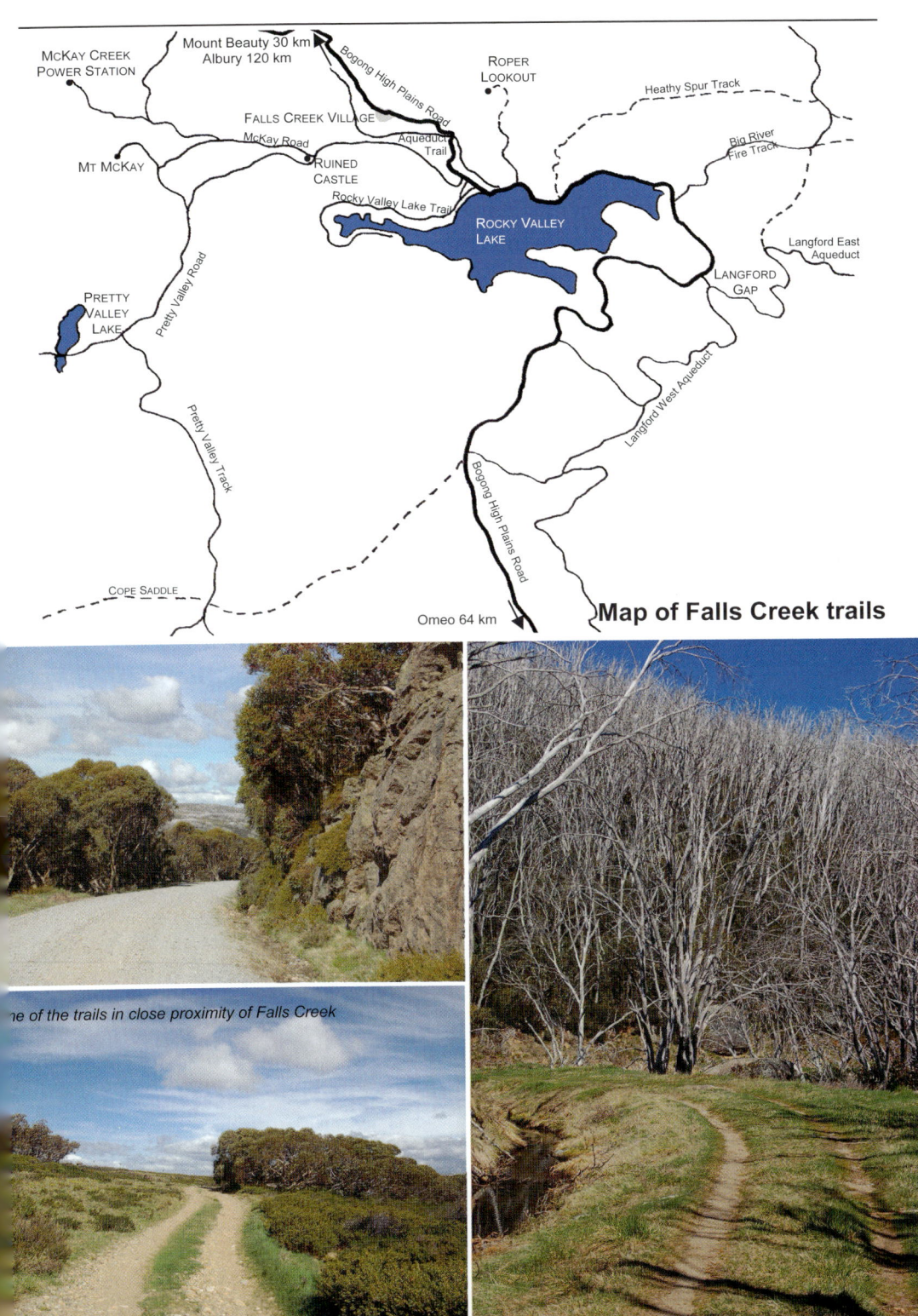

tennis courts at the Village Bowl, with bookings and racquet hire from Max's Restaurant opposite the courts. There is also a half-size basketball court. Open water swimming is possible on Rocky Valley Lake. Canoeing and kayaking is also possible, and canoes and kayaks can be hired from the visitor information centre.

Sports medicine and sports science support

The nearest physiotherapy practice is Kiewa Valley Sports and Spinal Physiotherapy, located on Hollands Street in Mount Beauty.

Local races

The Falls Creek Triathlon and Trail Running Festival, held annually in February, features trail runs over various distances. Wodonga Athletics Club (www.wodongaaths.org.au) organises the North East Distance Runner Series with hill, trail, road and track races spread over the year and throughout the region, including events in Mount Beauty and Bright.

The Australian National Athletics Series runs from February (occasionally with even earlier races) through to April. Most of the events in the series allow guest entries from overseas athletes, and the standard is suitable for athletes at a high national and international level. The Melbourne meeting also forms part of the IAAF World Challenge series. Further information on these events can be found on the Athletics Australia website (www.athletics.com.au). The Athletics Victoria website (www.athsvic.org.au) and the Victorian Milers Club website (www.vicmilers.com) are also good sources of information on track races in the state of Victoria. Competing on the track circuit in Australia is becoming an increasingly popular alternative to an indoor season for many European middle-distance athletes.

Running community

Steve Moneghetti, Craig Mottram and Benita Willis are just some of the Australian athletes who have trained in Falls Creek. During her long and successful career, Irish athlete Sonia Sullivan spent much of her time here with Australian coach/husband Nic Bideau. The village is a relatively small one, and doesn't have a large running community (or large community of any kind for that matter), but most of the people who are staying in the village are athletes of some kind, or have an appreciation for recreation and the great outdoors.

Suitability for other sports

Falls Creek attracts athletes in a range of sports and recently top Australian Rules football and rugby union teams have used Falls Creek for preseason training. Falls Creek resort management are keen to maximise the village's potential as an altitude training destination, and they make every effort to facilitate groups looking to utilise the village as a training base.

Cycling Falls Creek is an ideal base for road cyclists looking to utilise the mountain roads and high country of the Victorian Alps for training. The road from Mount Beauty is a popular climb for cyclists of all levels, and cyclists can regularly be seen refuelling in Falls Creek after making the 31 km, 1,200 m climb from the town below. Beyond Falls Creek, the Bogong High Plains Road provides further riding options across undulating terrain. The Bogong High Plains Road forms part of the 230 km Bogong Alpine Way, a loop which circumnavigates the Alpine National Park and links the towns of Omeo, Mount Beauty and Bright. Maps and profiles of routes from Falls Creek can be found on the Cycle Profiles (www.cyclingprofiles.com.au) and the Visit Victoria (www.visitvictoria.com) websites. Falls Creek also plays host to some of Australia's elite road cycling events, and the 3 Peaks Challenge is a mass participation event on the Bogong Alpine Way. Prepare for all weather conditions, and note that temperatures can be 20 degrees higher in Mount Beauty than in Falls Creek.

Triathlon Falls Creek is a good option for triathletes. Though there is no swimming pool suitable for training in the village, there are excellent running and cycling options as detailed previously, together with open water swimming options at Rocky Valley. Mount Beauty Swimming Pool (www.mtbeauty.com) is a 33.33 m outdoor facility in which private lanes can be hired. It is located on Pool Road in Mount Beauty.

Team sports Geelong Cats (Australian Rules football) and Melbourne Rebels (rugby union) use Falls Creek for preseason training, where they combine mountain biking, hiking and other cross-training activities with running fitness work and basic skills drills. Grass areas are limited, and there are no specific sports facilities. Falls Creek is therefore most suitable for non-specific early preseason training for team sports.

Other sports Rocky Valley Lake is suitable for rowing and kayaking. The 2000 m long regatta course is the highest in the country.

Things to see and do between training

There isn't a lot to do in Falls Creek, though that could be one of its attractions. Hiking, mountain biking and fishing are popular and most people come to the village for outdoor activities.

In addition to mountain biking, canoeing and other activities mentioned in the 'cross-training' section, Segway tours, hiking tours and horseback riding are available. The hike to Falls Creek Falls, just below the entrance to the village is particularly scenic. Packhorse Heritage Trail leads from here towards Howmans Gap. Fishing equipment can be hired from the visitor information centre. Events and festivals held between Christmas and Easter include cricket matches, a tennis tournament, dragon boat racing, carnivals, and a billy cart derby. Christmas and Easter are the busiest times in the village, and the chairlifts are open for sightseeing trips to the summit over both holiday periods. An outdoor cinema on the 'village green' shows family-friendly movies during the summer school holidays. Programmes are available from the visitor information centre.

Ruined Castle, located on the way to Mt McKay, is a small outcrop of columnar jointed basalt, estimated to be 40 to 60 million years old. The hexagonal columns were formed during cooling, in a similar way to the Giant's Causeway in Northern Ireland. The uplifting which formed the Bogong High Plains approximately 1 million years ago was followed by denudation and erosion, and ruined castle is one of the few remaining examples of basalt columns in the area.

If you have your own transport, you'll be able to venture outside of Falls Creek for a day trip to nearby Mount Beauty or Bright. Canoeing, tennis, fishing, swimming, bush walks and dining are available at the Bogong Village resort (www.bogongvillage.com), halfway between Falls Creek and Mount Beauty. Fainter Falls are located just before you get to Bogong Village. There is an 18-hole golf course in Mount Beauty, where instructional flights in a lightweight glider are also possible. Bright is recognised as one of Australia's top hang-gliding, paragliding and microlighting destinations.

The Bogong Alpine Way (also known as the Queen Victoria Loop), a 230 km route which circumnavigates the Alpine National Park, takes in some of the most breathtaking views of Victoria. The Bogong High Plains Road forms part of the route, which you can drive either clockwise or anticlockwise from the village.

A note on living here long-term

Despite all its appeal, Falls Creek may not be the best place to live and train for prolonged periods. The weather is unsuitable for training during the Australian winter when the village is snow-covered, and the isolation, which may be therapeutic in the beginning, will lose its attraction for most athletes after time. The lack of a track may also be an issue for some athletes, and the distance to a major airport would make it difficult to get out for races during the year. The village is very quiet between the main winter and summer seasons, with not all of the amenities open, and though accommodation may be very cheap during the off seasons, having to buy food from a small supermarket, or drive to a larger one, will work out expensive. Job opportunities are also limited, and education opportunities non-existent. Falls Creek is a very nice place to spend a few weeks, but is more suitable as a focused training retreat than a permanent or semi-permanent training home.

Further information

Further information on visiting and staying in Falls Creek can be found on the visitor information website (www.fallscreek.com.au). The Falls Creek visitor information centre, located in the Falls Creek Resort Management building on the corner between Bogong High Plains Road and Slalom Street, is open daily from 10:00 to 15:00 throughout the year. The weekly Falls Creek & Mount Beauty 'This Week' newsletter includes contacts and opening times for business in the area and information on upcoming events. It can be picked up from restaurants and businesses, or accessed online at www.alpinehighcountry.com. The Victoria tourism website (www.visitvictoria.com) has useful information on travelling within the state of Victoria.

Other altitude training sites in Australia

Mount Hotham (1,861)
www.mthotham.com.au

Not far from Falls Creek, as the crow flies, Mount Hotham Alpine Resort is a particularly popular training base for cyclists during the summer months. Mount Hotham is 360 km from Melbourne, roughly the same distance as Falls Creek, but is accessed via the B500 via Bright, rather than via Mount Beauty. Mount Hotham like Falls Creek, sits on the popular Bogong Alpine Way. It has a similar range of accommodation and services to Falls Creek, and is similarly isolated outside of the ski season.

Potchefstroom

Potchefstroom, located in South Africa's North West Provence, is an ideal spot for European athletes looking for winter sun and moderate altitude exposure. The city's North-West University has excellent facilities, and many of the world's best athletes have trained here. There are grass and synthetic tracks, a designated cross country course, other grass fields for intervals and drills, and gym and recovery facilities for athletes training at the highest level. Potchefstroom is popular among middle-distance track athletes but its lack of trails make it less attractive for long distance runners.

Potchefstroom, South Africa (1,350 m)

Potchefstroom, referred to as 'Potch' for short and known as 'the City of Expertise', is situated in North West Provence, approximately 120 km south-west of Johannesburg. It is one of the oldest towns of the old Transvaal Republic, and dates back to 1838. The city is dominated by the Potchefstroom Campus of North-West University (NWU) and a permanent military base, and has a population of approximately 25,000.

Potchefstroom received city status in 1994. In 2004, Potchefstroom City Council changed to Tlokwe City Council, though the geographical name of the city remains Potchefstroom. The area has a strong agricultural economy. Industries include food processing, chemical and steel, and the city is home to a number of key players in the chicken processing industry. The annual Aardklop Festival (www.aardklop.co.za), an Afrikaans arts event, attracts thousands to the city every September.

Potchefstroom is known as the province's 'Home of Sport' and the regional headquarters of a number of sports are based here. The city hosted matches during the 2003 ICC Cricket World Cup, and was a co-host for the 2011 ICC Cricket World Cup qualifiers. The Spanish football team trained in Potchefstroom in the run-up to their FIFA 2010 World Cup win.

Some of the most famous track and field athletes in the world have spent time training in Potchefstroom. Famous athletes from Potchefstroom include Beijing Olympic long jump silver medallist Gofrey Khotso Mokoena; Jezekiel Sepeng who won silver in the 800 m at the 1996 Olympics; All-African Games javelin gold medallist Justine Robbeson; and Marius Corbett who was world javelin champion in 1997. Kennedy McArthur, the 1912 Olympic marathon champion, lived and trained here.

AUTHOR'S VERDICT

Winter sun and the excellent training facilities have put Potchefstroom on the map of altitude training destinations. Its altitude is scarcely high enough to induce a physiological response, though athletes can perform some quality sessions after a minimal period of acclimatisation. There are some trails for longer runs outside the city, but these are difficult to find. Many athletes from Europe train in Potchefstroom over the Christmas break, and you are likely to make friends (or find people that you know) if you hang around the track area long enough. I didn't always feel safe, but I think that may have been due to my preconceptions of South Africa. Eating out was cheap, but high carbohydrate meals were difficult to find, and even the spaghetti bolognese had much more meat than it did pasta. Cooking for yourself is highly recommended.

Running ★★★★★ - Excellent grass facilities for track workouts and repetitions; limited trails for longer runs; relatively low altitude; more suitable for middle-distance track athletes than marathon runners.
Convenience ★★★★★ - Long flights from Europe, but easily accessible from Johannesburg and Pretoria; many suitable accommodations located close to the facilities.
Safety ★★★★★ - Less crime than in the major cities, but caution should still be exercised; relatively safe around the university and training facilities; HIV and AIDS are endemic.
Cost ★★★★★ - Low cost of living; expensive flights from Europe; car not essential.
Cultural experience ★★★★★ - Getting out of the city required to get full South African experience; easy to forget you're in South Africa in relative comfort of the university training facilities.
Things to do between training ★★★★★ - Some sites to visit, shops to browse, activities to get involved in and sports events to attend; perfect weather for barbeques.
Suitability for solo travellers ★★★★★ - Opportunity to meet other runners at university training facilities; some safety risks, especially for female solo travellers; trip can be combined with other travels in South Africa; solo travellers not uncommon.

Must do Hang out around the track area after training and see how many famous athletes you recognise; organise a barbecue at your accommodation or in one of the local parks; get out of town and explore the Vredefort Dome.
Ideal for Track athletes looking for warm weather and mild altitude exposure during the Christmas break.

Did you know? The McArthur Stadium in Potchefstroom is named after Olympic marathon champion Kennedy Kane McArthur (also called Kenneth). McArthur was born in Co. Antrim in Ireland, but moved to Potchefstroom as a twenty-year-old, where he joined the police force. He won all six marathons that he ran in his career, including the Olympic event in Stockholm in 1912.

South Africa: A brief history

South Africa was settled by the Dutch in the late 17th century as a stopping point for their ships travelling to the East Indies. Fruit and vegetables, which would help prevent the problem of scurvy onboard passing ships, were planted in the area, and the Dutch built settlements across the southern tip of the African continent.

In 1815 South Africa became a British colony and many of the Dutch settlers travelled north to escape the British. As they travelled north, they met with African tribes who, over time, had travelled south down the continent. War ensued between the Dutch Boers and the Zulu tribes, and following victory, the Boers set up an Afrikaner state in the north of the country. The British later tried to annex this Afrikaner state in what were termed the Boer Wars. A coalition between the Afrikaner and British states resulted in the formation of the South African union in 1910.

A period of oppression, imposed by the white settlers on the native Africans and others of non-white decent, ensued, and apartheid was in full force by 1960 when South Africa gained independence from British rule. Decades of hardship followed, and it was only during the 1990s that all South Africans were granted equal rights.

South Africa has one of the largest economies in Africa, though the discrepancies in wealth between the rich and the poor give a very different impression. It is the world's largest producer of diamonds, gold, platinum, chrome ore, manganese and vanadium. Gold was discovered on the Witwatersrand, the area of land in and around modern-day Gauteng, in 1886, and resulted in the influx of workers, and rapid growth of cities such as Johannesburg and Pretoria.

South Africa's history is typified by conflict, not just between the Dutch, British and Zulu people, but between the area's many diverse ethnic groups. Today it is a country of great hope, diversity, and vibrancy. Racial division, is, however, still evident, and it's likely that many more decades will pass before all South Africa's people are truly equal.

PREVIOUS *Path through the Fanie Du Toit sports facility which forms part of a 3 km off-road circuit*

South Africa quick facts

Capital Pretoria
Largest city Johannesburg
Official languages Afrikaans, English (main language of the government), Ndebele, Northern Sotho, Sotho, Swazi, Tswana, Tsonga, Venda, Xhosa and Zulu.
Currency Rand (R; ZAR); divided into 100 cents
Public holidays New Year's Day (Jan 1), Human Rights Day (Mar 21), Good Friday*, Easter Monday*, Freedom Day (Apr 27), Workers' Day (May 1), Youth Day (Jun 6), National Women's Day (Aug 9), Heritage Day (Sept 24), Day of Reconciliation (Dec 17), Christmas Day (Dec 25), Day of Goodwill (Dec 26)
Time zone South African Standard Time (SAST; GMT+2); no daylight saving
International dialling code +27
Outgoing access code 00
Emergency contacts 112 (from mobile), 10111 (police and fire) and 10177 (ambulance)
Power 220-230 V; 50 Hz supply; Type M (SANS 164-1) South African plugs and sockets with three large round pins
Driving Left side
Measurement Metric

* vary according to Christian calendar

Some suggested reading

There are a number of great books which highlight the injustices of apartheid, and that demonstrate the power of peaceful rebellion, hope and forgiveness. Nelson Mandela's autobiography (*Long Walk to Freedom*, 1994) is a good starting point, and *No Future Without Forgiveness* (1999), the memoirs of Desmond Tutu, gives some insight into how South Africa overcame its darkest days. John Carlin's brilliant *Playing the Enemy* (2008; later called Invictus after the 2009 film based on the book), charts South Africa's path to winning the 1995 Rugby World Cup, and documents one of the greatest examples of sport's ability to heal and unite. *More than Just a Game: Football v Apartheid* (Chuck Korr and Marvin Close, 2010) looks at the role that sport played in the lives of political prisoners on Robben Island.

For a more lighthearted read, *Comrades Marathon: the ultimate human race* (John Cameron-Dow, 2012), traces the history of the world's oldest and largest ultramarathon.

Getting in

Potchefstroom is very accessible from both within and outside the country. It is located just 120 km from Johannesburg, and 180 km from Pretoria. Johannesburg's international airport is the busiest in Africa, and many coach services between South Africa's major cities stop in Potchefstroom.

By air

OR Tambo International Airport (JNB) in Johannesburg is located 150 km north-east of Potchefstroom, and 22 km from Johannesburg's central business district. More than 40 airlines offer direct flights from 80 destinations including Amsterdam, Atlanta, Bangkok, Frankfurt, Hong Kong, London, Munich, New York, Paris, Perth, Singapore, Sydney, Washington, and Zurich. Flights take approximately 11 hr from London and 10 hr 30 min from Paris.

From the airport, hire a car, get a direct bus to Potchefstroom, or take the Gautrain taxi or a private shuttle to Johannesburg or Pretoria and complete the journey from there by bus.

The Gautrain (www.gautrain.co.za), Gauteng's high-speed rail service, links the airport to Park Station in Johannesburg, and the main station in Pretoria (change at Marlboro or Sandton). Travelling on the Gautrain requires the one-off purchase of a tag-in card (Gold Card) onto which your fare is uploaded. Services run every 15 min during the week, and every 30 min at weekends and on public holidays. Services run from approximately 05:30 until 20:30.

Turn left once you exit the airport to find a line of licensed taxis. Do not accept an offer of a taxi from individuals approaching you in the terminal building, as these are unlicensed taxis. Magic Bus (www.magicbus.co.za) operates scheduled shuttle services to most of the major hotels in and around Johannesburg, while Airport Shuttle (www.airportshuttle.co.za), Buzz Around Tours and Shuttles (www.buzzaround.co.za) and Cab4U (www.cab4u.co.za) operate unscheduled 24-hour shuttle services around Johannesburg which should be booked in advance.

When returning to the airport by car, don't be confused by the fact that some signs still refer to the airport by its old names of Jan Smuts Intl or JHB International.

By bus

Citybug (www.citybug.co.za) operates a daily minibus shuttle service six days a week (Mon–Sat) to Potchefstroom (NWU Campus, corner of Steve Biko Avenue and Gerhard Dekker) from OR Tambo International Airport on their Nelspruit–Potchefstroom route. The service leaves from the bus terminal near the Intercontinental Hotel. The journey takes approximately 2 hr. Web bookings must be made at least five days in advance.

A number of coach services operate services to Potchefstroom from Pretoria Station and Johannesburg's Park City Transit Centre. Journey times on all services from Pretoria are approximately 3–4 hr, and just under 2 hr from Johannesburg. Tickets should be booked in advance, particularly if travelling during holiday time. Most of the coach services leave in the morning or early afternoon, so if your flight is scheduled to arrive in the early afternoon or evening, consider an overnight stay in Gauteng. The Computicket website (www.computicket.com) allows you to book Greyhound, SA Roadlink and Intercape services, and to compare times and prices for the three operators in one place.

Greyhound/Citiliner (www.greyhound.co.za) operates up to four services per day that stop in Potchefstroom (Cape Town, Bloemfontein and Mossel Bay services via Kimberley). Services stop at the junction between Nelson Mandela Drive and Parys Avenue, and at Jenny's Quality Foods (the Sasol Garage) further along Nelson Mandela Drive. SA Roadlink (www.saroadlink.co.za) services travel via Potchefstroom on their daily Cape Town (via Kimberley) service from Pretoria and Johannesburg. Intercape (www.intercape.co.za) operates one service per day from Pretoria and Johannesburg to Potchefstroom. The service stops at Jenni's Quality Foods on Nelson Mandela Drive. Translux (www.translux.co.za) operates one daily service between Johannesburg and Potchefstroom.

While the Park City transit centre in Johannesburg is relatively safe, it can get very busy during peak times. Beware of pickpockets in and around the station and keep all your belongings with you at all times. The area outside the station is less safe. Exercise caution, don't wander the streets aimlessly, and make connecting travel plans in advance. While most bus services are well maintained and comfortable, buses are a cheap form of transport, and your fellow travellers are likely to be poor. You should avoid wearing expensive jewellery and displaying valuables.

Taxis in South Africa are rare away from airports and the main city centres. Arrange for your accommodation providers to pick you up from the bus stop in Potchefstroom prior to your arrival, and as a matter of courtesy, keep them updated on any delays to your service.

By car

All the major international car hire companies, and some national ones, operate from OR Tambo International Airport. Car hire desks are located between the two terminals near the Intercontinental Hotel. Cars can also be hired from central Johannesburg and from Pretoria. Europcar have a number of pick-up spots in both cities.

Potchefstroom is located approximately 150 km south-west of OR Tambo International, a journey which takes approximately 1 hr 30 min by car. Johannesburg is 125 km from Potchefstroom and Pretoria is 180 km away. The roads are in relatively good condition, but can be dangerous to drive on (see p. 264).

Visa requirements

Visas are not required for stays of up to 90 days by passport holders from UK, Ireland, most Western European countries, Australia, New Zealand, Canada and US. Many other European residents can enter for up to 30 days without a visa. Up-to-date visa information can be found at www.home-affairs.gov.za.

GETTING AROUND

Though Potchefstroom isn't quite small enough to get around on foot, most of the sports facilities, accommodation, and best restaurants are located in a small area around the NWU campus. A car is useful to get to and from the shops, and to trails on the outskirts of the city, but is not essential.

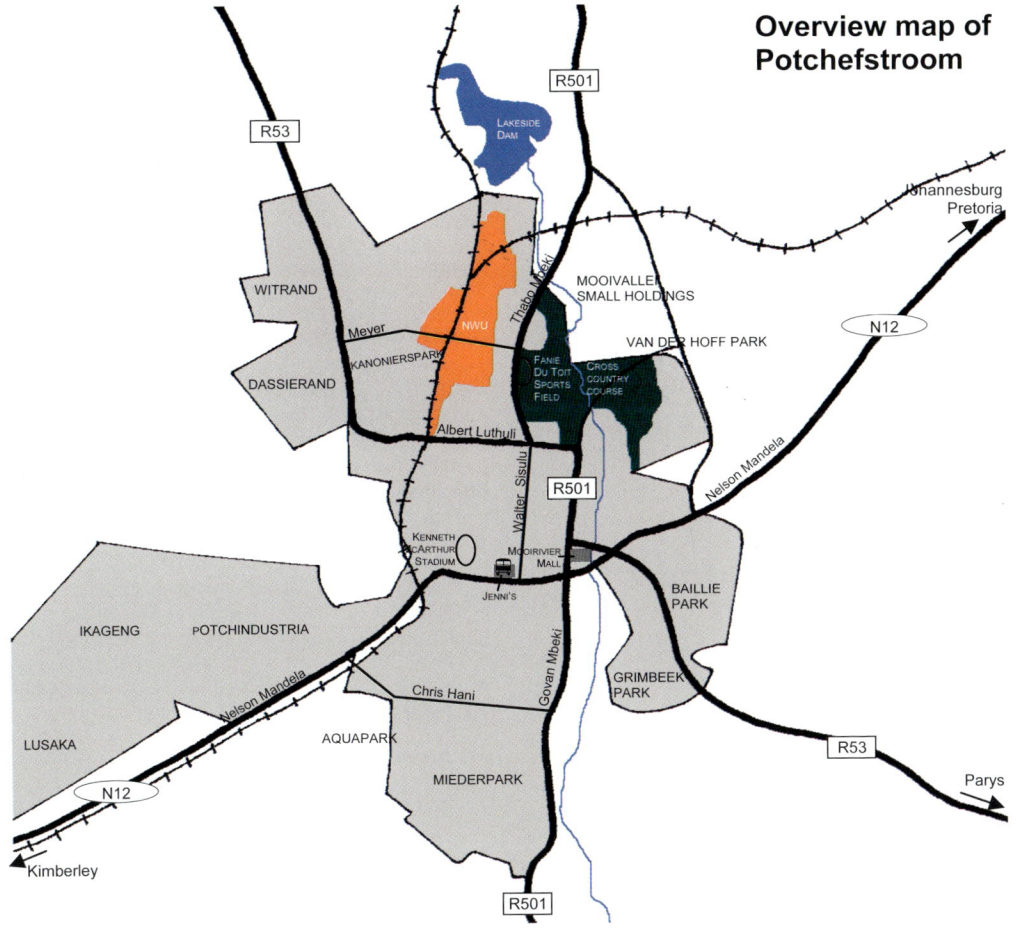

Overview map of Potchefstroom

DRIVING IN SOUTH AFRICA

Public transport in South Africa is relatively underdeveloped, and driving is the preferred way for Westerners to get around the country. Driving is, however, incredibly dangerous and more than 14,000 people are killed on South African roads each year. That's 38 people each day!

Extreme caution should be exercised at all times, but especially at night. The key is to drive defensively rather than aggressively and expect other drivers to do something dangerous, stupid and/or illegal. Pedestrians can step out onto the road at any time, and cyclists don't always cycle on the left. It's not unusual, in rural areas, for animals, including antelope, to venture onto the road, especially in the evening.

Car-hijackings are common, particularly in and around the cities. Drive with your doors locked and your windows up, and be aware of your surroundings at all times. Never leave valuables on display and always park in well-lit, busy areas. Don't pick up hitchhikers.

Four-way stops are common at quieter intersections (and particularly around Potchefstroom). All cars must stop, and the car which arrived first proceeds first. Vehicles entering a roundabout should yield to the traffic approaching from the right. South Africans generally use indicators in a sporadic and unreliable fashion. Proceed with caution.

South African roads are not always well signposted, and drivers are advised to purchase a good map, use a GPS, and plan routes in advance of setting out on a journey. Petrol Stations are usually open 24 hours a day and are located along all the main routes. Fuel prices are fixed and controlled by the government.

Cycling is generally not advised in most areas of South Africa, but is popular in and around Potchefstroom. The streets are normally quiet enough to get around without too much hassle. Bicycle hire is just one of the services that Altitude Training Potchefstroom (ATP) offers as part of their all-inclusive training packages *(p. 268)*.

If you choose to get to Potchefstroom by bus, but want to hire a car once you're there, both Avis and Budget have offices in the city.

A number of street names changed in 2004, so it is good to double-check that you have an up-to-date map of the town, and the modern name of the street you are looking for. Some old street names are still used by locals, and you may hear Steve Biko Avenue, particularly the section around the Cachet Square Shopping Centre still referred to as Toms Street. The other street name changes are listed on the Tlokwe City Council website (www.potch.co.za). Most businesses have separate postal and physical addresses. Physical addresses are normally given as a pair of intersecting streets similar to the system used in the US (e.g. cnr of Nelson Mandela and Govan Mbeki). Brabys (www.brabysmaps.co.za) produces a free street index/map of the area, which is available from the tourist information office and other businesses. Map Studio (www.mapstudio.co.za) has a good interactive map on which you can search shops, post offices, police stations, accommodations, restaurants, other businesses, and places of interest.

WEATHER AND WHEN TO VISIT

Monthly average daily highs between October and March are in the region of 26–27 °C. June and July are the coolest months, with monthly average daily highs of 18–19 °C, though even then temperatures can rise above 20 °C. Daily lows are in the region of 14–16 °C during the summer months, and can drop to low single figures during June and July, when nights are typically cold. The majority of Potchefstroom's rain falls during the summer, with heavy rain showers, and occasional thunderstorms in November, December, January and February. Heavy rainfall may disrupt training from time to time, though there is bright sunshine at some stage on most days. There is practically no rainfall in the cool winter months of May, June and July.

Christmas is a very popular time for athletes from Europe to visit. Accommodation can quickly fill up at this time, and larger groups and teams are advised to book well in advance. Students are on holiday at this time, so the city can still be relatively quiet. The spring and autumn months, when there is less rainfall but temperatures are still high, can also be a good time to visit.

ACCOMMODATION

The majority of accommodation is guesthouse and B&B style, with some properties offering additional self-catering and full board options. South Africa online (www.madbookings.com) and Gateway Potchefstroom (www.potchefstroom.co.za) are good starting points for accommodation. Cosy Cottage B&B (www.cosy-cottage.co.za; 38 Parys Avenue, Baillie Park) features private cottages with self-catering facilities, and dinner and breakfast available on request. Accommodations along Meyer Street and Thabo Mbeki Drive are within walking distance of the Fanie du Toit Sports Fields, and Huys ten Bosch, Vonkel en Koljander and Annelie's, all offer excellent facilities and services for athletes. Accommodation can be arranged for non-residents on the NWU campus (www.nwu.ac.za). This is a particularly good option for teams. The PUK Sports Village has an onsite restaurant; Astrovilla, on the grounds of the PUK Hockey Academy, has rooms with fully equipped kitchens; and Dennepark comes with communal kitchen facilities. Most of the accommodation is within easy reach of the sports facilities.

Food

Finding good food to meet the dietary needs of an endurance athlete can be difficult. Takeaway food is plentiful, and chips are the standard carbohydrate served with most meals, even in restaurants. Pasta dishes even tend to come with minimal portions of pasta. It's a good idea to have access to cooking facilities, even if you don't plan to cook for yourself every day, or to arrange suitable food in advance if you are availing of a full board option.

There are restaurants located off Meyer Street close to Cachet Square, and at the Mooi Rivier Mall off Nelson Mandela Drive. There is a Nando's, a favourite among many athletes, on the corner of Nelson Mandela and Beyers Naudé Avenue, and a couple of decent fish restaurants in the city. Meat in South Africa tends to be well done, so if you want something rare or medium, be sure to explain just how well cooked you would like it.

Supermarkets are relatively cheap by European standards, and there is a good range of medium to large supermarkets carrying a broad range of goods. There is a medium-sized Friendly supermarket on Meyer Street, close to the university/sports facilities, SPAR stores throughout the city, a Pick 'n' Pay at West Acres Shopping Centre on Walter Sisulu Avenue, and an outlet of Checkers in the Mooi Rivier Mall. Megasave, located on Tieroog Street in the Industrial Zone (west along Nelson Mandela Drive), is a wholesale store, which also sells groceries direct to the consumer. This may be a good option for groups spending considerable time in the town, but a car will be required to get there.

BELOW Grass area at the Fanie Du Toit sports fields

Shopping

MooiRivier Mall (www.mooiriviermall.co.za), located on Nelson Mandela Drive (N12), just after the junction with Parys Avenue (R53) is the main shopping centre. It is a modern centre, opened in 2008, and has over 100 stores including a large supermarket, bookshops, sports stores, department stores and clothes shops. There are also fast-food restaurants, and entertainment facilities. You are likely to find most things that you will need in the mall.

There is a small area of shops and businesses, including a medium-sized supermarket, a pharmacy and a bookshop, just off Meyer Street by the university (Cachet Park Shopping Centre). West Acres Shopping Centre, on Walter Sisulu Avenue, also has a range of shops.

As the city is not a major tourist destination, souvenirs and crafts are difficult to find. The monthly art market, held in the city council gardens, is a good place to make interesting purchases.

The large Mr Price Sport (www.mrprice.co.za) store in the MooiRivier Mall sells a variety of sport and leisurewear, including some running kit and footwear. The smaller sports shops in the mall (Sportscentre; Total Sport), sell mostly leisurewear. There is a Des Fontaine Sports store on Walter Sisulu Avenue in the centre of town.

Language

Though over 85 percent of Potchefstroom's people speak Afrikaans as their first language, English is widely spoken, as it is elsewhere in South Africa and English-speaking visitors shouldn't have any problems communicating.

Communications

Mobile phones in South Africa operate on the same GSM frequency (900/1800 MHz) as Europe and the rest of Africa. 3G (UMTS) networks are also widely available and European or African phone users should be able to pick up a signal with at least one of South Africa's mobile phone network providers (Vodacom, MTN, Cell-C, Virgin Mobile and 8ta). Prepaid SIM card starter kits are the cheapest mobile phone option if staying in South Africa for longer than a few days though you normally need a residential address to purchase and register a starter kit. There are a number of phone shops in the MooiRivier Mall and prepaid credit is available in almost every shop.

There are several internet shops around the city and access is relatively cheap. An increasing number of cafes and small restaurants also provide free Wi-Fi access for customers. Examples include Mugg and Bean at the Mooi Rivier Mall, and McDonalds just behind the mall. Most of the guesthouses also have free Wi-Fi access.

The South African postal service (South African Post Office) is slow. Delivery by international airmail service can take up to 10 days, and national city-to-city services take approximately 4 days. There are post offices located right around the city, with one in Baillie Park, outlets on OR Tambo Avenue and Hucle Malberry in the centre of town, and one on Esselen Street, close to the university.

Health and Safety

Potchefstroom is located within the malaria-free area of South Africa. The north-west of the country, including the Kruger National Park, does have a seasonal malaria risk. If you plan to travel around South Africa during your stay, seek medical advice on whether or not prophylactics are required. Anyone travelling through a yellow fever risk area (including Ethiopia, Kenya and Uganda) will need a valid yellow fever certificate to enter South Africa. Vaccination against tetanus, diphtheria, hepatitis A and typhoid is also recommended. AIDS is endemic in South Africa, and an estimated 15 percent of the sexually active population are HIV-positive. Blood for transfusions is carefully screened and treated, so the risk of hospital transmission is minimal.

Potchefstroom Hospital, the main public hospital, is located south-west of the city centre on the corner of Kruis Street and Chris Hani Drive. Mooi-Med Hospital (Albert Luthuli Drive, by the junction with Thabo Mbeki Drive) and Potchefstroom Medi-Clinic (Meyer Street) are both multidisciplinary private hospitals.

Potchefstroom is relatively tidy, but some streets are littered with plastic waste and broken glass bottles. Keep an eye out for broken glass and avoid walking the streets in flip-flops. Tap water is generally safe to drink, though bottled water, which is widely available, is advisable.

Potchefstroom is generally a safe place, especially by South African standards, and violent crime is much rarer than in the large cities. Take normal precautions, and take care not to flaunt your wealth or belongings (this also shows

Staying safe in the cities

Most of South Africa's major cities have a reputation for violent crime. Illegal firearms have made their way onto the streets, and car-jackings and muggings are common. Some areas are worse than others, but if you are travelling through Johannesburg or spending time in any of the other major cities, you may find the following advice useful.

- Try not to look affluent or show off valuables in public. Leave jewellery, cameras, watches and other valuable items at home, or keep them hidden when out in public.
- Avoid carrying large amounts of cash. It's a good idea to have a small amount of cash within easy reach, so that if you are approached, you can claim that it's all the cash you have on you.
- Never walk alone after dark.
- If you are attacked, hand over valuables without resisting. Attackers may have a gun. Phone the police once the assailant is out of sight.
- Don't stop to help people who appear to be in trouble, even if you genuinely think that they need assistance. Phone the police instead and report what you have seen.

respect, and can help reduce hassle from beggars). The police station is located on OR Tambo Avenue. Violent crime is common in Johannesburg and other major cities. Driving on South African roads is dangerous and care should be taken (p. 264).

Money

The rand (sign: R; code: ZAR) is the currency of South Africa. It is also used in the common monetary area that includes Lesotho and Swaziland. Avoid using the currency exchange offices in the airport as they apply heavy exchange charges. There are many ATMs in the airport and around Potchefstroom, and South African banks don't charge a fee for using them (though your own bank may). There are branches of ABSA, FNB, Nedbank and Standard Banks in the Mooi Rivier Mall, and elsewhere around the city.

Power

South Africa operates on a 220–230 V; 50 Hz electricity supply, and uses Type M (SANS 164-1) South African plugs and sockets with three large round pins. Combined/multi adaptors do not normally have the pins to fit South African sockets. There is good power supply in South African cities, but there may be sporadic power cuts in rural areas.

Time

South Africa operates on South African Standard Time (SAST; GMT+2). There is no daylight saving or summer time, and South Africa is only an hour ahead of Britain during British Summer Time. Daylight lasts for just under 14 hr in midsummer, and for almost 10 hr 30 min in midwinter.

	Mar	Jun	Sep	Dec
Sunrise	06:12	06:58	06:08	05:12
Sunset	18:28	17:26	18:04	19:01

Laundry

Laundry facilities are plentiful and many offer reasonably-priced service washes. There is a coin-operated self-service laundry at Cachet Park Shopping Centre (by the Friendly Supermarket on Meyer Street). Some accommodations also have washing machines or offer laundry facilities. Unlike other parts of Africa, you are not expected to wash your clothes by hand.

Culture and respect

South Africans are generally friendly, and particularly welcoming to tourists. Males normally greet by shaking hands and women by the typical Continental kiss on the cheek. Begging, though less than in the large cities, does exist. To avoid unwanted attention you should dress conservatively and avoid looking like a tourist.

Most South Africans have an interest in sport, and are used to athletes visiting the city. Anyone working in the tourist industry is likely to be friendly and to ask you about your sport. Don't be surprised if they want to stay in touch after you leave.

Most food bills do not include a service charge, and a tip of 10-15 percent is appreciated. A service charge may be included in the bill for large groups (6 or more), in which case there is no need to tip. Parking attendants and petrol station attendants are normally tipped a few rand for their services. If you take a guided tour, it is normal to tip the guide and driver at the end of the day (usually R10.00–R15.00 per person which is divided between guide and driver).

Sports facilities and services

The main facilities, including a grass track, playing fields and a cross country course, are located next to the FNB High Performance Institute of Sport (HPI) at the Potchefstroom Campus of NWU. Team sports are well catered for and there is a variety of cross-training, recovery and rehabilitation options for athletes of all levels.

Training camps and tour operators

Altitude Training Potchefstroom (ATP; www.atp-sports.com) arranges all-inclusive packages. In addition to accommodation and access to training facilities, physiotherapy and sports massage, transfers to and from the airport in Johannesburg, transport within Potchefstroom, sightseeing and adventure trips, bicycle hire, training partners, and coaching, if required, can be arranged.

Trails and running routes

The Fanie Du Toit Sports Fields on the NWU Campus is the most popular place to run, but there are other options, and the more adventurous visitors can make use of scenic trails in the Vredefort Dome.

NWU Campus
Many athletes complete grass efforts and recovery runs around the grass track and adjacent cricket and rugby fields at the Fanie Du Toit facility or around the nearby purpose-built cross country course. The total perimeter around both areas is approximately 3 km.

Lakeside Dam
From Fanie Du Toit Sports Fields, you can follow the river north, across Thabo Mbeki, and continue north along grass and paths to the Lakeside Dam Recreation Resort. There are some quiet and flat roads there which may be suitable for road efforts.

Dirt roads and farm tracks
Outside the city you will find some dirt roads and farm tracks which are good for off-road running. Finding ones that are longer than a few hundred metres is tricky. Try to find one that looks like there are a number of houses along, or that gets a good bit of use. The further you get from the city, the more likely you are to find unsurfaced and dirt roads. In this respect, a car is very useful.

Vredefort Dome
There are some challenging out-of-town options. Deelfontein Trails (www.deelfontein.co.za) is a 60 km network of multi-use tracks, trails and farm roads across intermediated terrain in the heart of the Vredefort Dome (p. 271). Located 21 km from Parys and approximately 45 km from Potchefstroom, the trails offer spectacular views of the surrounding countryside and are open all year-round. There are changing rooms and showers on site, which are useful for those visiting from Potchefstroom and day visitors are required to pay an access fee. In the same general area, the Meteorite Hiking Trails (www.domehiking.co.za) also comprise more than 60 km of trails. Thabela Thabeng Trail (www.thabelathabeng.co.za) near Parys, and the trails at Dome Adventures (www.domeadventures.co.za) in Venterskroon, are also suitable for running.

Track facilities

There is a 400 m grass track, with synthetic run-ups for horizontal and vertical jumps and javelin, a synthetic 60 m sprint straight, and concrete throwing circles, at Fanie Du Toit Sports Fields. There are always hurdles available for drills, and steeplechase barriers, but no water jump. The 400 m synthetic PUK-McArthur Stadium track (Kenneth McArthur Oval) is located in the centre of town between Nelson Mandela Drive and Beyers Naudé Avenue.

Gym facilities

There is a fully equipped gym, which includes cardio equipment (bikes, rowing machines, treadmills), free and fixed weights, Olympic lifting platforms, a Hammer Strength Super Circuit, and other strength and rehabilitation equipment within the High Performance Institute at NWU. Virgin Active (virginactive.co.za), located on Meyer Street, has free weights and super circuits areas, cardiovascular equipment and a 25 m pool.

Cross-training options

Road cycling, mountain biking and swimming are good options for low impact activity. Facilities at the High Performance Institute include a rehab pool which can be used for aqua jogging, and a good range of cardiovascular training equipment. There are outdoor fields and courts, and tennis, basketball, volleyball, netball, cricket and football are all good options for those who like to add variety to their training. Canoeing and kayaking are available at Lakeside Dam. For those willing to travel, activities such as climbing, white-water rafting and hiking are available in the Vredefort Dome area.

Opposite Parts of the route around the Fanie Du Toit sports facility

SPORTS MEDICINE AND SPORTS SCIENCE SUPPORT

The High Performance Institute (www.puk.ac.za/hpi) located at the corner of Thabo Mbeki Drive and Meyer Street is a one-stop shop for high performance athletes. It houses a recovery ice bath, a core area, a salinated pool for rehabilitation and aquajogging, a 45 m synthetic running track, steam rooms, sports science laboratories, consultation rooms for sports medicine and sports science practitioners, biomechanical and game analysis facilities, and training and lecture rooms. There are other physiotherapists around the university area. Sentrum Physiotherapy, on the corner between Steve Biko Avenue and Meyer Street, is particularly popular among athletes.

LOCAL RACES

South Africa's track and field season runs from early January, through to April when the South African Senior Championships are normally held. Combining training in Potchefstroom with racing on the South African athletics circuit can be a good alternative to racing indoors. The KK McArthur Stadium Permit Meeting and the NUK-Pukki Invitational meeting are held at McArthur Stadium in Potchefstroom. There are also regular road races in and around the town.

South African Athlete (www.saathlete.com) is a good source of information for track events, and Runnersguide.co.za (www.runnersguide.co.za) and Runner's World South Africa (www.runnersworld.co.uk) are good sources for on and off-road race listings in South Africa.

RUNNING COMMUNITY

The grass track at Fanie Du Toit Sports Fields is the best place in town to hang out and meet other athletes. As the city attracts field event athletes, sprinters and multieventers as well as distance runners, you're likely to encounter a broad range of track and field stars. The British cross country team prepared for the 2007 World Cross Country Championships in Potchefstroom, and many top British athletes have spent time training in the city. Kelly Holmes trained in Potchefstroom during her career, and brought a group of talented teenage middle distance athletes to train here as part of the On Camp with Kelly programme. More than 800 visiting athletes, the majority of them from France, used the HPI during 2010. A number of world-class athletes hail from Potchefstroom, and Josia Thugwane, the 1996 Olympic marathon champion, spent time training in the town.

SUITABILITY FOR OTHER SPORTS

The mild climate, moderate altitude and excellent facilities make Potchefstroom a great training destination for a variety of sportspeople, and not just endurance athletes looking to boost their red blood cell count. Tlokwe City Council's Parks and Recreation unit (www.potch.co.za) is a good starting point for booking sports facilities. Facilities within the city, which they maintain, include swimming pools, netball, volleyball, tennis and basketball courts, football and rugby fields, softball and baseball fields, and cricket facilities. There are additional training facilities at NWU, and ATP can help with locating sports facilities to meet the needs of most sportspeople.

Swimming There are 50 m swimming pools at the Lakeside Recreation resort in the north of the city, and by McArthur stadium in the city centre. There is a 25 m indoor swimming pool at the Virgin Active Health Club on Meyer Street, and a pool alongside the other facilities at Fanie Du Toit.

Cycling Competitive cycling is relatively popular, and country roads can be reached quickly from anywhere within Potchefstroom. Dingo Cycles (www.dingocycles.co.za), located on Thabo Mbeki Drive, is a particularly well-stocked bike shop.

Triathlon Decent running facilities and trails, swimming pools and good cycling options make Potchefstroom suitable for triathletes.

Team sports Cricket, rugby, hockey and football teams are all well catered for. The Spanish football team trained here in the run-up to the 2012 FIFA World Cup, and a number of national teams compete in the city. The cricket stadium at Senwes Park (previously known as Sedgars Park) hosted matches during the 2003 Cricket World Cup, and regularly hosts one-day internationals and first class test matches. There are good hockey facilities at PUK Hockey Academy. A number of accommodations, including the PUK Sports Village, are well equipped to cater for large groups and teams. Consultation rooms, suitable for team doctors, physiotherapists and massage practitioners, can be booked at NWU's HPI and classrooms, which may be required by large teams, can be booked at both the HPC and the PUK Sports Village.

Other sports There are numerous tennis courts around the city. Lakeside Dam is suitable for kayaking, canoeing and rowing. There are four golf courses, providing good variety to golfers who wish to practise at altitude.

THINGS TO SEE AND DO BETWEEN TRAINING

Potchefstroom is a student city, and much of its tourism industry is built around sporting events and visiting athletes. While far from a sightseeing hotspot, there is plenty to do in the city.

There are a few buildings of historical and cultural interest. Andrew Carnegie Library and City Hall, both located on Nelson Mandela Drive, are national monuments. The town is home to one of the oldest Reformed Churches in South Africa and Saint Mary's Anglican Church built in 1891, features exceptional stained glass windows. Oak Avenue, which stretches for 6.84 km from Lakeside Dam to the Agricultural College in Aquapark, was planted in 1910 and is the longest avenue of its kind in the southern hemisphere.

Water sports, fishing and mini-golf are available at Lakeside Dam. OPM Prozesky Bird Sanctuary, located in the very south of the city, is home to more than 200 species of bird. The sanctuary is open at all times, and there is no entry fee. The botanical garden at NWU also has free admission. There is a cinema at the MooiRivier Mall. Sanlam Ouditorium (auditorium) hosts regular concerts and music performances.

Boskop Dam Nature Reserve, approximately 25 km north of Potchefstroom, is a popular picnic site and fishing and yachting location. Black wildebeest, zebra, springbok and more than 250 bird species can be spotted within the reserve. Nearby Buffelsvlei Wild Animal Park (www.buffelsvlei.co.za) is home to giraffe, zebra, ostrich, impala and springbok, and is a good place for quad biking, horseback riding, target shooting, paintballing and clay-pigeon shooting. Volleyball, rugby and obstacle course racing are also offered.

REST DAY EXCURSIONS

In addition to the obvious destinations of Johannesburg and Pretoria, there are a number of interesting places to visit from Potchefstroom.

Vredefort Dome, the oldest and largest clearly visible meteorite impact structure on earth, is situated approximately 50 km from Potchefstroom. Activities available within this UNESCO World Heritage site include mountain biking, hiking, horse riding, birdwatching, stargazing, fly fishing, rock climbing, hot-air ballooning, and canoeing. Activities are located around Deelfontein (www.deelfontein.co.za), Parys (www.parys.co.za) and other small villages. The hiking and mountain bike trails in the area can be used for trail running.

Tours of Soweto, South Africa's best-known township, are available though Themba Day Tours (www.sowetotour.co.za) and Taste of Africa Tours (www.tasteofafrica.co.za), among others. The township, where both Nelson Mandela and Desmond Tutu have lived, is located south-west of Johannesburg (Soweto is an abbreviation of South Western Township), just off the main route to Potchefstroom.

Sun City, a major resort and casino located approximately 200 km north of Potchefstroom is one of South Africa's main tourist destinations, and features cinemas, restaurants, golf courses, the world's longest zip wire ride and water rides and slides in the valley of the waves. Pilanesberg National Park (www.pilanesbergnationalpark.org), which features the big five (buffalo, elephant, leopard, lion, rhino) is located close by.

A NOTE ON LIVING HERE LONG-TERM

Potchefstroom's biggest drawback is its lack of trails and running routes. While the grass facilities at NWU are excellent, and more than adequate for a middle distance athlete training here for a few weeks, distance runners, particularly marathon runners, will quickly tire of what the city has to offer. Potchefstroom's altitude is minimal, and training benefits may be negligible. This should be considered before spending a lot of money moving to the town. There are advantages (e.g. warm weather training; quality training can be performed), but there may be more suitable places in the world to train in warm temperatures. The city, though relatively small, has a variety of shops and amenities, and is within easy reach of Johannesburg and Pretoria. The sports facilities are excellent, and the track is a great place to meet people and make friends. There are some work, volunteering and educational opportunities. The city's proximity to Johannesburg's major international airport makes it easy to get to races, and the climate is suitable for training year-round.

FURTHER INFORMATION

Further information, including event listings, emergency contact, and information about the city, can be found on the city council website (www.potch.co.za). There is information on towns and attractions in North West Provence on www.tourismnorthwest.co.za, and www.potch.info and www.potchefstroom.co.za are useful business directory websites. The Potchefstroom Tourism Information and Development Centre is located on the corner of Nelson Mandela Drive and Walter Sisulu Avenue.

The grass track at the Fanie Du Toit sports facility

Dullstroom

Dullstroom is an ideal training venue for athletes wishing to experience South African culture, countryside and cuisine, and benefit from the southern hemisphere's summer. The small town, which is located approximately three hours east of Johannesburg, is trying to grow its reputation as an altitude training destination and is a friendly place for runners to train. Dullstroom is arguably South Africa's best training location for long-distance runners. A double-track dirt trail stretches from the town alongside the railway line, through beautiful rolling countryside. An abundance of rental cottages and other self-catering accommodation offers excellent value for money, and there is a fine collection of restaurants and cafes.

Dullstroom, South Africa (2,080 m)

Dullstroom is located in the heart of Mpumalanga Province in north-east South Africa. It was established in 1883 for Dutch immigrant settlers by Wolterus Dull, after whom the town is named. The original settlement was all but destroyed during the Second Boer War, and most of the original settlers returned home. Today the town thrives thanks to tourism. Rolling hills, quaint country inns, fly-fishing reservoirs and mountain biking trails make it a popular weekend getaway for the city-dwellers of nearby Pretoria and Johannesburg. Its location also makes it a popular stopping point for those travelling between Gauteng and Kruger National Park, one of Africa's largest game reserves.

The Drakensberg Escarpment divides Mpumalanga, which means 'there where the sun rises', roughly in half. An area of high altitude (1,700–2,300 m) lies to the west (Highveld), and a region of lowlands (Lowveld/Bushveld) to the east. Dullstroom is located in the Steenkampsberg Mountain Range, though the area is not particularly mountainous.

Dullstroom train station, at 2,078 m is the highest station in South Africa. The town is one of the coldest in the country. It has a whiskey bar with the largest collection of whiskeys in the southern hemisphere and the town's clock shop has the largest collection of clocks in the southern hemisphere. Dullstroom has a population of approximately 600, and is sometimes known as Dullstroom-Emnothweni, which means 'Dullstroom: the place of prosperity'.

Author's verdict

Dullstroom is a very pleasant venue; the small town is both beautiful and welcoming. There are plenty of trails, lots of nice cafes and restaurants in which to relax and excellent value for money when it comes to accommodation. Even though there is no track or fancy facilities, it has a number of advantages over Potchefstroom, and it is surprising that there are not more athletes training here. I was glad to be self-catering as carbohydrates don't seem to feature in South African restaurant meals, but the trout, for which the town is famous, is definitely recommended if you are eating out. The trails were particularly good for longer runs, though most tend to be out-and-back options. Dullstroom is situated close to one of South Africa's most important tourist areas, so there are good choices for rest day excursions.
Running ★★★☆☆ - Some good routes through beautiful countryside, though most are out-and-back in nature; some trails become muddy after rain; no track.
Convenience ★★☆☆☆ - Long flight from Europe; limited public transport access from Johannesburg; car useful; small town easy to get around on foot; trails accessible from all accommodations.
Safety ★★★☆☆ - Very peaceful by South African standards; minor risk of theft; caution should be exercised; HIV and AIDS are endemic; vaccination against hepatitis A, typhoid and polio is recommended; some distance to nearest hospital.
Cost ★★★☆☆ - Low cost of living; plentiful accommodation offering excellent value-for-money; flights expensive; car useful.
Cultural experience ★★★☆☆ - Feels more like Africa than Potchefstroom; offers insight into South African culture and way of life; excursions can be arranged to further enhance the cultural experience.
Things to do between training ★★★☆☆ - Limited activities that don't involve physical exertion and the great outdoors; good day-trip options; malaria prophylactics essential if exploring Kruger National Park.
Suitability for solo travellers ★★★☆☆ - Travelling in a group makes accommodation and car sharing cheaper, but solo travellers can easily survive; females travelling alone may attract some unwanted male attention but shouldn't feel threatened.

Must do Try some locally caught trout in one of the local restaurants (or catch your own); make the leisurely hike to the top of Groot Suikerboschkop; explore some of the local natural beauty.
Ideal for Those who want to experience the beauty of rural South Africa, and enjoy pleasant temperatures over Christmas.

GETTING IN

Dullstroom is located approximately 250 km from Johannesburg and 230 km from Pretoria. The large international airport in Johannesburg offers direct flights from many major cities around the world, and the town is easily accessible by car. There is an infrequent bus connection from Pretoria and the airport in Johannesburg.

By air

Most visitors from abroad will travel via Johannesburg's OR Tambo International Airport (JHB). There are direct flights from Amsterdam, Atlanta, Bangkok, Frankfurt, Hong Kong, London, Munich, New York, Paris, Perth, Sydney, Singapore, Washington, and Zurich, among others. Direct flights take just over 11 hr from London and approximately 10 hr 30 min from Paris. The airport is located approximately 22 km from Johannesburg's central business district, and 57 km from central Pretoria.

Those who are not hiring a car or getting a direct bus service from the airport, can take Gautrain (www.gautrain.co.za), Gauteng's high-speed rail service, to Johannesburg's Park Station, or to Pretoria Station (change at Marlboro or Sandton). Travelling on Gautrain services requires the one-off purchase of a tag-in card (Gold Card) onto which the fare is uploaded. Services run every 15 min during the week, and every 30 min at weekends and on public holidays from approximately 05:30 until 20:30. Taxi and private luxury shuttle transfers are also available from the airport as far as Johannesburg.

When returning to the airport by car, note that some signs still refer to the airport by its old names of 'Jan Smuts Intl' or 'JHB International'.

By bus

You may be told that there is no bus service to Dullstroom. This is not true. Bushveld Link operates a small minibus service from OR Tambo International Airport (bus and coach terminal behind the Intercontinental hotel) via Pretoria (McDonalds on the corner of Hamilton Street and Church Street) to Dullstroom (PB garage at the top of town). The service runs on Monday, Wednesday, Friday and Sunday, and takes just under 4 hr. Advance bookings, which are essential, can be made by email (bushveldlink@vodamail.co.za) or by phone (+27 (0)13 750 1953 or +27 (0)83 284 5382).

BELOW One of the amazing views from the railway trail
OPPOSITE View from the top of Suikerbosch Koppie
PREVIOUS A railway bridge with Dullstroom Dam and Dullstroom campsite in the background

Getting around

Dullstroom is easy to get around on foot. Most of the businesses, shops and restaurants are situated along the main road through Dullstroom (R540; Hugenote Street/Naledi Street). Your own transport is useful if you want a greater variety of trails, you wish to explore Mpumalanga's attractions, or you want to get to some of the larger supermarkets to pick up supplies. It is possible to get to some of the nearby towns by minibus service, though this form of transport is dangerous, and rarely used by tourists or white South Africans.

The town consists mainly of two small centres, both located along Hugenote Street. 'The top of town' or 'the top end' is centred around the supermarket, PB petrol station and Duck and Trout Restaurant close to the railway crossing. Just 1 km down the R540 in the direction of Lydenburg, 'the bottom of town' or 'the bottom end' is centred on a number of restaurants and cafes close to the Dullstroom Inn. The vast majority of shops, restaurants, cafes, and other services, including the Dullstroom Reservations and Dullstroom Accommodation office, are located in or between these two areas, or along Teding Van Berkhout Street at the bottom of town. Most of the other streets contain residential and rental accommodations.

Maps, with the major services and accommodations marked on them, are available from the information centres at Dullstroom Reservations and Dullstroom Accommodation. Dullstroom Reservations has an interactive map on their website (www.dullstroom.biz) which includes locations of accommodations, shops and restaurants. Recent street name changes have not been widely publicised, and many maps (and addresses) contain the old names.

Weather and when to visit

Dullstroom has a cool, sub-alpine climate, with mild summers and cool winters during which frost is common and snow occasionally occurs. Summers are wet, with regular thunderstorms, and winters (Jun–Aug) are typically dry, with minimal rainfall. The warmest months are between September and March when average daily temperatures are in excess of 20 °C, and average daily lows are 7–14 °C. June and July

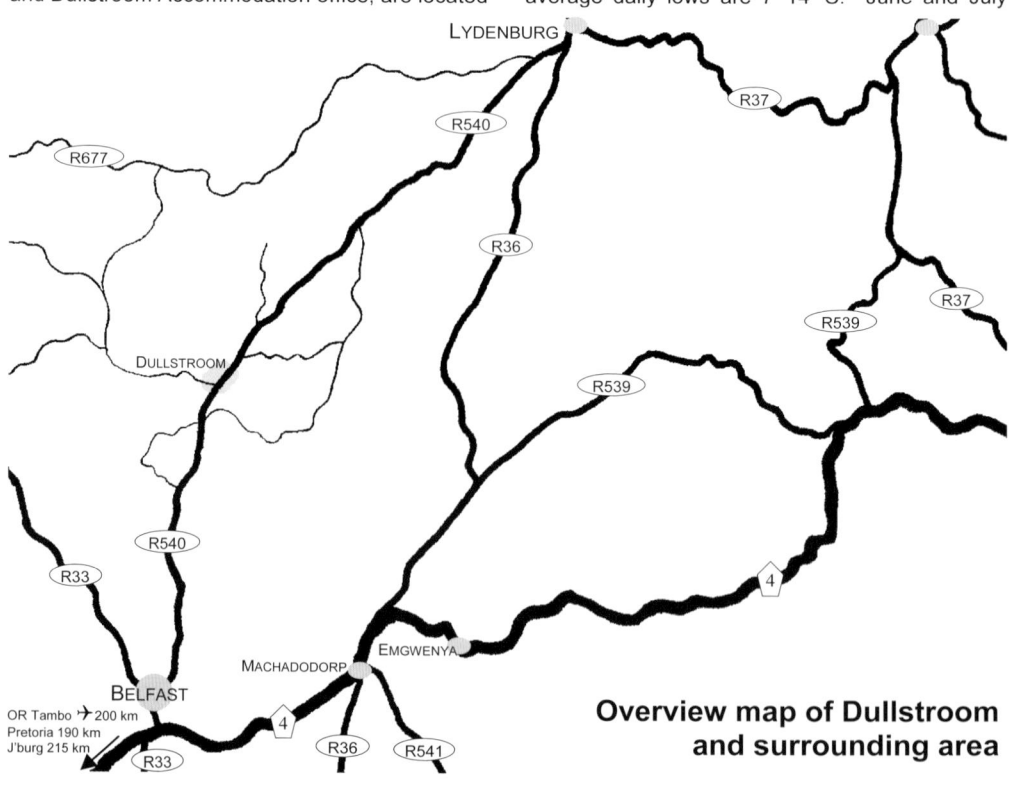

Overview map of Dullstroom and surrounding area

are the coldest months, with average daily highs of 12–16 °C and daily lows which can drop below freezing.

The town's altitude and location mean that weather can change quickly, and while summer mornings are normally bright and sunny, clouds tend to gather in the afternoon, and thunderstorms are common in the early evening. The dirt roads can become sticky after heavy rainfall, and running in thunderstorms is not advised. Where possible do your main training session in the mid morning (after the previous nights rain has dried up, and before the clouds start to gather), and prepare for all weathers when you are out and about.

South Africa is a popular destination for European athletes during and immediately after the Christmas holidays because of the warm temperatures. Visiting slightly before or after the main summer season, particularly during April, May or September, can mean that you avoid the worst of the rain, but still benefit from warm temperatures.

There is adequate accommodation to cater for even the busiest holiday periods, but booking well in advance is required if you have specific needs or want to stay in a specific property. Services and businesses are open year-round.

ACCOMMODATION

As a largely tourist town, Dullstroom contains a great selection of high standard, excellent-value, self-catering cottages. The town boasts more than 1,800 beds between hotels, lodges, B&Bs, guesthouses, apartments, and self-catering houses. Reservations can be made through Dullstroom Reservations (www.dullstroom.biz) and Dullstroom Accommodation (www.dullstroom.co.za). Both have offices, from where you pick up the accommodation keys, along Dullstroom's main road. You should take note of office closing times when planning your arrival in Dullstroom, particularly at the weekend. Most of the accommodations are situated within easy reach of the amenities and the trails, and those that are on the outskirts of the town are usually right next to the trails. You will need your own transport to get to the out-of-town accommodations.

Most self-catering accommodations have excellent cooking facilities, and many come with barbecuing (braai) facilities. In some cases, full board options are available by prior arrangement.

Satellite TV and DVD players are standard, though only the most expensive hotels have Wi-Fi internet connections. Some accommodations have laundry facilities, and bed linen and towels are usually provided.

A typical, well-equipped rental property

FOOD

Most of the restaurants and cafes are situated along Dullstroom's main road. Many of the eateries serve a variety of European and South African foods, with a broad range of meats. The trout, for which the town is famous, is highly recommended. Apart from rice with curry-style dishes, and the occasional pasta dish, chips are the normal carbohydrate food served with meals. Even when potatoes are served, the portions are small. Don't be afraid to ask for extras or sides. Most eateries also have takeaway services. Service in some of the restaurants may be slow.

The town has some good bakeries and pancake cafes, so there is no shortage of places for desserts and the occasional treat. Pancakes come in savoury and sweet forms, and tasty light meals, which make a great addition to self-catered dinners for hard-training athletes, are cheap and easy to find.

Restaurant reviews, opening times and links to restaurant websites and menus are available on the Eatout SA website (www.eatout.co.za). Dullstroom Online (www.dullstroom.co.za) has additional restaurant listings, locations and contact details.

There are a few small supermarkets. Freshpick Foods is located by the PB petrol station at the top of town, and Arbee's Supermarket is located at the bottom of town on Lesedi Street by the church. Bergen Cheese Shop (the top of town), the Bread Shop, Cakes and Things and the Butchery (by the BP Garage) also sell fresh produce, and there are usually some fruit and vegetable stalls along the main road. The supermarkets are moderately well stocked, and sufficient for the basics, but don't expect the same variety as you would get in a modern European supermarket. If you are a picky eater, don't like bland food, are spending a prolonged period in Dullstroom, or are planning on cooking all your meals, it would be a good idea to pick up additional supplies at one of the large supermarkets off the motorway before you exit for Belfast (for example, the large Pick n Pay in Witbank) on your way to Dullstroom. Most of the self-catering accommodations have excellent cooking facilities, and many have barbecues (braais).

SHOPPING

In addition to the supermarkets, which sell mainly food products, there are a variety of stores and shops. While you wouldn't come to Dullstroom just to shop, and you may not find everything that you need, it certainly is a good place to pick up some gifts and souvenirs to take home. Shops sell tacky nick-knacks, genuine handcrafted South African products, and decent works of art. Prices are much lower than in the airport. The Clock Shop on Teding Van Berkhout Street has the largest selection of clocks in the southern hemisphere, so that is a good place to pass some time, so to speak. There are outdoor and clothing stores, shops that sell supplies for fly fishing, a hardware shop, a phone shop, a DVD rental outlet, and even a Christmas shop. Most of the shops are situated along the main road.

There are no running shops, or specialist sports shops. There are a few outdoor shops, which may sell a very limited stock of leisurewear, but you are unlikely to find anywhere selling running footwear.

LANGUAGE

English is widely spoken in Dullstroom, as it is elsewhere in South Africa, and English-speaking visitors shouldn't have any problems communicating. Northern Sotho and Afrikaans are the most popular non-English first languages in and around Dullstroom.

COMMUNICATIONS

Mobile phone reception in and around Dullstroom is good. There is a Cellnet mobile phone shop in Dullstroom (at the top of town by the BP petrol station), where you can purchase SIM cards and starter kits. See *p. 266* for other information on mobile phone access in South Africa.

Internet access is available in Dullstroom Video Shop by the BP petrol station in the top of town. This is relatively expensive, but the connection speed is fast, and you don't need your own laptop. Apart from the more expensive hotels, most accommodations do not have internet or Wi-Fi access.

There is a small post office located at 117 Lethabo Street (formerly Gunning Street) in the bottom of town.

HEALTH AND SAFETY

Dullstroom is a malaria-free area so prophylactics are not required unless you intend to travel to the Lowveld and Kruger National Park where there is a seasonal malaria risk. Yellow fever vaccination is required for anyone travelling from or through a yellow fever infected area. Vaccination against tetanus, diphtheria, hepatitis A and typhoid is also recommended. South Africa has one of the highest HIV infection rates in the world with an estimated 1 in 4 females between the ages of 20 and 40 being HIV-positive. Tap water is generally safe to drink, though bottled water, which is easily available, is advised.

Dullstroom is a very small town and does not have a hospital. The nearest hospitals are in Belfast (Vermooten Street), 36 km away, and Lydenburg (Berg Street), 55 km away. Both hospitals have emergency departments. Life Med operates an ambulance service from Nelspruit. Dullstroom has one pharmacy, located by the Duck and Trout at the top of town. There is one doctor based in the town. Contact details can be found in the Dullstroom Emnothweni essential info booklet or on any of the online directories.

Dullstroom is a safe place, especially by South African standards, and violent crime is rare. There is, however, a large gap between the rich and the poor, and robberies do happen. Take normal precautions, and take care not to flaunt your wealth or belongings (this also shows respect, and can help reduce hassle from beggars). The police station is located on the corner of Lethabo Street and Lesedi Street in the bottom of town.

Take particular care if travelling through Johannesburg. Violent crime is common, and certain areas within the major cities should be avoided.

Driving on South African roads is dangerous *(p. 264)*.

Money

See p. 257
There are three ATMs in Dullstroom, two in the top of town, and one in Arbee's Supermarket at the bottom of town. There are no banks.

Power

See p. 267
There may be sporadic power cuts in Dullstroom. A torch is a useful item to pack.

Time

See p. 267
South Africa operates on South African standard time (GMT+2). There is no daylight saving or summer time, so South Africa is only 1 hr ahead of Britain during British Summer Time.

Laundry

Some, but not all, of the accommodations have washing machines or access to laundry facilities. There are a number of cleaning and laundry services operating in the town. The essential information booklet will have contact details. Unlike other parts of Africa, you would not be expected to wash your clothes by hand.

Culture and respect

South Africans are generally friendly, and the locals very helpful. Males tend to greet each other by shaking hands and women by the typical Continental kiss on the cheek. Begging, though less common than in the cities, does exist, and to avoid unwanted attention you should dress conservatively and avoid looking like a tourist.

Most food bills do not include a service charge, and a tip of 10 to 15 percent is appreciated. A service charge may be included in the bill for larger groups (six or more), in which case there is no need to tip. Parking attendants and petrol station attendants are normally tipped a few rand for their services.

Racial division is still evident, and the vast majority of the local black population still live in a township (Sakhelwe) on the edge of Dullstroom. While you are unlikely to experience any problems because of this, you are likely to become very aware of it.

BELOW Dullstroom Dam
FOLLOWING Distant view of the township on the edge of Dullstroom from the railway trail

Sports facilities and services

Dullstroom is a small town, and you are never very far from a dirt road or trail which crosses the beautiful rolling landscape. While sports facilities, in the typical sense, are practically non-existent, athletes who are happy to just run and explore, won't have any trouble putting in a good block of training in Dullstroom.

Much of this area of Mpumalanga is situated at or above 2,000 m of altitude, so while a 'live high, train low' approach is possible if you have a car, it does require considerable driving, and a good knowledge of the area. Lydenburg is situated at approximately 1,400 m above sea level, but is about 55 km away. If you travel about 20 km to Tonteldoos, or south of the town towards the R36, you'll come to ground that is at an altitude of approximately 1,800 m. However, because of the undulating terrain here, you may find yourself at an altitude close to that of Dullstroom a couple of kilometres into a run.

Dullstroom is suitable for distance runners, and has some good surfaced roads for marathon runners and other road racers. There is no track, which may be a drawback for middle distance runners. There are some technical trails for fell runners, though these are a little less obvious than the dirt tracks and roads, and while the area is very hilly it wouldn't be described as mountainous. Race walkers do sometimes train here, but surfaces suitable for walking are largely limited to the surfaced roads on the outskirts of the town.

Trails and running routes

Apart from the R540 which runs through the town, most of the roads in the area are unsurfaced. These dirt roads provide good options for running. The jeep track, which runs alongside the railway, is one of the most popular options. There are some specially constructed technical trails in the area.

Most of the roads off the R540 in the direction of Belfast are unsurfaced. As a rule, any road that is not marked with an 'R' code on a map is a dirt road beyond the first kilometre or two. To avoid private farm roads or dead ends, take only the roads that have signposts.

Railway
The main trail through Dullstroom is a jeep track that runs alongside the railway line as it heads out of town towards Lydenburg. It is a soft clay double-track trail that undulates slightly as it winds through beautiful countryside. This trail in particular can become muddy and waterlogged after heavy rain, but has usually dried out by lunchtime. Unless you are planning on a very long run, this trail is an out-and-back option. You can access the trail either where the railway crosses Blue Crane/Slachters Nek Street close to the mosque and water tower, or by Dullstroom Dam/Campsite. The trail continues for approximately 7 km in a roughly north-easterly direction until it intersects a surfaced road (De Berg Road), just 200 m from the R540. To the left this road turns into a dirt road, and can be used to add additional distance to a run.

Bird of Prey Centre/Kruisfontein Loop
As you travel towards Belfast along the R540, there is a dirt road to your left just before you reach the Bird of Prey Centre. This road is a good option if you want to get a decent workout over hills. It continues in an anticlockwise direction for a loop of approximately 40 km and rejoins the R540 a couple of kilometres below the bottom of town. The route drops to 1,750 m at one point and has some serious climbs after you turn left just beyond Wickhams Country Estate and head back to Dullstroom. Though you are unlikely to do the whole loop, sections can be used for various different runs or sessions.

Bosman Street/Tonteldoos
Bosman Street, and the first 3 km section of the road which leads past Sakhelwe in the direction of Tonteldoos is a good option for those looking to do some road sessions. It is quieter than the R540, relatively flat by Dullstroom standards, and has a good surface. It may also be suitable for race walkers. About 3 km from the town the road turns to a dirt road and begins to drop gradually to 1,800 m as it heads towards Tonteldoos, 23 km away. Other dirt roads off this road offer additional variety.

Dunkeld Adventure Trails
The recently constructed multi-use trails at Dunkeld Country Estate (www.dunkeldestate.co.za) offer more technical terrain than the dirt roads and trails around Dullstroom. Single-track pathways, totalling 36 km, wind over bridges and streams through the estate, and form three separate challenging courses of 7.8 km, 12.7 km, and 14.9 km. Dunkeld Estate is located approximately 3 km from Dullstroom along the Tonteldoos Road and welcomes day visitors for a small conservation fee (per car).

OPPOSITE Various sections of the railway trail

Map of Dullstroom trails

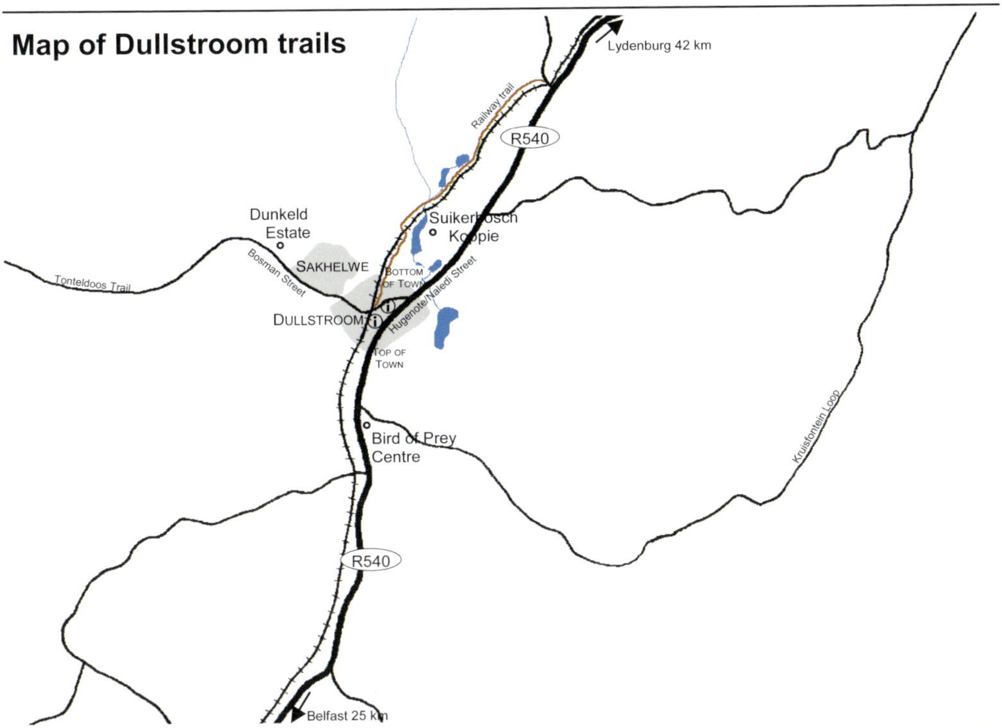

Other trails in area

There are many other trail runs within a 60 km radius of Dullstroom. The Num-Num Challenge Trail (www.thenum-numtrail.co.za) includes a technical and challenging route totalling 36.5 km through gorges, sandstone labyrinths, and open grasslands. The trail, which needs to be pre-booked, hosts an annual race each July or August and is located 22 km from eNTokozweni. Misty Valley Lodge (www.mistyvalleylodge.co.za), located 27 km from eNTokozweni, has 10 trails of varying difficulty over distances of 5 km–20 km. Game, including zebra, springbok and wildebeest, can be spotted in the area. Prior booking is required, and there is a small charge for using the trails. Emgwenya Waterval Boven trails (www.rocrope.com) has options of between 5 km and 30 km through mountains, ravines, exotic forest and along steep single track. A permit should be obtained from Roc 'n' Rope Adventures in Waterval Boven before running on the trails. Waterval Boven is also a popular climbing town.

TRACK FACILITIES

There is no track in Dullstroom.

GYM FACILITIES

Dullstroom Altitude Training Centre, a small gym on Teding Van Berkhout Street (beside the Dullstroom Inn) has spin bikes, machine and cable weights, a punch bag, and core equipment.

CROSS-TRAINING OPTIONS

Mountain biking is the best form of cross-training in Dullstroom. You'll have to travel to Longtom Cycle and Sport on Voortrekker Road in Lydenburg to hire a bike, though bikes can be hired at Dunkeld Country Estate (www.dunkeldestate.co.za) for use on their specially constructed multi-use trails. The tennis courts at Critchley Corner can be used for free. Keys for the courts can be collected from Milly's Trout Store. Exercise classes are available at the Dullstroom Altitude Training Centre.

SPORTS MEDICINE AND SPORTS SCIENCE SUPPORT

There is one physiotherapist operating in the town (Gudrun Combrink; +27 (0)13 254 0143; +27 (0) 82 550 1903), who is available by appointment.

LOCAL RACES

Many of the races around Dullstroom are trail runs and off-road ultra runs through estates and resort lands. Options include AdventureLisa's Forest Run (www.forestrun.co.za), a 62 km ultra trail run starting from Lakenvlei Forest Lodge, 10 km from Belfast; the Num-Num Challenge Trail (www.thenum-numtrail.co.za) near eNTokozweni with 15 and 36.5 km options; and a trail run event, held over 7 km and 14 km on the outskirts of Dullstroom and around the beautiful Lost Valley Residential Estate as part of the annual Dullstroom Winter Festival.

SUITABILITY FOR OTHER SPORTS

Dullstroom has some potential for training in other sports, but the opportunities are limited by a lack of tarred roads and sports facilities.

Cycling Mountain biking is particularly popular, and the abundant dirt roads in the area provide a good variety of routes. Information on some of the best rides, which are typically undulating or hilly, can be found on the Dullstroom MTB website (www.dullstroommtb.co.za). There are specially constructed mountain bike trails at Dunkeld Country Estate (www.dunkeldestate.co.za) which welcomes day visitors for a small conservation fee (per car).

The area is less suitable for road cyclists. The R540 Belfast–Lydenburg road, the only tarred road in the area, is narrow, and unsafe for cycling.

Triathlon The lack of swimming and road cycling options make Dullstroom a poor destination for triathletes unless they are focusing on their running, and happy to maintain cycling fitness on tough mountain bike rides.

Other sports Dullstroom and the surrounding areas are popular among orienteers, and the town is often a base for orienteering competitions. Just remember to pack a southern hemisphere compass. There are no specific facilities for team sports in Dullstroom.

BELOW Dullstroom Dam

THINGS TO SEE AND DO BETWEEN TRAINING

Dullstroom is a very small town, and lacks the entertainment opportunities that go with a city packed with cinemas, theatres and shopping malls. That said, Dullstroom is built around country retreat tourism, and if you enjoy outdoor activities, you won't easily get bored.

The Bird of Prey Rehabilitation Centre (www.birdsofprey.co.za), located just a kilometre from Dullstroom on the R540 towards Belfast is an excellent place to spend a few hours. The flying displays are particularly interesting to those that are new to falconry, and the centre owners put on an entertaining show. It's well worth the small entry fee.

Take a walk around the wetlands, just off the main road (entrance just off Idube Street), or for a spectacular view of the town and surrounding countryside, take a walk to the top of Suikerbosch Koppie (2,200 m) from Dullstroom Campsite. Fly-fishing is one of the main reasons that people come to Dullstroom. There are a number of well-stocked dams close to the town. Permits and tackle are available in Mavungana Flyfishing Shop and Village Angler.

There are a number of other activities available within easy reach of Dullstroom, including horse and pony rides (Dullstroom Riding Centre; www.dullstroomhorseriding.co.za), clay-pigeon shooting (Field and Stream), paintballing (Go Country), and archery (Hide-out). There are also regular darts, bingo, quiz and poker evenings in Dullstroom's pubs and restaurants.

REST DAY EXCURSIONS

Having access to a car can provide the opportunity to explore some of Mpumalanga's many attractions east of Dullstroom. Malaria prophylactic may be required if you intend to explore the sites in the Lowveld.

Kruger National Park (www.krugerpark.co.za) is one of the most visited sites in South Africa, and one of the most famous nature reserves in the world. The park contains almost 150 different species of mammal (including the big five of lion, elephant, buffalo, leopard and rhino), 100 different reptiles and more than 500 bird species, and covers an area the size of Wales. Dullstroom is located on one of the routes from Johannesburg and Pretoria into the park and is situated approximately 200 km from the Paul Kruger Gate.

Sudwala Caves (www.sudwalacaves.co.za), the world's oldest known caves, are situated just over 100 km east of Dullstroom via the R539. There is a fish spa and a dinosaur park located next to the caves, and just 3 km away is Mankele Mountain Bike Park (www.mankele.co.za), one of the best places in South Africa to mountain bike.

The town of Nelspruit is the capital of Mpumalanga Provence, and the gateway to Kruger National Park. It is located approximately 130 km from Dullstroom. Lowveld National Botanical Garden is located just outside Nelspruit and has a number of walks through humid rainforest and past spectacular natural waterfalls. Pilgrim's Rest, essentially a living museum to the 1870s gold rush, with many original buildings from that era, is located 110 km from Dullstroom. There is the opportunity to try gold panning and visit House Museum, which shows how the upper class used to live.

There are a number of natural landmarks and breathtaking views along the Drakensberg Escarpment overlooking the Blyde River Canyon. Take the Panorama Route (R532 and R534) north from Graskop to view the Pinnacle, Berlin Falls, Lisbon Falls, God's Window, Bourke's Luck Potholes, Wonderview, the Three Rondavels (Three Sisters) and Echo Caves. Graskop is located 120 km from Dullstroom.

BELOW Birds at the Bird of Prey Rehabilitation Centre just outside dullstroom

A NOTE ON LIVING HERE LONG-TERM

If you're the type of person that likes to pass the hours between training doing some fishing or birdwatching, Dullstroom may be a suitable place for you to live. The laid-back atmosphere make it easy to meet new people and make friends, but many will find the pace of life a little too slow for a prolonged stay. There is no track, little opportunity to implement a 'live high, train low' training approach, and a lack of local races to test yourself in, particularly if you're a track runner. On the plus side, the cost of living is low, there is a good choice of self-catering accommodation, pollution is minimal and the crime rate is low. The weather is favourable for training most months of the year, though it can get cold in June and July, and regular evening thunderstorms in the summer months may become frustrating. Work, volunteering and study opportunities are rare.

FURTHER INFORMATION

Tourist information is available at Dullstroom Accommodation (www.dullstroom.co.za) and Dullstroom Reservations (www.dullstroom.biz). Copies of Dullstroom Emnotweni Essential Info guide (www.essential-info.co.za), a small booklet containing a directory, an events calendar, suggestions of things to do, and maps of the town can be picked up from the information centres and shops in town. The Proudly Dullstroom website (www.dullstroom.info) also contains useful information about events and things to do.

OTHER ALTITUDE TRAINING SITES IN SOUTHERN AFRICA

Much of north and central South Africa is located at or above 1,300 m but few towns or villages are located above 2,000 m. Johannesburg and Pretoria are used, but are scarcely high enough. An altitude training centre is planned for Belfast, 35 km south-west of Dullstroom. The proposed centre will be located just south of Belfast Dam at an altitude of 1,850 m. Lesotho, a country with its borders completely within South Africa, is also used for altitude training.

Pretoria, SA (1,350 m)

Pretoria is a popular destination for athletes in team sports. The facilities at the University of Pretoria are excellent, and the High Performance Centre (www.hpc.co.za) is a one-stop facility for elite athletes. Training facilities, medical services, sports science support, food, accommodation and transport are all part of the all-inclusive package offered at the centre. Over 70 hectares of land are dedicated to sports, and facilities include a large sports hall for basketball, volleyball and netball; halls for judo, karate, badminton, table tennis, fencing and gymnastics; a heated indoor swimming pool; rugby fields; a cricket oval and cricket nets; grass and synthetic hockey fields; all-weather netball courts; football fields; tennis courts; outdoor basketball and volleyball courts; an outdoor 50 m swimming pool; a climbing wall; a dam for rowing and canoeing and a four-hole golf course. Facilities for athletics include an athletics track and stadium, hammer throwing circles and a cross country course, though the city environment is far from ideal for distance runners. The altitude of Pretoria at approximately 1,500 m, like Potchefstroom, is not high enough for maximum altitude training benefit. Its location brings with it the hazards of South African cities.

Lesotho (2,000 m–3,200 m)

Lesotho is the only country in the world which lies completely above 1,400 m of altitude. Unsurprisingly, the Lesotho authorities have recognised the country's tourism potential, and are looking to develop altitude training opportunities there. Two areas are currently suitable for altitude training.

AfriSki resort (www.afriski.net) is located at 3,030 m of altitude in the Muluti Mountains near Lesotho's northern border, 405 km by road from Johannesburg . Chalets, lodges, apartments and a hostel are available within the resort (book through the resort website), and meals can be booked at the resort's Sky Restaurant. The spring and summer months (Sept–Apr) offer warm temperatures and occasional rain.

Mohale Village, which was used to accommodate workers during the construction of the nearby Mohale Dam, is being developed into a tourist resort. Mohale Lodge (www.mohalelodge-lesotho.com) provides suitable accommodation for sportspeople looking to take advantage of the beautiful surroundings of Lesotho's sparsely populated interior. Wi-Fi access, laundry facilities, an onsite restaurant and a library are available at the lodge which also has squash courts, tennis courts and a volleyball court. The lodge is situated at 2,200 m above sea level and is located 520 km south of Johannesburg.

Lesotho is covered with rugged mountains and spectacular scenery, crystal clear rivers and streams, traditional dwellings, and sandstone caves. Pony-trekking, hiking, 4x4 off-roading and mountain biking are popular downtime activities.

Some of the sites of Dullstroom CLOCKWISE from TOP LEFT The cargo railway which runs through the town; view of Suikerbosch Koppie; the railway trail; one of the ponds viewed from the railway trail

Ifrane

In the pretty town of Ifrane, with its European-style parks and streets, it's difficult to believe that you are in Africa. With budget airlines now operating between Europe and Fez, Ifrane is easy to get to, and a perfect alternative to the more expensive European training destinations. The Cedar forests of the Middle Atlas surround the town and there is an abundance of gravel tracks and well-surfaced asphalt roads suitable for training. There is a 400 m track just on the edge of the town. The locals are less reserved than in other areas of Morocco, and many women, as well as men, can be seen training here. Ifrane is ideal for marathon runners who would like to experience Africa without spending a lot of time, or a lot of money, getting there.

Ifrane, Morocco (1,665 m)

Located less than 1 hr from the cities of Fez (*Fès*) and Meknès and nestled in the cedar forests of the Middle Atlas in the Meknès-Tafilalet region, the beautiful town of Ifrane (pronounced 'E-Frahn') is Morocco's most popular altitude training spot. Good food, comfortable accommodation and cheap transport make Ifrane an attractive destination, and plentiful trails through beautiful rocky countryside and dense cedar forests make running enjoyable, exciting, and full of variety. The town is a popular training base for Moroccan distance runners, but is quickly increasing in popularity among athletes from across the world.

Ifrane was developed as a hill station—a place for the colonials to retreat to and feel like they were at home—during the French protectorate era. The cool alpine climate was a welcome relief from the desert heat, and Ifrane became a popular summer retreat for French families from the Saïss Plain, Fez and Meknès. Hill stations, originally used by British in India, were designed to remind expatriate European inhabitants of their homelands. Hill stations tend to feature European architectural styles and trees and plants imported from Europe. Lilac, chestnut and plane trees were introduced to Ifrane in such a fashion.

Ifrane was designed as a garden city, an urban design which was popular in Western Europe between World War I and World War II. Garden cities were originally developed to overcome some of the social problems associated with 19th century industrial cities, but later became a fashionable urban design with no particular social purpose. Garden cities are typified by low-density housing surrounded by gardens, wide curving tree-lined streets, and many public parks. Ifrane's initial town plan was incomplete, and no housing provision was made for the Moroccans who worked as guards, gardeners and maids for the colonial homeowners. They made their homes in a shantytown, known as Timdiqin (officially called Hay Atlas) on the north of the town.

Today Ifrane combines characteristics of its various functions as a historical station, imperial city, university town, and ski resort. The town is overlooked by a palace, has areas of wide streets and gardens, features markets and has a thriving student population. Despite its European influences, Ifrane is true to Moroccan and Berber traditions. Like the French colonial expatriates, you are likely to feel comfortably at home, while experiencing one of the world's most vibrant cultures.

AUTHOR'S VERDICT

It was difficult to find information about Ifrane and getting there. I didn't know anybody who had trained there, and thought that it was going to be more hassle than it was worth. I had apprehensions about travelling and training in a Muslim country, and at one stage almost scratched it from my itinerary. To do so would have been a mistake. I thoroughly enjoyed my trip. The food was great, living and travel costs were low, and the variety of trails was excellent. It was a great place to practise my basic French. A good variety of day trips can be organised from the town, and there are many opportunities to sample North African culture. I never felt threatened or unsafe; to the contrary, everyone was very welcoming. I did find it comforting to have a travel partner for this leg, French (or Arabic) would definitely be an advantage, and it rained a lot. Apart from that, it was an excellent trip!

Running ★★★ - Lots of beautiful runs, though off-road, the underfoot conditions are often rocky; track on edge of town for interval sessions; level road-surfaces for quality marathon sessions.
Convenience ★★★★ - Easy to get to; car not required; easy to get around; limited self-catering accommodation; good choice of restaurants.
Safety ★★★ - Peaceful and safe town; some caution required if spending time in the cities; be respectful of the Muslim culture.
Cost ★★★★ - Low cost of living; budget flights available; rental accommodation scarce; day-trips cheap and easy to organise; car not required.
Cultural experience ★★★★ - Morocco is a completely different world, less than a 4-hr flight from London; a trip to the Fez medina will give a good insight into Moroccan culture.
Things to do between training ★★ - Not a huge amount to do in the town itself, but a number of short excursions within easy reach; Fez's wonderful medina is just 60 min away.
Suitability for solo travellers ★★ - Female solo travellers may feel uncomfortable; less conservative than other areas of the country; welcoming as long as you remain respectful; friendly locals make an effort to communicate across language barrier; lack of things to do may make it less interesting for those travelling alone.

Must do Make a day trip to Fez and explore its Medina; try a Moroccan tajine; spend some time relaxing by the waterfalls.
Ideal for Europeans who want to experience Africa without the long-haul flight.

Moroccan history in a nutshell

African, Arab and European influences have shaped Morocco's history and modern culture. The area which makes up present-day Morocco was ruled by the Romans, conquered by the Arabs (who converted the area to Islam), invaded by the Spanish and Portuguese following the decline of Moorish control of Europe, and later colonised by the French and the Spanish. All have left their legacy.

Around 1000 BC Mediterranean traders known as the Phoenicians, and originating from an area along the coastline of what is now the Lebanon, found this area of Africa to be inhabited by people they called *barbaroi* ('not our people', later known as the Berbers).

Around 150 BC The Romans added the costal part of what is now Morocco and Algeria to their empire. After the fall of the Roman Empire, these coastal regions were taken over by barbarian peoples known as the Vandals and the Visigoths, and by the Byzantine Empire from Constantinople.

7th century AD Arab armies entered northern Africa and spread west into Morocco where they joined with the Berbers, who they had converted to Islam, and invaded most of what is now Spain. The Arab-Berber armies, known as Moors to the Europeans, had a presence on the Iberian Peninsula for approximately 600 years.

AD 788 Moulay Idriss, a descendant of Prophet Mohammed, and a rebel Arab prince, became king of the Berber tribes. Despite becoming influential and powerful, Idriss was murdered by a rival, and his son, Moulay Idriss II, took over the throne. He founded the city that is now Fez, and which became the capital of Morocco. When he died in 828, power was divided among his sons, resulting in a weakened leadership.

10th century Control of Northern Africa alternated between the Fatimids of Tunisia and the Ommayad dynasties of Moorish Spain.

Mid 11th century The Almoravids, a group of strict Muslims from a desert monastery, formed an army and conquered south Morocco. After establishing their own capital at Marrakech, they captured the city of Fez.

Mid 12th century The Almohads, another group of even stricter Muslims, took control of northern Africa and much of Spain.

Mid 13th century The Beni Merin Berber tribe (the Merinids) took over from the weakened Almohads. More materialistic than their predecessors, the Merinids built fine buildings throughout their territory including Granada's Alhambra *(p. 178)*.

15th century After the Christians pushed the Moors out of Spain, the Portuguese and the Spanish invaded the Moroccan coastline.

Morocco Quick Facts

Capital Rabat
Largest city Casablanca
Official languages Modern Standard Arabic and Berber (French unofficial but widely spoken third language)
Currency Moroccan dirham (Dh; MAD), divided into 100 santimat
National holidays New Year's Day (Jan 1), Proclamation of Independence (Jan 11), Labour Day (May 1), Enthronement (Jul 30), Oued Ed-Dahab Day (Aug 14), Revolution of the King and the People (Aug 20), Youth Day (Aug 21), Green March (Nov 6), Independence Day (Nov 18), Muslim New Year*, Birth of Prophet Muhammad*, Eid ul-Fitr*, Eid ul-Adha*
Time zone Western European Time (GMT+0), with daylight saving (Apr–Sept)
International dialling code +212
Outgoing access code 00
Emergency contacts 177 (police); 15 (fire and ambulance)
Power 220 V; 50 Hz power supply; Type C (CEE 7/16) and Type E (CEE 7/5) Europlug-compatible plugs and sockets with 2 small round pins
Driving Right side
Measurement Metric

* varies according to Muslim calendar

Mid–late 16th century The Saadi Arab tribe (the Saadians), encouraged by the invasion of the Spanish and Portuguese, moved north from the Draa Valley and took control. King Ahmad el-Mansur came to power. Marrakech had much wealth lavished on it by the Saadians.

Early 17th century Saadian power crumbled following King Ahmed's death, and under the sultan Moulay Ismail, the Alaouites took control.

19th century Following the colonising of Africa, the Moroccans became increasingly dependent on the French, who had taken control of neighbouring Algiers.

1912 With an Alaouites sultan chosen by the French, Morocco became a protectorate for the French (central and southern areas) and Spanish (northern Morocco). Rabat became the capital. Schools, railways and roads were built throughout the country, and new towns were built beside many of the old towns.

Second World War The French control was weakened, and there was a Moroccan move for independence. Mohammed V, the sultan, was exiled to Corsica, but this only strengthened the independence movement.

1956 Independence was declared and Mohammed V was made king.

GETTING IN

By air

The closest airport is Fez-Saïss Airport (FEZ), about 60 km north of Ifrane. The airport is located just off the N8 (the main road between Fez and Ifrane), about 10 km south of Fez. Budget airlines fly between many European cities and this small airport. Ryanair operates flights from London Stansted twice per week, and budget airlines Ryanair, EasyJet and Jetairfly operate flights from mainland Europe (including, among others, Barcelona, Brussels, Dusseldorf, Frankfurt Hahn, Paris and Rome Ciampino). Royal Air Maroc operates flights from Casablanca and Paris Orly.

From outside Europe, you are likely to fly via Casablanca or Paris Orly with Royal Air Maroc. The budget airlines may provide more options, and cheaper prices, but remember that budget airline flights are non-transferable and if you miss your check-in, you will need to pay for a new ticket. When transferring onto a budget airline flight, you will also need to pick-up and re-check luggage (for which there is an expensive additional fee), and you'll likely have to clear immigration and customs.

Take the airport shuttle bus from directly outside the arrivals door to Fez, and swap onto a grand taxi to Ifrane, or take the more convenient and comfortable option of a direct taxi from the airport. Taxis are fixed price (prices to the main destinations are displayed just outside the arrivals door), so you should be charged a fair price. The taxi ride takes 40–60 min depending on weather conditions. To find the taxis, walk out of arrivals, across the road, and down some steps. Write the address for your accommodation in Ifrane clearly on a piece of paper for the driver, and include some directions if you're not staying at one of the main hotels.

Car hire is available from the airport through the large international companies (Avis, Alamo, Hertz, Budget, Europcar, Sixt, and Thrifty) and some small local ones (e.g. AirCar; www.aircar.ma). The journey from the airport to Ifrane is quite direct. Drive out of the airport and join the N8. Follow this road south (opposite direction to Fez) for approximately 55 km (1 hr) until you reach Ifrane.

Driving on the roads of Morocco is dangerous, and, where possible, should be left to the locals. However, driving is likely to be the best option if you're flying into one of Morocco's other airports or if you're arriving by ferry. There are some sharp bends and steep sections of road. Be particularly careful if driving at night. Distances and speeds are in kilometres and kilometres per hour respectively, and road signs are in both Arabic and English. The maximum speed limit in built-up areas is 60 kph.

By train

The nearest train stations are in Fez and in Meknes, both approximately 1 hr drive from Ifrane. There is no advantage to travelling by train rather than flying, unless travelling from elsewhere within Morocco.

BELOW The Alpine-style houses of the town of Ifrane

Visa requirements

Visitors from the EU, Schengen agreement countries, Australia, New Zealand, Canada and the US, do not need a visa to enter Morocco for tourist stays of up to three months. Tourist visas are required for citizens of South Africa, and most African, Asian and Central American countries. All passports are required to be valid for at least six months from the date of entry.

GETTING AROUND

Ifrane is small enough to get around on foot, and if required, taxis are cheap and plentiful. The best running routes are accessible on foot. Taxi hire is very cheap, and if you want to explore the country, it's probably best to hire a driver for the day. The main taxi rank/grand taxi station is located on the west side of Parc des Ombres Noires near the marché. French (or Arabic) is very useful when arranging a taxi, but if you don't speak French, writing your directions on a piece of paper beforehand should suffice. Petit taxis (the small green ones) are used to get around town, and grand taxis travel between towns.

As you travel to Ifrane from Fez along the N8/Avenue Hassan II, you will first pass the university on the right. As you enter the town, there is a lake area with fountains to your left, and just at the top of the hill beyond the lake is a large statue of a lion, one of the main focal points of the town. Beyond the lion, situated in the forest on the left in the direction of Azrou is the Royal Palace, a summer residence of the King of Morocco. There are two main areas in central Ifrane. Centre Ville, located immediately west of Avenue Hassan II (turn right at the lion), has most of the main restaurants and cafes, and is the more modern, touristy end of town. The marché (market) area, further west along Avenue Mohamed V (S309) has the market stalls and shops, and some traditional food stalls and eateries. It is where most of the locals shop and eat.

Map of Ifrane

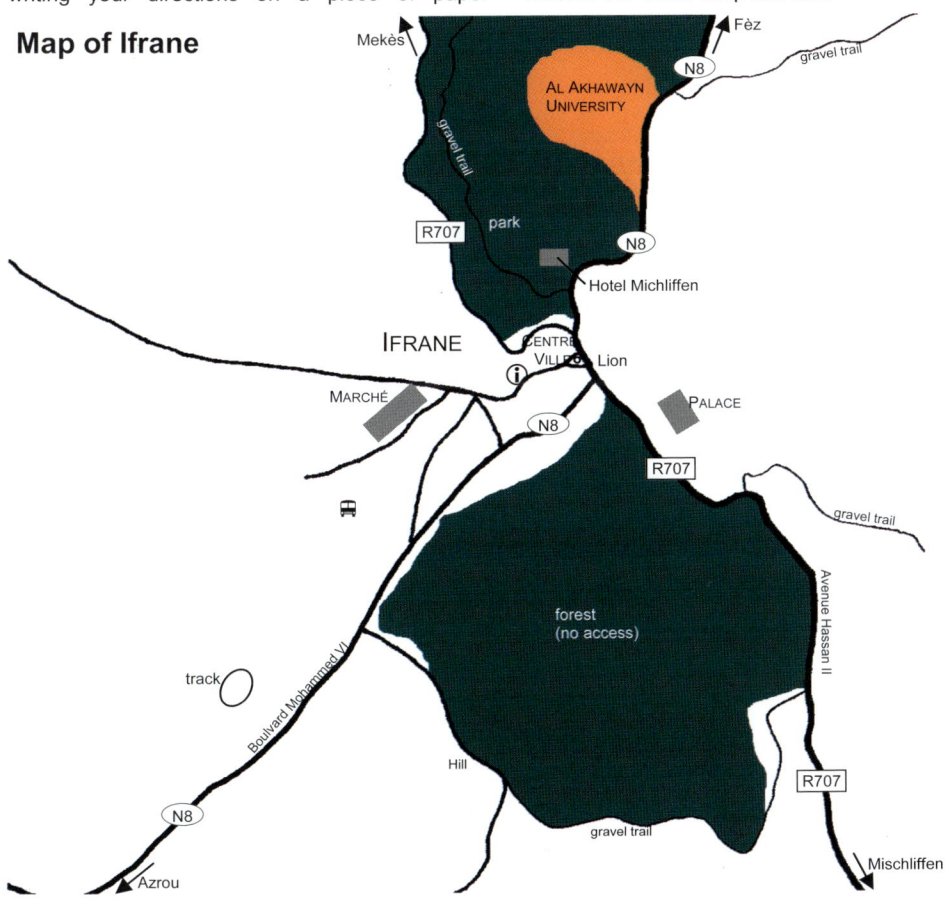

Weather and when to visit

The Middle Atlas is known for changeable and unpredictable weather conditions and there is heavy rainfall whenever weather fronts meet in this region. Temperatures are much lower than in other parts of Morocco because of the altitude, and the coldest ever temperature on the continent of Africa was recorded in Ifrane. On 11th February 1935, the mercury dropped to -24 ºC.

Ifrane has a mild Mediterranean climate with a cool winter, warm summer, and cool to cold evenings and nights throughout the year. Average daily highs for the months of December through to February are in the region of 9–10 ºC, the average highs for July and August, the warmest months, are above 28 ºC. July and August are also the driest months with an average of just 4 rain days per month, compared with between 10 and 15 precipitation days between November and May. Snow is unpredictable, with snow cover during the coldest months, and snow showers up to and including April.

Ramadan, which moves forward approximately 11 days each year, may be a difficult time to visit Morocco. Muslims fast during daylight hours, and though they don't expect foreigners to observe their religious fasts, some visitors may feel uncomfortable eating before dark. Some restaurants may also be closed during the day, and become particularly busy after sunset.

Accommodation

Accommodation is not as plentiful as it is in the other venues featured in this book, and some effort is required to find suitable lodgings for a training trip. Most of the accommodation that is available is of a high standard, and prices are low compared to European ski resorts. Gabinohome (www.gabinohome.com) and Maisons Maroc (www.maisondemaroc.com) list some apartments and chalets in Ifrane. Searching for 'appartement', the French spelling of apartment, or for 'gîtes', a common type of holiday rental in French-speaking countries, may yield slightly better web search results.

The Best Western Farah Inn Hotel and Resort (Nouvelle Station Touristique), located 20 min walk from the town centre, features chalets and suites, each with a refrigerator and kitchenette, as well as a restaurant and sports facilities on-site. The hotel and resort forms the centre of the ARZ Village, a tourist complex designed to attract visitors to the area. Relais Ras El Maa (Avenue Mohammad VI; www.relaisraselmaa.com), a motel located very close to the athletics track and the roads used for training, has rooms and suites for 1-4 people. There is a restaurant on-site, and a petrol station and small shop next door. Other accommodations include Club Sequoia, which has 1 and 2-bedroom apartments and villas; Gîte de Charme Ras Al Ma (www.rasalma.ma); Auberge Tourtite (www.aubergetourtite.com), Le Chamonix (www.lechamonix.com), Les Residences d'Ifrane, Hotel Grande and Hôtel Perce Neige. The luxury Hotel Michlifen (www.michlifenifrane.com) is expensive, but does have a swimming pool, fitness centre and other facilities.

Food

Eating out in Morocco is very cheap, and may be a more attractive option than self-catering. The more modern restaurants are located in Centre Ville, though there are much cheaper traditional options in the marché. La Paix and Forest Restaurant, both in Centre Ville, are good options. La Paix serves excellent salads, wonderfully fresh bread, and traditional meals such as tajines and pastille. Forest Restaurant serves pasta and other European dishes. Many of the hotels, including Hotel Chamonix and Hotel Michlifen, also have restaurants.

Many of the accommodations mentioned previously come with cooking facilities, and self-catering is just about feasible. The small supermarkets and shops in Centre Ville sell a moderate range of non-perishable goods and some fresh fruit. Fresh bread can be bought from La Paix in Centre Ville and the shops and stalls in the marché sell a variety of goods including fresh meat, fruit and vegetables. Fresh fruit and vegetables are available to purchase in large quantities, when, at the weekend, a travelling souk (market) visits the Timdiqin residential area. Fresh milk (non-UHT) is difficult to find, but a few shops do sell it (look for milk in a refrigerator labelled 'lait frais'). If you're in Ifrane for a prolonged stay and have your own transport, it may be worth stocking up on foodstuff in one of the larger European-style supermarkets on the outskirts of Fez.

Moroccan cuisine is a mix of couscous and tajine dishes from the Berber tribes, spices from the Arabs, olives and citrus fruit brought back from Andalucía by the Moors and some French influence from colonial times. Morocco has a largely self-sufficient food supply and any land which is not desert or rock is cultivated with crops of almonds, olives, grapes, pulses, dates, vegetables, sugar cane and sugar beet. Chicken and lamb are the most commonly available meats, and the country's long Atlantic and Mediterranean coastlines result in a good availability of a variety of seafood. Though vegetables are plentiful, and nutritious side salads are widely available, vegetarian meals are difficult to find.

Tajines are slow roasted, slightly spiced dishes made in shallow earthenware pots with a conical lid, also called tajines. They are usually made with chicken, lamb or mutton cooked with vegetables and/or olives. *Pastilla* (pronounced and sometimes spelt 'Bastila') is a lightly-spiced chicken or pigeon filling wrapped in filo pastry and topped with sugar and cinnamon. Though quite tasty, the contrast of savoury and sweet takes some getting used to. Couscous, a basic Berber food which is served with vegetables, meat and in some cases fruit and nuts, is made from semolina which comes from coarsely ground wheat. While Westerners may be used to making couscous from a packet, the traditional method takes much longer. Restaurants may require couscous dishes to be pre-ordered, and couscous is not widely available in Ifrane. *Harira*, a thick soup or broth containing chicken or lamb, chickpeas, lentils, onions, tomatoes and herbs, is traditionally eaten to break the daily fast during Ramadan. Most dishes are served with fresh bread. Bread is used as an eating tool and to soak up food juices. Tea, flavoured with mint, and sweetened with lots of sugar, is traditionally served in a glass.

SHOPPING

Ifrane is not the place to come to if looking to shop. The marché area has a number of small shops selling a range of goods including kitchen utensils, hardware, items of clothing, and toiletries, but don't always expect to find what you need. Many shops close for lunch. There are few places to purchase souvenirs—there are some stalls by the lake and in the park, but these tend to sell very tacky items. The medina in Fez and the roadside pottery stalls between Ifrane and Fez are much better for Moroccan crafts and pottery items.

The souks and markets of the larger towns and cities are great places to purchase dates, leatherwear, tajines and other pottery, carpets and Moroccan teapots. Bargaining is expected in the souks, and is very much part of the shopping experience. The items in most shops won't have price tags so either gauge a price from those that do, or have some idea about how much you are willing to pay for an item. Offer less than you think the item is worth, but not so little as to be ridiculous. Show a genuine interest, take time to bargain, and most of all enjoy the whole process.

There are no sports shops in Ifrane. Sport Plus (www.sportplus.ma), which has stores in Fez, has a running department.

BELOW One of the beautiful ponds in Ifrane
FOLLOWING A trail through the rocky Mid Atlas countryside

LANGUAGE

Standard Arabic and Berber, spoken by almost a third of the population, are the official languages of Morocco. Moroccan Arabic, a dialect of Maghreb Arabic which is influenced by both French and Spanish, is widely spoken. The language is very different from standard Arabic, and Arabic speakers from outside of Morocco would find it difficult to decipher a conversation between two Moroccans. Moroccans do learn standard Arabic in school though, so can understand and converse in the standard form of the language. Tamazight is the regional Berber dialect spoken around Ifrane.

French, often used in business and commerce, is taught in schools, and is the unofficial third language. Spanish is widely spoken and understood in the very north of the country around Tangier, but by few in and around Ifrane. English is spoken by some in the main tourist areas, for example in the median areas of Fez, but less so in Ifrane, particularly among older individuals. Al Akhawayn University teaches its classes through English, French and Arabic, and at least some of the student population have a good level of English. Basic French will suffice, and Moroccans speak French slower and with less of an accent than the French do. They are also a little more patient than the French with non-fluent French speakers who make an effort. Menus are normally available in French.

There is a mini French phrase list in Appendix 1. Some useful Moroccan Arabic phrases, written phonetically, are listed at the bottom of the page. Moroccan Arabic doesn't have a written form (standard Arabic is used in writing).

COMMUNICATION

Mobile phone signal in most of Morocco, including in and around Ifrane, is good. Morocco operates on 900 Hz GMS, and 2100 Hz UMTS networks. Roaming charges are expensive, but European phone users shouldn't have any problem getting network coverage. Cheap handsets and pay-as-you-go SIM cards (Carte Jawal) can also be purchased (try the market area). Morocco's two competing networks Maroc Telecom and Méditel offer favourable rates for calls and texts, and reasonably priced international rates.

Some of the larger restaurants, including the Forest and La Paix have Wi-Fi internet access, and athletes can often be seen on their laptops hanging out at these restaurants between training.

The post office is located in Centre Ville opposite La Paix. The Moroccan postal system is generally reliable, though international post has a reputation for being slow.

HEALTH AND SAFETY

Violent crime is not prevalent in Morocco, and the country has one of the lowest homicide rates in the world. Ifrane is particularly peaceful. Common sense should be applied in the cities, dark alleys avoided, and valuables kept out of sight. Females travelling alone are likely to be harassed, usually in the form of hisses or catcalls—much less so in Ifrane than in the cities—and women shouldn't feel the need to be polite to the perpetrators. Be firm, and attract the attention of a passer-by if harassment is persistent.

OPPOSITE *Tree-lined pond in one of Ifrane's parks*

Driving is one of the main 'health' hazards in Morocco. Animals, pedestrians and other obstructions, speeding, poor and narrow roads, badly maintained vehicles, and general bad driving combine to make Moroccan roads a treacherous place. Travelling at night should be avoided where possible, and if driving yourself, be aware of the numerous hazards on the roads.

There are no vaccination requirements for travelling in Morocco. Routine vaccines such as diphtheria, polio and tetanus, together with hepatitis A and typhoid, are recommended. Morocco is malaria free apart from a few isolated cases of the disease near Mauritania. Individuals travelling to Ifrane and Fez should not be at risk. There may be a risk of rabies if bitten by an infected animal, and there are some dogs around Ifrane. Avoid straying too far off the beaten track, or wandering close to farm enclosures that are protected by dogs. Carrying a stick is also a useful defence against a nasty dog.

Many travellers to Morocco experience stomach discomfort at some stage during their stay. Those staying in Ifrane shouldn't be at too much of a risk, so long as all food, especially meat and fish, is well cooked and that fruit and vegetables are peeled or cooked before eating. It is not advised to drink tap water as it has higher mineral levels than in Europe, and has been known to cause stomach upset. Bottled water is widely available in Ifrane. Of the popular brands, Sidi Harazem, Sidi Ali and Danone Aïn Saïss are still, and Oulmès is sparkling.

Morocco's health system is comprised of public, semi-public and private sectors. There is a small public hospital in Ifrane, and a larger one 17 km away in Azrou. Some of the larger hotels have a doctor on call. Remember that few doctors will speak English. English is spoken at Pharmacie Les Iris, located south of the marché, and at Pharmacie Michlifen in Centre Ville. Pharmacies are open all day.

MONEY

The Moroccan dirham (sign: Dh; code: MAD) is the currency of Morocco. The dirham is a closed currency, which can only be traded within Morocco, though small quantities of the currency can be obtained through travel agents and airports abroad. Import and export is tolerated up to 1,000 dirham per person (approximately €90/£75). Travellers should keep foreign exchange receipts which will be required to exchange unspent dirham when leaving the country. ATMs are

Special Feature
MOROCCAN GLOSSARY

The following words are used to describe Moroccan clothing, architectural features, landscapes, religious traditions and feasts, and other items in everyday life. While many are common words used in Islamic countries, Arabic countries, or North African areas, some are uniquely Moroccan or Berber in origin.

medina a traditional enclosed Arab town, surrounded by ramparts. Typically has narrow streets not navigable by car, and with the grand mosque as its central point.
souk a type of market, usually located within the medina, which is laid out so that stalls selling similar goods are placed together.
rampart defensive city wall, usually with a walkway
minaret the tower of a mosque from the top of which the call to prayer comes
muezzin a religious official who calls the people to prayer
Hadj pilgrimage to Mecca
qibla direction of Mecca indicated in a mosque by a niche known as a *mihrab*
sharia religious law which is based on the teachings of Koran
burnous, *haik*, *jellaba*, *kaftan*, *seroual*, *hendira*, and *shamir* all types of traditional clothing. The hooded jellaba, with wide sleeves and hand woven from wool is one of the more distinctive items of Moroccan dress, and, worn by both men and women, is often seen in rural areas
hanbel carpet woven by Berbers
wadi a river bed which, apart from during the rainy season, is dry. Wadi can also mean river, or river valley.
bled countryside or village
adrar mountain
reg stony desert

Some useful Moroccan Arabic phrases

hello (formal) SALAM
hello (informal) AHLAAN
please AAFAK
thank you CHOUKRANE
yes NAAM
no LLLAA
excuse me (to get somebody's attention) ESSMAHHLIYA
excuse me (to beg pardon) BALLAK

widely available, and it is easy to obtain currency within Morocco. As with many countries with closed currency, there isn't much difference in exchange rates in airports, in the city, or at ATMs. Some hotels quote prices in euro as well as dirham. Torn or damaged banknotes, small coins and New Zealand and Australian banknotes are difficult to exchange, and new design banknotes, in any currency, can be problematic. Euro, US dollars and GB pounds are the most widely accepted, though most major currencies are accepted at airport Bureaux de Change. Duty-free shops in Moroccan airports will not accept dirham. There are some ATMs, and a bank (Banque Populaire) in Centre Ville.

Power

Morocco uses 220 V; 50 Hz power supply and Type C (CEE 7/16) and Type E (CEE 7/5) Europlug-compatible plugs and sockets with 2 small round pins. It is unlikely that you will find power adaptors to purchase in Ifrane.

Time

Morocco operates on GMT, and currently has a period of daylight saving (late Apr–late Sept) which was introduced in 2008 and lengthened in 2012. For short periods of the year (between the start of British Summer Time and the start of Moroccan daylight saving and again between the end of Moroccan daylight saving and the end of British Summer Time), Morocco is 1 hr behind Britain. Daylight saving is suspended during Ramadan, and clocks are readjusted to the winter time if Ramadan falls between late April and late September. This is to make evenings shorter and daylight fasting more manageable for Muslims. Daylight hours range from just over 10 hr in mid December, to just under 14 hr 15 min in mid June.

	Mar	Jun*	Sept*	Dec
Sunrise	06:34	06:19	07:09	07:18
Sunset	18:33	20:32	19:30	17:23

* When Ramadan falls between April and September, daylight saving is suspended, and these times will be 1 hr earlier.

Laundry

Many of the accommodations have washing machines or a laundry service. There is also a dry-cleaning and laundry service in the marché.

Customs and respect

Approximately 99 percent of Moroccans are Muslim, and the customs and practices of the country reflect their Islamic faith. Shops and market stalls may close around midday on Fridays, the Muslim holy day. Muslims largely don't drink alcohol, eat pork or expose their bodies. Muslims don't eat, drink or smoke between sunrise and sunset during the Islamic holy month of Ramadan. Most mosques are out of bounds to non-Muslims.

Despite its Muslim majority and associated conservative customs, non-Muslims shouldn't be overly apprehensive about travelling and training in Morocco. Moroccans recognise the value of tourism to their economy, and Morocco is less conservative than other Islamic countries. Ifrane, as a university town, is even more liberal in its attitude than other Atlas Mountain towns and villages. Because of the difficult travelling conditions within the desert and mountainous landscape of Morocco, Moroccans are incredibly hospitable and following a few simple guidelines should make a trip enjoyable.

During Ramadan, Muslims recognise that non-Muslims have a need to eat, and so long as eating and drinking are done out of public view there should not be a problem. Restaurants will be quieter than usual during the day, and some may even be closed. After dark restaurants come to life, and may even become very busy.

It's sensible to be cautious in both behaviour and dress, so as not to offend others. Shorts (or three-quarter length leggings) and tee shirts are acceptable running kit around Ifrane, even for females, but anything too revealing or unnecessarily skimpy will draw attention. At the track, away from the public, almost anything goes.

Muslims find it unusual to see a woman travelling alone, and become suspicious if they see women alone after dark. Ifrane's function as a university town and a tourist stop helps, but females travelling alone may be treated with suspicion.

A 10 percent service charge is normally already included in restaurant bills for tourists, in which case no tip is required. Moroccans will usually just leave a couple of dirham tip in a restaurant, and this is acceptable if no service charge is included. Taxi fares should be rounded up to the nearest five dirham, and a small tip should be given if somebody helps you with your bags. If you visit the Medina in Fez, you may find unofficial 'guides' helping you with directions and then demanding a tip for their services. Be cautious with such individuals, and if you do not require their service, make sure that you make this clear.

The town's parks are full of interesting streams and trees

Sport facilities and services

Sport is relatively popular in Morocco, and Ifrane, which has long been a training base for Moroccan distance runners, is well equipped to support athletes. There is a 400 m track and lots of roads and trails, in addition to some training facilities suitable for team and indoor sports. Many people come to Ifrane to train, and the locals have a good understanding of athletics.

Training camps and tour operators

Training camps of various lengths are organised in the town by Atlas Altitude Training (www.trainingatlasaltitude.com). Camps, which are run at various times of the year, are designed for runners of all levels, and include full-board hotel accommodation in Auberge Tourtite Hotel (owned by marathoner Abdelkader El Mouaziz), access to weights and cardiovascular equipment, massage and hamman (Turkish baths) and the opportunity to train with champion French and Moroccan athletes. Race walkers, mountain bikers and triathletes are also welcome. Note that the English version of the website may not have the most up-to-date information on upcoming training camps, but the French version does.

Trails and running routes

Decent running routes can be found as you head from the town centre in any direction. While the small park on the northern edge of the town centre is great for shorter recovery runs, the roads through the forest off Boulevard Mohammed VI close to the track (*Centro Sportif*), is where you will find most Moroccans training. Once you get past the sections of road with pavements within the town itself, the road surface is incredibly smooth and great for doing road sessions and runs on. The trails are quite stony, but lead through beautiful countryside and forested areas.

North of Centre Ville

As you head north past the lion, and down the hill, you'll see a lake on your right. Take the left turn opposite this lake, and about 100 m down this quiet road, a pair of black stallions mark the entrance to a small park. This park is popular for evening recovery runs. The surface is slightly gritty, and ever so slightly undulating. The whole park is approximately 2 km long, but can form part of a longer run. If you continue past the cafe and souvenir stalls at the end of the park, and up the hill by the river, the track twists around the hill, into the forest and eventually meets up with the main Fez road beyond the university.

If you continue along Avenue Hassan II towards Fez, past Al Akhawayn University, and down the hill, a non-paved road will appear on your right. This meanders through slightly undulating countryside in a roughly north-easterly direction from the town until it comes to a dead-end. It's a beautiful run during which to appreciate the open space and beauty of the mid-atlas landscape. On the way back you will get a beautiful perspective of the town.

South of Centre Ville

Heading south along Avenue Hassan II past the Royal Palace, take the first left, across a small bridge. Take a quick right turn, and follow the road up around the hill. As you reach the top of the hill, a trail appears on the right. This trail undulates and curves across the mountainside for approximately 3 km.

If you continue southwards without taking this turn past the palace, the road climbs for another bit, before flattening out to a beautiful road surface, ideal for long road runs and sessions.

The track area

There are trails, and quiet roads with good surfaces suitable for road efforts, just off Boulevard Mohammed VI, as you leave town. Just before the track, immediately after the petrol station, a road to the left rises into the forest. This surfaced road is where you'll often find Moroccans doing hill sessions. A 200 m hill is marked out along here. At the top of this hill, a dirt track leads off to the left through the forest, and eventually onto Avenue Hassan II. The road continues for approximately 8 km and joins the N8 south-west of the town.

Track facilities

There is a 400 m Tartan track just off Boulevard Mohammed VI, in the south-west of town. Take the N8 south towards Azrou. At the time of publishing the surface is very worn, but is relatively soft to run on. The track is open to all.

Gym facilities

Some of the hotels have gym facilities, including the Michlifen Hotel which has fitness and weights rooms, and there is a weight-training centre under the stand at the track.

Opposite Various trails within easy reach of the town

CROSS-TRAINING OPTIONS

There is an outdoor (50 m) municipal pool at the end of Rue de la Piscine off Avenue Hassen II just north of the town. Mountain biking is also a popular form of cross-training, though there are no bike rental shops in the town.

LOCAL RACES

Marathon des Cedars is an annual four-stage, 90 km ultramarathon trail run through Ifrane and the surrounding areas. More information can be found on www.marathondescedres.com.

RUNNING COMMUNITY

Some of Morocco's most famous athletes have trained in Ifrane, and there are often large groups of Moroccan athletes in the town. Ifrane is also popular among French distance runners, and each year more and more European runners and race walkers can be found training there.

SUITABILITY FOR OTHER SPORTS

Ifrane is known primarily as a base for distance runners, and is less capable of supporting athletes in other sports than other venues featured in this book. The well-surfaced roads are suitable for cycling, though without any bike shops in the town, spare parts may be difficult to find. That aside, the combination of good cycling and running surfaces, and the municipal swimming pool, may make Ifrane attractive to some triathletes. The 2500 m^2 multi-sport hall (L'Omnisport) at the Michlifen Hotel (www.michlifenifrane.com) can cater for basketball, volleyball, table tennis, and futsal.

ABOVE LEFT and OPPOSITE Some of the excellent road surfaces around Ifrane which are suitable for training
BELOW The track located on the outskirts of Ifrane

Special feature
MOROCCO'S DISTANCE RUNNING SUCCESS

Like most other African countries, football is the sport of choice for most young males. Athletics, however, is highly popular, and Moroccan distance-running champions are treated as celebrities. Moroccans have won 22 medals at the Olympics (as of 2012) and all but three of these are in distance races.

World 1500 m and mile record holder and double Olympic gold medallist **Hicham El Guerrouj** is probably Morocco's most famous distance running success. The 'King of the Mile' won 4 consecutive world 1500 m titles, won three consecutive golden leagues, and broke numerous world records during his illustrious career. After a fall at the Atlanta Olympics in 1996, and a defeat to Noah Ngeny, his former pacemaker, in Sydney, it appeared that he would become more famous for his failures than for his victories. El Guerrouj demonstrated just how difficult Olympic titles are to come by, even for those that are clear at the top of the world rankings. It wasn't until Athens in 2004 that El Guerrouj eventually came good, and like the preverbal bus, won not one, but two Olympic gold medals. His victory in the 5,000 m denied Kenenisa Bekele the first Olympic 5,000 m/10,000 m double since Miruts Yifter in 1980, something which Bekele himself rectified in Beijing four years later.

Saïd Aouita was not only the first great Moroccan champion, but the first Arab athlete of any nationality to gain global recognition. He was the 1984 Olympic 5,000 m champion and the 1987 world champion over the same distance. Aouita was among the first to use Ifrane as a training base. **Khalid Skah** is infamous for the controversial way in which he won the 1992 Olympic title. He received assistance from fellow Moroccan Hammou Boutayeb, when lapping him on the way to winning the race by a single second from Kenyan Richard Chelimo. Skah was initially disqualified, but reinstated on a technicality, and was booed by the crowd when being awarded his medal. **Salah Hissou** set new world record figures for the 10,000 m in Brussels in 1996 (26:38.08), and was the 5,000 m champion. More recently, female athlete **Hasna Benhassi** added Olympic medals to Morocco's collection. Morocco staged the World Cross Country Championships in 1975 (Rabat) and 1998 (Marrakech).

It would be wrong to write about Morocco's distance running success and not mention their less than commendable doping history. Brahim Boulami, a former world steeplechase record holder tested positive for EPO and received a two-

year ban in 2002 and Moroccan-born Belgian Mohammed Mourhit who holds the European records in both the 3,000 m and 5,000 m, and who has twice won the world cross country championships, was banned for doping offences in 2002. Abdelkader Hachlaf, a former world indoor bronze medallist over 1500 m, former world junior 1500 m champion Adil Kaouch and two-time Olympians Asmae Leghzaoui and Amine Laâlau have also been banned for drug offences. Former Moroccan marathon record holder Abderrahim Goumri, who died in a car crash in 2013, was provisionally suspended by the IAAF in 2012 on the basis of biological passport abnormalities. Morocco's reputation, however, received it's greatest blow when Mariem Alaoui Selsouli tested positive for a banned diuretic just before the London 2012 Olympics. Selsouli had raised suspicion among the athletics community when, after just returning from a two year ban for a previous offence, she knocked more than 4 seconds from her 1500 m personal best and ran the fastest time by a female for six years.

If you have a particular interest in reading more about the success of Moroccan distance runners, Moroccan Success: The Kada Way (Greg Rowlerson, 2009) may be of interest. The book relives the careers of Hicham El Guerrouj, Salah Hissou and Ali Ezzine, who were all coached by Abdelkader Kada, and relives many of their races in some detail. Sadly, it does not cover coaching and training methods.

BELOW Moroccan athletes utilising the trails trough the cedar forests for a warm-up jog
ABOVE and OPPOSITE Athletes performing a hill session on perfectly smooth and almost traffic-free roads

A THOUSAND CAMEL?
Adapted from the blog, 14 and 15 April 2012

Although it was almost dark as I touched down in Africa again, the greenness of the countryside was visible, and surprised me yet again. Even though all my previous preconceptions of Africa have been wrong, I was sure Morocco would be dry and barren! Wrong again it seems!

As I take the hour-long taxi ride from Fez to Ifrane, I can tell that there is a stark contrast between North Africa, and the sub-Saharan countries like Kenya, Ethiopia and South Africa. But there are also similarities. In the dark and teeming rain, the drive up the mountains to Ifrane has all the dangers of all roads of Africa. Darkly clothed people walk on the verge of the unlit road making their way home in the downpour; the lights of the taxi silhouetting them, and saving them, at the last moment. As the road twists and turns further into the Middle Atlas, the driver makes half-hearted attempts to pass laden trucks, pulling alongside them, before the lights of an oncoming car makes him think better of it. When we eventually arrive in Ifrane, the light dusting of snow, which has just fallen, reminds me that I'm a long way from the sundrenched plains of the Rift Valley.

I woke early the next day to the sight of a stork on a nearby rooftop. I quickly crept out of bed, grabbed my camera, and carefully opened the window to take a picture without frightening her away. Ten days later she didn't seem to have moved, and I've since realised that there are about eight other storks nesting within sight of my bedroom window. In fact the town is full of them. Later that day, I also discovered some monkeys playing at the edge of the forest; the closest of them were within touching distance. Unfortunately, my camera wasn't so close this time, and I didn't spot them again. Just my luck!

I was very apprehensive about coming to Morocco. I was worried about running around a Muslim country, particularly on my own, and was very glad when AnnMarie joined me on Sunday for the remainder of the trip. Now it's difficult to see what I was so apprehensive about, and why I would ever have left a place like this out of my research! Apart from our distinct lack of French, we're doing just fine.

This morning we left the rain of Ifrane behind. After 10 days of training in the fresh air, it was time to travel back to London. Just a short trip to Fez, and another leg of the journey would be over.

Storks nest in the chimneys of Ifrane

Though I'm disappointed to be heading home, I've had a huge smile on my face all day today. Usually when I come to the end of a trip I'm ready to go home; ready to get on with the rest of my life. This time around, another week would have been greatly appreciated. As hard as I wished though, it was not to be.

Cascades just north of Ifrane

This morning after inadvertently bargaining with a taxi driver (the gist of the story is I walked away from the taxi driver because I couldn't understand what he was saying, he thought that I thought the price was too high, he gave us the ride for an absolute song), we headed down the hill towards Fez. It was nice to see the country in daylight, even if it was through the pouring rain. As we approached the city the rain stopped, and I knew then it was going to be a great day.

One of the stallions that guard the park entrance

We got a mini taxi from the new town to the gates of the medina in the old town and then stepped into what can only be described as a dream. The tiny shops along the narrow winding streets sold everything from colourful pottery, wooden carvings and intricate silverwork to tacky plastic toys and big cotton knickers. The smell of food from the small restaurants and stalls was divine, and the sight of a fully laden donkey trotting down steps in alleyways barely wide enough for two people to meet, only added to the feeling that we were in a different world.

One of the gates to the medina in Fez

As we're flying later today, both AnnMarie and myself had our small trolley suitcases with us. Because of these, we were offered all manner of accommodation for the night, and one guy even promised the luxury of an indoor shower! Such a shame we couldn't take up the offer. We quickly warmed to all the attention, and it was nice to hear English being spoken again. In fact we really got into the swing of it, and smiled as we said 'no hotel required' and made an aeroplane imitation before the friendly locals could even get the word 'hotel?' out of their mouths.

And it wasn't just hotels that we were offered. One young man seemed particularly obliging. 'What is it you're looking for?' he said. 'Hotel?' 'Food?' 'Husband perhaps?' Alas, the thousand camels I thought he was offering turned out to be just a cow and camel. Beggars can't be choosers I suppose, but I didn't think even that offer was completely genuine, and passed on this occasion.

We seem to be getting the hang of the 'point-and-hope-for-the-best' approach to ordering food. For 10 dirham (about 80p), we managed to get a large selection of cookies and pastries from a small bakery where nobody spoke English, and before we left the medina, we had a delicious three-course meal for the equivalent of just £6. And just like that, our few hours in Fez were over and a very enjoyable trip to Morocco complete.

Things to see and do between training

Ifrane isn't the most appealing venue in terms of things to do between training, but with cheap food and drink, and free internet access, the cafes and restaurants in Centre Ville are a pleasant place to pass some time, and to spot other runners who are staying in the town.

If birdwatching is your thing, Ifrane has a multitude of birds to look out for. Storks seem to have nested in just about every roof crevice and tree in the town. The tailless macaque (or Barbary) ape, Morocco's only monkey, can also be spotted close to the town. The majority of the world's population of macaque are found in the cedar forests of the Middle Atlas.

The statue of the lion in Centre Ville (opposite Le Chamonix) is popular with tourists passing through the town. If you wish to have your photo taken with it, be prepared for a long wait, as coach loads of tourists have the same agenda.

There is a series of waterfalls and cascades in the area. Some are in the park, and others are a short drive away. Though not particularly spectacular, they are beautiful, and with many of the locals hanging out there, they are a good place to get a taste of Moroccan life.

Apart from the spa treatments available at the Michlifen Hotel, there aren't many indoor activities. Rain can be heavy and prolonged, so ensure that you bring reading material and other forms of indoor entertainment with you.

Rest day excursions

Ifrane is just 1 hr by car from historic Fez, Morocco's third city. Meknes, Fez's long-time rival for attention, and ruins of the ancient town of Volubilis are also about 1 hr away. Azrou, a market town in the centre of a volcanic basin, is just 48 km south-west of Ifrane. To the east of the town, the lakes of Dayet Hachlaf, Dayet Ifrah and Dayet Aoua make for a beautiful 60 km drive.

Fez is the oldest of Morocco's imperial cities. It was the capital for four centuries, and is the country's cultural and religious centre. Take a grand taxi from Ifrane to the centre of Fez's new town (Ville Nouvelle) and from there take a petit taxi to the Medina (Fès el-Bali). Ask the driver to take you to one of the main gates of the medina and wander among the narrow, winding streets and market stalls. Take time to sample traditional Moroccan cuisine from one of the many rooftop terraces, and bargain over the prices of colourful pottery, intricate silverwork, and smooth wooden carvings. The Jewish quarter (Fès el-Jedid) is located south-west of the medina and features the Royal Palace.

Meknès and Volubilis lie in the centre of Morocco's agricultural area. Meknès is famous for its mint tea, wine and olives. The finest buildings are located within the imperial city, while the souks and kissaria of the medina are perfect for experiencing Moroccan culture, and bargaining for handcrafted items. The Roman ruins of Volubilis, the ancient town and once capital of the Roman province of Mauretania, are located just 31 km north of Meknès. Most impressive are the Triumphal Arch, the Basilica, and mosaics dotted around Morocco's most impressive Roman ruins.

Azrou, less than 50 km south of Ifrane, has a large weekly souk and a crafts centre selling handcrafted wood and iron items and carpets. The town is a health resort, and trout, roach and pike fishing is available on the nearby lakes. The Middle Atlas Arts Festival is held in Aïn Louh, a Berber village 30 km south of Azrou, each July.

A note on living here long-term

Athletes may find Ifrane a difficult place to live long-term. A lack of things to do between training may concern athletes who like to keep busy. There are also few employment opportunities (though speaking English in addition to French or Arabic may help). Athletes could undertake a semester of classes at the university as part of a study-abroad programme. While the trails are good for a few weeks, the lack in variety of surface may become an issue. The limited cross-training options may be a problem if an athlete becomes injured. Athletes who don't speak French or Arabic may struggle, though Ifrane is an ideal place to practise and improve your French.

Further information

The town gets a passing mention in many guidebooks, but more detailed information for athletes looking to train in Ifrane is almost non-existent. Ifrane is easy to get to from Fez airport, and is straightforward, so a lack of information shouldn't stop you from visiting. There is a small visitor centre in Centre Ville. The Morocco National Tourist Office Board website (www.visitmorocco.com) may be helpful, and the Al Akhawayn University website (www.aui.ma) usually contains some useful information for visitors to the town.

One of the gates to the medina in Fez

St. Moritz

The beautiful town of St. Moritz, quaintly situated around Lej da San Murezzan in the glacial valley of the upper Engadin and surrounded by dramatic mountain peaks, is a popular training destination for athletes in both winter and summer sports. The town has hosted two Winter Olympics (1928 and 1948) and more world bobsleigh and skeleton championships than any other venue. Well groomed trails, a relaxed atmosphere, an abundance of high quality accommodation and an altitude of 1,856 m make it a popular destination for distance runners. Switzerland is expensive, but for those looking to train in peace, beauty and clear mountain air, it's worth every penny.

St. Moritz, Switzerland (1,856 m)

St. Moritz is located in eastern Switzerland in Graubünden, the largest of Switzerland's 26 cantons. The almost completely mountainous region borders Liechtenstein, Italy and Austria, and is characterised by glaciers, imposing mountain peaks, high mountain passes, and some of the most scenic train rides in the world. The Engadin, meaning 'Valley of the River Inn', together with the nearby Swiss National Park, forms the heart of the region. St. Moritz is located in the upper portion of the Engadin between the Engadin Dolomites and the Silvretta Alps.

St. Moritz is one of the oldest winter resorts in the world and has more 4- and 5-star hotels than anywhere else in Europe. The first altitude training facilities were built here in 1967 and 1968, and were used by the Swiss team in preparation for the 1968 Olympic Games. The town remains the official Swiss centre for altitude training, and offers an excellent training infrastructure for athletes in a variety of sports.

Author's verdict

St. Moritz is incredibly beautiful, and one of my personal favourites. It is a paradise for those that love the outdoors, and has just about everything an athlete needs. The ease of access to facilities and the moderate altitude of the town make it an ideal place for altitude first-timers. The incredible choice of trails was a personal highlight and I managed to do a different route each day during my stay. The high cost of living is the only downside of an otherwise wonderful destination, but by booking well in advance, and choosing to cater for myself, it worked out well even on that front.

Running ★★★★★ - Excellent variety of flat and hilly trails with spectacular views and good conditions underfoot; easily accessible track; good cross-training options.

Convenience ★★★★☆ - Long but spectacular trip from Zurich; accommodations, shops and facilities all conveniently located; well-stocked supermarket; English widely spoken; self-catering accommodation plentiful and easy to book.

Safety ★★★★★ - Peaceful and safe town; no major crime or health risks; good, though expensive medical care; travel/health insurance highly recommended.

Cost ★☆☆☆☆ - High cost of living; shared accommodation, self-catering, budget flights and surviving without a car, can keep costs on par with other destinations.

Cultural experience ★★☆☆☆ - Beautiful place, welcoming people and active outdoor culture; but nothing culturally extraordinary for central Europe.

Things to do between training ★★★☆☆ - Mountain biking, hiking, fishing, and shopping for designer goods are popular activities; some attractions are closed outside of the main seasons; most activities available involve the great outdoors and physical exertion.

Suitability for solo travellers ★★★★☆ - Friendly locals; English widely spoken; easy to find trails and training facilities are attractive to solo travellers, though travelling in a group helps to keep costs down.

Must do Take the funicular to the top of Corviglia and admire the town below; explore a new trail each day; complete at least part of the historic train journey between Thusis and St. Moritz.

Ideal for Anybody who appreciates a good variety of trails, and beautiful surroundings.

BELOW Lej da St. Murezzan
PREVIOUS Fishing boats on the lake with St. Moritz Dorf in the background

A BIT ABOUT SWITZERLAND

Switzerland is the ultimate playground for outdoor enthusiasts. Fresh mountain air, endless kilometres of beautiful Alpine trails, pine forests, green meadows and tranquil glacial lakes, which typify rural Switzerland, combine to create one of the best places in the world for hiking, mountain biking, road cycling, skiing, running, horse-trekking and rock climbing.

Switzerland is landlocked in the centre of Europe, surrounded by Germany, Austria, Liechtenstein, Italy and France and bordered by the Alps and the Jura Mountain ranges. The Swiss have used the mountainous landscape to their advantage and the seemingly harsh topography has not stopped Switzerland becoming one of the wealthiest countries in the world.

Switzerland remained neutral through both World Wars, and has historically avoided political and military alliances. This has enabled Switzerland to maintain strong links with all of its neighbours. Switzerland is not a member of the EU, and only joined the United Nations in 2002.

Despite the blending of French, German and Italian cultures within the country, Switzerland has its own distinct identity. Alphorns, clocks, watches, cow bells, yodelling, banks, muesli and chocolate are just some of the words synonymous with the country, and though not entirely comfortable with the stereotype portrayed to the outside world, the Swiss are very patriotic and inherently proud of their unique 'Swiss-ness'. The Swiss flag, which is, coincidentally, the only square flag in the world, has become a symbol of a country like no other national flag. The red flag, with a white cross, was created to easily identify Swiss soldiers in battle and features on Switzerland's best-selling postcard!

The Swiss are a very sporty people, and approximately quarter of the population are active sports club members. Winter sports are enjoyed by natives and tourists throughout the country, while football and ice hockey are Switzerland's most popular team sports. In addition to the two Winter Olympics hosted by St. Moritz and the numerous winter sport championships hosted throughout the country, Switzerland was a joint host of the 2008 UEFA European Football Championship. The country's past and present sports stars include tennis players Rodger Federer and Martina Hingis, 2012 Olympic triathlon champion Nicola Spirig, and 2001 world 800 m champion André Bucher.

SWITZERLAND QUICK FACTS

Capital Bern
Largest city Zurich
Official languages German, French, Italian (Romansh is also a national language)
Currency Swiss franc (Fr/sFr; CHF), divided into 100 centimes (or rappen)
National holidays New Year's Day (Jan 1), Good Friday*, Easter Sunday* Easter Monday*, Ascension Day*, Whit Sunday* and Whit Monday*, National Day (Aug 1), Christmas Day (Dec 25), St Stephen's Day (Dec 26), plus some canton-specific special holidays and religious observations.
Time zone Central European Time (GMT+1), with daylight saving.
International dialling code +41
Outgoing access code 00
Emergency contacts 117 (police); 118 (fire); 144 (ambulance)
Power 220 V; 50 Hz supply; Type J Swiss (SEV 1011) Europlug-compatible (Type C; CEE 7/16 only) plugs and sockets with two round prongs.
Driving Right side
Measurements Metric

* vary according to Christian calendar

GETTING IN

St. Moritz is normally approached from Zurich, the nearest major city, though travel from Italy in the south and Austria in the east is also possible, particularly if travelling by car.

By air

The small airport in Samedan, just 20 min from St. Moritz, serves only charter and private flights. Zurich Airport (ZRH), also known as Kloten Airport, is the closest Swiss international airport. The airports around Milan in Italy (Milan Linate, LIN; Milan Malpensa International, MXP and Bergamo Orio Al Serio, BGY) and Innsbruck International Airport (INN) in Austria are also convenient if driving, but take considerably longer by public transport. Lugano also has a small airport operating internal flights from Zurich, Geneva and Bern, though this is of little advantage as it is still 4 hr by bus or a 130 km (2 hr 15 min) drive from St. Moritz.

Zurich and Innsbruck are served by the budget airline EasyJet, and Bergamo Orio Al Serio is one of Ryanair's hubs. Zurich Airport is an international hub, serving most European cities. Swiss International Airlines and its partners operate direct flights to Zurich from cities across the world, including Atlanta, Bangkok, Boston, Cairo, Delhi, Hong Kong, Johannesburg, Los Angeles, Miami, Montreal, Newark, New York, Shanghai, Singapore, Seoul, Toronto, Tokyo and Washington.

Zurich airport is located 12 km north of Zurich city centre, a journey which takes 10–12 min by train. Connections on the S16 commuter train, and the IC and ICN intercity lines operate at least every 10 min during the day, and less frequently during the early morning and late evening. The train station is located in the shopping mall directly opposite the exit of the arrivals building. You must purchase a ticket before boarding the train. Trains arrive at Zurich's main train station (Hauptbahnhof/HB), from where you can catch a train towards St. Moritz (see below).

By car
Switzerland's refusal to let geography hinder its transport network has resulted in an impressive network of mountain roads and multiple access points to the Engadin. The Julier Pass and the Albula Pass allow access from Chur; access from Davos is via the Flüela Pass; and the car-transporter rail service, operating every 30 min via the Vereina tunnel, is the main access point when travelling via Klosters. Travellers from Austria and Germany should travel via Landeck, and the Maloja, Ofen and Bernina passes allow access from Italy. Not all passes are open during the winter and access should be checked in advance.

The journey from Zurich Airport is approximately 210 km (3 hr). Milan is 175 km away, and the journey from any of the Milan airports takes between 3–4 hr depending on the route taken. Innsbruck is 185 km (2 hr 30 min) from St. Moritz.

All the main car hire companies, including Sixt, Budget, Alamo, Hertz and Avis, operate from the Zurich and Milan airports. Car hire may be cheaper from Milan, but you should let the hire company know that you will be driving in Switzerland. Fuel prices in Switzerland are significantly lower than in the UK.

The Swiss drive on the right. Traffic offences are taken seriously, and those who exceed the speed limit or commit other driving offences can expect an on-the-sport fine. Speeding is a legal offence, and if you are caught on a camera your fine will be followed up, even if you live outside the country. Speed limits are 50 kph in built-up areas, 80 kph on open roads and 120 kph on motorways. Dimmed headlights are required in tunnels, and advised at all times. When navigating sharp mountain bends with limited visibility you are advised to sound your horn (during daylight hours) or flash your headlights (at night). A vignette (motorway sticker) is required on motorways. Most hire cars already have a vignette (but this is worth checking) and they can be purchased at the border.

By train
Switzerland has an excellent rail network, and Swiss trains are renowned for their punctuality. The journey from Zurich is a pleasant one. Take the fast intercity Swiss Federal Railways (SBB) train to Chur or Landquart, and the Rhaetian Railway (RhB) line through the Albula Valley towards St. Moritz. This line, together with the Bernina line which travels via the Bernina Pass from St. Moritz to Tirano in Italy, has had UNESCO World Heritage status since 2008 and features an intricate series of spiral tunnels and viaducts (p. 319). The total journey takes just less than 3 hr 30 min, with services at least every 60 min, and 19 services per day.

The train journey from Innsbruck takes just over 5 hr, and requires changes at Sargans and Chur. The quickest trains from Milan take at least 4 hr 30 min and involve train journeys to Colico and Chiavenna before changing to bus at Chiavenna.

French high-speed trains travel from Paris, Dijon, Avignon and Nice, hourly trains from Milan and the rest of Italy, hourly German high-speed trains from Frankfurt and Mannheim and nightly trains from Amsterdam, Paris, Berlin, Hamburg, Vienna, Prague, Belgrade, Barcelona, Venice and Rome are just some of the many trains linking the rest of Europe to Zurich.

Train tickets can be purchased from ticket offices or ticket machines, which provide instructions in English, in the larger stations. Single journeys are half the price of return journeys, so if you are likely to lose your ticket, just buy a single. Few locals pay the full price for tickets, and half-fare cards are so common that the SBB website quotes half-price fares by default. Half-fare cards can be purchased from ticket offices at any of the main stations, and may be worth considering if you are making multiple return journeys across Switzerland. Tickets can also be booked online in advance (www.rail.ch), and non-refundable print-at-home supersaver tickets, with reductions of up to 50 percent, are sometimes available for travel in the next 14 days.

Zurich HB is a big station, with platforms on a number of levels, so it's worth checking departing

Special Feature
THE ALBULA/BERNIA WORLD HERITAGE RAILWAY

The Albula (Thusis–St. Moritz) and Bernina (St. Moritz–Tirano) lines of the Rhaetian Railway form only the third railway in the world to receive World Heritage status. As the line transverses the Alps and surrounding countryside between Thusis and Tirano, it winds through the mountains, gaining and losing altitude using a series of clever spiral tunnels.

The 122 km of track passes through 55 tunnels and crosses almost 196 bridges and viaducts. Most spectacular of these man-made structures seamlessly fitted into the mountains are the Solis Viaduct which stands at 90 m high and the Landwasser Viaduct which seemingly disappears into a sheer rock face. The highest point on the line is the 2,253 m Bernina Pass. Between Bergün and Preda the line gains 400 m in altitude within a horizontal distance of just 5 km. As the train crosses over and back the valley and does 360 spirals through the mountains, you sometimes think that you're about to head back home. This section of the line alone involves nine viaducts, five loop tunnels, two standard tunnels, and a lot of mental confusion.

The Glacier Express is another spectacular train line to grace this part of the country. It runs from St. Moritz and Davos, via the UNESCO region to Thusis and across the country to Zermatt at the foot of the Matterhorn. The journey takes 8 hr each way and is spectacular in both winter and summer.

platforms in advance via the website. There are a number of different train lines within Switzerland and the system can, at first, appear confusing. The website is useful for working out routes and connections in advance. Transfer times are often less than 5 min but as long as you know your arrival and departure platform (available via the website), you'll easily make the connection. If, unusually, the train from Zurich to Chur is delayed, the connection to St. Moritz may wait for arrival of the Zurich train.

By bus
If you prefer to travel by road, St. Moritz is served by the PostBus (www.postauto.ch) from both Chur and Lugano. The scenic route from Lugano (the Palm Express) takes approximately 4 hr and runs once in each direction each day. Reservations are essential. The drop-off point in St. Moritz is by the train station.

Visa requirements
EU and EEA citizens, and citizens of America, Canada, Australia and New Zealand do not require a visa for visits of up to 90 days. Switzerland is a member of the Schengen agreement and holders of a valid Schengen visa can enter. Citizens of most African, Asian and South American countries do require a visa to visit Switzerland. Those requiring visas should apply in advance of travel via the local Swiss Foreign Mission (www.bfm.admin.ch).

GETTING AROUND

St. Moritz is divided into two main areas. St. Moritz Dorf (village), the area built on the mountainous north shore of Lej da San Murezzan, is the more expensive part of town and contains most of the exclusive hotels, many of the restaurants, the tourist information centre and the entrance to the funicular. The valley region to the west and south of the lake is known as St. Moritz Bad (spa). It contains the cheaper apartments and hotels, and the athletics track and training facilities, is closer to the trails, and due to the flat ground is easier to get around.

Despite having two distinctive areas, St. Moritz is small and can be easily negotiated on foot. The main train station is no more than 2 km from the furthest accommodation. A local bus service, runs regular services from the train station to most areas of St. Moritz Dorf and St. Moritz Bad, and to nearby towns and villages, including Pontresina, Samedan, Celerina, Champfèr, and Silvaplana. Timetables, an online planner, and other information on bus services can be found on the Engadin Bus website (www.engadinbus.ch). Taxis also operate from the train station.

ONE LAST TRIP
Adapted from the blog, 2 June 2012

Yesterday I left work at three in the afternoon in a sort of excited haste. Not only was it nice to leave the office early, but I was excited to be commencing my final journey for this project. Not that I'm glad that the travelling is ending, but I'm buoyed by the sense of satisfaction that comes with reaching the home straight. At times there seemed to be little chance of me completing the journeys while still owning the clothes on my back, and now I've almost done it. Just after six o'clock yesterday evening I was on a plane to Zurich.

This trip is memorable in more ways that one. It marks the final trip of the most exhilarating phase of my life, but just over a decade ago, my last visit to Zurich was the start of another very significant period in my life—the PhD years. During the past week I was trying to recall that first visit, but could remember little of it. I couldn't even remember what time of year it was. As the plane touched down on the tarmac at Zurich Airport the memories started flooding back. It was not long after 9/11 and security was tight. I had nearly missed the flight; my only close call in years of travelling, and in the end it wasn't that close as the flight ended up being delayed by two hours. When I arrived in Zurich I was confused by all the signs in the airport—I had mistakenly thought that French was the main language in this part of the world. Everything was expensive. There were lots of churches. It was very pretty. It was a crisp autumn day. I only had 24 hours in the place. It was my first trip outside the EU, and only my second time to Continental Europe. I took lots of photos with my little film camera. I bought a lot of chocolate. A lot has changed since then. Nothing has changed at all. Zurich is still expensive and I'm still taking lots of photos.

Like then, I had little time to spend in Zurich, and this morning I left for St. Moritz by train. Not long after leaving the station the beautiful Lake Zurich appears on our left. As the train makes its way away from the city I see the picture-postcard Switzerland that seems so familiar: rugged mountain tops, green meadows reaching right to the forests; grazing cows precariously hanging on to the steep slopes, triangular-roofed log houses set into the hills. The rivers and lakes are a beautiful turquoise colour; the clearest I've ever seen. The houses seem to have no boundary fences; the Alps provide all the garden they need, the fields and forests their playground. The train makes its way along the valley floor, past all this beauty, until we reach Chur. There I change trains, from the fast moving intercity one, to one that is built more for climbing and twisting and winding. This train is for sightseeing, and not for speed. And that's okay, because I have all the time in the world.

At every corner there is breathtaking beauty, meadows full of flowers, snow-capped mountain peaks, trees, trails, waterfalls, rivers. And then we enter a tunnel and everything goes dark. Moments later, like a well kept secret, St. Moritz is revealed before us. I can't wait to explore!

Map of airports close to St. Moritz

Overview map of St. Moritz

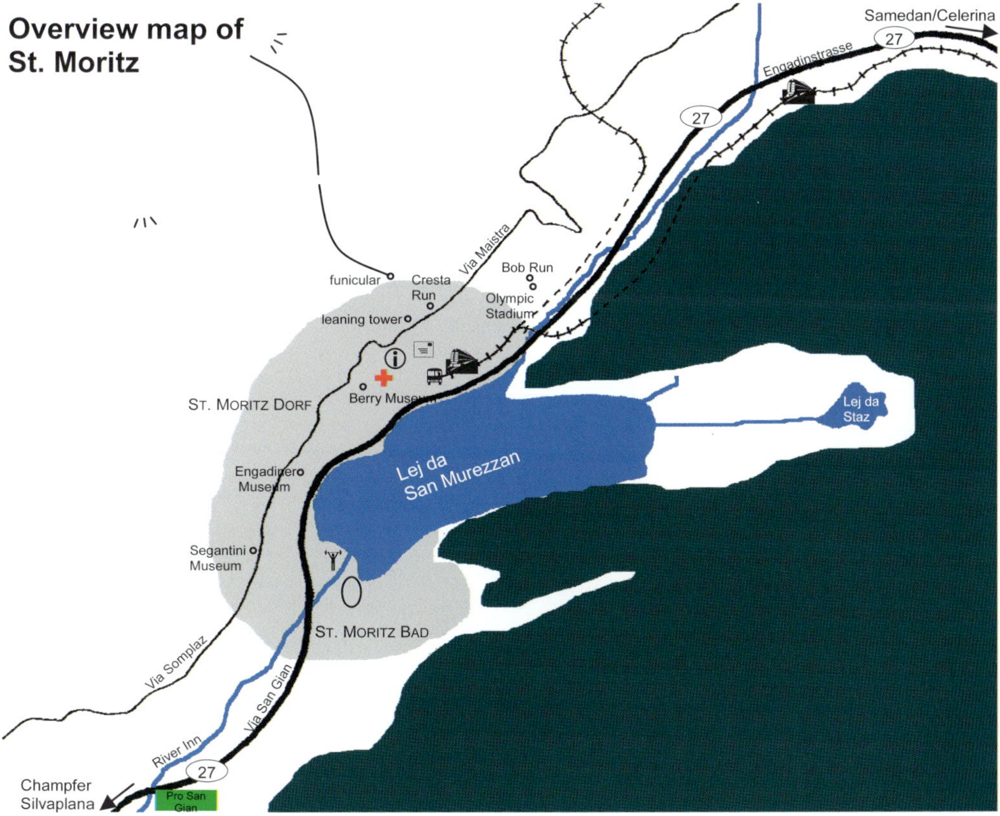

ABOVE One of the many beautiful trails in St. Moritz
OPPOSITE The grass fields by Pro San Gian sports fields

Weather and when to visit

St. Moritz has an Alpine climate, with cold, moderately snowy winters, and wet, but mild summers. Average monthly highs are above 15 °C between June and September. July and August are the warmest months, but also the wettest, with 10–12 rain days on average per month.

Snow can fall in any month of the year. During the summer months this usually amounts to no more than a few centimetres of overnight snow which has usually melted by late morning. Weather during the summer months should not hinder training once you are flexible enough to adapt to the conditions. Afternoons tend to be windier than the mornings and the prevailing Maloja wind begins to blow around midday, particularly on sunny days.

There is a short off season between the ski and summer seasons when some of the funiculars, shops and other attractions are closed. While training is still possible and accommodation cheaper during this down-time, the weather is less predictable, and there is less to do between training. The ski season usually ends in mid April, and the majority of the chairlifts, gondolas and funiculars operate between late June and early September, the main summer season.

Accommodation

In addition to the wide range of exquisite and spa hotels, there is an excellent choice of self-catering accommodation and apartments. Accommodation may be more expensive than elsewhere in Europe, but the standard is very high. Most of the exclusive hotels are in St. Moritz Dorf, and the cheaper apartments are in St. Moritz Bad. Accommodation can be booked through the St. Moritz or Engadin St. Moritz websites. All accommodation is within easy reach of the trails and other training facilities. In most instances accommodation is charged per week (Saturday to Friday usually), irrespective of how many days you stay. If you are staying for shorter periods hotel accommodation with self-catering facilities may be a cheaper option. The Sports Hotel Stille offers hotel rooms, and self-catering apartments charged per night, for individuals and groups, and in addition to having onsite cooking staff, the hotel offers use of its kitchens to chefs travelling with large groups of athletes. The youth hostel (Youth Hostel St. Moritz Bad) just beside Hotel Stille on Via Surpunt would be a more cost-effective option for large groups staying together, or individuals willing to share with strangers.

For those travelling on a budget, Camping TCS Olympiaschanze (www.campingtcs.ch), a campsite on the east of the town, halfway

between St. Moritz and Champfèr, is open between mid-May and early October.

Because most of the trails form part of a larger network right through the valley, individuals don't have to stay in St. Moritz. Pontresina (altitude: 1,805 m; *p. 335*), Samedan (1,721 m) and Champfèr (1,792 m) also have plentiful accommodation and are within easy reach of the facilities in St. Moritz. Pontresina and Samedan also have good sports facilities of their own, though no athletics track.

FOOD

Everything in St. Moritz is expensive, and eating out is no exception. Food is of a very high standard and a number of the restaurants have been awarded Gault Millau points. The online gastro guide (www.engadin.stmoritz.ch/gastronomy) has suggestions for restaurants to suit all tastes. In addition to fine dining, there are some nice bakeries and cafes.

Though groceries are not cheap, cooking your own food is highly recommended. The local supermarkets are well stocked with both fresh and non-perishable products. Larger supermarkets like Coop, located on Via dal Bagn, offer big savings on some products when purchased in

SHOPPING

Shops include supermarkets, sports shops, gift shops and designer boutiques. Most of the shops are in St. Moritz Dorf, with designer shops located along Via Serlas, one of the world's most exclusive shopping streets.

Many businesses, including all the supermarkets, are closed on Sundays and close early on Saturdays (17:00). Some shops and businesses close for lunch during the week. Swiss employment laws forbid working on Sundays with two exceptions—family-owned businesses which don't employ anybody, and businesses within railway stations which are deemed to be serving travellers. If you need to find a shop while travelling on a Sunday, look out for small corner shops, or head to the nearest large railway station.

There are no specialist running shops. The few sports and outdoor shops stock a limited range of running clothing and footwear, but are expensive.

LANGUAGE

St. Moritz is officially located in a Romansh and German-speaking area of Switzerland, though Italian, and to a lesser extent French, are also widely spoken. Most signs, notices and menus are in three languages. English is also widely understood, and all tourist office literature is published in both German and English. While a basic understanding of German, Italian or French is an advantage, it is not essential.

COMMUNICATION

Orange, Swisscom and Sunrise, the main mobile networks, are used by a number of mobile virtual network operators who also offer services. Service is good on all networks, and Swisscom coverage is close to 100 percent right across the country, even in sparsely-populated mountainous areas. All European phones should have coverage on one of the local networks. Prepaid SIM cards and handsets can be purchased for those who wish to make calls and send internal text messages. Call and text prices on prepaid plans are similar to elsewhere in Europe, with same-network calls significantly cheaper than calls to other networks. Swisscom's Natel Easy Befree plan is a prepaid option for iPhone and iPad. Public phones are relatively cheap.

LEFT The River Inn as it enters Lej da St. Murezzan
OPPOSITE Lej da Staz

Internet cafes are rare in Switzerland, though Bobby's Pub on Via dal Bagn has internet access. Approximately half the rental accommodations have free Wi-Fi access.

The post office is located at Via Serlas 23. Stamps can also be purchased from some newsagents. The postal system (Swiss Post) is fast and reliable.

HEALTH AND SAFETY

There are generally no problems with food or water. Tap and fountain water is safe to drink, unless otherwise indicated (*Kein Trinkwasser*), and hygiene levels in restaurants are strictly controlled. Organic food is widely available, and it is illegal to sell genetically modified foods. No vaccines or prophylactics are required for travelling to Switzerland.

Switzerland doesn't have free state health care, so health insurance is essential. A European Health Insurance Card (EHIC) is also highly recommended for EU and EEA citizens. Klinik Gut St. Moritz (www.klinik-gut.ch), located on Via Arona, is the main medical practice. It has an accident clinic and sports medicine facilities. St. Moritz has an emergency GP medical service (+41 (0)81 833 1414) and there is a larger hospital (Spital Oberengadin; www.spital-oberengadin.ch) in Samedan. Pharmacies (*apotheke*) are located throughout the town. Medicines are expensive and visitors should bring adequate supplies.

There is a very low crime rate, and visitors should not expect to be targeted. Normal precautions should be exercised when travelling through major train stations and other crowded areas.

MONEY

The Swiss franc (sign: R; code: CHF), made up of 100 centimes, is Switzerland's currency. Prices are often also marked in euro. Some larger shops around the country may accept euro, though this is unlikely in St. Moritz. Credit cards are widely accepted, and there are ATMs around the town which accept credit and debit cards. Most of the major banks have branches in St. Moritz Dorf.

POWER

Switzerland operates on a 220 V; 50 Hz electricity supply and uses Type J Swiss (SEV 1011) Europlug-compatible plugs and sockets with two round pins. European plugs and travel adaptors may not fit into recessed sockets normally used in kitchens, bathrooms and other wet areas.

Typical European adaptors and plugs don't fit into recessed Swiss sockets

TIME

Switzerland operates on Central European Time (CET; GMT+1) with summer time operating between the last Sunday in March and the last Sunday in October.

Daylight varies from approximately 8 hr 30 min in mid December to almost 16 hr in mid June.

	Mar	Jun	Sept	Dec
Sunrise	06:33	05:27	06:59	07:58
Sunset	18:26	21:15	19:32	16:34

LAUNDRY

Most rental accommodations have washing facilities, and some hotels have a laundry service. Laundrettes are not common, so if you are staying for a long period, you may want to check washing facilities before booking accommodation.

CULTURE AND RESPECT

Though most people in Switzerland speak good English, learning a few greetings in German is a great way of showing respect. The Swiss greet each other with three alternate (left-right-left) 'fake' kisses on the cheek, and this is the normal greeting when introduced to somebody new.

Jaywalking and littering are treated seriously and can result in on-the-spot fines. The Swiss are less concerned with litigation than other European countries, and warning signs are usually a notification of actual danger. Failing to obey signs can have a detrimental effect on your health or safety.

The Swiss are incredibly punctual (they are, after all, known for their clocks and watches), and even a minute after the agreed appointment time is considered late. Talking loudly on a mobile phone in public, or talking loudly on the train, is not appreciated. Discretion and understatement are appreciated while show-offish ways and exaggerated friendliness are looked upon with suspicion. Asking about someone's private income and wealth is considered rude.

A service charge is included in restaurant, bar and hotel bills, and tipping is not required. That said, rounding up to the nearest Swiss Franc, or adding some small change is usual, particularly in more expensive restaurants.

Special feature
SWISS GERMAN

Though German is the main language spoken in this part of Switzerland, visitors who learnt German in Germany, or from a textbook, may be in for a bit of a surprise. Indeed Swiss German, in its spoken form, can sometimes have little resemblance to German. Swiss German uses many different words from standard (High) German, uses some different pronunciations, and has its own grammatical rules. To make matters more confusing, there are a number of different dialects of Swiss German. Most Swiss speak standard German, having learned it as a somewhat foreign language at school, and since Swiss German is not an official language, and doesn't have a written form, the Swiss write using standard German.

Some useful phrases include *Grüezi* (Hello, pronounced [Grea-atsie], similar to Italian), rather than the German *Guten Tag*, and *Merci Vilmal*, meaning thanks a lot, which combines the French word for thanks, said with a Swiss pronunciation, with a typically standard German word.

BELOW Apartment blocks and the athletics track in St. Moritz Bad
FOLLOWING The forests of St. Moritz offer an exceptional variety of mildly undulating routes for running, mountain biking and hiking

SPORTS FACILITIES AND SERVICES

As Switzerland's main altitude training base, St. Moritz has facilities to cater for a wide range of sports. St. Moritz Sport, located within the town's tourism information centre, maintains and co-ordinates sports facility use, and provides facility access cards to athletes training in the town. Athletes should complete and submit the online registration form (www.sports.stmoritz.ch) in advance of travel. Passes can be picked up from the St. Moritz Sport offices (in the tourist information centre on Via Maistra), in St. Moritz Dorf upon arrival.

Yellow elite passes are issued to members of national teams and entitle the holders to use the weight-training facilities at Ludains Ice Arena, the running track on Corviglia, the athletics track in St. Moritz Bad, and summer use of the funiculars around town. While this card doesn't automatically entitle the holder to access of the swimming pool in Pontresina, separate tickets (one per week for athletes and coaches) can be obtained from St. Moritz Sport. Additional tickets can be negotiated, with a doctor's certificate, for injured athletes. Green passes, issued to regional standard athletes, entitle the holder to use of the running and athletics track and the weight-training facilities, and to child fares onboard the funiculars. Individuals, groups and teams are eligible for these cards.

TRAILS AND RUNNING ROUTES

St. Moritz has an excellent variety of trails within easy reach of the town. Most routes start at the lake (Lej da San Murezzan) which forms the focal point of the town. A part-asphalt, part-gravel flat route, approximately 3 km long, circles the lake. In the unlikely event that you do become bored of the trails in and around town, a short drive up or down the valley will lead to a whole new set of off-road trails and paths.

Trail runners have a variety of options. Taking any of the smaller trails off the main routes will usually lead you over areas of challenging trail, with particularly good options south-east of the lakes between Champfèr and Silvaplana. The best options for mountain runners are pretty obvious, with a number of peaks surrounding the lakes. Beware of patches of ice and snow up the mountains even as late as early summer. Orienteers should also find suitably challenging terrain. Race walkers can use the route around the lake, or travel to Samedan where there are flat routes in the valley around Engadin Airport including a 5 km inline skating route at the airport, a 2 km bike route between Punt Muragl and Samedan, and an inline route of 8.6 km between La Punt and S-chanf.

Hiking and mountain biking maps which help give an overview of the local terrain and routes are available in most book, gift and grocery shops. The Scott Engadin St. Moritz Mountain bike map in 1:50 000 has clearly marked routes along the upper Engadin and surrounding valleys, together with difficulty ratings and terrain profiles of each route. The Schweizerische Eidgenossenschaft St. Moritz (1257) map at 1:25 000 offers more detail of the valley between Silvaplana and Samedan.

Towards Celerina and Samedan
From the bridge just beyond the train station a route leads out of town beside the main road (Via Grevas). This gravel route takes a short but sharp drop shortly after running beneath the railway bridge, flattens soon after and continues adjacent to the river and railway line towards Pontresina (to the right) and Celerina, Samedan and Bever (to the left; cross under the road at Celerina). This out-and-back route is good for long runs. It can be made into a loop lap for those with a good sense of direction by cutting into the forest on the right of the route just beyond Celerina.

Forest routes towards Pontresina
Routes from the forest entrance just beyond the youth hostel on Via Surpunt, and the valley path past Melerei Hotel on the eastern edge of the lake lead into the forest and head towards Pontresina. These trails are undulating, but with a pleasant, soft running surface. There are a number of interconnecting loops, and the mountains should help with direction. A fitness loop, with various outdoor gym exercise stations, starts at the edge of the forest in St. Moritz Bad.

Towards Champfèr, Silvaplana and the other lakes
Running south-west along the foot of the mountain, head past the playing fields at Pro San Gian, the campsite, and the base of the ski-jump, before reaching Champfèr and a choice of off-road lake-side routes around Lej da Champfèr, Lej da Silvaplauna and Lej da Segl.

Up the mountain
For those who prefer to run up and down steep hills, there are routes up the slopes behind St. Moritz Dorf. They offer fantastic views of the town, lake and surroundings once you reach the top. There are also some runs up the mountains south of the town from St. Moritz Bad.

Map of St. Moritz trails

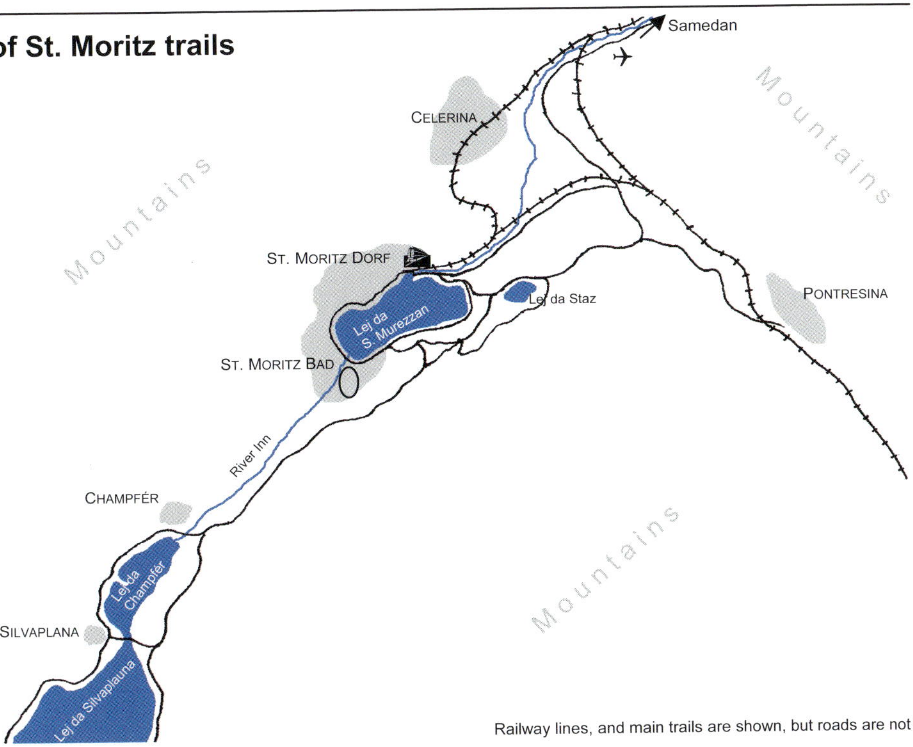

Railway lines, and main trails are shown, but roads are not

Some of the trails in St. Moritz

Track Facilities

A four-lane 400 m Tartan track is located close to the lake in St. Moritz Bad, between Via Sela and Via Mezdi. All users of the athletics track, which has facilities for jumping and running events (except steeplechase water jump), are asked to register with St. Moritz Sport. Athletes who fail to register will be charged a daily fee. The soft jogging track near Corviglia (use the funicular) at an altitude of 2,500 m is perfect for those looking for the ultimate altitude exposure. The funicular doesn't operate in the period between the winter and summer seasons. The large grass area around the Pro San Gian playing fields can be used for grass repetitions.

Gym Facilities

The well-equipped weight-training room at Ludains Ice Arena, close to the athletics track, looks out onto Lej da San Murezzan. In addition to free and machine weights, there are spin bikes, cross-trainers and treadmills. Use of this facility is free to yellow and green card holders (p. 328), though pre-booking must take place, and Swiss elite athletes have priority access. The fitness loop, with various outdoor gym exercise stations in the edge of the forest in St. Moritz Bad provides additional variety for strength training.

Cross-training Options

Mountain biking, road cycling, swimming and inline skating are popular forms of cross-training. Tickets for the swimming pool in Pontresina are available through St. Moritz Sports. Mountain and road bikes can be hired from Engadin Bikes in St. Moritz Bad, and city bikes from the rent station next to the sailing club restaurant. There are guided and GPS mountain bike tours in the area. There are inline skating paths in and around Samedan and skates can be hired from Fähndrich Sport in Pontresina (www.faehndrich-sport.ch). Other facilities suitable for recreational sport and cross-training include playing fields by the camping grounds, indoor and outdoor tennis courts, squash courts, and indoor multi-purpose sports halls.

Sports Medicine and Sports Science Support

Massage and physiotherapy services are available through Gut Training St. Moritz (www.gut-training.com), an approved Swiss Olympic sport medicine base. Body composition analysis and other support for athletes is also available.

Local Races

The Engadiner Sommerlauf (www.engadiner-sommerlauf.ch) is an annual 26 km race along a relatively flat course by the lakes and through the forests between Sils and Samedan. There is a 10 km option along the later part of the course from Pontresina to Samedan. Sporthotel Pontresina organises a running camp in the week preceding the race, which is normally held in August. The Engadin St. Moritz Alpinathlon (www.alpinathlon.ch) is a popular annual adventure race for individuals and teams. The 130.2 km course between Bergün and the Corvatsch mountain terminal features approximately 5,500 m of climbing and 3,600 m of descents, and is covered in road bike, mountain bike and running stages.

St. Moritz Sports organises evening runs over a 4.3 km loop around the lake during the summer months. There is a small entry free and prizes for the first three finishers in each category. A little further afield, the annual Jungfrau and Davos marathons are popular mountain marathons which attract runners from around the world.

Running Community

Viktor Röthlin, Switzerland's first European marathon champion and leading distance runner, uses St. Moritz as his altitude training base. A number of other distance runners, triathletes and race walkers, from across Europe, regularly train here, and some athletes from further afield, including Mo Farah and his American-based training group, use it as their training base during the European track season. The track area is a good place to meet other runners.

Suitability for Other Sports

Swimming There is a 25 m indoor swimming pool, and an outdoor pool (open summer only) at Bellavita Pool and Spa (www.pontresina-bellavita.ch) in Pontresina. The new Ovaverva (www.ovaverva.ch) 25 m indoor swimming pool is due to open in St. Moritz in 2014.

Cycling With relatively quiet roads, challenging terrain and a cycling-friendly community, St. Moritz is a great place for cyclists to train. Mountain bikers are also well catered for and during the summer months the ski slopes, particularly around the Corviglia, are used for downhill biking and BMX. Mountain biking maps are available free of charge at information points and mountain railway ticket offices.

The 4-lane track in St. Moritz Bad

Triathlon The area is popular among triathletes who make use of the swimming pools in Pontresina, the track in St. Moritz, and the cycling routes through the Engadin Valley.

Team sports St. Moritz is suitable for preseason training in team sports. There are grass playing fields at Pro San Gian Sports Ground and a FIFA-standard artificial grass pitch at Promulins Sports and Leisure Centre (Center da Sport Promulins) in Samedan. The centre in Samedan also has a multi-purpose indoor facility with three separable sports halls, suitable for basketball, volleyball and other indoor sports. St. Moritz Sport is a good starting point for locating other facilities.

Other Lej da San Murezzan and Lej da Silvaplauna are suitable for rowing, canoeing, sailing and windsurfing. Corviglia Tennis Centre has four indoor and three outdoor courts, as well as two squash courts. There is a large dojo near the ice rink, and shooting ranges for air rifle and pistol shooters. The locality is also suitable for rock-climbing and mountaineering. During the winter months skiers (alpine and cross country), ski jumpers, bobsleighers, skaters and ice hockey players flock here to hone the physical and technical elements of their training.

BELOW The Cresta Rider monument in St. Moritz Dorf
OPPOSITE St. Moritz has hosted the Winter Olympics twice

Special feature
ST. MORITZ AND WINTER SPORTS

St. Moritz is the birth place of resort holidays, is one of the oldest ski resorts in the world, has hosted the world bobsleigh and skeleton championships a record 21 times and was the venue for both the 1928 and 1948 Winter Olympics. Today it features the world's only ice bobsleigh run, has an ice skeleton run, and hosts spectacular events such as horse racing, show jumping, cricket and golf on snow and ice.

The 1928 Games was only the second running of the Winter Olympics, and featured 464 competitors from 25 nations competing for 14 sets of medals in six sports (bobsleigh, figure skating, ice hockey, Nordic skiing, speed skating and tobogganing/skeleton). Switzerland won a single bronze medal.

St. Moritz was chosen for the 1948 Games because of Switzerland's neutrality during World War II, and because the 1928 facilities gave them the head start needed with only 18 months lead-in time. These Games featured 22 events across alpine and Nordic skiing, bobsleigh and skeleton, figure skating, speed skating and ice hockey. Alpine skiing made its Olympic debut, 669 participants from 28 countries took part, Germany and Japan were not invited because of their involvement in World War II, and Switzerland won 10 medals, including a gold and silver in the two-man bobsleigh.

Sites from both Olympics can still be spotted around town, and two, the Cresta Run and the St. Moritz-Celerina Olympic Bobrun, are still in use today. The Cresta Run is a 1,200 m skeleton course that twists and turns down the hill from the centre of town, past the hamlet of Cresta, and on to the village of Celerina. Each year the run is built from scratch using earth banks and the natural topography of the hill as a framework on which to pack snow and ice. The track was first built in 1884. Across the road from the Junction start of the Cresta run is the start of the St. Moritz-Celerina Olympic Bobrun. This run was opened in 1904, making it the oldest, and only naturally refrigerated, bobsleigh run in the world.

Olympiaschanze St. Moritz hosted the ski jumping events of both games, and was in operation until 2006. It is located just by the Olympiaschanze campsite on the west of the town. The site of the original Olympic stadium, now used as a driving range, is located close to the bobrun. The original stadium building, overlooking the range, is, externally, unchanged from 1948. Internally it has been converted into residential apartments. The stadium hosted the opening and closing ceremonies and skating events.

THINGS TO SEE AND DO BETWEEN TRAINING

There aren't many major sites though there are a few places of minor interest. What's left of the town's Olympic past (p ?) is worth checking out. The town has its very own leaning tower dating back to the 12th century and located by the Cresta monument just opposite the Kulm Hotel, but don't get too excited—this is mostly just a shabby old tower. There are a few small museums including the Engadiner Museum which houses a collection of artefacts of Engadin cultural history, the Segantini Museum displaying a collection of works by artist Giovanni Segantini who spent his final days in the area, the Berry Museum, dedicated to painter and doctor Peter Robert Berry, and Museum St. Moritz which displays works of art from around the world in an escalator mall which runs from lake level to Via Serlas in the centre of St. Moritz Dorf.

A film of the story of Heidi was shot in the Engadin, and the Heidi hut used for the film is located above the town. The futuristic Chesa Futura, designed by Lord Norman Foster, a renowned English architect, houses ten private apartments and sits like a giant capsule on stilts above St. Moritz close to the entrance to the Corviglia funicular. The 'big 5' of St. Moritz are not animals but the exquisite 5-Star hotels (Kempinski Grand Hôtel des Bains, the Carlton, Suvretta House, Badrutt's Palace and Kulm) for which the town has gained its exclusive reputation.

Hiking in the beautiful forests and mountains is a wonderful way to spend an afternoon. Canyoning is possible from Pontresina. Boat trips are available from Sils and rowing boats can be hired for use on Lej da Silvaplauna and Lej da Segl from Silvaplana. Helicopter and light-aircraft sightseeing flights can be arranged from Engadin Airport. There is a bowling alley in the Grand Hotel Kronenhof in Pontresina. Shooting and horse riding are also possible.

During the summer months (late Jun–early Sept) a funicular runs from St. Moritz Dorf to Corviglia, offering spectacular views of the town and lakes. There are restaurants, again with late June to early September opening, throughout the mountains and in easy reach of the mountain railways. Shopping is expensive and almost completely limited to the exclusive Via Serlas. The local cafes are a relaxing, if somewhat expensive, place to pass some time. There are spa options throughout St. Moritz and the surrounding towns.

Details of exhibitions, performances and festivals which run during the summer months can be found in the news booklet produced by St. Moritz tourist office every few weeks, and distributed in shops and business throughout the town.

REST DAY EXCURSIONS

If you fancy getting out of town, and shopping really is your thing, there is a shopping outlet in Landquart. Reduced price branded articles and great dining bring shoppers of all ages to this Alpine outlet village, just north of Chur and accessible by train.

The area is particularly interesting for those who love trains. Steam trains, restored 'crocodile' locomotives and open carriage trains operate on the UNESCO line on Sundays during the summer months, and the railway museum in Bergün is a must for anyone interested in railways. Check out www.rhb.ch for further information.

From Zernez you can explore the Swiss National Park (www.nationalpark.ch), home to ibex, deer, chamois and bearded vulture, and visit the national park visitors' centre. Chur, the capital of Graubünden, is an ancient town with a historic centre consisting of a maze of quaint cobbled streets and pretty squares, and overlooking the rest of the town is a Romanesque cathedral that is well worth a visit. There are beautiful drives and quaint villages throughout the region.

A NOTE ON LIVING HERE LONG-TERM

So long as you have an adequate source of funding, St. Moritz would not be the worst place to live for long periods of time, at least during the snow-free months. Zurich Airport, approximately 3 hr 30 min away, provides direct flights to many European cities, and getting to and from races during the European track season should not be a problem. Facilities are suitable for training at any stage of the season, and a variety of trails, and multiple cross-training options, means that athletes should never tire of the town from a training perspective. There are things to do between training and opportunities for employment, particularly in the hotel industry. Unlike other resort towns, people do actually live in St. Moritz, and there are opportunities to make friends and become part of a community. English is widely spoken and the laid-back atmosphere is appealing for those seeking a better quality of life.

FURTHER INFORMATION

The St. Moritz website (www.stmoritz.ch) has lots of useful information including accommodation and restaurant listings, news and events, and details on sports facilities. It has a summer and a winter version in both English and German. The Engadin St. Moritz official website (www.engadin.stmoritz.ch) has useful information and an accommodation booking facility. It comes with a summer and winter version and is available in English, German and five other languages. The official website of Switzerland tourism (www.myswitzerland.com) has useful information on travelling in Switzerland

St. Moritz and Engadin St. Moritz produce a number of useful publications in German and English which can be picked up from the tourist office or downloaded from the website. The former has a downloadable altitude magazine available on its website which includes information on the training facilities available.

Other altitude training sites in Switzerland

Pontresina (1,805 m)
www.pontresina.ch

Nearby Pontresina is also a popular training destination. Its proximity to the training facilities in St. Moritz, access to the same trail network, a similar altitude, and the added bonus of a swimming pool make it a popular choice among triathletes. There are further sports facilities at Cuntschett Sports Grounds.

Pontresina is located in the Val Bernina, a branch valley off the Upper Engadin, and though often overshadowed by St. Moritz, is in itself a noted tourist destination. The Spaniola Tower, Grand Hotel Kronenhof and the Church of Santa Maria are listed as nationally significant Swiss heritage sites. The town has rail, road and bus links with St. Moritz and other nearby towns and villages.

Davos (1,560 m)
www.davos.ch

Davos is another popular Swiss altitude training venue, and like St. Moritz is used as an official Swiss Olympic training base. The small city, with a population of just over 11,000, is located north of St. Moritz and Pontresina on the Landwasser River between the Plessur and Albula Ranges of the Swiss Alps. Davos is the largest city in the canton of Graubünden, and, situated at 1,560 m of altitude, is Europe's highest. It is one of Switzerland's largest ski resorts, attracting Dutch and British tourists in particular, and has hosted numerous international speed skating championships. It is also famous for cross country skiing with 97 km of trails, has 320 km of alpine slopes, and has Europe's largest natural ice skating field. From the mid 1700s, Davos became a destination for convalescents; its high valley microclimate deemed excellent for recuperation from respiratory and lung diseases. Robert Louis Stevenson was among those to winter here while recuperating from tuberculosis.

Training facilities at Davos Sports Centre (Davos Sportzentrum, Davos Platz) include a 6-lane 400 m track, a UEFA artificial grass football pitch, a training pitch for ball sports, plus a restaurant and sun terrace for hanging out with other athletes after training. Färbi Sporthalle AG (www.sportdavos.ch) in Davos Platz has tennis courts, and indoor squash, badminton, climbing and archery facilities. There are 700 km of hiking trails and 1,500 km of biking trails around Davos, Klosters and Prättigau.

Klosters, located just 15 km and 20 min by train north of Davos also has good facilities including an athletics track, tennis courts, football fields and a public swimming pool (www.sportzentrum-klosters.ch). It is situated at 1,179 m, making Davos a suitable venue for a 'live high, train low' approach to altitude training.

Outdoor facility usage, bus transport within Davos and train travel between Davos and Klosters is free with the Davos Klosters Inclusive Card which is available to anyone staying in a Davos hotel.

Temperatures in Davos are similar to those in St. Moritz, though Davos receives more rain, and more wet days, particularly during the summer months. It is located less than 2 hr 30 min from Zurich, with an hourly train connection via Landquart. The city's location close to a good transport network, together with its moderate altitude, may make it a preferable location to those looking for a base with mild altitude exposure.

BELOW Another scenic trail through St. Mortiz
OPPOSITE Lej da Staz

335

Well groomed trails like this one provide ideal running terrain through the forests of St. Moritz

FIFTEEN VENUES LATER
Adapted from the blog, 10 June 2012

I'm sitting in yet another airport. The final destination has been visited, and another Olympic venue has been added to my list. St. Moritz was everything that I'd hoped for, and more. It was the perfect place to finish my travels.

To say that the weather is temperamental is an understatement. In the space of eight days I saw rain, snow, wind, cloud, and sunshine. The snow I guess was the biggest surprise, but it wasn't a great deal—five centimetres is easily melted by lunchtime, and for once my 'owl' personality had its benefits! This morning I had no choice though, and I was out in the snow for my final run before heading home. The beauty of running in the snow at that time of the morning is that the only footsteps are yours—there's a certain sense of pride in knowing that you're up, out and at it while everyone else is sleeping. The downside of course is that, despite being alone, it feels like you're in the middle of a giant snowball fight—the trees periodically lightening their branches of their load.

The town of St. Moritz after snow

St. Moritz is ideally set up for training in almost any sport. For athletes like me who love a bit of variety, and prefer off-road routes, it's like heaven on earth. I did 14 runs while I was there, and no two of them were the same. In fact if I had stayed another week, I would still be discovering new routes. And the best bit? The trails started just 10 m from the door of my apartment and the athletics track was only about 500 m away. For a runner, you can't ask for much more than that.

Apart from the running, there hasn't been much to report. I celebrated a birthday—well I spent all my pocket money on a small pastry, enjoyed it with a cup of tea, and acknowledged the passing of another year. Adamant to overcome the high food prices that I'd been warned about so much before coming here, I cooked every single meal for myself. The local supermarket was somewhat affordable when goods were purchased in bulk. Getting through 1200 grams of spaghetti in eight days was a challenge I was more than up for, though I'm still traumatised from the after-effects of eating a kilogram of asparagus over the same time period.

Birthday cake for one

Incident-wise it's been pretty uneventful—no missed trains or flights, no last-minute hiccups, no clumsy accidents. Okay, that's a lie. But I was doing well, until an incident with an escalator yesterday! Absorbed in getting photos of the fine artwork displayed I managed to forget that I would reach the top at some stage. The escalator delivered me to my destination, I was standing still, back facing the wrong direction, and almost fell over right in front of a group of people. Luckily I do the embarrassed look very well (years of practice I suppose), so they didn't need to say anything. I walked away, proverbial tail between my legs, nothing hurt but my pride, and they got a smile out of it. Everyone's a winner!

And just like that, just as I'm getting used to all this travelling malarkey, it's all over. It seems like only a moment ago I was squeezing belongings into a suitcase at four in the morning, on half an hour sleep, heading to Mexico, with not even my first night's accommodation booked. Now I'm here, over two years later, still alive, and still incredibly unorganised.

Anyway, I mentioned something about not missing a flight—better go catch this one back to London. It would be a shame to mess up at this stage.

Altitude Training Sites in South America

No South American venue has been featured in this book. For European athletes, the jet lag and travel fatigue may outweigh the benefits of training there. That said, South America is a popular destination for gap-year travellers and those looking to learn Spanish, and with a large proportion of the continent at altitude, there are many opportunities for altitude training. Pollution can be a problem in the larger cities, good Spanish or Portuguese (depending on country) is essential, the risk of contracting food-related illness is high. Beautiful scenery, a rich culture and history, a low cost of living, and a southern hemisphere summer are just some of the attractions. The following are just some of the options available.

Bogotá, Colombia (2,625 m)
www.bogotaturismo.gov.co

Colombia's capital city Bogotá (officially Santa Fé de Bogotá) is a large city of almost nine million. The main training facilities are located north-west of the city centre. Parque Simon Bolivar offers running trails and is situated just west of the Centro de Alto Rendimiento en Altura (altitude training centre), which has facilities suitable for a range of sports. Bogotá has Latin America's largest network of bicycle routes, and many of the city's roads are closed to cars on Sunday mornings, leaving over 120 km of routes free for cycling, running and inline skating.

The Spanish spoken in Bogotá is considered the clearest and most neutral in the world, making the area a great place to learn the language. Bilingual schools are plentiful and English is widely spoken by the city's youth. There is a significant demand for English teachers and teachers of other languages. El Dorado International Airport (BOG) offers direct flights from Paris, Madrid, Barcelona and Frankfurt and many North American cities. The climate is relatively mild, with two rainy seasons (Apr–May and Sept–Nov).

Paipa, Colombia (2,577 m)
www.paipa-boyaca.gov.co

Paipa is a town of approximately 27,000, located at 2,577 m above sea level, approximately 200 km north-east of the capital Bogotá. Paipa has a mild climate, and, as the main tourist centre of the region, has a plentiful supply of hotels. Among the attractions is a range of hot springs. El Dorado International Airport (BOG), 200 km away in Bogotá, is the nearest commercial airport. The best way to get to Paipa from Bogotá is by car. Lago Sochagota, a large lake south of the town, is suitable for a range of water sports, and has trails around its shores. The athletics track at Estadio de Paipa, is located just north of the lake.

Cuenca, Ecuador (2,350 m)
www.cuenca.com.ec

Cuenca, which has a population of approximately 300,000, is officially situated at 2,350 m above sea level, though altitude varies between 2,350 and 2,550 m above sea level. The city is home to 1997 champion Jefferson Perez (of whom there is a statue in Parque de la Madre) and some of Ecuador's other world-class race walkers. The hills outside the city are popular for trail running and mountain biking. Running is also popular in the city parks, and along the banks of the rivers, which run through the city. The cobbled streets of the city centre are best avoided. Running holidays offered by Running Treks (www.runningtreks.com) include daily runs and hikes, yoga sessions and excursions to local sites.

Cuenca has a subtropical highland climate with mild temperatures year-round, and a rainy season, characterised by bright sunny mornings and afternoon showers, between January and May. There are daily flights to Cuenca from the capital Quito, and the country's largest city Guayaquil, both of which offer direct flights to Europe. The city centre is a UNESCO World Heritage site and many North Americans retire to the pretty city. It is a good place to learn Spanish, and to engage in volunteer work.

Quito, Ecuador (2,850 m)
www.quito.com.eu

Quito, the capital of Ecuador, has a population of just over two million people and is situated within a few kilometres of the equator. The city's official altitude is 2,850 m, and there are trails at and above 3,000 m in the surrounding mountains. Traffic pollution makes it difficult to run, and trails are largely limited to Parque Metropolitano Guanguiltagua which is located at almost 3,000 m. Cycling is a good way to get around and several shops rent bikes. Approximately 30 km of roads are closed to traffic every Sunday, and become run, cycle and rollerblade routes. The Flying Dutchman offers single- and multi-day mountain biking trips to surrounding hills, lakes and valleys.

According to UNESCO, Quito has the largest and best-preserved historic centre in Latin America. Average daily temperatures are above 19 ºC year-round. Humidity is high and sunshine plentiful. June through to September are the driest months. There are direct flights to Quito from Madrid (Iberia) and Amsterdam (KLM), and from many US airports.

OTHER ALTITUDE TRAINING SITES IN EUROPE

Turracher Höhe, Austria (1,763 m)
www.turracherhoehe.at

Run2gether (www.run2gether.com) offers runners of all levels the opportunity to train with Kenyan athletes in Kiambogo in Kenya *(p. 208)*, and in Turracher Höhe, a small ski town approximately 60 km north-west of Klagenfurt, Austria. During week-long, all-inclusive camps, participants have the opportunity to train with Kenyan athletes, follow Kenyan training practices, eat Kenyan food, and experience a Kenyan athlete's way of life in the scenic mountains of southern Austria.

The town offers running routes on the high plateau on which the town is located, and in the surrounding mountains up to the summit of Kornock Mountain (2,205 m). There is a 2.4-km flat, part-asphalt, part-gravel, circular trail around Lake Turracher See, a moderately hilly trail along the three-lakes tour, and other hillier loops through the forests.

The town boasts 'pollen-free' air, and offers tennis, fishing, mountain biking, horse riding, golf and rafting to fill the time between training. Turracher Höhe is best reached by car, though trains do stop at Predlitz, 12 km north of the town. Accommodation can be booked through the Turracher Höhe website (www.turracherhoehe.at).

Kühtai, Austria (2,020 m)
www.kuehtai.info

Kühtai High Altitude Training Centre (www.hoehentraining-kechtai.at) is a sports facility and organisation, owned by the Tourism Association of Innsbruck, which can organise accommodation and training facility access for athletics, speed skating, football, rowing, beach volleyball and beach football. There is a four-lane 400-m synthetic track, a floodlit 500-m oval woodchip trail, and a variety of running trails. Facilities are open between May and October. 'Live high, train low' training is possible with Innsbruck, at just 574 m, less than 1 hr away.

Visitors can choose from 3-star and 4-star hotels, traditional inns and serviced apartments, and opt for full board, half board or self-catering options. Camp prices include training facilities for two 90-min training sessions each day.

Kühtai, renowned for its clear mountain air, is located just 40 km west of Innsbruck. There are regular flights to Innsbruck's small airport from Vienna (Austrian Airlines) and Frankfurt (Lufthansa) and regular trains to the city from Zurich, Munich, Vienna, Graz and Venice.

Tenerife, Canary Islands (2,146 m)

Mount Teide, an active volcano, is, at 3,718 m, Spain's highest point. It dominates the island of Tenerife, and much of the land surrounding it (Teide National Park), rises above 2,000 m. Parador Hotel de Cañadas del Teide (www.paradores-spain.com), the only building within the National Park, is situated at 2,146 m. Many professional cycling teams stay there when they are making use of the island's excellent roads, and the sunny climate. The hotel is slightly isolated and relatively expensive, but it does offer special rates for 5 night stays, and has half board and full board options available. It is located approximately 45 km (60 min by car) from both Tenerife South Airport (TFS), and the beaches and amenities of Los Cristianos and Playa de las Americas. 'Live high, train low' is, therefore, possible. Some organisations (e.g. TKO Gym Tenerife) advertise under the altitude training banner, but, in fact, provide training rather than accommodation at altitude.

Tenerife is well connected by plane to most of Europe With budget airlines such as Ryanair operating 4–5 hour flights from a number of cities in the UK and Ireland, it is both accessible and affordable. Year-round warm temperatures are an added bonus.

Rila Mountains, Bulgaria (2,050 m)

Belmeken Alpine Sports Complex (www.nsb.bg) is situated on the plains where the Rhodope and Rila mountain ranges meet, 120 km (1 hr 50 min) south of Sofia. Velingrad, the nearest settlement, is 35 km away. The complex provides excellent facilities and hotel accommodation for teams and individuals. Facilities include a 25 m swimming pool, indoor sports halls suitable for volleyball, basketball and other sports, a gymnastics hall, a boxing gym, biathlon shooting ranges, a football pitch, fitness areas, a weightlifting gym and a medical centre. There is also a rowing centre and regatta course on nearby Belmeken Reservoir. The complex provides airport transfers, but a car is required for any additional travel.

Acknowledgements

Even for somebody like me, never one to do things by-the-book, my 'at-the-drop-of-a-hat' decision to quit a secure job during a recession to travel the world and write a book, must have seemed a little extreme, even to those that know me best. If they were shocked, they didn't show it, and I'd like to extend a special thanks to all my friends for being so enthusiastic about my idea in the few hours before the crucial decision was made. Without their support this book may just be another unfulfilled dream.

A special mention must go to Bud for all the people that he put me in contact with along the way, and for putting up with all my stuff in his spare room for so long.

My family, despite thinking that I'm a bit crazy, have supported me emotionally, financially and logistically all the way. I could never have done this without the Bank of Barmoney behind me. John and Patrick's responses to my text telling them that what I had decided to do were something along the lines of 'Eliz, you're mad' and 'You're crazy'. Only they would have know that I took their comments as compliments! Mam has exceeded my expectations on the proofreading front; Dad, like a true investor, guided and motivated me with his constant questioning, and Nicholas was patient with my overuse of his broadband.

A big thanks to all those who helped me with my travels and research along the way. Luke and Hannah picked me up from the airport in Mammoth Lakes, showed me around the town and drove me to training. They should also be thanked for providing the opportunity to spot a bear, and for teaching me how to do cryptic crosswords. Thanks to Durk for arranging accommodation and providing transport and support on training runs, and Scott and Audrey for driving me to San Francisco. The athletes and coaches at University of New Mexico were extremely welcoming and helpful. Special thanks to Nicky and Del.

Flagstaff was a turning point, and where this project started to gather momentum (at least in the metaphorical sense – something that takes over three years to complete can hardly have had much momentum in the literal sense!). Thanks to the athletes at McMillan Elite and the staff at Run Flagstaff for being so enthusiastic about my project, to Greg and Karen for answering all my questions, and to all the people who were so forthcoming with information about the facilities in the town. Thanks to Angelina and her friends and family for making me so welcome in Boulder, for providing a bed, some great food and lots of giggles, and for showing me the best trails that Boulder has to offer. Jukka and the other staff at CAR Sierra Nevada were also extremely helpful with my research.

Lornah and Pieter and all the staff at HATC in Iten were, as always, helpful and welcoming. Juma cooked some excellent food; and Hatti and Dave provided great company. Iten will always have a very special place in my heart, and it is all the great people that I have met there on my six trips that have made it so special—a special thanks to you all.

Thanks to Gudisa for meeting me at the airport in Addis and for his help and hospitality throughout my stay, and to all the lads at Running Across Borders for their company on runs, their card playing skills, and their entertainment. Jacob ('Zuma') was great company on excursions, and I'm grateful that he let me beat him in the Great Ethiopian Run. Though her French wasn't as good as expected, AnnMarie brightened up what could have been an otherwise dull week in Ifrane. The staff at Sport St. Moritz were extremely helpful, and Wilko provided some great advice on the town before I travelled.

Ryan McLeod, Deena Kastor (Mammoth Track Club), Malcolm Anderson (Running Across Borders) and Joseph Kibur (Yaya Village) provided vital photos. Claire and Cienna did an excellent job at taking over the 'Hawk Eye' mantle with their proofreading skills. Wayne came up with a publishing name that epitomises everything that this project has been about, challenged me to draw the best running man that I could, and supported in many other ways during the project. Andy, Lee, Luke, Rachael and Tatiana, among others, provided assistance along the way.

Those who read my blog posts showed enthusiasm and positivity for what I was doing, kept me motivated and focused throughout this project, and the random people who engaged in conversation with me on various flights and train journeys around the world and showed genuine interest in what I was doing, even if they didn't know what altitude training is, helped me more than they will ever know.

Appendix 1 - Basic French, Spanish and German phrases

English	French	Spanish	German
Hello	Bonjour	Hola!	Guten Tag
Good morning	Bonjour	Buenos días	Guten Morgen
Good evening	Bonsoir	Buenas noches	Guten Abend
Goodbye	Au revoir	Adiós	Auf Wiedersehen
See you	Â bientôt	Hasta la vista	Bis später!
My name is…	Je m'appelle …	Me nombre es …	Ich heiße …
How are you?	Ça va/Comment ça va?	¿Cómo está usted?	Wie geht es ihnen?
All right	Ça va	Muy bien	Gut
Very well, thank you	Tres bien, merci	Muy bien, gracias	Sehr gut, danke
And you?	Et vous?	Y usted?	Und ihnen?
Thank you (very much)	Merci (beaucoup)	(Muchas) gracias	Danke (viel)
Please	S'il vous plaît	Favor de	Bitte
Do you speak English	Parlez-vous anglais?	¿Habla usted inglés?	Sprechen Sie Englisch?
I do not understand	Je ne comprends pas	No comprendo	Ich verstehe nicht
I understand	Je comprends	Comprendo	Ich verstehe
Yes	Oui	Sí	Ja
No	Non	No	Nein
Excuse me	Pardon	Dispénseme	Entschuldigung
Why?	Pourquio?	¿Por qué?	Warum?/weshalb?
When?	Quand?	¿Cuándo?	Wann?
Who?	Qui?	¿Quién?	Wer?
What?	quoi?	¿Qué?	Wie bitte?
How?	comment?	¿Cómo?	Wie?
How long?	combien de temps?	¿Cuánto tiempo?	Wie lange?
How far?	à quelle distance?	¿A qué distancia?	Wie weit?
here/there	ici/là	aquí/ allí	hier/dort or da
to/from	à/de	a/de	zu/von
with/without	avec/sans	con/sin	mit/ohne
the airport	l'aérodrome	el aeropuerto	der Flughafen
the bus station	la gare des autobus	la estación de autobuses	der Busbahnhof
the dock	le quai	el muelle	der Kai
the train station	le gare	la estación de tren	der Bahnhof
to the left	à gauche	a la izquierda	zu links
to the right	à droite	a la derecha	zu rechts
Monday	Lundi	Lunes	Montag
Tuesday	Mardi	Martes	Dienstag
Wednesday	Mercredi	Miércoles	Mittwoch
Thursday	Jeudi	Jueves	Donnerstag
Friday	Vendredi	Viernes	Freitag
Saturday	Samedi	Sábado	Samstag
Sunday	Dimanche	Domingo	Sonntag
one	un	uno	eins
two	deux	dos	zwei
three	trois	tres	drei
four	quatre	cuatro	vier
five	cinq	cinco	fünf
six	six	seis	sechs
seven	sept	siete	sieben
eight	huit	ocho	acht
nine	neuf	nueve	neun
ten	dix	diez	zehn
eleven	onze	once	elf
twelve	douze	doce	zwölf
thirteen	treize	trece	drizehn
fourteen	quatorze	catorce	vierzehn
fifteen	quinze	quince	fünfzehn

sixteen	seiz	diez y seis	sechzehn
seventeen	dix-sept	diez y siete	siebzehn
eighteen	dix-huit	diez y ocho	achtzehn
nineteen	dix-neuf	diez y nueve	neunzehn
twenty	vingt	veinte	zwanzig
twenty-one	vingt et un	veintiuno	einundzwanzig
twenty-two	vingt-deux	veintidós	zweiundzwanzig
twenty-three	vingt-trois	veintitres	dreiundzwanzig
thirty	trente	treinta	dreißig
forty	quarante	cuarenta	vierzig
fifty	cinquante	cincuenta	fünfzig
sixty	soixante	sesenta	sechzig
seventy	soixante-dix	setenta	siebzig
eighty	quatre-vingts	ochenta	acgtzig
ninety	quatre-vingt-dix	noventa	neunzig
one hundred	Cent	cien	hundert
one thousand	Mille	mil	tausend
I would like…	Je voudrais…	Quisiera…	Ich hätte gerne…
breakfast	le petit déjeuner	el desayuno	das Frühstück
lunch	le déjeuner	el almuerzo	das Mittagessen
dinner	le dîner	la comida	das Abendessen
the bread	le pain	el pan	das Brot
the butter	le buerre	la mantequilla	die Butter
the sugar	le sucre	el azúcar	der Zucker
salt/pepper	sel/poivre	sal/pimienta	Salz/Pfeffer
the sauce	la sauce	la salsa	die Soße
jam	confiture	conserva	konfitüre
an omelette	une omelette	una tortilla	ein Omelette(e)
eggs	œufs	huevos	Eier
ham	jambon	jamón	Schinken
chicken	poulet	pollo	Huhn
beef	bœuf	carne de vaca	Rindfleisch
lamb	gigot	cordero	Lammfleisch
pork	porc	puerco	Schweinefleisch
steak	bifteck	Bisté	Steak
veal	veau	Ternera	Kalbfleisch
minced meat	viande hachée	carne picada	Hackfleisch
fish	pêche	pescado	Fisch
beans	haricots	frijoles	Bohnen
cabbage	chou	col	Kohl
carrots	carottes	zanahorias	Karotten
olives	olives	aceitunas	Oliven
mushrooms	champignons	hongos	Oilze/champignons
lettuce	laitue	lechuga	kopfsalat
peas	petits pois	guisantes	Erbsen
potatoes	pommes de terre	patatas	Kartoffel
tomatoes	tomate	tomates	Tomate
rice	riz	arroz	Reis
peppers	poiverons	pimientos	Paprika
apple	pomme	manzana	Apfel
orange	orange	naranja	Orange
peach	pêche	melocotón	Pfirsich
cheese	fromage	queso	Käse
black coffee	café noir	café solo	schwarzer Kaffee
coffee with cream	café crème	café con crema	Kaffee mit Sahne
milk	lait	leche	Milch
tea	thé	té	Tee
cake/pie	gâteau	pastel	Torte
ice cream	glace	helado	Eiscreme

Appendix 2 - Conversions tables

Pounds to kilograms
For when you're in the weight training room and trying to work out whether you're a weightlifting animal, or should just be adding some more iron to the bar.

lbs	kg	kg	lbs
0.5	0.23	0.5	1.10
1.0	0.45	1.0	2.21
1.5	0.68	1.5	3.31
2.0	0.91	2.0	4.41
3.0	1.36	3.0	6.61
4.0	1.81	4.0	8.82
5.0	2.27	5.0	11.02
6.0	2.72	6.0	13.23
7.0	3.18	7.0	15.43
8.0	3.63	8.0	17.64
9.0	4.08	9.0	19.84
10	4.54	10	22.05
20	9.1	20	44.1
30	13.6	30	66.1
40	18.1	40	88.2
50	22.7	50	110.2
60	27.2	60	132.3
70	31.8	70	154.3
80	36.3	80	176.4
90	40.8	90	198.4
100	45.4	100	220.5
150	68.4	150	330.7
200	90.7	200	440.9
300	136.8	300	661.4

Miles to kilometres
For when you're driving, and not sure how far you still have to travel (or what speed you can do).

km	Miles	Miles	km
1.0	0.6	1.0	1.6
2.0	1.2	2.0	3.2
3.0	1.9	3.0	4.8
4.0	2.5	4.0	6.4
5.0	3.1	5.0	8.0
6.0	3.7	6.0	9.7
7.0	4.4	7.0	11.3
8.0	5.0	8.0	12.9
9.0	5.6	9.0	14.5
10	6.2	10	16
20	12	20	32
30	19	30	48
40	25	40	64
50	31	50	80
60	37	60	97
70	43	70	112
80	50	80	129
90	56	90	145
100	62	100	161
150	93	150	241
200	124	200	322
300	186	300	483
400	249	400	644
500	311	500	805

Fahrenheit to Celsius
For when you need to work out whether you should be packing the bikini and Bermuda shorts, or the long johns and winter coat.

Fahrenheit	Celsius	Celsius	Fahrenheit
-5.0	-20.6	-20.0	-4.0
0.0	-17.8	-15.0	5.0
5.0	-15.0	-10.0	14.0
10.0	-12.2	-5.0	23.0
15.0	-9.4	0.0	32.0
20.0	-6.7	2.0	35.6
25.0	-3.9	4.0	39.2
30.0	-1.1	6.0	42.8
35.0	1.7	8.0	46.4
40.0	4.4	10.0	50.0
45.0	7.2	12.0	53.6
50.0	10.0	14.0	57.2
55.0	12.8	16.0	60.8
60.0	15.6	18.0	64.4
65.0	18.3	20.0	68.0
70.0	21.1	22.0	71.6
75.0	23.9	24.0	75.2
80.0	26.7	26.0	78.8
85.0	29.4	28.0	82.4
90.0	32.2	30.0	86.0
95.0	35.0	32.0	89.6
100.0	38.7	34.0	93.2
105.0	40.6	36.0	96.8
110.0	43.3	38.0	100.4
		40.0	104.0

Feet to metres
For when you're just not that sure how far in the sky you are.

Feet	Metres	Metres	Feet
4,000	1,219	800	2,625
4,200	1,280	900	2,953
4,400	1,341	1,000	3,281
4,600	1,402	1,100	3,609
4,800	1,460	1,200	3,937
5,000	1,524	1,300	4,265
5,200	1,585	1,400	4,593
5,400	1,646	1,500	4,921
5,600	1,707	1,600	5,249
5,800	1,768	1,700	5,577
6,000	1,829	1,800	5,906
6,200	1,890	1,900	6,234
6,400	1,951	2,000	6,562
6,600	2,012	2,100	6,890
6,800	2,073	2,200	7,218
7,000	2,134	2,300	7,546
7,200	2,195	2,400	7,874
7,400	2,256	2,500	8,202
7,600	2,317	2,600	8,530
7,800	2,377	2,700	8,858
8,000	2,438	2,800	9,186
8,200	2,499	2,900	9,514
8,400	2,560	3,000	9,843
8,600	2,621	3,100	10,171
8,800	2,682	3,200	10,499
9,000	2,743	3,300	10,827

Legend for maps

✚	hospital
'Y'	gym
≷	view point
🖃	post office
🚍	bus or public taxi station
🚂	train station
🚇	metro
✈	airport
++++	railway line
\\\|//	cliff edge
○	point of interest
ⓘ	information point
(C 51)	road number
(4)	road number
[B500]	road number
▬	camp or other important building
▬	park or forest
⬭	athletics track
▬	pond or lake
▬	sea or ocean
⌒	river
▬	built up area
▬	university campus

The maps that are included in this book are outlines only, and are not intended to replace detailed city or regional maps. Sources of detailed maps, where relevant, are mentioned in the 'Getting around' section of each chapter

Photo credits

Deena Kastor p. 83
Ryan McLeod pp. 90/91, 92, 100/101
Yaya Village pp. 230, 231 (all)
Running Across Borders p. 238 (all)

Author All other pictures

...our deepest fear is that we are powerful beyond measure
(Marianne Williamson, 199